HOUSE OF DISCIPLES

HOUSE OF DISCIPLES

*Church, Economics, and Justice
in Matthew*

MICHAEL H. CROSBY

Maryknoll, New York 10545

The Catholic Foreign Mission Society of America (Maryknoll) recruits and trains people for overseas missionary service. Through Orbis Books Maryknoll aims to foster the international dialogue that is essential to mission. The books published, however, reflect the opinions of their authors and are not meant to represent the official position of the society.

Copyright © 1988 by Michael H. Crosby
Published by Orbis Books, Maryknoll, NY 10545
Manufactured in the United States of America
All rights reserved

The Scripture quotations contained herein are from the Revised Standard Version Bible, copyright 1946, 1952, 1971 by the Division of Christian Education of the National Council of the Churches of Christ in the USA, and are used by permission.

Imprimi Potest
Kenneth W. Reinhart, Capuchin
Provincial Minister
Midwest Province, O.F.M. Cap.

Nihil Obstat
Francis Dombrowski, O.F.M. Cap.
John F. X. Sheehan, S.J.

Imprimatur
Most Reverend Rembert G. Weakland, O.S.B.
Archbishop of Milwaukee
August 12, 1987

LIBRARY OF CONGRESS
Library of Congress Cataloging-in-Publication Data

Crosby, Michael, 1940–
    House of disciples : church, economics, and justice in Matthew /
Michael H. Crosby.
        p.   cm.
    Bibliography: p.
    Includes index.
    ISBN 0-88344-610-3.   ISBN 0-88344-609-X (pbk.)
    1. Bible. N.T.   Matthew—Criticism, interpretation, etc.
2. Economics in the Bible.   3. Justice—Biblical teaching.
4. Sociology, Biblical.   I. Title.
226'.206—dc19   88-5347
                                                                CIP

While he was still speaking to the people, behold, his mother and his brothers stood outside, asking to speak to him. But he replied to the man who told him, "Who is my mother, and who are my brothers?" And stretching out his hand toward his disciples, he said, "Here are my mother and my brothers! For whoever does the will of my Father in heaven is my brother, and sister, and mother"

[Matt. 12:46–50].

Contents

Preface

This book began as a paper for one of the first courses I took in pursuing my doctorate at the Graduate Theological Union at Berkeley, California. For their class on "Scripture and Ethics," Jesuits John Donahue and William Spohn asked that a fifteen-page paper be written on some economic theme in the Bible. By the end of the semester that paper had become 250 pages. Ultimately it became my dissertation and the basis for this book.

In the three years that have elapsed since that time I have been helped immeasurably by professors, classmates, acquaintances, and Capuchin brothers. My first thanks go to John Donahue and Bill Spohn for the assignment that stimulated the idea. My work was further encouraged by other members of the G.T.U. faculty, notably Charles McCoy, Andrew Christensen, S.J., Robert H. Smith, Robert B. Coote, William R. Herzog, II, and Wilhelm Wuellner. David S. Steward was especially helpful as the head of my Area Committee. Above all, the development of this book was nourished by interaction with the members of my dissertation committee. Bill Spohn graciously took the place of Martha Stortz on the committee when she went on sabbatical. He, along with William Short, O.F.M., and John Elliott, of the University of San Francisco, proved most helpful. Jack's unique expertise on house churches and his points of difference with me challenged me to make important distinctions and nuances that have made my arguments much more cogent.

My peers at the G.T.U. gave special help, especially Douglas Oakman, Camilla Burns, and David Hester. The librarians patiently helped track down sources. I benefited greatly from critiques offered by ethicist William Johnson Everett and scripture scholars Donald Senior, C.P., and John Reumann in the United States and David Sanders in England. Conversations with other theologians helped as well, but their names are too many to be mentioned here. As has been the case with my other books, my Capuchin brother, Dan Crosby, acted as early sounding board and initial editor. Laurie Michalowski, SSSF, gave helpful comments to keep me from using exclusive language. I have tried faithfully to employ inclusive terminology, although in scripture studies such as this it is often impossible to avoid using terms such as "kingdom." My Orbis editor, Hank Schlau, proved to be the best one could imagine or desire. He not only grasped the issues I tried to deal with; he was able to help in developing clarity, consistency, and persuasion. Above all, he and his peers at Orbis did not throw out the whole project when I kept making changes.

Three acquaintances deserve special mention. When the final version of the manuscript was being delivered to Orbis, that version as well as an earlier copy were swept up in a wind at La Guardia Airport. Three strangers—Woodrow Greggs and Mari and Gary Paolillo—came from nowhere to help salvage what otherwise would have been a manuscript lost to the environment at the Eastern shuttle.

Finally I want to thank my brothers at the Capuchin House of Studies in Berkeley for their many forms of support. This includes Robert Barbato and Kendall Jones for their help in translations and especially Christopher Thiel for his expertise in teaching me how to use a word processor and for his patience in helping me through many technological problems. I sometimes imagine that, without Chris, I would still be in chapter 1. To these, and to all in the house who were so hospitable to me during my stay in Berkeley, I dedicate this book.

HOUSE OF DISCIPLES

Introduction

THE RATIONALE FOR THIS BOOK

This book seeks to uncover the ecclesial and economic dimensions of Matthew's notion of justice and how these justice-dimensions touch upon ethics and spirituality. My search revolves around two primary "poles" or "horizons"[1]: (1) the data in the gospel of Matthew; and (2) the moral and spiritual implications of that data for economics and ecclesiology today. While the vast majority of this study focuses upon the former, my ultimate concern is to develop an interchange between the two horizons, especially as the gospel data regarding justice can touch upon contemporary economics and ecclesiology.

Creating a language to facilitate this interchange and fusing first- and twentieth-century "horizons" are extremely difficult and risky because our contemporary "economics" as well as "church" differ so vastly from those of the first century. It is necessary, then, that in this Introduction I explain my method. However, before explaining the method I have decided to use to investigate a possible fusion of these horizons, I want to explain how this book came about.

In my first semester at the Graduate Theological Union I took a course on "Scripture and Ethics." We were asked to find some economic theme in the Bible and deal with the interplay between scripture and economics. I decided to investigate the meaning of *oikía/oikos,* the Greek words for "house."[2] Why, it might be asked, did I choose to consider "house"?

The gospels were written for house-based communities. Further, when the gospels were written church (religion)[3] and economics[4] were house-based—the church was based in the house until the third or fourth century; economics remained house-based until the industrial revolution. Given that data, I reached the conclusion that "house" is key to understanding church and economics in the gospels. Part of that conclusion has long been accepted by New Testament scholars: they have long recognized the connection between house and church; however, similar links have not been made between house and economics. But that connection is clear: the root word for "economy" (*oikonomía*) means house-management or house-ordering (*oikos/oikía* + *némein* [management] = *oikonomía*).[5]

I might have considered Mark, because "house" not only plays a central role as his locale for Jesus' teaching but also serves as the framework for his understanding of Jesus' community as a new kind of family.[6] Similarly, because Luke makes it clear that Jesus was of the "house and lineage of David" (Lk. 2:4) and because he stresses hospitality, reflections on "house" in Luke might have proved quite fruitful.[7] John's gospel also highlights hospitality as well as "dwelling with" to refer to discipleship. In addition, John writes about the royal official at Capernaum who "himself believed, and all his household" (Jn. 4:53). This phrase alone could have launched a fuller investigation into just one theme related to households—namely the implications of individual and household conversions in the early church.

Even though it might be possible to argue that in some ways Matthew is the weakest of the gospels as regards the use and meaning of *oikía/oikos,* I chose to investigate "house" and its related concepts in his gospel[8] for various reasons.

First, like all the gospels, Matthew's redaction was conditioned by dynamics within his house-based audience. It was meant to be used as a guidebook to assist members of household churches to implement the basic teachings of Jesus in their religious and social life (those two dimensions of life never being separated at that time). Another reason for choosing Matthew is that, with one exception, he alone uses both the words "church" (16:18; 18:17) and "justice" (3:15; 5:6, 10, 20; 6:1, 33; 21:32).[9] Since the right-ordering of households reflected justice, I wanted to probe his connection between church and economics from the perspective of justice,[10] even though he did not use the word "economics" as such. Furthermore, while house-order refers to economics, the root word for order or management (*némein*) of households originally had religious overtones.[11] This realization led me to believe Matthew might offer an especially fertile ground for probing the connections among "church," "economics," and "justice."

Besides these more academic reasons there were personal reasons to choose Matthew. After working five years in a changing parish and then in the ministry of corporate responsibility and social justice, I wrote a book on the Beatitudes in Matthew's gospel. It considered the implications of wealth in Matthew's house churches.[12] That study resulted from my realization of the need to bring "gospel values" (as the term was used in the late 70s) to bear upon our political economy. Eventually that effort led me to pursue a masters degree in economics. Course work in traditional socio-economic formations afforded me many more insights into religious and economic activity in the first century.

Since, as it will be shown, Matthew's households reflected urbanization and prosperity,[13] I decided to investigate what, if any, connections could be made among church, economics, and justice from his perspective, especially for affluent peoples in the First World. I felt it important to make that investigation even though Matthew's more egalitarian church and precapitalist "system" were vastly different from today's patriarchal ecclesiastical structures and post-industrial capitalism.[14]

In the end I developed the hypothesis of this book: that Matthew's ordering of the house—be it church-order or economics (house-order)—demands justice at its core. This justice can be identified as the salvific (re)ordering of relationships with God and others, as well as the socio-political (re)ordering of resources not only in the house church, but throughout the world (*oikouménē*) and throughout the earth itself (ecology).

ECONOMICS AND RELIGION IN MATTHEW'S GOSPEL

In the first century, each independent household was held together not only by economic ties, but religious bonds as well. Religious and economic bonds undergirded the household itself. Since the household was the basic political unit, religion and economics had a macro, socio-political dimension as well as a micro, kinship dimension. At the time of Matthew, religion as well as economics were embedded within bonds of kinship that constituted the household. However, kinship bonds of individual households also constituted the wider polity and, as such, the wider social sphere. Therefore, as Bruce Malina notes, "just as there was domestic economy and political economy in the first-century Mediterranean, but no economy pure and simple, so also there was domestic religion and political religion, but no religion pure and simple."[15] Religion was substantive, embedded in kinship ties and politics; so was economics. The household was the unifying force for all.

Matthew's ecclesial perspective was influenced on the day-to-day faith-level by and with human beings who lived and worshiped in houses and who ministered and evangelized from houses. The same households which manifested a faith or religious dimension also served as the foundation of the economic world of the first century.

In part because of his unique use of the word *ekklēsía* (16:18; 18:17), Matthew's ecclesial perspective has been considered central to understanding the first gospel. This has taken place at the expense of his economic perspective. This dimension cannot be limited to a few stories here and there; it too underlies the whole gospel.

Matthew's narration of Jesus' life reveals definite economic overtones. His birth was a threat to Herod; in a house wise men shared their wealth (2:11) with the newborn child. The first disciples were small businessmen (4:21) and probably knew the art of bartering quite well. Perhaps his fishing and bartering skills enabled Peter to own a house (8:14) large enough for an extended family, including his mother-in-law. Indeed, we shall see, there is good reason to believe that, according to Matthew, Jesus had a house of his own (9:10, 28; 12:46; 13:1, 36; 17:25).[16] Matthew's Jesus interacted with people like the centurion (8:5) who had incomes large enough to own their houses (see 8:6). Even more, people of wealth were counted among his followers. Joseph of Arimathea was a wealthy man as well as a disciple. However, he proved his discipleship by sharing his wealth with someone in need (27:57–60).

The evangelist Matthew realized how material things could become addictive and the source of household worrying (see 6:19–34). He knew that acceptance of Jesus' message had economic implications not only for individuals (4:20; 8:20; 19:21); it might affect local economies such as the Gadarene territory (see

8:34). We shall see that Jesus' message had effects even on the underlying social order.

When Matthew wrote his gospel, multinational banks or corporations did not exist. However, people were growing wealthy, and not always justly. To keep their wealth from being dissipated by Rome's taxation, they rapidly converted liquid assets into large estates. Thus, in a reflection on his environment, Matthew's Jesus speaks about landowners, some of whom were absentee. Neither could the first gospel be divorced from stories about wages (20:1-16), leases (21:33-43), and ways to enhance property values (25:14-30), even though this practice reflected an aberration of Jewish law.

Because small land-tenants and householders often lost their assets through debt (18:23-35; 21:33-46), Matthew's Jesus understandably spoke about the good news of debt-forgiveness (6:12; see 18:23-35). With debts forgiven, people could experience a kind of jubilee or fresh start.

Toward the end of Jesus' life, in the house of Simon, a woman with costly perfume shared her affluence (26:6-13). From the apostles' interpretation, hers was an economic activity; from Jesus' interpretation it was religious as well. What she did, Jesus said, was to be memorialized whenever the good news would be preached (26:13). The very proclamation of the gospel, then as now, could never be divorced from economic or religious implications.

Throughout the gospel, especially in the parables—which, following Mark, often were told in the setting of the house (13:36-53; 18:21-35)—Matthew's Jesus used economic themes to talk about God's reign: planting and sowing, wealth and poverty, buying and selling, hiring and firing, the just and the unjust. Almost all of these deal with the (re)ordering of relationships and resources. Because house-ordering is economics and because rightly-ordered relationships with God and others reflect justice, Matthew's economics and ecclesiology had to witness to justice. Those who performed economic/ religious activities according to God's will would be called just (13:49; 25:37).

THE RELATION OF THE GOSPEL TO ECONOMIC ETHICS

Despite such economic indicators in the gospels, many biblical scholars have paid scant attention to socio-economic structures and the subculture of early Christian communities in the gospels.[17] Consequently, most of them, as well as most ethicists, spend little time bringing any explicit scriptural values to bear upon economic thought and decisions. This lacuna is evidenced in someone like Thomas W. Ogletree, who wrote in his *The Use of the Bible in Christian Ethics* (1983):

> In comparison with their paramount interest in the internal relations of Christian communities, the Synoptic authors give relatively scant attention to established economic and political structures. By and large, they perceive these institutions to be external to immediate Christian concern; they consider them effectively out of reach of initiatives by the first disciples.[18]

Ogletree's thesis might be tenable had not these disciples lived in houses and related to and among specific Christian communities. As such these disciples were members of households whose internal relations were not only religious or churchly;[19] those households were also basic economic units of society. Internal religious relations in Christian households were economic relations. Economic relations were religious. "Where two or three are gathered" (18:20) Jesus was present; but "where two or three are gathered" in a household, there also was a division of labor. Spiritual relations involved relations of production. Relations of faith could not be separated from economic activity. Because the very structure of the household was not only spiritual but economic, how the Christians related to each other and their resources had religious *and* economic implications. In fact, at the time when Matthew wrote the first gospel no fundamental economic institutions existed without religious components. Unlike today, economics and religion could not be divorced. Embedded as they were in the household, they were united in a common bond, a *Gemeinschaft*.

The common bond cementing religion and economics in Matthew's *Gemeinschaft* was justice, or rightly-ordered relationships. In fact, it can be safely induced that, more than any other gospel writer, Matthew considered economics, as well as church itself, closely connected with the effort of individuals and groups connected to households to be just and to practice justice.

DEVELOPING A METHODOLOGY FOR AN INTERACTIVE HERMENEUTIC

The way I have chosen to discover a possible underlying link or fusion between religion and economics "then" and "now" is by investigating Matthew's use of and the dynamics surrounding the word "house" (*oikía/oikos*) and its related concepts, especially as they image justice.[20] In *The Semantics of Biblical Language,* James Barr includes *oikos* as a word which underwent development in the Bible.[21] However he cautions against a purely lexicographic approach to biblical theology.[22] This procedure can tend to collapse a theological concept (e.g., *ekklēsía*) by over-identifying it with a particular word (e.g., *oikía/oikos*). Instead of being sensitive to the context of the word, such an approach can force a word and its meaning to fit the theological presuppositions and ideology of the exegete. To use traditional categories, this reveals a reading-into (*eisegesis*) the scriptures rather than a reading-out (*exegesis*).

Exegesis, in a broad sense, means interpretation. Hermeneutics has been traditionally defined as the *study of the locus and principles of interpretation*— particularly as it is applied to the interpretation of ancient texts.[23] However all interpretation is historically-conditioned and reflects what Hans-Georg Gadamer calls the interpreter's "horizon."[24] For instance, as author of this book, I have my own horizon. The readers of this book will have their horizons as well. When someone with a twentieth-century horizon returns to such an ancient text as the gospel of Matthew he or she should not forget that it too reflects the historically-conditioned horizon of its author. Consequently any contemporary interpretation of Matthew's text (which reflects his horizon) will be made more difficult and fruitful by readers' recognition of their own historical conditioning or horizon. Gadamer notes that "every encounter with tradition that takes place within historical consciousness involves the experience of the tensions between the text and the present. The hermeneutic task consists of not covering up this tension by attempting a naive assimilation but consciously bringing it out."[25]

What Gadamer describes as "horizons" at the level of communication are closely related to what Thomas S. Kuhn has called "paradigms."[26] When applied to the sciences, paradigms represent an interpreter's historically-conditioned worldview or "horizon"—including assumptions, beliefs, key metaphors, and accepted patterns—which underlie scientific inquiry.[27]

1. The Historical-Critical Method and Social Sciences

Until recently, the paradigm guiding the science of biblical interpretation reflected the "scientific method" of the Enlightenment. Biblicists assumed that scriptural texts were stable and objective realities, the details of which could reveal certain meanings to the unbiased observer. From this assumption (or "paradigm"), scripture scholars developed the "historical-critical method." It aims to apply the Enlightenment's "scientific method" to biblical materials. The desired objectivity of the historical-critical method in scripture studies is enhanced when interpretation also incorporates methodologies and findings from the social sciences.

When the scientific method is applied to the scriptures, hermeneutics involves textual, historical, literary, and theological analysis.[28] Generally and briefly, for my treatment of Matthew's gospel, textual analysis considers the socio-historical meaning of precise words like *oikos/oikía*. An understanding of a word (for our purposes, "house") is aided by historical analysis, which tries to set the date and authorship of the gospel within a specific socio-economic, political, and cultural environment. This demands tools of social-scientific analysis. My primary tools have come from economics, sociology, political science, and anthropology. Literary analysis views the words being considered within literary units—for example it would examine Matthew's use of *oikía/oikos* in his various pericopes, as well as in his overall gospel—and it focuses especially upon how the words and units would be understood by Matthew's original readers. While literary criticism deals with how a passage relates to its larger literary unit, *form criticism* is more narrowly concerned with the passage itself; *tradition criticism* uncovers earlier stages of development through which a text has passed, while *redaction criticism* focuses on the final form of the passage and asks what the author or final editor intended to say through the passage in its final form.[29] Once textual, literary, and historical analysis have taken place, the interpreter is able to do theological analysis.

Theological analysis considers the explicit and implicit relationships among the words and concepts and their underlying assumptions and connections which articulated the faith of a past generation; theological analysis then shows the implications of that faith for the present.

The approach to the scriptures that is based on the Enlightenment paradigm or the scientific method revolves around three main presuppositions. It assumes that all interpretation is neutral, that the text being interpreted can be divorced from the paradigmatic assumptions of the interpreters, and that objectivity can be assured by simply using the correct interpretive tools, especially if those are enhanced by material from the social sciences. However, these presuppositions have been proven vacuous ever since Thomas Kuhn's work on paradigms has demonstrated that all "objective" observation is preceded by an interpreter's theories ("paradigms") which are conditioned by his or her world of meaning or "horizons." Because all people are conditioned by and interpret reality from their horizons, the Enlightenment "paradigm" itself has proven insufficient for thorough hermeneutics.

2. The Literary-Critical Method

Partially in response to this realization, a new approach (or "paradigm") emerged which focused on the relationship between the text and the interpreter. This paradigm has been called the "literary-critical approach" or narrative criticism. It views the gospels as unified narratives. Narrative criticism studies the content of these narratives and the rhetorical techniques used by the author (redactor) to elaborate the narrative. All narratives encompass "what" is told ("the story") and "how" it is told ("discourse").[30]

The "story" involves three elements. *Events* revealing the plot involve various incidents which are weaved throughout the story; in Matthew,[31] conflict is central to the plot. *Characters* in different events are the vehicle used to show how the plot develops; in Matthew Jesus is the main character; the disciples, the Jewish leaders, and the crowds act as other key characters, and there is an assortment of minor characters. *Settings* refer to the time, place, and/or social circumstances in which the events involving the characters take place.

The "discourse" of the Matthean narrative includes three main factors as well. The first is the *author* and the *narrator*; though there are distinctions, "Matthew" would be both author and narrator. The second involves the *point of view* or "paradigm." It includes the evaluative point of view (God's perspective [16:23]), as well as other points of view: the phraseological (which reveals reliability and truth), the spatial and temporal (whose historical grounding reveals the evaluative paradigm), and the psychological (whose purpose is to evoke within the readers positive and negative feelings regarding the events and characters). The *implied reader* (24:15; 27:8; 28:15) "denotes no flesh-and-blood person of any century but an imaginary person who is to be envisaged, in perusing Matthew's story, as responding to the text at every point with whatever emotion, understanding, or knowledge the text ideally calls for."[32]

Despite the fact that the "implied reader" in narrative criticism can be any reader, including the First World reader-interpreter in the twentieth century, I have found that this approach, like that of historical criticism, lacks the necessary elements that people of faith can use to make the words which they read concrete in their lives and history.

As long as people conduct their inquiry within a certain paradigm and achieve expected results, they will not tend to call that paradigm into question. However when one's paradigm no longer seems relevant to a task, a new paradigm is sought to help one's subsequent interpretation. When it is found, a "paradigm shift" takes place. My uneasiness with historical and literary criticism signals my own "paradigm shift."

3. Toward a New Interactive Paradigm for Interpreting Matthew

Matthew used what I have called his "horizon" to project the situation of his readers and hearers of the 80s and 90s back to the life of the disciples during the earthly activity of Jesus in the 30s.[33] In other words, he equated the time of the church of the 80s and 90s with the presence of the earthly Jesus. But since this "church" is to continue, even to our day and beyond, Matthew obviously intends that his narration will make all his readers through history into contemporaries of the historical Jesus—they will be brought into the presence of the Christ. This construction is based on the presence of the Risen Christ in the congregation (18:20; 28:20).

However, some scholars have viewed the relation between Matthew and contemporary readers differently. Walter Wink has argued that the historical-critical method, in its attempt to imitate the scientific method, gradually transferred the gospel's context from a vital faith community to a guild of biblical scholars.[34] No longer is biblical criticism part of a dynamic community for whom the results of biblical scholarship might offer applied meaning for their day-to-day lives. I believe that Wink's critique of the historical-critical method can also be applied to narrative criticism. Consequently, it seems more important to me that my method of hermeneutics or interpretation reflect my interaction with the text in a faith dialogue which admits my concerns and then attempts to determine how the text might challenge my "horizons." This effort demands a "fusion of horizons."[35]

Having challenged the assumptions behind my horizons I can better apply the scriptures to the world in which I am called to implement faithfully the teachings of Jesus. In this light, my hermeneutic will be interactive. I will try to find a fusion or interaction between how Matthew's narrative tried to apply the pattern of Jesus' life to Matthew's own house churches—which were to manifest Jesus' life and works fifty years after they had occurred—and how this same pattern must continue to be reflected in us, Matthew's readers, "to the close of the age" (28:20). The interactive process should help me in being faithful to what Dan Via concludes is the purpose of true narrative:

Narrative incorporates the past into an ongoing process, creating a continuity between past, present, and intended future. This continuity makes it possible for us to accept our past as our own, both as flawed and as forgiven, and that acceptance provides the coherence of self that is necessary for moral responsibility.[36]

Not only should this reflection on the Matthean narrative have implications for moral responsibility or ethics; it should come alive in spirituality itself. According to Wolfgang Iser, a literary work involves the actual text of the author as well as its *realization* accomplished in and by the reader. This represents fusion or interaction. Consequently, my approach to Matthew as a literary work involves not only the use of good textual, historical, and literary criticism aided by the social sciences and the best of the insights gained from narrative criticism, but, above all, it involves my interaction with the text as a subjective reader.[37]

This interactive hermeneutic contains elements of what has come to be known as "reader-response criticism."[38] According to Iser, the reader must act as co-creator of the work, supplying that portion of it which is not written but only implied. This "concretization" of a text in any particular instance requires that the reader's imagination be employed actively. The reader's activity is only a fulfillment of what is already implicit in the structure of the work. The engagement of the reader with the text, in this perspective, is essential. According to J. Severino Croatto, "All reading is production of meaning, and is done from a locus or context. As a result, what is genuinely relevant is not the 'behind' of a text, but its 'ahead,' its 'forward'—what it suggests as a pertinent message for the life of the one who receives or seeks it out."[39] What was written then must come alive now in my life as a reader. Thus Matthew's christology must not only become ecclesiology; his ecclesiology must also become lived-out in our ethical decisions and become the foundation for our spirituality itself. Matthew's Jesus could not have put it better: "Make disciples of all nations, . . . teaching them to observe all that I have commanded you . . . always, to the close of the age" (28:19–20).

As I stated above, in the scientific field, the move from one paradigm to another is what Thomas Kuhn calls a "paradigm shift." My shift from the historical-critical method I learned in the early sixties and my realization of the limits of narrative criticism have been conditioned by subsequent factors that have shaped my horizon as I interpret the gospels. The fact that I also have developed a certain way of interpreting the political economy of the First World, especially the United States of America where I live, is an element of this horizon as well.

In my previous writings, as well as at the beginning of this Introduction, I noted some of the specific factors that contributed to the shaping of my horizon, such as work in a changing parish—which inserted me in another race of people and among the economically marginated—as well as my ministry of corporate responsibility and social justice. These have forced me to struggle with the issue of what it means to be a disciple of Jesus Christ in an affluent society.[40] What does it mean to live the gospel today?

While I have tried to be a faithful exegete, my main concern has been to offer a contemporary hermeneutic. My interactive hermeneutic is geared to understand Matthew's final redaction of the gospel for his church's life and what implications his narrative may have for ethics and spirituality today. The specific literary vehicle I have chosen to use to accomplish this interpretation is the metaphor.

a. The Function of Metaphor in the New Paradigm

In trying to find a common ground for dialogue between our "horizons" and the text itself, as well as between ethics and the social sciences, we must begin by considering the nature of communication itself. Gibson Winter has shown that human beings express their inmost being to others in gesture and communication.[41] This is "language." Language, Heidegger says, is "the house of Being" (*das Haus des Seins . . . die Hut des Anwesens*).[42] Over time, interpersonal interaction through these gestures and communication— "language"—gradually becomes symbolically represented through comprehensive or root metaphors. These lead to the creation of patterned ways of thinking and behaving. Consequently, according to Winter, "certain metaphoric networks become dominant in a total society, shaping modes of thought, action, decision, and life."[43]

When this understanding of "metaphoric network" is applied to the interpretation of the method of communication contained in a narrative like Matthew's gospel, it becomes clear that metaphors are not just devices for embellishing a story. Metaphors imply *a way of thinking* and *a way of seeing* that pervade readers engaged with the text and the way in which they understand Matthew's world and their own. Metaphors represent a key element in paradigms. Sallie McFague writes: "Metaphor is basically a new or unconventional interpretation of reality, whether that interpretation refers to a limited aspect of reality or to the totality of it."[44]

Metaphors help to transform the unintelligible into the intelligible. Because they are specific, yet sufficiently different from the usual interpretation of reality, they are meant to provide a simple network of language to make something unfamiliar clearer. In this sense, *oikía/oikos* are not just words; they represent an entire cultural referent, a world of meaning. When terms such as *oikía/oikos* are viewed and studied with that in mind, the world of meaning they represent can be uncovered and becomes applicable to contemporary life. This broad notion of *oikía/oikos* is captured in the following comment by John Elliott: "The *oikos* or household constituted for the Christian movement as well as for its environment a chief basis, paradigm and reference point for religious and moral as well as social, political, and economic organization, interaction and ideology."[45]

b. House as Assumed Primary Metaphor

Given this understanding of reader-response criticism and the meaning of metaphor, and building on Winter's notion of "root metaphor,"[46] this book considers *oikos/oikía* as the "assumed primary metaphor" in Matthew, much like "air" is an assumed primary "metaphor" to human life or "water" is to fish. Without air, human life could not exist; without water, fish would die. Without the house, church and economics did not exist at the time when Jesus lived and Matthew wrote. Thus, just as air and water are assumed for those entities dependent on them, so it must be assumed that at the time of Jesus and Matthew "house" was the center of economic and political life as well as religious and ecclesial life. What is implicit in Matthew about house and the dynamics taking place in and around it can be made more concrete if house is viewed as an assumed primary metaphor.

My notion of "assumed primary metaphor" parallels what Anders Nygren called, many years ago, "the self-evident in history." The self-evident is the assumption on which an age builds. It is held in common by all. Precisely because these assumptions are self-evident, they are not subject to scrutiny except by later historians. Because they are "taken for granted, like the air we breathe, the atmosphere in which we live," the role of the biblicist is to enter "so fully into the spirit of the past that its presuppositions become his own. Only thus will he be able to view events as the age itself saw them."[47]

Viewing "house" in Matthew as a self-evident, "primary assumed metaphor" enables us to discover how various Matthean concepts referring to relations and resources in "church" and "economics"—which today seem dichotomous— can be interwoven. In this sense, a Matthean theology (including ethics and spirituality) is revealed by considering his use of the notion of "house" and related concepts, especially if one continually remembers that, at the time of Matthew, the household represented the basic unit of economic and social life as well as the life of the local church. As John Elliott writes, "The household had a dominant influence not only on the structure and internal conduct of the early Christian groups but also upon their theological perspectives and sociological symbols."[48]

In the following pages I try not to "read into" every Matthean use of the words *oikos/oikía*. Neither do I presuppose that "house" is Matthew's central focus. However, for reasons already stated which will be developed throughout the book, the following chapters do see "house" as the assumed primary metaphor of the first gospel. Since Matthew's redaction was oriented to specific issues related to a specific house-based community and how the disciples in those households could order their lives around the teachings of Jesus, "house" as a theological metaphor can help make other metaphors in the gospel more comprehensible. Furthermore, since metaphors play a significant role in engaging readers in the narration, focusing on "house" in Matthew should affect not only our minds but our feelings and have an impact on our actions as well. After all, as reader-response criticism insists, the narrative is to be considered as alive; it cannot be understood apart from its effect on one's mind, values, and behavior.

At this point one might legitimately ask why "house" has never been highlighted in the study of Matthew. Possibly because "house" was self-evident and commonplace at the time of Matthew it has not been highlighted by modern exegetes as were other Matthean metaphors such as "Son of man" and "Son of God" or "reign of God" and even "church." Another reason for the neglect of "house" may have to do with the theological approach and social perspective of modern theologians. Given an insufficient use of social-scientific criticism, an over-consciousness of conceptual metaphors like "Messiah" and "Teacher" has been developed to the neglect of socio-anthro-pological metaphors like "house." The result too often has been a lack of appreciation of and attention to underlying similarities as well as basic differences between ancient and modern cultures and social structures.

When Matthew wrote his gospel, "house" included family and kin as well as buildings and property. Thus, when Jesus "entered a house," he did not merely walk into a building[49]; he entered into relations among people that were religious as well as productive. In his gospel what happens in and around the house reflects Matthew's stated and presumed assumptions about Jesus' vision of religious and economic values and of social order vis-à-vis family, kin, buildings, and property (19:29). In this sense what was commonplace for Matthew must become clear to us. The "assumed primary metaphor" of house must always be kept in mind as the interpretive construct for this book if its thesis will be understood and made applicable to current economic realities and problems.

4. Determining a Model to Study the Social Environment

Besides stressing the role of metaphor in the paradigmatic approach I have outlined, I intend throughout this work to emphasize a second methodological point—that is, the need to understand the social and cultural environment within which Matthew composed his work. Including this wider, social dimension seems essential if we are to understand the implications of Matthew's gospel for our social reality today, especially vis-à-vis contemporary ethics and spirituality. A study of Matthew in its first-century setting should help us see that gospel's relevance to our contemporary context, which may be radically different but whose internal relational dynamics have basic parallels to Matthew's context.

In outlining an approach to the study of New Testament ethics, Wayne Meeks insists on the need to begin from an understanding of the broader context or environment which gave rise to the narrative: "I believe we cannot claim to understand the morality of a group until we can describe the world of meaning and of relationships, special to that group in its own time and place, within which behavior is evaluated."[50] What Meeks says about the need to understand the "world of meaning and of relationships" for New Testament ethics is echoed in Karl Polanyi's reflections about the priority of social relationships in economics:

> The outstanding discovery of recent historical and anthropological research is that man's economy, as a rule, is submerged in his social relationships. He does not act so as to safeguard his individual interests in the possession of material goods; he acts so as to safeguard his social standing, his social claims, his social assets. He values material goods only insofar as they serve this end.[51]

Understanding the world of social relationships helps ground ethics, be it theological ethics or economic ethics (or a mixture of the two). Thus it is necessary for us to understand Matthew's particular "world of meaning and relationships." These relationships, we will see, imply a certain house-order.

In social-scientific research, in order to understand this world of meaning and social relationships, researchers operate consciously or unconsciously from some sort of model which serves as the construct for their investigation and theories. In the social sciences, conceptual models help concretize a researcher's assumptions regarding the social world, its relationships and meanings. While a model is like a metaphor insofar as both compare entities and provoke the imagination in order to advance understanding from the more well-known to the less well-known, there also are important differences between the two. According to John Elliott (building on the work of T. F. Carney), "the difference between a model and . . . metaphor lies in the fact that the model is *consciously structured* and *systematically arranged* in order to serve as a *speculative instrument* for the purpose of organizing, profiling, and interpreting a complex welter of detail."[52]

In order to understand the world of meaning and social relationships revolving around *oikía/oikos,* some kind of speculative instrument is needed to interpret "house" in its wider social environment and show how a vision of morality and spirituality flowed from this wider world. I have chosen to follow the model of T. F. Carney,[53] especially as it is applied to the New Testament world by John Elliott.[54]

The brunt of T. F. Carney's work on models involves one which he terms "cross-cultural."[55] The cross-cultural model investigates historical and social data in order to explain the interrelationships between society and its major sub-systems. It is sociologically impossible to study a sub-system without comprehending the wider social reality of which it is a part. For my purposes this wider "society" encompasses the Greco-Roman world of the 80s and 90s, while the particular "sub-system" is Matthew and his audience. In examining society, the cross-cultural model considers socio-economic and political-legal factors as well as the cultural elements (belief system and mores) which affect individual and group interests, ideas, thinking (ideology), and behavior.[56] Studying the various sub-systems better enables one to articulate the overall system: "The institutions, practices and values—economic, political and social—of such societies complement and reinforce one another. These societies thus constitute distinct entities, social systems."[57]

This cross-cultural model has helped me investigate available historical and social data in order to build a structure within which I have been better able to understand the broader world of meaning and social relations in the first-century environment that was the context of the first gospel. However, as Elliott argues, "its very capacity as a *large-scale* model limits its utility for analyzing particularized areas and aspects of conflicts within the system."[58]

Central to this book's thesis is the conviction that Matthew's house churches reflected and interrelated with each other within a context of deep ethnic/social tensions representing different interests, values, ways of thinking, and patterns of acting. This demands a consideration of the relationships among the wider socio-economic, political-legal, and cultural factors—including the faith and belief systems (ideology) of the members of those house churches. Another model from Carey—the "multivariate or matrix model," which relates the wider social variables of the cross-cultural model to the specific sub-groupings in tension with each other—has facilitated making these connections.

From these considerations on "model," it should be clear that this book will investigate in varying degrees these major components of the social system in order to deepen our understanding of the world of meaning and the relation of social structures and processes that impacted Matthew's narrative; the book will also examine how the message of Matthew is a creative response to that situation. This will be done by studying bureaucratic and urban social ordering from the perspective of the metaphor of the basic unit of first-century bureaucracy and urbanization—the house.

Metaphors lay the foundation for a "world of meaning" with others; the social sciences help us understand the "world of meaning" of the first century and how that world of meaning generated social codes for valuation and behavior. This is what Barrington Moore calls "social causation." Social causation reveals the process of moving from an innate sense of morality that is contained within metaphors[59] to the recognition of "the need to cooperate with other human beings. . . . It is in this sense that the fact of living in society generates moral codes."[60] How did Matthew develop a moral code for his house churches in their particular urbanized, bureaucratic setting? How was this moral code an attempt to bring resolution to community problems? How did that moral code influence the development of a vision for house-ordering and house-discipleship?

In their attempt to live together, human beings experience certain recurring problems. These problems, Moore writes, can be identified under the general notion of "the problem of social coordination." How can order be established among differing peoples? The problem of social coordination, perceived from the metaphor of the household, involves three dimensions of human relationships in and around the *oikía/oikos*: the problem of authority, the division of labor, and the allocation of goods and services:

There is the problem of authority. In very small and simple societies it amounts to hardly anything more than who is going to make suggestions and who is going to follow them. There is the problem of the division of labor: who is going to do what work and when and how. Then there is the problem of allocating the resources available to the society and distributing among its members the goods and services that they collectively produce.[61]

We shall see in the following chapters that basic issues involving the problem of social coordination within households faced the Roman Empire and Matthew's house churches in their own ways. They face us today. Thus the need to understand the model of house in Matthew and its setting in the wider environment.

CAUTIONS ABOUT COLLAPSING A TWENTIETH-CENTURY HORIZON INTO THE FIRST-CENTURY HORIZON

Before moving to the outline for the development of my argument, an important caution should be made regarding an over-identification of first-century economics with that of the twentieth century. As Max Stackhouse has written:

It is no more possible to derive a contemporary normative economics directly from the pages of Scripture than it is to derive a biology from Genesis, a platform for democratic politics from Amos, a medical ethic from Luke, or a university curriculum from the letters of Paul. Several of the best contemporary efforts to relate biblical materials to issues of modern social ethics all recognize the necessity of a certain indirection of connection.[62]

Jesus and Matthew lived in a traditional society: individual, independent economic units were bonded by a common religious sense and a set of social and cultural relations. Today's culture of post-industrial capitalism is vastly different. A common familial bond no longer unites an entire society in a *Gemeinschaft*. Today, with economics and religion separated, the most we can hope to share is a *Gesellschaft* wherein individuals, who precede the group, decide for individualistic reasons to establish social relations, to create a society.

The "horizon" of Matthew is separated by twenty centuries from our own. For this reason, I do not propose that any contemporary, intelligent human order, much less economics, can operate simply on the counsels of the gospel. Organizing a capitalist economy according to the highest Christian principles certainly would destroy corporate capitalism as it presently exists. Similarly, as François Houtart has shown so convincingly, the fact that religion was central to agrarian-based, precapitalist economies and has become separated from economics in post-industrial capitalism argues against a simple application of first-century realities to twentieth- and twenty-first-century complexities.[63]

Even though an identification cannot be made between the traditional economy of the first century and ours almost two thousand years later, we must search for some kind of "fusion" of horizons. This fusion, I believe, can be found by considering the underlying relational meaning of justice.[64] I insist that there are certain principles about justice in the former that need not be divorced from the latter.[65] In this book I am careful and cautious about fusing the two "horizons," yet I don't doubt that I will be criticized for trying to make a simplistic identification of first-century traditional economics with twentieth-century post-industrial capitalism. I can only hope that my readers will carefully consider my text before launching such criticisms.

Although the specification of Christian principles embedded in the gospels of the first century cannot be identified with specifics in our economic system, democratic and/or post-industrial capitalism cannot ignore underlying principles and ethical values, especially when those principles and values reveal the criteria of justice. At the least, for Christian ethics, these values and principles must not contradict basic values. At the most, they should nourish and facilitate them. Without becoming unnecessarily bogged down in specifics, which will always elicit differing approaches (Keynesian, Marxist, Rational Expectationist, Friedmanian, etc.), one must consider the gospels' underlying assumptions about justice and how these might be applied to the overall, if not the specific, functioning of today's political economy as it operates in capitalist nations. If Matthew's gospel offered a vision to the individual households for their economic and religious ethics, we must ask how the core of his narrative and ethic, if not its specifics, can be appropriated today. This I shall try to do at the end of the book where I attempt to apply the specific redaction criticism and narrative to our contemporary environment. This is where "reader-response" criticism becomes so important.

If "house" was the "primary root metaphor" of the first century and if its relevance is questioned today, one might ask if there is any other image with which we can understand better our contemporary religious and economic systems. I would submit that this image would be that of organization itself. However, while organization might be a more appropriate image today, "organization" too can be considered from the metaphor of the house. In fact, my conversations with organizational theorists who have used metaphors to understand the nature and functions of organizations support the connection between first-century "house" and twentieth-century "organization."[66]

Despite the link between organization now and house then, Matthew's gospel does not promote a gospel-oriented, clerical, religious bureaucracy or economic system as we understand "bureaucracy" and "systems" today. Neither can we find any step-by-step Matthean blueprint for ecclesiastical or economic justice. However, because Matthew's christology reveals a highly-sculpted ecclesiology and because the teachings in his gospel are to be observed "all days," his basic organizational approach to (re)ordered relationships and resources must stand as an ultimate goal toward which all Christian life, including religious and economic life and decisions, is ordered and organized. Thus this book, like the documents on the economy from various First World church bodies, is geared to help avoid a tragic separation between faith and everyday life, between the scriptures and economics.

Hoping that this book on Matthew will be used to elaborate on this theme of the Catholic bishops of the United States, as well as similar reflections from other denominations,[67] I can ground myself in Matthew's horizon and say with the bishops about our own era:

> We write to share our teaching, to raise questions, to challenge one another to live our faith in the world. We write as heirs of the biblical prophets who summon us "to do justice, to love kindness and to walk humbly with our God" (Mi. 6:8); and we write as followers of Jesus, who told us in the Sermon on the Mount: "Blessed are the poor in spirit. . . . Blessed are the lowly. . . . Blessed are those who hunger and thirst for justice. . . . You are the salt of the earth. . . . You are the light of the world" (Mt. 5:1–6, 13–14). These words challenge us not only as believers, but also as consumers, citizens, workers and owners. In the parable of the Last Judgment, Jesus said, "I was hungry and you gave me to eat, thirsty and you gave me to drink. . . . As often as you did it for one of these the least of my brothers, you did it for me" (Mt. 25:35–40). The challenge for us is to discover in our own place and time what it means to be "poor in spirit" and "the salt of the earth" and what it means to serve "the least among us" and to "hunger and thirst for justice."[68]

If contemporary First World Christians bring a clear and deep understanding of the scriptures to bear upon religious and economic life, then that will help insure that good news comes to the poor in our own lands and in the Third World. This study of church, economics, and justice from the perspective of Matthew's house churches constitutes but one step in advancing that process.

OUTLINING COMING CHAPTERS

Working within the framework of the cross-cultural model, I intend to focus primarily on the three dimensions of social ordering mentioned above: authority, the division of labor (which will be treated under "relationships"), and the allocation of goods and services (which I will equate with "resources"). The procedure I shall use contextualizes problems facing Matthew's house churches within the wider environment. Since my approach means to create a continuity between the author's past, the reader's present, and society's future, Matthew's narrative will be examined to show how Matthew tried to apply Jesus' teachings to his house churches in their environment and how we can apply those values to today's problems in the hope of creating a better society.

The first chapter begins with a description of "house" in Greco-Roman times and then moves to its role in the New Testament and especially Matthew. With urbanization, a gospel once addressed to migrating and marginated people now was preached to wealthier people, while the poor remained alienated. Matthew offered his pattern of Jesus to inspire those disciples still faithful and to bring about conversion in those who had grown tired.

The second chapter outlines Matthew's gospel and shows how its five central discourses feature "house" as a key element. By understanding the dynamics between people (relations) and their possessions (resources) in the "house," one understands Matthew's vision for church and economics.

The next two chapters consider three dimensions of social relations: the nature and use of authority, the division of labor, and the distribution of goods and services. Chapter 3 shows how Jesus' authority (*exousía*) opposed the dominant exercise of authority within his social environment. Jesus shared his *exousía* with the house churches and with all those who would be baptized.

The fourth chapter considers rank and patriarchy as part of the structure within which the division of labor occurred in Matthew's time. His vision for household ordering will be shown to represent a more collegial model. In response to forms of reciprocity sustaining inequity, Matthew's broader economic will reveal his goal of a community wherein resources of all kinds (material and spiritual) were to be shared.

Having discussed notions regarding Matthew's approach to an embedded first-century religion and economics in the first four chapters, I show in the fifth chapter how he developed, via narrative or story, a household or communitarian ethic as the context within which individuals would realize their individual dignity and their responsibility to each other. His narrative reveals the norm by which members of the households would witness to their fidelity by doing good. The temptations of Jesus will serve as one such story dealing with property or wealth in the form of power, possessions, and prestige.

The sixth chapter demonstrates how the Beatitudes center around the notion of justice while the seventh highlights love and justice as the underlying characteristics of all moral activity in Matthew. His gospel, especially the Sermon on the Mount, will be shown as featuring love-in-justice as central.

The eighth chapter shifts from ethics to the heart of spirituality—conversion. Given the fact that prosperity in Jesus' day, Matthew's, and our own is addictive—leading humans to "serve mammon rather than God"—Matthew's call to conversion via an experience of God (i.e., contemplation) will be shown as the only effective way to challenge injustice in a manner that offers an alternative way of life for people living in the midst of prosperity.

Jesus' message in Matthew about converting toward God's reign (discussed in the ninth chapter) did not bring about a change of the social order of the first century. We have not seen radical structural change in corporate capitalism either. Thus the tenth and concluding chapter will try to analyze our present ecclesial and economic reality, discuss the need for a morality of public householding which highlights justice, investigate its obstacles in the notion of society-as-addictive, and conclude with a vision for the creation of contemporary "house churches" modeled on Matthew's gospel as a concrete way of addressing the problems of authority, relationships, and resource-sharing in today's affluent First World cultures.

A SUGGESTION ON HOW TO READ THIS BOOK

Although this book relies heavily on redaction criticism and its stress on narrative points to the goal of having Matthew's "house" put into practice in a way that bears fruit, its ultimate goal is to have that done today. This demands that the reader interact with my reflections as mine interact with Matthew's. Through Matthew's narration, his audience was to move from the story, to the paradigm or metaphor, and then to praxis, or life-translation. This faith-approach should apply not only to the readers of his day, but for all days. With the "primary assumed metaphor" of house, this demands that we consider it not only as an interpretive construct or way of understanding the setting of the gospel, but as an interpretant and framework of action today.[69]

The reader of these reflections on Matthew, using "house" as assumed primary metaphor, should better be able to understand how Matthew's gospel of the kingdom on earth is now to become housed in the hearts of the disciples and, through them, in the entire world. Thus Jack Dean Kingsbury concludes his book *Matthew as Story* with the words:

> The disciples, whom the risen Jesus commissions to a worldwide ministry at the end of Matthew's story, understand this, and so does the implied reader. It is apparent that the first evangelist, who wrote this story, would also have wanted the real reader both to understand this and to act on it.[70]

Given this understanding, I have tried to order the ten chapters in such a way that they lend themselves to an application of Matthew's first-century gospel to our twentieth-century lives. Thus, as I said in the opening paragraph, gospel data and life today become the two poles or horizons of the book. According to William Herzog, "The power of any reading of a text will not reside in its accuracy in stating *the* meaning of the text but in creating its meaning so that it is applicable to the contemporary world."[71] However, he notes in the same breath that, for this very reason, this approach will be open to debate, challenge, and questions from others whose horizons differ.

While a single word should not easily be made the basis for a book about an entire gospel, given a proper understanding of *oikía/oikos* as assumed primary metaphor, neither should it be easily discounted. Only further investigation which studies the use of *oikos/oikía* in Matthew, and, indeed, in all the gospels, will furnish support for or against the hypothesis of this book, which makes (re)ordered relationships and resources central to Matthew's vision of house-order, i.e., which makes justice central to Matthew's church and economics.

If this book can elicit this debate in a way that will not only bring about another way of interpreting Matthew's gospel, but, more importantly, a way which will "put into practice its teachings" in these last days of the second millennium, my effort will have borne fruit.

1

The Environment of Matthew's Gospel

THE SOCIO-ECONOMIC ENVIRONMENT OF THE FIRST CENTURY

Hellenism was saved for the first six centuries of the Common Era when Pompey annexed Syria and Palestine (64 and 63 BCE) for Caesar and Rome. With his victory at the Battle of Actium (31 BCE) Gaius Julius Caesar Octavianus ("Augustus" after 27 BCE), the adopted son and heir of Julius Caesar, began the process of the establishment and complete reorganization of the Roman Empire. His reign inaugurated what is called the "Principate." Under Augustus the entire Mediterranean world and a large part of northern Europe became united. By 23 BCE he had realized his goal of heading the Roman state as a constitutional patriarch. However, despite these successes at imperial expansion,[1] first-century Roman economy remained quite primitive.[2] No economic structure or "system" existed as such.[3]

As Alexander had begun urbanization for the purpose of inclusive Hellenization, Augustus continued the process of urbanization as his means of romanizing the area within the empire. Despite his efforts, agriculture still dominated economic activity.[4] With agriculture governing the economy, most products were consumed within the producing household rather than traded. Each household, village, district, and region grew and made nearly everything that it needed. Consequently, as with all subsistence forms and land-based modes of production, manufacturing and commerce (i.e., "business") were secondary.[5] While the state promoted home trade and craft production,[6] any surplus realized from crafts and trade tended to be immediately funneled to land purchases. According to Kevin Greene:

> Traders and craftsmen were modest in their operations, and of low social status; any who did make fortunes promptly bought land, and became "respectable" landowners to whom commerce was a side issue. Land bought status, and status involved displays of wealth by private consumption and expenditure on public benefactions—never productive investment.[7]

Although there was not a large-scale economic system supported by accumulation as in present-day capitalism, first-century economic life involved production, distribution (trade), and consumption. While subsistence characterized the overall economy, there were pockets of growth and a trend toward greater surplus. Greater surplus spurred population. In fact, population growth was the most fundamental economic factor during this period.[8] First-century population was between 50 and 60 million—greater than it was 1000 years earlier (and 500 years later). Between 5 and 6 million people lived in Palestine and Syria, with probably about 4 million located in Syria. The population of first-century Antioch, according to Heichelheim, was "twice or three times its later size."[9] Increasing population spurred agricultural production; consequently more land was cultivated.

With increasing urbanization, a greater proportion of workers entered non-agricultural production and services, especially in towns, but around the countryside as well. Increased agricultural and non-agricultural production facilitated increased division of labor; this led to an increase in per capita production. Per capita production also increased because of slavery, Augustus's attempt at common coinage[10] (which facilitated trade), voluntary associations, and prolonged peace. The levying of money stimulated long-distance trade, better modes of transportation, the production of goods for sale, and the use and volume of coinage. Although trade (especially long-distance trade) tended to be limited to grain and luxury goods, the entire constellation of economic relations in the first century stimulated the growth of towns.[11]

Agricultural production constituted the base of the whole economy, economic relations were tightly bound up with nature, and nature was envisioned as inseparable from the supernatural. Because of this connection among agricultural production, economic relations, and nature, production was not viewed as ultimately controlled by humans, but by extra-human forces, mostly divine. The social order and the natural order overlapped; both depended on the divine.

The divine was at the center of the world. However the house was a microcosm of the world. The ritual of constructing a house was to reflect the original creation of the world. House-order was to reflect the original order intended for creation, the *oikos tou theou*. Mircea Eliade has shown that "traditional man" continually felt "the need to reproduce the cosmogony in his construction, whatever be their nature; [and he felt] that this reproduction made him contemporary with the mythical moment of the beginning of the world."[12] Indeed, the Jews saw the cosmos as God's household; God was its builder. In this household, heaven was the throne of God; earth was God's footstool (5:34–36); no human house—even the temple—could compare to it (Is. 66:1). Despite this, the sanctuary of the temple in Jerusalem had three parts to correspond to the three cosmic regions: the Court representing the sea (the lower region), the Holy Place representing the earth, and the Holy of Holies representing heaven. Given the centrality of house in the cosmogony of traditional peoples as well as in their daily lives, the unity between religion and economics was as embedded as the divine and the human. The metaphor of house represented a microcosm of the universe for non-nomadic peoples.

1. The House as the Basic Economic Unit of Society

Despite instances when people transferred their accumulated wealth into purchase of land, wealth was usually fixed by inheritance within families. Thus household economics was grounded in kinship. Kinship formed the foundation for the wider polity. Economic functions such as production and consumption, planting and sowing, hiring and firing, were determined ultimately by kinship (belonging or family) and political (power or honor) considerations, rather than "market" or "economic" factors.

According to Karl Polanyi, economies at that time (and until the end of feudalism in Western Europe) were organized around three poles: reciprocity, redistribution, and householding. Sometimes, as in the first century, all three were combined.[13] Reciprocity involved a kind of implicit, nonlegal, contractual obligation between ranked peoples enforceable by codes of honor and/or shame. Redistribution represented the collection, storage, and reallocation of goods and services determined by some center (usually some form of government or temple). Taxes and rents often constituted the main form of redistribution.[14]

The third pole, householding, grounded relations of reciprocity and redistribution. Polanyi notes that, as the "third economic principle," householding was destined to play an important role in history because large amounts of goods were produced domestically for the family's use:

> As far as ethnographical records are concerned, we should not assume that production for a person's or group's own sake is more ancient than reciprocity or redistribution. On the contrary, orthodox tradition as well as some more recent theories on the subject have been emphatically disproved. . . . Indeed, the practice of catering for the needs of one's household becomes a feature of economic life only on a more advanced level of agriculture; however, even then it has nothing in common either with the motive of gain or with the institution of markets. Its pattern is the closed group. Whether the very different entities of the family or the settlement or the manor formed the self-sufficient unit, the principle was invariably the same, namely, that of producing and storing for the satisfaction of the wants of the members of the group. The principle is as broad in its application as either reciprocity or redistribution.[15]

Within this traditional first-century economy, household members interacted with each other vis-à-vis their resources and in such a way that the wider community was able to function.

a. The Relation among *Oikía, Pólis,* and *Basileía*

Along with reciprocity and redistribution, householding constituted the basic operational unit of society. The household served also as the foundation of the *pólis* or city, as well as of the *basileía,* the empire. To the degree the household would be properly ordered, so would the city, and, ultimately, the empire. This natural order at the human level would reveal the divine order. The inseparable link between *oikía/oikos* and *pólis/basileía* explains Rome's preoccupation with proper order throughout the empire. This right-ordering (justice) started with the household.

Generally various households organized themselves according to lineage into villages not only for protection and proximity to water but also better to ensure basic reciprocal relations.[16] The organizing principle was kinship. An adaptation of a model developed by Robert David Sack reflects this interaction of traditional reciprocity and redistribution within and among households and how this relationship of household members and their resources created a village or community. By community, Sack means any social unit larger than the household. Sack's model applies equally well to agricultural and non-agricultural households and communities:

Aerial View of an Urban-based,   Reciprocity and Redistribution
Traditional Agricultural Economy   in Traditional Household Economy

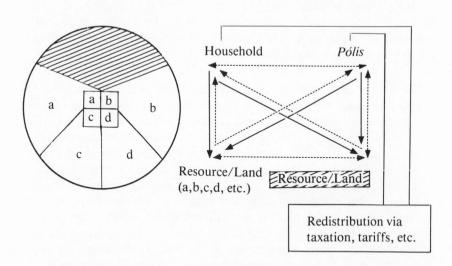

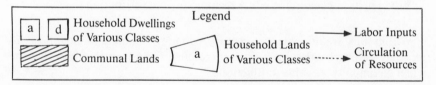

The two main actors were the household and the village or community, which controlled resources. The solid arrows indicate flows of labor inputs; the broken lines indicate output flows.[17] The entire socio-political system included independent households—some peasant, some of the higher classes, including the imperial lands ("a" to "d"). When household resources were extended beyond one's village or city to land elsewhere, absentee ownership and tenant farming resulted. Resources were also extended via tributes and taxation as the principle means of redistribution.

Given Rome's desire for urbanization in order to better solidify the empire, the households that were organized in and around villages gradually became attached or "attributed" to cities from which administration took place.[18] By the second and third centuries, this policy of urbanization gradually transformed most non-urban territories into areas administered by cities.[19]

During the first century rich landowners often lived in towns and cities which were administrative centers for regions and the base for modest production of crafts for local markets. As the towns and cities grew in numbers and power, their relations with the rural areas grew more tentative. Both depended on each other, but by every measure of physical and social advantage, the symbiosis was one-sided, favoring the city. Ownership of productive land became increasingly concentrated in the hands of fewer and fewer proprietors who lived in the city or its extension, their villas. Consequently small, independent landowners living on their own land gradually began to disappear only to become tenants or slaves, day laborers based in the cities, or recruits for the army.[20]

Despite exceptions like Antioch, Alexandria, and Rome, cities of the Roman Empire were generally quite small. While there were more spacious houses for the upper classes, the majority of people (the lower classes) seem to have lived in the equivalent of one- or two-room apartments.[21] Ramsey MacMullen has estimated that the average population density in some of the larger cities of the empire may have approached two hundred per acre, a density not found today except in highrises and industrial slums.[22] Tensions resulting from the overcrowding within tenement-type households were eased somewhat through public areas open to all (as much as one-fourth of a city) for festivals, religious rituals, and sports; an abundance of voluntary associations for work and entertainment also helped lessen those tensions. There were also street-people.

Where reciprocity took place within and among households, redistribution insured the link between households and the wider polity. The instruments for this redistribution were rents, taxes, tithes, and tributes.[23] Besides taxes, tithes, and tributes, the state leased land (*ager publicus*) in various places and got directly involved in the grain market to fulfill the needs of the dole and of government personnel.[24] It allowed its soldiers to seize produce and demand to be billeted in villages. Not surprisingly, some of its agents abused their offices by various forms of exploitation. However, outside of these situations, the state generally did not become directly involved in independent household economies beyond redistributive practices (taxes and tributes).

The Roman state needed two kinds of economic services which it didn't perform itself. The first was the provision of supplies—for religious rituals, the army, secular civic purposes (i.e., public construction). The second flowed from the first: the collection of monies to pay for the essential state services. In peace-time, the army performed some of the construction projects. However, as François Houtart has shown, the family of Caesar created employment through public construction projects such as roads and aqueducts, palace buildings, monuments, and murals. By its involvement in the reconstruction of the temple, Rome helped establish strong ties between the official governing bureaucracy and a local religion. Furthermore, Houtart shows, "By the collections of taxes, the temple recouped for the State a good part of the surplus product of the people."[25]

Outside the above activities, Rome tended not to enter into the economy directly. For instance, it left the general trading in grain (except for the situations noted above) to private dealers.[26] It usually arranged for its work to be done through contracts for public works and services with *publicani*.[27] The publicans engaged in public contracts, tax-farming, and large-scale money-lending. The Jews saw this group as sustaining the imperial presence. Consequently, they were ostracized and known as "sinners" (9:10, 11; 11:19). To have a "sinner" of this type within one's *oikía* was to support the *basileía*.

While imperial Rome made its presence felt directly through the contract system, the imperial household was primarily reinforced indirectly through a culture of patriarchy which cyclically extended from it to the community and local household and back from the household and community to the Principate. Thus the patriarchal connection between the *politeía* and the *basileía* as ultimately grounded in the *oikía/oikos*.

Having examined the environment within which the households existed, we can now examine the two major kinds of households of the first century: the patriarchal form and the voluntary associations.

b. Patriarchal Households in a Patriarchal System

The entire cultural system of the first century was constitutively patriarchal. The patriarchal form of the household, especially in the areas under the influence of Rome, served as the foundation and reinforcement for the patriarchy of the empire itself. Behavior patterns of man to man (and to woman) were graded and fixed, immobile within various ranks.

Even though the family was the entire context for the household, the Greeks had no word (the only possible exception to this being *oiketeía* [24:45]) to express the modern notion of family except *oikos/oikía*.[28] The Latin word *familia* generally represents what the Greeks meant by *oikía;* however there were strong legal implications connected to the former term. For the Romans—whose legal system dominated the first century—*familia* had various meanings: the descendants of a common ancestor ("the house of David"); one's property; one's servants (the *familia Caesaris* comprised all the personal slaves and freedpersons in the imperial service, but not the emperor's wife or children); or, more commonly, all the persons, free or unfree, under the authority of the *paterfamilias* (*kýrios* in Greek), the lord or head of the household. The *paterfamilias* was not the biological father as much as the authority over the household.[29]

Wayne Meeks has shown that "family" was defined not primarily by kinship but by relations of dependence and subordination: "The head of a substantial household was thus responsible for—and expected a degree of obedience from—not only his immediate family but also his slaves, former slaves who were now clients, hired laborers, and sometimes business associates or tenants."[30] This authority of the *paterfamilias* was reinforced by Roman law. It divided that authority into three elements: *potestas,* or power over his children (including adoptees), his grandchildren, and his slaves; *dominium,* or power over his possessions; and *manus,* or power over his wife and his sons' wives.[31]

Marriage *in manu* was one of two types of legal marriage in Roman law. It transferred the father's *patria potestas* over the woman into the hands of the husband. The wife had no distinct legal position, but was like a daughter. The second legalized form of marriage was the *sine manu.* These were "free" marriages in which the wife was not subject to her husband's *patria potestas.* Here the woman, under the technical authority of her father, would seek formal emancipation upon his death to become a person *sui iuris,* legally competent to conduct her affairs.[32] The growing economic power of some women at this time brought about greater legal and household independence. While this served as a potential threat to the city and empire, the basic pattern of household division of labor dominated: generally the husband worked outside the house; the woman worked inside.

At the heart of householding was a system of patronage. Formal training, administrative skills, official expertise, and influential connections all tended to be part of inherited wealth and social relations. If a man did not have these and did not participate in a voluntary association that would provide sustenance,[33] his sole recourse was to put himself under the patronage of a household which had these resources and relationships. Household patronage affected the wider polity in such a way that society resembled a mass of little pyramids of influence, each headed by a major family—or one giant pyramid headed by an autocrat—not the three-deck structure of upper, middle, and lower classes familiar to us from industrial society.[34]

In reflecting on society's organization, Greek writers discussed the household (*oikos/oikía*) and its ordering or management (*oikonomía*) in two different but related ways; both ways assumed patriarchy. One approach equated a household with its property—the material possessions of the household head—and the means of production within that household. The other viewed the household as constituted primarily by the persons subject to the household head; the property was secondary. Both interpretations were framed within the context of a patriarchal polity and bureaucracy.

Xenophon represents the first position in the oldest extant and most influential treatise on house-ordering (*Oeconomicus*), written about 386 BCE. For Xenophon, the *oikos* comprised more than the house itself; it extended to the fields and possessions, wherever resources might be (even outside the boundaries of a city). He quotes Socrates as saying that "a household then looked to us to be the totality of possessions, a possession we asserted to be whatever would be beneficial for the life of each, and beneficial things were found to be all things that one knows how to use."[35] Possessions constituted the household; these encompassed social relations and activities.[36] These activities were connected to a certain lifestyle and ethical order.

While the husband was overall lord of the household, the wife was a key figure in household management and governance. The husband's activity brought provisions into the house; the wife's management regulated their use. The partnership established between husband and wife was not dichotomous; rather it was mediated by a common purpose: household maintenance and success. Reflecting on Xenophon's idea of house-ordering, Michel Foucault wrote:

> Hence each of the two marriage partners has a nature, a form of activity, and a place, which are defined in relation to the necessities of the *oikos*. That they remain steadfast partners is a good thing in the eyes of the "law," the *nomos*—i.e. the regular custom that conforms exactly to nature's intentions, assigns each person his role, and defines what is good and fine to do and not to do. . . . To alter this division, going from one activity to the other, is to be in contempt of this *nomos;* it is at the same time to go against nature and to abandon one's place.[37]

Aristotle can be considered representative of the second position, which grounds household relations in persons rather than a totality of possessions. His *Politics* responded to Plato's discussion of marriage, the family, and the private household. For Aristotle a complete household consisted first of people and then of property, both under the husband. "Thus it is clear that household management attends more to men than to the acquisition of inanimate things, and to human excellence more than to the excellence of property which we call wealth, and to the virtue of freemen more than to the virtue of slaves."[38]

Three basic groupings determined relationships among household members: master and slave, husband and wife, father and children. How members of these three groups should interact was codified by specific household codes which the Germans have called *haustafeln*. Since the household not only included the three groups of people but also involved "the so-called art of getting wealth" or property,[39] *haustafeln* often included this dimension as well.

The first level of Aristotle's politics deals with goods or primary resources (*chrēmata*) within the basic household unit. The title of the male (perceived to be a free male) as *oikonómos* shows how human identity linked both freedom and economics. The second level of Aristotle's politics considers people in their interaction with each other in the context of the house. Under the title *despótēs,* the individual householder (perceived to be the husband) is seen as citizen with certain rights and responsibilities regarding his wife, children, servants, and slaves.

According to Aristotle, individual households were organized into small village units. Several villages constituted a self-sufficient "city-state." The households of resident foreigners and other classes of non-citizens did not qualify. The way individuals relate to each other (second level) with their resources (first level) constitutes the common good of the *basileía*. When people relate to each other through their resources in such a way that the commonweal is achieved, justice results. Justice refers to the right-ordering of relations among the three groups of persons as well as the way they deal with wealth or resources. From that right-ordering, justice results as the first virtue of society.[40]

As indicated previously, an important way to insure the preservation of the patriarchal order was through *haustafeln* or household codes. These codes were part of the writings of Plato and the Middle Platonists, Aristotle and the Peripatetics, as well as the Stoics and Hellenistic Jews. David L. Balch shows how the local household was politically ordered to preserve the city and the imperial, patriarchal system as a whole:

> Greco-Roman political science often drew an analogy between the house and the city: the rejection of the husband's authority by the wife, or of the master's authority by the slave, or of the father's authority by sons led to anarchy in both home and city, to the rejection of the king's authority, and to the *degeneration* of the constitution from monarchy to democracy.[41]

From these considerations, it is not surprising that an entire way of life which was meant to cultivate the authority of the patriarchal system within the Greco-Roman world depended on the order exercised in the household. According to Abraham J. Malherbe:

> The household members' loyalty to the interests of the household was so strong that it could rival loyalty to the republic. The closeness of the household unit offered the security and sense of belonging not provided by larger political and social structures. The head of the household had a degree of legal responsibility for his charges, but the solidarity of the group was based more on economic, and especially psychological, social, and religious factors.[42]

The solidarity of the household unit that could challenge the closely organized patriarchal ordering within the empire under the head of the emperor himself potentially existed in all households. However, the nonpatriarchal form of households/associations represented a special kind of threat to the patriarchal constitution of the empire.

c. Collegial Households/Associations in a Patriarchal System

Marshall Sahlins has shown that, in addition to traditional, house-based kinship patterns, tribal groups have always ordered their lives through another means, that of associations or "brotherhoods" which may have been perceived as divisive of the dominant patriarchal system.[43] Throughout Greek and Roman cities, people organized themselves into various voluntary associations for social and economic purposes—such as taking meals and drinking, division of labor, burying the dead, etc. Rather than being hierarchical and patriarchal, these voluntary associations were more egalitarian. The Greek tradition referred to these voluntary associations generically as *koina*. The Romans called their groupings *collegia*. Though having economic purposes, religion was at the core of their organization. E. A. Judge noted as early as 1960: "As with the republic and the household, they were always religious societies to the extent that they gave formal expression to their unity in the worship of a god."[44]

The worship of Dionysius in small house churches (fourth century BCE) and particularly the worship of the goddess Isis in the first centuries before and after Christ were particularly threatening to the patriarchal system. The cult of Isis was the dominant faith around the first century BCE. Its household mix of slaves and freepersons, women and men, blacks and whites, undermined the very system of Roman patriarchy. According to Witt: "It was an international religion. In the service of the Queen of the Whole Universe fellow slaves would band themselves together and feel free, coloured Africans could join with Romans, and women could claim the same power as men."[45] Whether the cult of Dionysius or Isis, both depended on the *koina* or *collegia* for their nourishment and reproduction. Within a patriarchal system their more egalitarian ethos constituted a threat.

Although many of these voluntary associations functioned in a more egalitarian form than the patriarchal mode of household (especially in their treatment of women), they shared in common with the patriarchal model the same basic organizing principle of the households.[46] To the extent that the *koina/ collegia* were households they fit within the wider bureaucracy, but to the extent they were alternate, they served as a potential subversive element in society, especially in their stress on the equality of women. Thus, many first-century Romans believed that the cult of Isis subverted proper distinctions between men and women.[47]

Wayne Meeks notes that membership was established by the free decision to associate rather than by birth.[48] People created these associations to pursue common economic interests and also to find solidarity in face of the pervading status system. In the process, these assemblages served not only as support groups for society's alienated; they also represented an alternative to some of the existing (patriarchal) familial and status modes.

The potential of even the most social group to take on political characteristics led the authorities to limit such organizations to three main types under the Principate.[49] According to John Stambaugh and David Balch, professional societies composed of businesspeople sharing a common trade (shippers, porters, bakers, merchants of livestock, carpenters, and the like) constituted one kind of *collegia*. Another category was *collegia sodalicia*, devoted to the worship of specific gods. Often foreigners who worshiped the gods of their home territories belonged to such groups. Jewish synagogues in the various cities probably appeared barely distinguishable from other *collegia* of this category. The poor organized themselves into voluntary associations of a third kind called *collegia tenuiorum,* especially for purposes of being assured a proper burial.

Collegia had definite organizational forms and ways of sustaining themselves financially, such as patronage and contributions of members, gifts and return on investments. Smaller groups met in an area of a public temple, in rented halls, or in private households. More prosperous groups built their own meeting places, which normally had a small temple dedicated to the group's patron divinity, an open courtyard for meetings, dining rooms for the common meals, and various kitchens and service rooms.[50] Others had patrons.

Although there were different types of voluntary associations, it can be stated that in general their members experienced community more intimately and less patriarchically. While not all gatherings were exclusively religious, they, like all institutions of that age, had religious dimensions built into their functions.

d. The Basic Ordering of All Households

From these considerations, we can conclude that from Homeric times through the advent of Roman rule, the house served as the basis and model for social and cultural life as well as economic and political life. Besides referring to the *members* of the immediate household which occupied the building called the house, the terms *oikía/oikos* also included the household and its goods and means of production. At the *relational* level it could encompass the immediate and extended family, slaves and freedpersons, servants and workers, as well as tenants and business clients (and even "household gods"). At the level of *resources,* "house" included the building itself as well as land and property, including the means and forces of production peculiar to that house. The household was the center around which life was organized in a way that served to satisfy material, social, and psychological needs, including security. Certain ethical norms and values, duties, obligations and responsibilities, social relationships and allocations of resources were part of house-management. Hence house-management involved economic and ethical assumptions, rules, and norms about relationships and resource allocation among members within the house.[51]

Within the context of the management of household relationships[52] and resources[53]—which included kinship relations, position, freedom, wealth, and property rights—the basic forms of social relations and interaction, status and class, were determined in such a way that the dynamic of reciprocity and redistribution was never fundamentally altered.[54] This dynamic reflects an embedded economy wherein economic roles and goals, production and planning, hiring and firing, etc., are determined by kinship or political considerations, either alone or primarily, rather than purely economic relations and forces.[55] And, of course, religion was core.

2. The House as the Basic Religious Unit of Society

In the Roman world that provided the wider cultural system for the writing of the first gospel, the household was not only the basic economic unit. The household was a religious community as well. Just as no economics existed apart from the wider socio-political reality, so all religion, through the household, was embedded in either kinship or polity. According to Bruce Malina, "There was no freestanding social institution recognized as 'religion,' no discernible separation of church and state or church and family, even if one wished to make such a separation."[56] All members of the household (patriarchal or collegial) passed into the service and under the protection of the household gods. Wives passed from the gods of their fathers to those of their husbands. Wives trained the children in worship of the gods. Newly bought slaves were expected to worship the household gods as well; thus conversion of slaves to other forms of worship was a violation of household codes. If it happened it was considered subversive to right order. Thus Tacitus wrote of the slaves' independent cultic activities: "But now that we have in our households nations with different customs than our own, with a foreign worship or none at all, it is only by terror that you can hold in such a motley rabble."[57]

Religion and economics were organized through the house. Thus, when one considers the meaning of "church" in the first century, it cannot be divorced from the household. Indeed, one might well wonder why this theme has not played a more important part in recent exegeses on the gospels. As early as 1939 Floyd V. Filson wrote his ground-breaking article in the *Journal of Biblical Literature* entitled "The Significance of the Early House Churches." Yet, to my knowledge, the English-speaking world has yet to have a book on the gospels written from this perspective.[58] In concluding his article Filson summarized five reasons for the significance of the house in early church history:

> It thus appears that the house church was a vital factor in the church's development during the first century, and even in later generations. It provided the setting in which the primitive Christians achieved a mental separation from Judaism before the actual open break occurred. It gave added importance to the effort to Christianize family relationships. It explains in part the proneness of the apostolic church to divide. It helps us gain a true understanding of the influential place of families of means in what has sometimes been regarded as a church of the dispossessed. It points us to the situation in which were developed leaders to succeed apostolic workers. Obviously the apostolic church can never be properly understood without bearing in mind the contribution of the house churches.[59]

Having examined the way households fit within the wider social order, we can now examine the role of house in the New Testament.

HOUSE IN THE NEW TESTAMENT

The Hebrew word for house, *bayith,* was usually translated in the Septuagint as *oikos* and *oikía,* with little distinction between the words. Different scholars have offered different—and often conflicting—textual analysis of the words in the New Testament. For instance Hans-Josef Klauck argues for *oikos* representing lodging, room, and property, and *oikía* signifying relatives, clients, and servants.[60] In a book which appeared the same year as Klauck's article (1981), John Elliott argued exactly the opposite:

> *Oikía* in the literal sense of "house" or "building" denotes the *place* where the ministry of Jesus and the Christian mission originated and developed. *Oikos* denotes a *group of persons,* a household as well as the domicile in which they lived; that is the basic *social community* to which the message of salvation was addressed.[61]

I will show later in this chapter that, while there are some uses of *oikos* in Matthew that have very specific and limited meanings, no clear-cut distinctions between the words can be found in Matthew; this lack of clarity generally supports interchangeability between the words.[62]

The repeated New Testament use of the term *oikos* (112 times) and *oikía* (94 times) indicates the gospels' and epistles' contextualization within their environment. Historically, "household" and its related terms described the foundation and context of the Christian movement. Religiously, the movement originated in and owed its growth to the conversion of entire households or of certain individuals within households; generally cultic activities like the eucharist took place in the house. Economically, the household constituted the context for the sharing of resources among co-believers as well as the wandering charismatics. Socially, the household provided a practical basis and theoretical model for Christian organization as well as its preaching.[63] These various dimensions of "house" help support my focus on the concept as an assumed primary metaphor.

Assumptions about the ethics of the household and its ordering of relations and resources (read "economics," or the relations and forces of production) must be investigated beyond the mere use of the word; that investigation must also include the word's semantic and social fields. John Elliott has touched upon the semantic field of words directly connected to *oikos* and, at the same time, outlined the wide social fields they encompassed up to the state itself:

> The *oikos* . . . provided the model, the terminology and the ideological framework for the organization of the state as a whole, its smaller parts (e.g., *epoikia,* "villages"), its various types of subjects (e.g., *metoikoi, paroikoi,* "resident aliens"; *katoikoi,* "military colonists"), and its administrative officials (e.g., *diokētēs,* chief financial officer; *hypoikētēs,* his subordinate supervisor of several nomes; and *oikonomos,* the financial administrator of a nome).[64]

1. The Relationship between Oikía and Ekklēsía

Whereas the *oikía/oikos* referred to the basic unit of the empire, the *ekklēsía* was a more political entity that referred to the regularly-assembled political body of free citizens gathered for deliberation.⁶⁵ Thus not all households were *ekklēsíai.* Although all formal gatherings of people had some religious overtones, the original meaning of *ekklēsía* did not involve inherent religious or cultic meanings.⁶⁶ As Banks notes, "It simply means an assembly or gathering of people in a quite ordinary sense so that, as in Greek usage, it can refer to meetings that are quite secular in character."⁶⁷ Meeks described four kinds of *ekklēsíai*: the synagogue, the philosophical or rhetorical school, patriarchal households, and voluntary associations.⁶⁸

At the time of Jesus and for the first decades afterwards for the Jews, the *qahal* (congregation) assembled in house-based synagogues. The house-based congregation was known as the *ekklēsía* in Greek. As the central religious institution of Judaism, the Jewish house-synagogues were an attempt to extend the holiness of the temple to bed and board. In time the village synagogue became the Pharisees' power-base. Under them the synagogues stood opposed to corrupt temple practices.

The first stage of the house-based church in Christianity was short lived. Followers of the Way went daily to the temple and then met together in houses (see Acts 5:42). During the second stage the synagogue served as the primary setting for missionary preaching (Acts 9:20; 17:1–4; 18:4), while eucharistic worship continued to be ordered around individual homes.⁶⁹ However, as in Judaism, the house and church, *oikía/oikos* and *ekklēsía,* cannot be equated.

Paul referred to the *ekklēsía* in various ways. Romans alone reveals at least five different implications. *Hē kat' oikon* (+ possessive pronoun) *ekklēsía* designated "the assembly at the house of N." In Romans the church met in the house of Prisca and Aquila (Rom. 16:5; see 1 Cor. 16:19; Col. 4:15; Philem. 2). However, the church not only localized itself in the *oikía/oikos.* It was linked to groups (Rom. 16:4), to the *pólis* (Rom. 16:1), and to the whole body as well (Rom. 16:16). In the case of Gaius, it seems his house served as the center for the whole church at Corinth (Rom. 16:23); it is probably from there that Paul wrote to the Romans. John Elliott points to some of the local and universal dimensions of the terms:

> Both terms, *oikos* and *ekklēsía,* originally were employed by Christian missionaries to depict local individual households or public assemblies of believers, respectively. In the eventual expansion and consolidation of the Christian movement both terms also were used subsequently in a comprehensive manner to designate the sum total of Christian *oikoi* and *ekklēsíai* as constituting the one universal household or assembly of God.⁷⁰

If *ekklēsía* in the New Testament cannot be considered synonymous with *oikía/oikos,* what distinguished it from the other political *ekklēsíai* of the Greco-Romans and the synagogues of the Jews? While elements of the latter remained, especially in the notion of an actual gathering of people which met regularly, the connection to God (Acts 20:28; 1 Cor. 1:2; 10:32; 11:22; 15:9; 2 Cor. 1:1; Gal. 1:13; 1 Thes. 2:14; 1 Tim. 3:15) and to Jesus Christ (Rom. 16:16;

see Eph. 5:23–32; Col. 1:18–24) distinguished the Christian *ekklēsía*. The people who met as an *ekklēsía* were those called[71] by God and baptized in Christ Jesus; they gathered because of their faith in him and their baptismal bonds with each other.

2. The Household Church in Early Christianity

For the first centuries after Jesus' death-resurrection, the early church did not own buildings specially erected for religious purposes.[72] In the first decades Christians assembled in the house-based synagogues[73] and then in their own houses (see Acts 1:13; 2:46; 5:42). These ranged in size from smaller places (where 10 to 20 gathered) to locations able to hold as many as 30 to 50 and even 100 people. While mobility and urbanization contributed to the rapid growth of early Christianity, some advance the theory[74] that growth also was generated when the head of a house converted; often the household "believed" along with him or her (see John 4:53; Acts 16:15; 18:8; 1 Cor. 16:15).

These same dynamics seem to have been repeated in urban settings as the Christian movement spread throughout the empire. New foundations imitated the model of the Jerusalem house church. In fact, as Elisabeth Schüssler-Fiorenza has noted:

> The house church was the beginning of the church in a certain city or district. It provided space for the preaching of word, for worship, as well as for social and eucharistic table sharing. The existence of house churches presupposes that some rather well-to-do citizens—who could provide space and economic resources for the community—joined the Christian movement.[75]

The gathering of the faithful in household churches continued long after the resurrection/Pentecost event. The role of household gatherings in manifesting the unique, abiding presence of Jesus, his preaching, healing, and teaching, can be seen throughout the New Testament. In fact, as Filson noted, a study of the New Testament which does not take into consideration the house church will be sadly lacking:

> All of these studies are useful and necessary. However, all of them would be still more fruitful, and the New Testament church would be better understood, if more attention were paid to the actual physical conditions under which the first Christians met and lived. In particular, the importance and function of the house church should be carefully considered.[76]

While there now is no doubt about the significance of the role of the house in New Testament communities, the question of which model they adapted—the patriarchal or voluntary-association form—has become the focus of debate for decades. Originally it was generally accepted that a patriarchal form was followed. However, in 1876 Georg Heinrici proffered the idea that house churches were structured according to the form of the associations.[77] In a series of lectures four years later Edwin Hatch developed the theory further.[78] The implications of the association-model of house churches in Matthew will be described in chapter 4.

Almost from the time of Pentecost, major tensions existed in the church in Jerusalem. While the role of women within the house churches was bound to be a focal point of tension, given the changing position of women in society,[79] the first noted tension in the New Testament revolved around discrimination in the way Hebrew and Hellenist women were treated. The specific Hebrew-Hellenist tension—that the Hellenist "widows were neglected in the daily distribution" in contrast to the Hebrew widows—was resolved through the creation of the first deacons, including Stephen (Acts 6:1-6).

3. Founding the Church at Antioch

After the stoning of Stephen, with its resulting persecution (Acts 7:1-8:4), some of those who were persecuted "traveled as far as Phoenicia and Cyprus and Antioch, speaking the word to none except Jews" (Acts 11:19). The Greek-speaking Jews (Hellenist faction) of the diaspora grouped in Alexandria, Antioch, and Rome, as did the Aramaic-speaking (Hebrew) disciples. Here further divisions between the Hellenists and Hebrews arose. While many of the divisions and hard feelings were caused by religious and cultural differences, they were wrapped in debates about the degree to which Moses' Law would be incorporated in the ethic of the early community. Considering themselves freed from the terms of the Law, the Hellenists lived in households apart from the Hebrew faction. As Floyd V. Filson notes, "Each group worshiped in the language that they knew, and the language background no doubt determined the grouping when they met and ate in homes of the disciples, somewhat as was done in the 'house churches.' "[80]

The mother of John Mark, Mary, identified in Acts 12:12-17 as a woman in whose Jerusalem house the Hellenists gathered, was kin of Barnabas (see Col. 4:10). Barnabas was one of the early leaders of the Antiochene (house) church(es) which, we will see, may have been the intended audience of the first gospel. As the account in Acts implies, the rapid expansion of the early church made it virtually impossible to meet as a whole group in one place. Rather, gatherings ordinarily took place in various smaller groups (of 30 to 40) which met in private homes. A good number of these, though not all by any means, occurred in homes of women and the financially secure. The latter was especially true in those places where the poor dwelling in small apartments could not provide space for a gathering.

THE SOCIAL SETTING FOR THE FIRST GOSPEL

The general view about the date and location of the first gospel, attributed to Matthew, holds that it was written around 80-90 CE for an audience living in an urban setting. That theory is reflected in the framework I use in this book.

However, others have located this general urbanized community more specifically by pointing to the Syrian coast, usually Antioch.[81]

I will not detail reasons why this period seems correct or why Antioch seems preferred to such possible locations as Jerusalem, Palestine, Phoenicia, Caesarea Maritima, or even Alexandria. The best defenses for the date and setting I suggest have been proffered by Jack Dean Kingsbury[82] and John P. Meier in their various commentaries on Matthew. This includes Meier's *Antioch and Rome*[83] (co-authored with Raymond E. Brown, who also holds to the Antiochan location). What I will primarily discuss is the notion that Matthew's gospel indicates an urban setting. But before doing that, a few words about Antioch as a possible setting for Matthew's gospel are in order.

In the East, the most strategic province for Rome was Syria. Its strategic importance was twofold: it was a center for trade and industry as well as the frontier (together with Cappadocia) against Parthia. The combined district of Syria and Palestine was the most important Eastern corridor of trade to the Mediterranean countries.[84] While the actual mineral resources of the Syrian province were poor when compared to the West,[85] there was self-sufficiency in grains. Figs, fruit, and vegetables were abundant enough for exportation. Textiles and glass were also exported, but more as luxury goods, not for general use.[86]

Antioch on the Orontes was the capital of Syria. About three hundred miles from Jerusalem, it had been founded around 300 BCE by Seleucus I Nicator. As early as the time of the ancient oriental empires, the districts from Syria and Palestine to Babylonia had close economic and cultural connections.[87] According to Rostovtzeff, because Antioch was a center for the caravan trade, it vied with Rome, along with the "capitals of the richest and most prosperous provinces."[88] By the time of the early Christian era Antioch was exceeded in size in the Roman Empire only by Alexandria and Rome.

In 64 BCE Pompey made Antioch the focus of Roman power in the Near East. Consequently, by Matthew's day Antioch was beginning to reflect the emerging Roman pattern of reorganization which attached or "attributed" native territories to cities and their administration. This encouraged urbanization in the sense that people in rural areas left for the cities, while "urban" attitudes seeped into the country. This urbanization was another reason for Antioch's rapid growth.[89]

Despite its importance in the first century, twentieth-century archeological research around Antioch has discovered no details about the actual physical structure of any Christian houses at that time.[90] This may be because the archeologists' primary interest is in temples, arenas, or other large structures. It also may be because house churches merely followed the pattern of other household structures throughout the Mediterranean. Size and style based on common patterns reflected the rank of the householders.[91] Suffice it to say, with Heichelheim, that the houses in the area "bear a very strong resemblance to the type of house usual throughout the Roman Empire."[92]

While no authenticated archeological findings reveal what houses looked like in Antioch during the first century, discoveries at nearby Dura Europos (destroyed in 250 CE)[93] have uncovered three houses dedicated to worship in the third century. One was a Mithraeum, another a synagogue, and a third was a Christian house church. Members of each were in close enough proximity to invite mutual comparison and contrast. Matthew's gospel seems to reflect that sort of situation: the Christian house church was not only aware of the older and better established Jewish tradition but also found itself required to understand and explain why it had come to meet and worship here and not in the synagogue down the street. According to Luke Timothy Jones, "Matthew's Gospel makes a great deal of sense if this pluralistic context is assumed, one in which rival and persuasive claims demand interpretation of one's own."[94]

1. "House" and Related Concepts in Matthew's Gospel

Oikos is used nine times[95] and *oikía* twenty-seven times[96] in Matthew. Nine uses of *oikía* and three of *oikos* are unique to Matthew.[97] A textual analysis of the uses finds *oikía* generally referring to the building. However, in at least six places (8:14; 10:13; 12:25; 13:36, 57; and 19:29), it can refer to persons *and* property. *Oikos* generally refers to the building, especially the temple (12:4; 21:13[2x]; 23:38), but it also can include persons (9:6, 7; 10:6; 15:24; and 23:38). Consequently, since there is no clear distinction in Matthew between *oikía* and *oikos* (except when *oikos* refers specifically to the temple and the house of Israel), I will use the words interchangeably.

John P. Meier has shown that the inclusion of two uniquely Matthean uses of *oikos* (10:6; 15:24) was due to Matthew's effort to reconcile Judaizers within the increasingly gentile house churches.[98] However, we shall show later that the third unique use of *oikos* (23:38) represents the extension of God's household, the church, to the gentiles. Those who believed in Jesus, no longer those of a certain blood line or of the circumcision, would be part of this household.

In order better to grasp house as "assumed primary metaphor," a simple word count is not enough. Since the household constituted *persons* in *relationship* with each other and vis-à-vis their *resources,* we must examine what constituted the household: the various kinds of persons (head of the household, the wife [and the bride], children, tenants, etc.), relationships (genealogy, reciprocity, debt forgiveness, etc.), and resources ("the house," land, gold, taxes, commodities, etc.). This also involves consideration of the semantic and social fields represented by these words and terms.

The charts in the Appendix are an extensive, if not complete, representation of the different kinds of persons, relations, and resources in Matthew's gospel. The charts illuminate the wider religious and economic dynamics and ordering of "house" in Matthew's gospel. The *persons* connected to "house" in Matthew's gospel make up a large group ranging from kinfolk and visitors to heirs and business associates. There are almost as many variations of *resources,* ranging from possessions and provision bags to grain and vineyards. The largest number of words deal with the *relationships,* dynamics, and activities that revolved around the household. Finally, there are words that entail all three elements of a household: persons, resources, and relationships. These include: age (6:13; 12:32; 13:22, 39, 40, 49; 21:19; 24:3; 28:20), deportation (*metoikesía* [1:11, 12, 17]), homeland (13:54, 57), household (*oikiakós* [10:25, 36]), inhabited world (*oikouménē* [24:14]), marriage (22:2, 3, 4, 9, 10, 11, 12; 24:38; 25:10), places (12:43; 15:13; 24:7, 15), region (2:16; 4:13; 8:34; 15:22, 29; 19:1), city (2:23; 4:5; 5:14, 35; 8:33, 34; 9:1, 35; 10:5, 11, 14, 15, 23 [2x]; 11:1, 20; 12:25; 14:13; 21:10, 17, 18; 22:7; 23:34[2x]; 26:18; 27:53; 28:11), and village (9:35; 10:11; 14:15; 21:2).

The purpose of this book does not demand that I present here a lexical approach for all words dealing with persons, resources, and relationships within the "house" as they appear in Matthew. Neither will I elaborate on how all these words might interrelate. Instead, the rest of the book will probe those social relations behind many of the words in order to examine more fully the broader economic, ecclesial, and justice implications of "house" and its semantic field. At all times the reader should keep in mind that the semantic field directly revolving around the words for *oikía/oikos* as well as the notions related to persons, resources, and relations noted in the lists above cannot be adequately understood apart from their connection to *oikos/oikía*.

2. Urbanization and Prosperity in Matthew's Community

During his ministry, Jesus seems to have been the leader of a kind of a rural and village-based sectarian faction of wandering charismatics that originally attracted the alienated within Jerusalem.[99] Jesus is portrayed as calling disciples from a patriarchal household (4:18–22) into a free association that reflected a more collegial grouping. While some of these disciples would remain house-based, others would join Jesus as he went from town to town (4:23–25; 9:35–38), always assuming the hospitality of households on the way (10:1–15).

However, within a few decades a gradual change took place. Those followers of Jesus who before had been mobile were becoming sedentary or house-based as well. What appealed to the marginated, now attracted the middle and upper strata of society. A transition was being made from the rural and village culture of Palestine to Greco-Roman city culture, from the Aramaic to the Greek language, from an ethnically homogeneous constituency that was largely unlearned, relatively poor, and of low social status to an ethnically heterogeneous one that included people more educated, more financially secure and successful, i.e., persons of higher status.[100] All these factors in the transition were grounded in the dynamics of urbanization.

I noted earlier that urbanization was a policy of Rome. This policy was hastened as a result of the Jewish revolt (66–70). Because the Romans realized that the cities had functioned as a form of pacification, they tried to increase the centering of life and activity around urban locations as widely as possible. According to Michael Avi-Yonah, "Both Jewish and Gentile localities were declared cities as soon as they could be ripe for municipal life. This urbanization is the fundamental process of the period [in which Matthew's gospel was written]."[101]

That Matthew's community, at least in comparison to Mark's, was more urbanized seems evident from an analysis of various words in the two gospels. While Mark used the word *pólis* for "city" eight times and the word *kōmē* ("village") seven times, Matthew uses "village" only four times but "city" at least twenty-six times. Furthermore, Matthew often connected houses (*oikoi*) and city (*pólis*) (10:14; 12:25; 17:24-25; 23:38; 26:18). Thus socio-historical data as well as text criticism point to Matthew's community as more urbanized. Consequently it can be called both a "household church" and a "city church."

Urbanization led to a degree of prosperity. According to Avi-Yonah, Greco-Roman culture in Syria and Palestine "was marked by a steep rise in material standards of living."[102] Given that the community that was Matthew's audience resided in an increasingly urbanized[103] and cosmopolitan milieu, its households were situated in an environment which manifested a basic pattern of urban exploitation of agriculturally-based households. With power gradually being absorbed by the urban elites, especially in those cities along major trade routes, reciprocal types of exchange and relatively self-sufficient household relationships were threatened. As Douglas Oakman has written:

> Urban exploitation of the agricultural producer often engendered in bourgeois landlords a "political" egocentrism and plans for self-aggrandizement insensitive to the suffering of the countryside. Under the early Roman empire this arrangement presupposed, of course, strong trade and administrative relationships between urban areas. In a very real sense, the cities were allied against the countryside. Peasant and urban households were set at odds, with mutually exclusive interests.[104]

With urbanization and increasing wealth the house churches could be called relatively secure economically. Accordingly, Robert H. Smith writes:

> Matthew's audience apparently included many landholders, merchants, businessmen, and entrepreneurs. They were people who would appreciate the words on debtors and courts in 5:25-26, be startled by the suggestions regarding generosity (so unbusinesslike!) in 5:39-42 and the casual attitude toward sound financial planning in 6:19, be captivated by the dealer in pearls (13:45-46) and confounded by the logic of the landowner in 20:1-16 and would need the warning about the fate of those who have this world's goods but fail to share their resources with "the least of these my brethren."[105]

Jack Dean Kingsbury also argues that Matthew's audience was a generally prosperous community. He buttresses some of the arguments above with his findings that Matthew's house churches seemed to have been accustomed to large sums of money:

> Whereas Luke mentions "silver" and a few kinds of money (cf. e.g., 7:41; 12:6, 59; 19:13) and Mark mentions an assortment of what on the whole were the lesser denominations, the first evangelist makes no

reference whatever to the *lepton,* the smallest unit of money cited in the Gospels (a small copper coin = ca. 1/8¢), but does refer to all of the following: the *kodrantēs* ("quadrans" = ca. 1/4¢), the *assarion* ("assarion" = ca. 1¢), the *dēnarion* ("denarius" = ca. 18¢), the *didrachmon* ("double drachma" = ca. 36¢), the *statēr* ("stater" = ca. 80¢), the *talanton* ("talent" = ca. $1,080), and to *chalkos* ("copper coin"), *argyrion* ("silver"), *argyros* ("silver") and *chrysos* ("gold"). Indeed, if one takes the three terms "silver," "gold," and "talent," one discovers that they occur in Matthew's Gospel no fewer than twenty-eight times, which may be compared with the single use of the word "silver" by Mark and the fourfold use of it by Luke. Against a background of wealth such as these terms indicate, it makes sense that the first evangelist should appropriate in 13:22 Mark's warning against riches (Mark 4:19) and sharpen the saying of Jesus at Matt. 19:23 so that difficulty in entering the Kingdom is predicated not merely to "those who have means" (Mark 10:23), but to the "rich man."

Accordingly, in light of the preceding there is further reason to postulate that the real readers of Matthew's Gospel lived in or near a city, such as Antioch of Syria, and it also seems safe to infer that they were prosperous and in no sense materially disadvantaged.[106]

While Matthew's house churches had a degree of material security, the reality of urbanization and accompanying increasing exploitation of the poor indicates deepening economic polarities. Samuel Dickey noted these over fifty years ago in his essay "Some Economic and Social Conditions of Asia Minor Affecting the Expansion of Christianity." According to him, one of these social conditions was a "continued struggle between the factions of the rich and the poor."[107]

As Christianity evolved from a movement into a distinctive cult, it was tempted to take on the social attitudes of the house-based cultures which surrounded it.[108] The consequence of this was that *within* both Hellenist and Hebrew gatherings, house churches also began to reflect tensions which arose from their members' origin and rank, their power or wealth. Thus, in considering Matthew's concern about order within his divided community, simple categorizations such as "Hellenist" and "Hebrew" need to be nuanced with additional divisions based on splits between rural-oriented and city-oriented members, as well as other divisions related to rank and status (which determined the stratification of rich and poor). Divisions existed between households and within them. Wayne Meeks has noted that these divisions represented a cross-section of the wider urban society:

Not only was there a mixture of social levels in each congregation; but also, in each individual or category that we are able to identify there is evidence of divergent rankings in the different dimensions of status. Thus we find Christians in the *familia caesaris,* whose members were so often among the few upwardly mobile people in the Roman Empire. We find, too, other probable freedmen or descendants of freedmen who have advanced in wealth and position. . . . We find wealthy artisans and traders: high in income, low in occupational prestige. We find wealthy, independent women. We find wealthy Jews. And, if we are to believe Acts, we find gentiles whose adherence to the synagogue testifies to some kind of dissonance in their relation to their society.[109]

Despite the conflicts which arose over the exploitation mentioned above, the special Matthean material contains very few sayings about wealth or problems connected with wealth. Where these may be found, they do not reveal the kind of severity toward possessions that can be observed in the other gospels. Where Matthew does make redactional comments about wealth we can conclude with David L. Mealand:

An examination of Matthew's treatment of sayings about wealth shows that such changes as there are, usually seem slight. On the other hand the tendency of the redaction seems clear. Matthew does not intensify the severity of sayings about riches, he makes such sayings somewhat less severe. This tendency may be correlated with the fact that the economic circumstances of Matthew's church seem to have been less harsh than those of the earlier Christian communities.[110]

W. D. Davies has noted that "nowhere does Matthew reveal an emphasis on poverty and ascetic rejection of wealth."[111] On the contrary, people with apparent wealth such as Simon the leper (26:6) and Joseph of Arimathea (27:57) are discussed in the context of discipleship. Although Matthew's community of household churches might have been more prosperous than poor, the poor were all around them. More than becoming poor, the disciples in Matthew's households needed to practice justice toward the poor as a manifestation that they and their households were experiencing the reign of God within their lives. This included their relationships—religious and economic. More than becoming poor and living in poverty, Matthew envisioned his households being just by practicing justice toward the poor. This interpretation seems warranted especially since of all the gospels only Matthew uses *dikaiosýnē* (justice) to outline a way of reordering church life and creation itself (3:15; 5:6, 10, 20; 6:1, 33; 21:32).

Although the majority of its households were generally financially secure (and may not have had the numbers of poor members evident in Luke), Matthew's community also seems to have contained a significant group of poor. As those of means converted to Christianity, reflection on the heart of the gospel message could not escape the simple fact that Jesus came to bring good news to the poor (11:5) and that discipleship was indisputably linked to a reordering of possessions on behalf of the poor (19:21). To a financially secure faith-community, such statements might have appeared scandalous (see 11:6) and very difficult to accept (see 19:22ff.). Thus the church at Antioch, whose early growth was reinforced by Barnabas—the man who had sold his property and given the proceeds for the needs of the community (Acts 4:36–37)—could not escape its responsibility vis-à-vis the poor. Rather than making a futile and misplaced call to his community to be poor, *Matthew's gospel offered a challenge for it to be just toward the poor.* Matthew's use of *díkaios* (just) more than all the other gospels combined reinforces this conclusion. Furthermore, of all the Synoptics (save Lk. 1:75), he alone stresses *dikaiosýnē,* or justice. While Luke's has been called the gospel of the poor, Matthew's has often been called the gospel of justice.

If good news would come to the poor, if the jubilee envisioned by Jesus, the Messiah, would be realized (11:2–6) and a new age would be ushered in, it would not be because Matthew's household churches had become poor. Rather it would occur because they witnessed to an economic ethos which today is called solidarity with the poor. This demanded a reordering of households so that they would be free of exploitative practices and would proclaim justice in word and deed.

One can probably discover in the Mediterranean world itself the reason Matthew does not have strong statements against wealth as such, but stresses justice instead. In a ranked society, like that in the Mediterranean area, some would be poor and some would be rich. This inequality in the possession of resources was considered part of the order established by God/the gods. However, if humans violated relations by exploitation, the divine order was considered violated. It was also a violation of the poor and was, therefore, unjust.

Bruce Malina has shown that the first-century perception of resources revolved around concepts of reciprocity (ranked groups relating to each other in a way which insured that basic needs would be met in exchange for allegiance) and limited good.[112] People believed any decrease in their resources meant an increase in another's. From this perspective the possession of more wealth than necessary indicated the possibility of unjust accumulation. This would violate the poor. Thus Malina concludes:

> It seems that a common perception in the ancient Mediterranean relative to rich and poor was that "Every rich man is either unjust or the heir of an unjust person." For this reason, it is not adequate to say that the biblical texts witness to a pervasive concern with the dangers of wealth as such. Rather, there is a pervasive conviction of the wickedness of the wealthy.[113]

The economics regarding rich and poor, from this perspective, necessitates patterns of redistribution that demand not "sharing" with the poor, but "justice" toward the poor as a way of fulfilling God's will in the world.

MATTHEW: SCRIBE AND HOUSEHOLDER BRINGING OLD AND NEW

Given problems between rich and poor and between rural-based and city-based disciples—problems which exacerbated the division between gentile (Hellenist) and Jewish (Hebrew) factions as well as between the more itinerant and sedentary factions—the question of the identity of the author of the first gospel becomes important. How was he going to develop a narrative which would respond to these issues?

Because Matthew's gospel deals with so many explictly Jewish issues, and because the author is so thoroughly familiar with the Old Testament and sees Jesus as the fulfillment of the Old Testament, many commentators have just assumed that the evangelist was a Jewish Christian.[114] However a minority believe that, even though Matthew's community had a strong Jewish-Christian base, Matthew was a gentile.[115] John Meier argues that Matthew's severity toward the Jewish leaders (15, 23, and 27:25) as well as various errors about Jewish matters argue for a gentile well-versed in the Jewish scriptures and traditions, but not grounded in them.[116]

There is no reputable support saying that "Matthew" as we know it was the work of the tax collector known in the gospel as Matthew-Levi (9:9), and I tend to lean to Meier's argument. The "Matthaios" of the first gospel appears more likely to have been a gentile highly versed in the Jewish scriptures in the style of the disciple who has understood Jesus' message (13:51). Such a disciple is likened to a "scribe who has been trained for the kingdom of heaven [and who] is like a householder [*oikodespótēs*] who brings out of his treasure[117] what is new and what is old" (13:52; see 8:19).

The connection between the word *Matthaios* and a disciple (*mathētēs*) who had been taught (*mathēteútheis*) and who understood (*synienai*) should not be lost. In Matthew, as in the other gospels, *mathētēs,* disciple, is the correlative concept to *didaskalos,* teacher. The first gospel continually links true discipleship with being taught, understanding what has been taught, and putting it into practice. As Gundry notes:

> One becomes a disciple, or scribe, through being instructed concerning the kingdom of heaven. *Mathēteútheis* occurs only in Matthew among the gospels (13:52; 27:57; 28:19), and "the kingdom of heaven" is a well-known emphasis of Matthew (25:7).
>
> "Is like a man [who is] a housemaster" echoes the parallel openings of the preceding six parables (vv 24b, 31b, 33b, 44a, 47a), especially those in vv 24b and 45a, where Matthew has used "a man" as his designation of a disciple. . . . *Oikodespótēs* is another favorite (2, 4) and echoes v 27, where it stands for Jesus. Here it stands for a true disciple of Jesus. Like master, like disciples (cf. 10:25)![118]

While the basis of discipleship is the call of Jesus, the essence of discipleship in Matthew revolves around understanding his teaching and putting it into practice. Matthew omitted or interpreted differently all the Markan passages which speak about the disciples' lack of understanding.[119] He also used the word for the understanding (*synienai*) of the disciples more than Mark and Luke (13:13, 14, 15, 19, 23, 51; 16:12; 17:13; see 15:10). Thus, at the end of the key discourse on the parables of the kingdom in chapter 13, only Matthew has

Jesus ask: "Have you [the 'disciples' who heard Jesus and read Matthew, i.e., the 'audience'] understood all this?" (13:51). "All this" referred to the parables of the kingdom that are contained in the previous section and that have been shared with the disciples (12:46–13:50), especially in contrast to the "them" (13:13–15). When they responded "Yes," Jesus spoke about the scribe trained for the "kingdom of heaven [who] is like a householder who brings out of his treasure what is new and what is old" (13:52).

Every person learned in the Law and the prophets (a scribe) and who understands Jesus' teaching about the kingdom of God in the parables (a disciple) is like a householder. But, we shall see, the ultimate householder in Matthew is God, and Jesus is the Lord, or head of the household.[120] Therefore, since the household of the church is made up of those disciples who hear the word of God and put it into practice, the link between disciples being taught and Matthew can be further deduced from the words of John P. Meier: "A scribe who has been so 'trained' (or 'instructed', *mathēteútheis*) for and in the kingdom has become a true disciple (*mathētēs*)." He goes on to note that: "Such Christian scribes may have been the leaders in Mt's church (cf. 23:34)."[121] Such Christian scribes were not merely the leaders in Matthew's church; they were any disciples who understood the teachings of Jesus and put them into practice. True disciples not only see and hear (13:14) but understand (13:51). Their lives bear fruit (13:19, 23) by doing God's will (12:49–50). Bearing such fruit "is the absolute foundation of the Christian existence (13:16f.)."[122] Bearing fruit in justice characterizes the house of disciples.

In this sense, in Matthew, *mathētēs* becomes an ecclesial word that unites the followers of Jesus with the later church. True disciples faithfully put into practice all the teachings of Jesus contained in Matthew until the end of time (28:18–20). Thus each disciple (*mathētēs)* is to be the final redactor, the final Matthew (Matthaios).[123] Each disciple, as reader of Matthew, must also interact with the "old" (the text itself) and with the "new" (contemporary situations) and be challenged to interpret the text so that it comes alive. Ultimately, then, "Matthew" can be considered a rhetorical device which stresses the concrete application of the words to the one (the reader) confronted by them. It represents the praxis (16:27) which demands continual rereading, reinterpreting, and re-imaging of that form of activity that is "inseparable from the wider social relations between writers and readers."[124]

If indeed "Matthew" is this householder-scribe, the Matthew who is author of the first gospel can be seen as a kind of head of the family, the servant of the household churches. Given their unique situation and problems, the members of Matthew's households needed a new redaction of the scriptures about Jesus. The times demanded a return to the sources, both new and old, that they might discover anew how they could be faithful to the words and teaching of Jesus. Through the use of various rhetorical forms, Matthew would help his community deal with these concerns. In the process he would elucidate an ethic for his communities which would enable the members of his house churches to realize the pattern of Jesus' life in theirs, until Jesus would return at the end of the age (see 25:31). In this way they would make the vision of God's reign as articulated by Matthew's Jesus as fully realized in their lives as possible.

From where in the storehouse of sources did Matthew get the material for his narrative?[125] The gospel of Mark, which seems to have been widely used in the Matthean church, served as the main source. Of Mark's 661 verses, over 600 are used in Matthew. Written sometime after 70, Mark was used not only in catechesis and apologetic debate but in the liturgy as well. Because of its openness to the gentiles and its open approach to the Mosaic Law, it found a home in places like Antioch that had large concentrations of gentiles and Jews.

As to the problem related to rich/poor and the allocation of resources, Matthew made only minor variations on Mark. For instance, eleven of his references to *oikía* and five to *oikos* come from Mark.[126] With Mark's economic themes, Matthew warns about taking delight in riches (13:22; Mk. 4:19), coveting and lack of generosity (see 15:19; 20:15; Mk. 7:22), and the futility of gaining the whole world at the forfeit of life (16:26; Mk. 8:36). Becoming a Christian did not mean keeping the Mosaic Law alone; it involved leaving one's livelihood (4:20; Mk. 1:18) and a re-ordering of possessions on behalf of the poor (19:21; Mk. 10:21). In the new community, with its house churches, the needs of the members were to be realized as they went on their mission journey (10:9–10; Mk. 6:8–9). For his part, since he was writing to another community with an economic that seems to reflect the existence of more numerous poor, Luke used all the material of Mark on possessions and most of what was in Matthew, except 5:5; 6:1–4; 13:44–46; 17:24–27; 18:23–35; 20:1–16; 25:31–46; and 27:3–10.

The second source the Matthean scribe found in the storehouse has been called the "Q Document." Q represented a collection of sayings and stories of Jesus. It probably had its source in Palestine and refers, for our purposes, to that material that is not found in Mark but that is common to Matthew and Luke. Seven uses of *oikía*[127] and one of *oikos* (23:38) are included in Q. At times Q can also include material reported in a different style than that employed by Mark. Again, focusing on economic themes, we find that the Matthean material drawn from Q says that the poor have good news preached to them (11:5; Lk. 7:22) and that those following Jesus must be willing to break home and family ties (8:19–22; Lk. 9:57–60), to make a choice about serving God or mammon (6:24; Lk. 16:13), and to avoid the practice of storing up possessions (6:19; Lk. 12:33). Possibly the Q source which best reinforces the thesis that Matthew's community reflected an economic situation different from Luke's is that which has to do with the beatitude about the poor experiencing God's reign. Both Luke and Matthew redacted material from that source. Luke, writing to a community with a sizable number of poor, wrote that the blessing was with those who were poor (Lk. 6:20), while, in Matthew, God's beatitude would come to those who were poor in spirit (5:3).

In the context of Luke's four beatitudes and Matthew's eight (or nine), it is unclear who redacted what from Q.[128] However, it is clear that different redactions were made because the house churches to whom the evangelists wrote were in different economic and religious situations.

Matthew's material from Q about household dynamics cannot be limited, we have seen, merely to his use of *oikía* and *oikos*. An investigation of his use of these words *and* their related concepts in Q, for instance, reveals more fully how Jesus' disciples of the 80s and 90s tended to organize themselves into social groupings. These groupings not only revolved around dynamics of faith; they reveal definite data with discernible sociological patterns.

The primary concepts used by sociologists to study how people tend to organize themselves into social groups involve *status, role,* and *act;* these are aspects of social groupings and social interaction. Status is "a moment in a social process, associated with one or more persons as individuals, which combines a number of *roles* into a whole." Roles are "patterned, routinized sets of typical *acts* and typical expected *acts.*" An act is "an arrangement of physical movements and mental intentions, given coherence by an anticipated result."[129]

Anthony J. Blasi has applied the notions of status, role, and act to the Q material in Matthew, specifically as these notions might touch upon the narrator of the Q text, its intended audience in the house churches, and others (third-party Christians and non-Christians) who might have opposed the message of Q. It is more than incidental that one of the main concepts highlighted by Blasi from the Q material is how status, role, and act are considered from the perspective of "house" and related household concepts involving persons, resources, and their interrelationships. Blasi's sociological approach to the Q material lends further support to stress house as "assumed primary metaphor" in Matthew.

The third source for Matthew was the Old Testament. Of the sixty-one times he refers to it, twenty are unique among the Synoptics and ten are found nowhere else in the New Testament. Indeed, more than any other gospel writer, Matthew used the Hebrew scriptures to show Jesus as their fulfillment (probably done, in part, in deference to the Judaizers). The "fulfillment passages" are central to his presentation of Jesus as the Messiah (1:22; 2:15, 17, 23; 4:14; 8:17; 12:17; 13:35; 21:4; 26:56; 27:9–10).[130]

The "new" treasures from the storehouse brought forth by the Matthean scribe/householder came from the so-called M material—an overall term for the traditions used in the first gospel not derived from Mark or Q. These traditions evolved from the various viewpoints found within the groupings which were part of the various households in the Matthean church.[131]

In conclusion, we can say that Matthew's final redaction of both the new and old material from the scripture storehouse tried to reconcile groups within his audience whose conflicts were based on ethnic differences and power (economic) differences. The first type of differences involved the more open Judaizers and Hellenists and the various degrees among them. To them Matthew tried to show that the Law binds but only according to Jesus' radical interpretation of it. The second area of conflict involved the implications of the urbanization and prosperity of Matthew's house churches.[132] Matthew urged the prosperous within those house churches to meet the needs of the poor in their midst and around their households by practicing justice and love. A third division, which will be discussed later, revolved around approaches to authority. Some debates considered whether authority should be more formalized (institutional and legal) or charismatic; others revolved around whether authority should be more traditional/patriarchal or collegial/communal. Despite these differences, we can, in conclusion, concur with Wayne Meeks's summary of the context for Matthew's gospel:

> Some features of Matthew's community are tolerably clear. He writes in Greek to a Greek-speaking church, probably in an eastern city; most scholars think this was the great metropolis of Antioch in Syria, sometime in the last quarter of the first century. There may have been many small household groups of Christians in Antioch at that time, however, and quite likely there was a certain diversity among them. Not all may have shared the history and perspectives that Matthew assumes.[133]

Given this understanding of the context for Matthew's gospel we can now consider its basic themes and structure.

2

Oikía in the Structure of Matthew's Gospel

THE CONNECTION BETWEEN HOUSE AND CHURCH
IN MATTHEW

Traditionally, Matthew has been regarded as the gospel of the "church." Writing about Matthew's gospel in *The Interpreter's Bible*, Sherman Johnson asked rhetorically: "But why did laymen and readers in the house churches of the Graeco-Roman world read Matthew so avidly?"[1] Sherman's question is answered by those arguments advanced during recent years by most Matthean scholars: Matthew's use by the church as the primary basis of its lectionary, the completeness and integrity of the narrative, its challenge to morality, and its unique qualification for ecclesiastical purposes ranging from apologetics to liturgy. It can safely be concluded that the house churches at Antioch and elsewhere found Matthew's gospel both constitutive and normative for their life and apostolic witness.

Another significant reason for the popularity of Matthew's gospel among early household churches may be that, of all the evangelists, Matthew alone uses the word "church" (*ekklēsía*).[2] The expression is attributed to Jesus twice: when he says his *ekklēsía* will be built (*oikodomein*) on the rock (16:18) and when he states that the *ekklēsía* constitutes a third, communal possibility for reconciliation, after the failure of individual and third-party correction (18:17–18).

Another reason the house churches of the Greco-Roman world read Matthew's gospel so avidly rests in the realization that Matthew writes from a "horizon" that simply assumes an intimate connection between the term "house" (*oikía/oikos*) and "church" (*ekklēsía*). This horizon reveals the "sense" of Matthew's gospel, or its underlying thematic. This chapter will consider Matthew's sense or thematic. Furthermore, the chapter will try to demonstrate that, given the overall sense and structure of Matthew's gospel, it is important to understand the dynamics of the household of Matthew's day.

Without elaborating on the debate about whether the three uses of *ekklēsía* indicate a special Matthean redaction reflecting the community's needs more than Jesus' words, my interpretation will try to be faithful to the demand to interact with the text in order to make it come alive now.

1. Mt. 16:16-20 and Mt. 7:24-25: The Universal House-Based Church Extended to All

Triads can be found throughout Matthew's gospel.[3] One such triad connects concepts for authority and blessing, the use of a name, and a commission.[4] Among other places, Matthew uses this triad at two key points in his gospel— the sharing of Jesus' authority with the apostles who are named and then commissioned (10:1-8) and at the final commissioning (28:16-20). Further, the controversial triadic passage in Matthew's gospel regarding the foundation of the church (16:17-19)[5] has been traditionally identified with Matthew's redaction in 16:13-20 of Mark (Mk. 8:27-30). Here, following Peter's confession of Jesus as the Christ (16:16), Matthew composes Jesus' response in the form of another use of this triad. The *blessing and sharing of authority* is given in the words: "Blessed are you, Simon Bar-Jona" (16:17). A new *name* is given when Jesus says, "And I tell you, you are Peter, and on this rock I will build my church" (16:18). The *commission* is extended to Peter in the words: " . . . whatever you bind on earth shall be bound in heaven, and whatever you loose on earth shall be loosed in heaven" (16:19).

Noting the significance of the change of name to "Peter" and its connection to the establishment of the church, John P. Meier also discusses the meaning of "rock" and makes a connection between this passage and 7:24-25: "The original Aramaic form makes clear that 'this rock' refers to the person of Simon, and not to his faith or to Jesus. The significance of the rock is that it is firm, supplying a solid foundation for building (cf. Mt.'s perfect explanation of the image in 7:24-25)."[6]

For our purposes, Meier makes a significant connection between 7:24-25 (the wise man who built his *house* on the rock) and 16:17-18 (the *church* built on the rock). In 16:18, Matthew's Jesus says: *epi taútē tē pétra oikodomēsō mou tēn ekklēsían* (on this rock I will build my church). In 7:24, Matthew has Jesus concluding the Sermon on the Mount by saying that whoever hears his words and puts them into practice is like the wise man *hostis oikodomēse tēn oikían autou epi tēn pétran* (who built his house upon the rock). Far from being isolated texts, these phrases reveal an underlying element in Matthew's horizon about his community: the equation of the church with house, with both being built (*oikodomein*) on rock.[7] "Every one" who puts the words of the gospel into practice are those disciples throughout the world who understand Jesus' teaching and make it come alive in their lives and relationships. Thus the universal dimension of Matthew's church.

What building on "rock" means has been the subject of great controversy over the years, especially between Protestants and Catholics. Again, we need not elaborate on those controversies here. However, while Catholics have tended to concentrate on the Petros/*pétra* wordplay, it seems the underlying stress, from the wider context of Matthew's ecclesiology, should be on his addition to the Markan version of the phrase "*my* church."

In the last chapter I noted how, at the time of the writing of Matthew's gospel, the synagogue of the Jews was house-based. It was the building within which the congregation met. The congregation was called the *qahal* in Hebrew and *ekklēsía* in Greek. However, by the 80s and 90s when Matthew wrote his gospel, the congregation or *ekklēsía* of the synagogue no longer contained Christians. In fact, the Christians were separated from[8] and even persecuted by the Jews in the 80s and 90s.[9] This separation theme is underscored in Matthew's comments about "their" scribes (7:29), in his continual reference to the synagogue as "theirs" (4:23; 9:35; 10:17; 12:9; 13:54) whenever the context fails to identify clearly the synagogue as the institution belonging to those who are unjust, the "hypocrites" (6:2, 5; 23:6, 34),[10] and in his use of the Markan notion of "outsiders" (the house of Israel) and "insiders" (the new household of faith). Thus Matthew's first use of *ekklēsía* significantly has Jesus refer to it as "his" ("*my*") church, possibly to distinguish it from "theirs." The house-based synagogue may be an *ekklēsía*, but it is theirs. The new house-based church of his congregation is "my" *ekklēsía*.

The church is Jesus' own household or inheritance (21:38), entrusted to him by the divine householder (see 21:33). As such Jesus is the Lord (10:24), *the* head of the household (10:25). As head of the household, he exercises his authority in the name of God. Not only will his authority be rejected by the builders (21:42); it will even be a stumbling block for Peter, who does not think God's thoughts (16:23).

Matthew 16:18 gives the wider tradition of the church founded on the rock—Jesus[11]—Matthew's own ecclesiological interpretation when "my church" (*mou hē ekklēsía*) becomes united with the tradition regarding Peter's change of name. Jesus is the rock (*eben*) but he is also the son (*ben*), and on him the church is built (from the Hebrew *banah*). Augustine Stock notes, "In 16:18 both 'rock' and 'build' appear and the word 'scandal' follows soon after (16:23). . . . The parable of the vineyard comes in Matthew 21 to explain that the rejected son (*ben*) of the parable is to be identified with the stone (*eben*) which the builders rejected."[12] "Son" is essentially a house-connected word; the line of house-based authority was extended from the head of the house through the sons. In this case, the divine householder shares authority with Jesus.

By linking "my church" with Jesus in 16:18, Matthew preserves the tradition of Christ as the cornerstone of the *ekklēsía*. With this established, the tradition about the church's foundation becomes open to a new usage; by the Petros/*pétra* wordplay the foundational function is transferred to Peter. In verse 18 the tradition takes on a new ecclesiological interpretation which finds expression in the stress on *mou hē ekklēsía* as it is united with another tradition about a change of name. As Edward Schillebeeckx concludes:

> In Aramaic a clear wordplay can be made between *ben* (Jesus, as "the Son"), *eben* (bedrock) and *ebeni* (= I shall build). (The Jewish Targum on the psalm in question, Ps 118:22, knows just such a wordplay.) Thus, by way of a wordplay the old tradition can be heard also in Matthew 16:18: the church is built on the Son, on Jesus Christ. But in the Jewish-

Hellenistic phase of the Matthean tradition a new wordplay appears: petros/*pétra*, which Matthew uses to mark off the Petrine church wherein Peter is tradition-bearer—to distinguish between the church and the synagogue of the Jews. Matt 16 places the "ecclesia of Christ" over against the "ecclesia of the scribes and Pharisees" (cf. Matt 16:21). Properly speaking Matt 16:18-19 is not concerned with "the primacy of Peter," though the Matthean tradition very clearly views Peter as "*ho prōtos*," the first among the apostles (Matt 10:2) and presents him as the spokesman of the apostles (14:28-31; 15:15).[13]

In Matthew's ecclesiology, Christ is always present in the whole church; Peter is the keeper of the keys with a function in the whole.[14] This leads to another important connection between *ekklēsía* and *oikía/oikos*, a connection found in Matthew's concept of the keys. The "keys to the kingdom" (16:19; 23:13) seems to have been a notion unique in Christian literature.[15] Receiving the keys meant having authority or the power to administer a house.[16] Thus the connection between house and kingdom in Matthew.

That the keys may be given does not preclude their being taken away. In Isaiah 22, the prophet delivered an oracle against Shebna, the steward (*oikonó-mos*) over Hezechiah's household. Because he abused his position, he was to be thrust from his office (*oikonomía* [Is. 22:19]) in favor of Eliakim: "And I will place on his shoulder the key of the house of David; he shall open, and none shall shut; and he shall shut, and none shall open" (Is. 22:22). However, Eliakim seems to have proved wanting as well.[17]

When the house of Israel itself proved wanting as God's kingdom, Jesus established *his* new household, the church, as the new entrance into the kingdom of God. Jesus would remain the rock (21:42), the foundation of the new house of Israel, his *ekklēsía*. Peter would be given the keys to his *ekklēsía*. But Peter the rock would prove wanting as well; he would be a stumbling block (16:23). Consequently, the power given to him to bind and loose also would be extended to the members of the church (18:18), who would do the will of their Father in the kingdom.

In this sense, the connection between the structure symbolizing the church in 16:18 and the implied structure to which Peter is given the keys symbolizing the kingdom of heaven in 16:19 should not be lost. The former is considered in light of the synagogue, which took the place of the temple; thus the connection between the temple and the church. The latter can be envisaged as a house of the king, a palace along the lines of Is. 22:22, or a temple, or even a city (the gates of which can be opened by the key). In the wider environment which integrated the *oikía/oikos* with the *pólis* and *basileía*, the notions about entering the house, city, and kingdom in Matthew cannot be overlooked.[18]

As early as 1928 Hans Windisch pointed to three precedents in the Old Testament for sayings related to entering the kingdom of God: entering the holy land (i.e., Dt. 4:1), entering the holy city (i.e., Is. 26:2), and entering the holy temple (Is. 56:1-8; see Pss. 15 and 24). While I see notions of land, city, and temple revolving around "house" in Matthew's portrayal of Jesus' entrance into Jerusalem (21:1-13), Windisch contends that each of these "types" is represented in various "entrance" sayings of Jesus. Entrance into the kingdom of God (the kingdom as the promised land) is noted in Mt. 19:23; Mt. 7:13-14 refers to the narrow gate (into the city); and our passage in Mt. 16:19—given 7:24-25—implies a house.[19]

According to Beasley-Murray, "If Jesus is to build on Peter a 'house' of God—that is, a community—and he gives Peter the key to the house of God's kingdom, the implication is plain that the community constitutes the people of the kingdom."[20] This notion of the house-based community living under the rule or will of God brings us to the next time *ekklēsía* is used in Matthew.

2. Mt. 18:18-20: The Church in the House and in the Gathering of Disciples

Because membership in the church is effected via baptism in that discipleship which observes all that Jesus commanded (28:20), the church built on Christ and his authority shared with Peter and the entire household must also be grounded on the solid rock of obedient and active faith in Jesus' words by disciples who constitute the house churches. The church in its local houses (18:17) as well as its universal expression as the new house of Israel (16:18) finds its ultimate foundation in Jesus and from him to Peter, but the members within those house churches who put into practice Jesus' teachings (7:24-29; 28:16-20) and thus fulfill God's will also constitute that foundation.

These notions must be seen as background to the only other instance besides 16:18 where Matthew uses the word *ekklēsía*. The house (17:25) sets the context; the context indicates division in Matthew's households. This appears evident in the main body of the section (18:1-35), which deals with the need for overcoming divisions and generating reconciliation within the churches.[21] Speaking of the "brother" (18:15) who is alienated from the community, Matthew's Jesus offers a final way which seeks reconciliation:

> If he refuses to listen to them, tell it to the *ekklēsía*; and if he refuses to listen even to the *ekklēsía*, let him be to you as a gentile and a tax collector. Truly, I say to you, whatever you bind on earth shall be bound in heaven, and whatever you loose on earth shall be loosed in heaven. Again I say to you, if two of you agree on earth about anything they ask, it will be done for them by my Father in heaven. For where two or three are gathered *synágein*, there am I in the midst of them [18:17-20].

Just as the Jews had "insiders" and "outsiders" based on the Law, so now, "outsiders" will be those refusing to be reconciled as disciples within the community.

In contrast to "their synagogue," Jesus would build "his church" (16:18). Now, while the church which shares the legal authority of binding and loosing may be "synagogued" in a new kind of household (17:25), it is not necessary to be house-based for "church" to occur. No longer would it take ten heads of households to constitute the authority within the synagogue; now wherever two or three disciples gather ("synagogue") there Matthew's Jesus is with them (18:20) in authority (28:18–20), forming church (18:18).

Given these reflections we can conclude that Matthew does not make a simple equation of *oikía/oikos* with *ekklēsía.* On the one hand, the former is a universal concept which assumes local households (16:16–18). On the other hand, the church (18:18) may be house-based (17:25), but need not be spatially-determined; it can extend beyond households to the gathering of at least two or three (18:18–20). This can be diagramed as follows:

	EKKLĒSÍA	NON-EKKLĒSÍA
OIKÍA	Disciples "inside" (12:46-50); Universal (16:18); Local (18:17)	Those "outside"; The building itself
NON-OIKÍA	Wherever 2 or 3 are gathered (18:20); Disciples "with" Jesus	"Them"; The United Front of Israel; The Crowds

The notion of disciples being gathered with each other and with Jesus, doing the will of the heavenly Father, is at the core of understanding Matthew's sense of the church as the true Israel. We turn now to examine the broad outlines of that church, the house of disciples.

THE STRUCTURE OF MATTHEW'S GOSPEL

Although other models are offered,[22] a traditional way of viewing the structure of Matthew's gospel has been based on some of the insights offered by Benjamin Bacon.[23] Those following Bacon find a Matthean arrangement of the teachings of Jesus and stories of his activities into a prologue (genealogy, birth, and infancy) and climax (passion, death, and resurrection) with five "books" in between. Some support Bacon further by suggesting that the five books reflect the five books of the Old Testament that the Jews believed were authored by Moses. Because Matthew presented Jesus as the one who fulfills the Mosaic Law and prophets, the five books of his gospel thus outline, in word (discourse) and action (narrative), the fulfillment of the Law which Jesus wanted to be continued in his church by his disciples.

My adaptation of Bacon suggests a chiastic format which structures the five books around the uniquely Matthean phrase which appears at the end of each discourse: *kai egéneto hote etélesen ho Iēsous* (and when Jesus finished these sayings [7:28; 11:1; 13:53; 19:1; 26:1]). The gospel can be structured as follows:

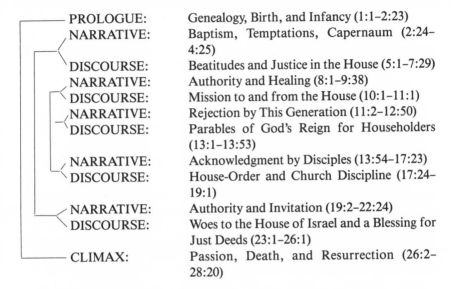

PROLOGUE:	Genealogy, Birth, and Infancy (1:1–2:23)	
NARRATIVE:	Baptism, Temptations, Capernaum (2:24–4:25)	
DISCOURSE:	Beatitudes and Justice in the House (5:1–7:29)	
NARRATIVE:	Authority and Healing (8:1–9:38)	
DISCOURSE:	Mission to and from the House (10:1–11:1)	
NARRATIVE:	Rejection by This Generation (11:2–12:50)	
DISCOURSE:	Parables of God's Reign for Householders (13:1–13:53)	
NARRATIVE:	Acknowledgment by Disciples (13:54–17:23)	
DISCOURSE:	House-Order and Church Discipline (17:24–19:1)	
NARRATIVE:	Authority and Invitation (19:2–22:24)	
DISCOURSE:	Woes to the House of Israel and a Blessing for Just Deeds (23:1–26:1)	
CLIMAX:	Passion, Death, and Resurrection (26:2–28:20)	

According to this chiastic structure,[24] Matthew's gospel centers around the third book: 11:2–13:53. In the narrative of 11:2–12:50 Jesus and his message are rejected by "this generation." The following discourse (13:1–53) has two parts: the sharing of the parables "outside" with the crowd (the Jews) who neither hear nor understand (13:1–35), and Jesus' entry "inside" the house to share and explain more parables with the disciples who hear and understand (13:36–53).

THE SENSE OF MATTHEW'S GOSPEL: THE PIVOTAL MEANING OF 12:46-50 IN THE THIRD BOOK (11:2-13:53)

Chapter 13, especially 13:35, represents the turning point of the entire Matthean narrative.[25] In the first half of the gospel, Matthew has Jesus directing his attention primarily to the Jews. However, there is growing conflict, especially with the leaders. By the end of chapter 12 the Jews—the members of Jesus' own family—clearly have become outsiders having nothing to do with his message.

Two times in the third narrative Matthew discusses the refusal of "this generation" to be converted (especially 11:16–24 and 12:41). Matthew's narrative reveals the underlying conflict between Jesus and the united front of the house of Israel.[26] In the context of a divided or united household (12:25–29), Matthew takes from Q the eschatological saying: "He who is not with me (*met emou*) is against me (*kat emou*), and he who does not gather with me (*synagón met emou*) scatters" (12:30).

Matthew's notion of discipleship involves "being with." Jesus is "with" us, his disciples (1:23; 17:17; 26:18 ,20, 29, 36; 28:20; see 9:15; 26:11). The disciples are "with" Jesus (12:30; 26:38, 40, 71; see 8:11; 9:11). According to Jack Dean Kingsbury, "Matthew utilizes the concept of 'being with Jesus' and the related idiom of his 'being with them' in order to restrict close association with Jesus almost exclusively to the circle of the disciples. . . . "[27] Thus the disciples are also those gathered ("synagogued" [3:12; 12:30; 13:2, 47; 18:20; 22:10; 23:37; 24:31; 25:32)[28] with Jesus. In 25:35, 38, and 43, the notion for hospitality, or welcoming in the house, is *synágein*.

Those in a house are welcoming if they receive not only the person but the one that person represents (10:40). In the case of those in the house with Jesus, they must receive the one who sent him by accepting the heavenly Father's will. Thus, realizing the lack of reception given Jesus, Matthew adapts his Markan source to offer a pericope that serves to hinge the end of the third discourse (11:2–12:45) with the beginning of the third narrative (13:1–53). As such, 12:46–50 reveals the theological heart of Matthew's gospel:

> While he was still speaking to the people, behold, his mother and his brothers stood outside, asking to speak to him. But he replied to the man who told him, "Who is my mother, and who are my brothers?" And stretching out his hand toward his disciples, he said, "Here are my mother and my brothers! For whoever does the will of my Father in heaven is my brother, and sister, and mother."

In this passage Matthew distinguishes between the blood family "outside" the house and those "inside." However, he changes his Markan source (which speaks about those "who sat about him" [Mk. 3:34]), points specifically to those "disciples" *in* the house who do God's will, and calls them his "brother, and sister, and mother." What Jesus earlier asked of his disciples—the breaking of patriarchal family ties (4:22; 8:21–22)—he himself now makes clearer. In the new family of disciples blood counts for nothing. What counts is being a disciple who does the will of the heavenly Father. The transition from one household to another also becomes clearer. Meier concludes, "the earthly family of Jesus, left cooling its heels *outside*, may represent the unbelieving members of Israel, cut off from the house where Jesus teaches, i.e., the church."[29]

Matthew's meaning of discipleship involves far more than a name;[30] it represents a dynamic involving children of the heavenly Father[31] who become such through baptism and implement the teachings of Jesus (28:18–20) by bearing fruit in works of justice. Thus this pericope (12:46–50) reveals a key theme in Matthew which links the disciples of Jesus' day with the house of disciples in the church for all time. It contains two discipleship themes that are essential to Matthew's morality: the notion of God's will and the need to do God's will.

The "will of God" is a key theme in Matthew. Mark uses *thélēma* as the noun for "will" in reference to God only once (Mk. 3:35), and Luke uses it directly of God once (Lk. 22:42) and indirectly twice (Lk. 12:47[2x]). Matthew uses *thélēma* of God six times (6:10; 7:21; 12:50; 18:14; 21:31; 26:42). He uses the verb form, *thélein*, of God in 9:13; 11:25–26; 12:7; and 20:14–15. Invariably God wills to yoke disciples in justice (20:14–15) and mercy (9:13; 12:7). Doing the will of Jesus' heavenly Father constitutes a new household, a new family of brothers and sisters who remain gathered with Jesus whether they are inside or outside the house. This is the church.

The concept of "doing"—in contrast to "saying"—is central to Matthew. Doing God's will is linked with putting morality and spirituality into practice (6:1; 23:3), bearing fruit (3:8, 10; 7:16, 17[2x], 18[2x],19, 20; 12:33[3x]; 21:19, 34, 41, 43), as well as being and doing good (5:45; 7:11[2x]; 12:34; 12:35[3x]; 19:16, 17[2x]; 20:15; 22:10; 25:21, 23). These notions of *praxis*, doing good, and bearing fruit are involved in Matthew's idea of being just (*díkaios* [1:19; 5:45; 9:13; 10:41; 13:17, 43, 49; 20:4; 23:28, 29, 35; 25:37, 46; 27:19, 24]), doing justice (*dikaiosýnē* [3:15, 5:10, 20; 6:1; 21:32] and *krísis* [23:23]), as well as experiencing justice (*dikaiosýnē* [5:6; 6:33]) or judgment (5:21, 22; 10:15; 11:22,24; 12:18, 20, 36, 42; 23:33).[32] Those in the household who do justice are those who will enter the kingdom of the heavenly Father. This identification of those doing the will of God in justice determines who in the households or those gathered with Jesus will enter God's reign.

The connection among "the will of the father," practicing it via justice, and membership in the household is reinforced in the parable of the two sons, which is unique to Matthew (21:28–32), and follows the whole section dealing with Jesus' conflict with the leaders over his authority (21:1–27).[33] After asking which one of the sons did the "will of his father" and being told it was the second who put into practice his father's will, Matthew's Jesus declares: "Truly, I say to you, the tax collectors and the harlots go into the kingdom of God before you. For John came to you in the way of *dikaiosýnē,* and you did not believe him, but the tax collectors and harlots believed him; and even when you saw it, you did not believe afterward and repent" (21:31–32).

Meier notes that the apocalyptic nature of the saying beginning with "Truly" (*amēn*) emphasizes inclusion and exclusion: that is, "they go in while you do not." This is reinforced if the translation is connected to the thrust of the two subsequent parables about the vineyard and the evil tenants (21:33–46) and the wedding banquet (22:1–14). The "you" (who may be the leaders of the Jews or any disciples who do not bear fruit) are the "outsiders." The "insiders" will be those who do *dikaiosýnē* (21:32).

In the parable about the wicked tenants in the vineyard (21:33–46), Matthew's Jesus makes it clear that the householder (21:33) will make sure that "the kingdom of God will be taken away from you and given to a nation producing the fruits of it" (21:43). In the parable about the vineyard, Matthew took over the basic Markan story but made two very important additions in verses 41 and 43. In 21:41 Matthew rewrote Mark's version about what the owner of the vineyard would do as a response to the tenant's murder of his beloved son: "He will put those wretches to a miserable death, and let out the vineyard to other tenants who will give him the fruits in their seasons." Given Matthew's stress on disciples' bearing fruit, he further adapts Mark to show that the new tenants of the householder will be those of any nation (*ethnos* [21:43]) who bear the fruits of the season. God's reign will be "taken away" from the old tenants and given to any nation bearing fruit—a definite image of the transfer of God's reign from the household of Israel to the church.[34] Those of any nation in this pericope become in the next pericope (22:1-14) those in the "thoroughfares" who are invited to the wedding, but who can remain inside only if they wear the "wedding garment" (22:11) of good works. The head of the household in the parable of the vineyard (21:33-43) becomes the king who reconstitutes the wedding feast in the next parable (22:1-14) in such a way that those once "inside" are thrown out and those "outside" come in.

While these passages help elaborate the overall sense of Matthew's theology as articulated in 12:46-50, those members of Jesus' blood family "outside" the house and those "inside" disciples—who constitute Jesus' true family—can be further understood in the context of the subsequent parables in chapter 13. Whereas 12:46-50 contrasts those of Jesus' blood family who are "outside" with the disciples "inside," the parables in chapter 13 revolve around the difference between those who see and hear but who don't understand and those who do *understand.*

In 13:1, Jesus goes "out of the house" to be with the crowd. There Jesus tells the parable comparing the reign of God to seed sown on various kinds of ground (13:3-9). Then, after explaining why he spoke to "them" in parables (13:10-17), the parable of the sower is explained to "them" (13:18-23).[35] After telling more parables (13:24-35), Matthew's Jesus leaves the crowds and goes "into the house" (13:36) where he explains the parable of the weeds of the field to his disciples (13:37-43). Then, after telling some more parables (13:44-50), he concludes them all by asking: "Have you *understood* all this?" (13:51). The disciples do the will of the heavenly Father and become united to Jesus and each other because they understand.

Whereas Mark keeps the disciples in the dark, not understanding, Matthew omitted or interpreted differently all the Markan passages that indicate lack of understanding on the part of the disciples.[36] A central element in Matthew's notion of discipleship is that they understand (*syniénai*).He uses it nine times in reference to the response to Jesus' words (13:13,14,15,19,23,51; 15:10; 16:12; 17:13). Matthean disciples understand; outsiders do not (13:13-15). However, understanding Jesus' message can never be separated from putting it into practice in the house churches. Thus, after finishing his discourse on the parables by asking if the disciples had "understood" *all* this, Matthew's Jesus discusses the scribe "trained for the kingdom of heaven" in terms of a "house-holder" (13:51-52) who acts on his words.

Immediately after the traditional formula ending a discourse ("when Jesus had finished"), Matthew adds one more "in" and "out" reference. Since the members of Jesus' own house of Israel do not understand, they do not believe; therefore his work will not be done in them:

> And coming to his own country he taught them in their synagogue, so that they were astonished, and said, "Where did this man get this wisdom and these mighty works? Is not this the carpenter's son? Is not his mother called Mary? And are not his brothers James and Joseph and Simon and Judas? And are not all his sisters with us? Where then did this man get all this?" And they took offense at him. But Jesus said to them, "A prophet is not without honor except in his own country and in his own house." And he did not do many mighty works there, because of their unbelief [13:53–58].

Even though Jesus taught in their synagogues, those who heard did not believe and put into practice his teachings. Those "of" his own house—those of traditional blood lines—no longer would constitute his disciples. Rather, as in 12:46–50—which distinguished between the patriarchal household of that day and Jesus' new household of those doing the heavenly Father's will—so, from now on Jesus will tend to concentrate his effort on those willing to bear fruit. Thus 12:46–50 and 13:53–59 serve as the hinges for the description of the kingdom of God that is elucidated via parables in chapter 13.

Having outlined the basic sense of discipleship in Matthew from the central third book and its pivotal pericope of 12:46–13:50, we can now determine how it was further nuanced through his structuring of the five basic discourses of Jesus. Our examination will demonstrate how Matthew features "house" in all.

HOUSE IN THE FIVE DISCOURSES OF MATTHEW'S GOSPEL

1. 5:1–7:29: Beatitudes and Justice in the House

In the *first discourse* the word *oikía* is used just after the end of the Beatitudes, within Matthew's triad of blessing, naming, and commissioning (5:15), as well as at the end of the Sermon on the Mount (7:24–27). The notion of *oikía* thus serves as bookends for Jesus' most important teaching.

The first eight beatitudes (5:3–10) all refer to those practicing them in the third person ("they," "theirs," "those"). The last part of the eighth beatitude, considered by some as the ninth, does not refer to "those" persecuted ones who are blessed (5:10), but to "you" who are blessed (5:11–12). The "you" in this case refers to Matthew's church and the church until the end of the world (28:20) that experiences the buffeting winds of persecution for putting into practice the Beatitudes and the rest of the Sermon on the Mount (7:24–27). While this "you" of the ninth beatitude ends the blessings (or makarisms), it also begins another uniquely Matthean triad of blessing/authority-naming-commissioning.

The first part of the triad begins "Blessed are *you* when men revile you and persecute you . . . " (5:11). The "you" refers to persecuted disciples of Matthew's era who put into practice the teachings of Jesus and thus were "blessed." In the second part of the triad, Matthew adapted the text to give a new name to such disciples: "*You* are the salt of the earth" (5:13) and "*You* are the light of the world" (5:14). At this point Matthew adapted his source from Q (not forgetting Mark) to explain that people do not "light a lamp and put it under a bushel, but on a stand, and it gives light to all in the *oikía*" (5:15). Here Matthew's Jesus images the church as a house filled with light. In the third part of the triad Christians are commissioned to act thus in such a house: "Let *your* light so shine before men, that they may see your good works and give glory to your Father who is in heaven" (5:16). Just as, in the beginning, God's good work created the world, the *oikouménē* (Ps. 19:5), through light, so now the good works of Jesus' disciples reveal a new light in the *oikía* for the whole world, especially persecutors, to see (see 1 Pet. 2:12 as a parallel).

It was shown earlier and will be shown in the last chapter that the performance of "good works" (*kala érga*), especially deeds of justice, constitutes a key ethical requirement in Matthew. However, here the connection among the concepts of "good works," "house," and exemplary behavior, especially by those persecuted for justice (*dikaiosýnē*), should not be overlooked as evidencing a unique household ethos in Matthew. Doing good would win over persecutors. Putting into practice the Beatitudes would be the best apologetic.[37]

Matthew adapted this section from Q to fit the needs of his households. Speaking to the members of his house churches being persecuted for justice' sake, Matthew's Jesus urges them to let their light shine in the *oikía* for all to see their good works. In this way their persecutors will be edified. Here, for the first time in Matthew,[38] the doing of good works in the household to edify persecutors is used by Matthew's Jesus. We have already seen that "doing good" is essential to doing the will of the heavenly Father. However, Kenneth W. Dupar makes it clear that the household tradition of "doing good" also implies a means of changing one's enemy:

> Proverbs 25:21f teaches that the doing of kindness towards one's adversary brings him to a sense of shame and a humble change of heart. . . . Further parallels to this are found in the Gospels, especially in the Sermon on the Mount, where Christians learn not to return evil for evil, but to let their good works so shine before men that men will come to glorify God who is in heaven, cf. Matthew 5:16. It is of particular interest that Matthew 5:16 refers to the *kala érga* of the Christians having an influence on men and bringing them to glorify God.[39]

It is difficult to understand Matthew's triad—ending with the light to be shown—separate from the "house." In fact, according to Hans-Josef Klauck: "To understand the concept [of the light to be shone], the image of house is indispensable."[40] Thus the Sermon on the Mount begins (after the prologue of the Beatitudes) by making it clear that the disciples' good works and justice are what will fill the house with light. This house-light[41] must be revealed to Jew and gentile alike—for everyone to see—and right house-ordering (= economics [as well as *ekklēsía*]) must be based on good works that bear fruit in justice.

The Sermon on the Mount ends with the passage (7:24-27) from the primitive sermon about the house built on rock, a passage I have already discussed. Those who put into practice what Jesus taught by the performance of good works (7:15-20) would be doing God's will (7:21-23).[42] Consequently, their actions would manifest the behavior of wise people who built their house on rock. Following Proverbs, they would be imitators of wisdom who "built her house" (Prov. 9:1; 24:3). When the persecution noted in 5:11-16 would be experienced (in the form of rains that fall, floods that come, and winds that blow and beat upon the *oikía*), their house would not fall, "because it had been founded on the rock" (7:25).

Justice, good works, nonretaliation, the "two ways," and persecution are all recurring themes in *haustafeln*. This makes one question if the entire Sermon on the Mount might not be considered an extended *haustafel*. In order to answer this question, we need to investigate what constituted an authentic *haustafel*.[43]

Haustafeln or "household codes" were first researched in depth at the beginning of the twentieth century by Alfred Seeberg.[44] He believed the Christian *haustafeln* found in key New Testament passages[45] had pre-Christian roots in the Jewish proselytical teachings. Shortly after, Martin Dibelius probed the notion of household codes in greater depth and suggested that the *haustafeln* were general ethical instructions (i.e., paranetic) adapted for everyday house-church life from Stoic household codes.[46] His student, Karl Weidinger, developed Dibelius's ideas further, showed examples of the Hellenistic *haustafeln* in Hierocles, an early second-century CE Stoic, and suggested that such codes would have been adapted by the Christians only after they began to alter their original concepts about the immediate expectation of the *parousía*.[47] Since Weidinger, major studies of *haustafeln* have tended to cover the same scripture passages, although they disagree as to their origin. The Dibelius-Weidinger thesis about the Hellenistic origin was challenged by Ernst Lohmeyer, who postulated a Jewish source.[48] Karl Heinrich Rengstorf argued that their origin rests in the Christian households themselves,[49] while David Schroeder found their roots in the Decalogue and first-century Hellenistic Judaism, especially Philo.[50]

Despite what they see as the origin of the *haustafeln*, these pioneers, as well as various contemporary writers, tend to limit the *haustafeln* to certain passages that share common structures. Two basic structures tend to reveal a *haustafel*. The first has two dimensions: one part dealing with submission to civic authority and the other dealing with submission of wives to husbands, children to parents, and slaves to masters (1 Pet. 2:18-3:7; Col. 3:18-4:6; 1 Tim. 2:1-8; Tit. 2:1-10). The second also includes two dimensions. One deals with relationships among various household members while the other part deals with wealth and the art of making money (1 Tim. 6:6–10,17–19). Ephesians 5:21–6:9 treats only the groups dealing with domestic submission.

John Elliott has argued that a clearer understanding of the *haustafeln* has been hampered, in part, by a tendency to treat all New Testament household codes *en bloc* rather than inquiring about a specific function of a code within a specific document. The question of function, for Elliott, "implies a certain relationship between social situation, authorial intention and conventional understanding."[51] For his part, Dupar shows that the general outline of a household code containing the three elements of form of address, instruction, and motives, tended to be quite fluid. While the form usually contained an *address* if it was meant for a specific group (wives, children, slaves), if it was addressed to a general audience, the address was omitted. While the *instruction* was oriented to the performance of duties, "it is obvious from the different arrangements of the duties of the *haustafeln* texts that the New Testament writers did not attempt to hold to a set traditional structure or sequence. The duties are arranged, edited and expanded according to the preference of the author."[52] Finally, Dupar notes that "motives are not [always] prominent in the *haustafeln* tradition."[53]

If one would combine the comments of Elliott with Dupar and apply them to Matthew—who wrote for a general audience of divided households—a case might be made for Matthew's adaptation of the traditional *haustafeln*—one of whose purposes was to reinforce patriarchy against equality[54]—as his way of promoting a more collegial house church. What can we conclude? While in Matthew no specific *haustafeln* exists that parallels the traditional forms, the characters addressed and the issues raised are key to Matthew's gospel. However, his ideal was not to use codes to reinforce the traditional patriarchal approach to *haustafeln*. Rather he used themes contained within them and offered another way to structure household living.

For instance, the first part of the Sermon on the Mount refers to the need to do good to persecutors so that the good can be seen in the "house," while the last part refers to the storms (of alienation and persecution) that buffet the house. Again, only those who do good will be able to be part of that household. Doing good, for Matthew, is the answer to the traditional patriarchal demand for domestic submission. According to Dupar, "Submission through the doing of good was the kind of behavior complying with the teachings of the Sermon on the Mount, where Christians are taught to be a light to the gentiles by doing good works and non-retaliatory actions. It was also the kind of behavior which follows the example of the suffering servant, Jesus."[55] This admonition not only applied to the gentiles, but to the Jews as well, especially those Jews from whom the Christians were now separated and at whose hands they had experienced various forms of rejection and persecution.

This brings us back to our pondering whether the entire Sermon on the Mount might not be considered "an extended *haustafel*." From strict literary analysis the answer would be a definite "no." The Sermon merely contains some themes contained in the *haustafeln*. The tone of Matthew's Sermon is also more general. However, while the Sermon on the Mount does not reflect a *haustafel* as such, it will be shown that Matthew knew the structure and was able to adapt it to serve as a vision for a new kind of nonpatriarchal household code (17:25–20:15).

In concluding the Sermon on the Mount with the reference to the house, the durability of the one and the weakness of the other, Matthew differs from Luke's version, which stresses a careful laying of the foundation. It also differs from the rabbinic parable which stressed the strength or weakness of the house's walls. Matthew stresses the house built on the rock. Furthermore, everything depends on a household putting into practice the words of Jesus (7:28–29). The church built on rock is the household of true scribes and disciples who perform all that Jesus taught (28:16–20). As in the Torah, those who would perform good works and justice and learn the Torah would now be the new students, the new disciples who are to build up God's world with a new teaching. Not even the powers of death (see 16:18) would be able to prevail against such a firmly-grounded house/church.

2. 10:1–11:1: Mission to and from the House

As the metaphor of house serves as the opening image and concluding paradigm in the Sermon on the Mount, so the *second discourse* also features *oikía*. In the second discourse the house is the context for missionary activity as well as the center for a new kind of hospitality of resource-sharing.

To contextualize this discourse, which covers the tenth chapter, one must refer back to the preaching, teaching, and healing of Jesus (4:23–25), which are further specified in 5:1–7:29 (teaching) and 8:1–9:34 (healing). Because Jesus' fame spread "throughout Syria" (a reference to Matthew's community at Antioch?), crowds following Jesus were so large that he needed others to share in his ministry (9:35–38). Originally authorized for mission by God's power, Matthew's Jesus extends his ministry; Matthew shows this by adapting Mark, and in so doing presents another triad of authority/blessing-naming-commissioning: "And he called to him his twelve disciples and gave them authority over unclean spirits, to cast them out, and to heal every disease and every infirmity" (10:1). "The names of the twelve apostles" (10:2–4) immediately follow. Next the commission is given: "These twelve Jesus sent out, charging them, 'Go nowhere among the gentiles, and enter no town of the Samaritans, but go rather to the lost sheep of the *oikos* of Israel. And preach as you go, saying "The kingdom of heaven is at hand." Heal the sick, raise the dead, cleanse the lepers' " (10:5–8a).

This triad, which only in Matthew limits the mission to "the lost sheep of the house of Israel" (10:6), seems to reflect Matthean communal tensions wherein the Judaizers or the "James faction" wanted to express Christianity within the Jewish mode. The limiting of the *exousía* or power of the apostles to the house of Israel alone also might reflect the influence of the wandering charismatics, who recalled that Jesus said his own ministry was limited to the *oikos* of Israel

(15:24).[56] The tension is further evidenced when both 10:6 and 15:24 are compared with the final triad of authority/blessing-naming-commissioning of 28:16–20. There Matthew's resurrected Jesus *authorizes* those baptized in the *name* of the Father and of the Son and of the Holy Spirit with the *commission* to go to "all nations, . . . teaching them to observe all that I have commanded you; and lo, I am with you always, to the close of the age."

Given the triad for the apostles limiting their mission to "the lost sheep of the house of Israel" (10:6) and the resurrection triad to "all nations" (28:19), one discovers, with John Meier, a Matthew who sought to integrate both dimensions in an unique approach to salvation history:

> In the early church, however, these words [of 10:6] may have been used by conservative Jewish Christians to reject any formal mission to the gentiles, perhaps to polemicize against the mission undertaken by the Hellenists and later by Paul. The conservatives would have felt that, in keeping with OT prophecy, it should be left to God to lead the gentiles in pilgrimage to Zion on the last day. The conservative-yet-liberal Mt. affirms vv. 5–6 as the venerable tradition of his Jewish-Christian church, yet modifies it by inserting it into a higher synthesis, namely his view of salvation history. The Twelve are sent only to the lost sheep which make up the house of Israel (a genitive of apposition; cf. Is 53:6; Ex 16:31). Jesus' prohibition stands during his public ministry; but, after the apocalyptic turning point of the death-resurrection, the exalted Son of Man, who now has all authority over the cosmos, commands the same group of disciples to undertake a *universal* mission. . . . Thus does Mt. preserve both the new and the old (cf. 9:17; 13:52).[57]

Recognizing the integrative element in Matthew's salvation history, one can rightly ask: How did Matthew resolve the apparent conflict in the two missions? Recalling the tensions between the Judaizers and Hellenizers in the house churches and Matthew's goal of reconciling them, it should not be surprising to find both missions highlighted in his gospel. Because Matthew wanted to reconcile his divided house churches, it is understandable that his gospel would include both strains. Schuyler Brown has noted the tension well in an article on the two missions in Matthew. He concludes:

> The importance that Matthew attached to the gentile mission is clear from the climactic position in which he has placed the universal mission mandate. From this, however, it can not be inferred that all the members of the evangelist's community were in agreement on the issue. Indeed, Matthew's inclusion of a particularist form of the mission mandate in his Central Section suggests that the gentile mission was controverted at the time of the gospel's composition.[58]

Prescinding from further debate about the two missions, we can ask: How was the mission to the house of Israel and, by extension, to the gentiles, to be exercised? Reflecting the earlier tradition which had the wandering charismatics going about from town to town (8:19–22), the first condition was that the preachers were not to be overly anxious about what they were to eat or wear, or how they were to be otherwise resourced: "Take no gold, nor silver, nor copper in your belts, no bag for your journey, nor two tunics, nor sandals, nor a staff" (10:9–10a).

Upon quick reading, such a requirement seems to have restricted Jesus' followers (and, by extension, Matthew's house churches) to a life of poverty. However, far from canonizing an economic of poverty (which cannot be found in Matthew's gospel), the first gospel reveals another way to manage households in the new Israel. Matthew's economics calls for a mutual sharing of resources among those sent and received, those welcoming and those welcomed. Those commissioned in *exousía* (10:1; see 28:18) should enter households in peace with their resources of preaching and healing (10:9–10a and teaching [28:20]); those who welcome them share their resources of food, shelter, clothing, and other forms of hospitality (10:11–13). The reason why those commissioned need not burden themselves with securing their own physical resources is simple economics: "the laborer deserves his food" (10:10b).[59]

Deviating from his sources, Matthew placed the aphorism about workers deserving their keep at this point in the tenth chapter. Unlike Luke, who places it at a different point (Lk. 10:7), Matthew's placement of the aphorism here reveals his basic economic ethic for the community. The preachers and healers (and teachers) could leave with no money because the community should be characterized by just social relations. Ideally, by the end of the day of sharing their resource of the gospel, the missionaries should have earned their keep in the house churches of the various villages, towns, and cities to which they went. "By placing our proverb as close as he could to the statement that a Christian missionary would have no money in his purse," A. E. Harvey explains, "he may have wanted to suggest that it could be used as Paul and the author of 1 Timothy used it, that is, as an argument that preachers should not be expected to support themselves, but should be supported by the church in which they work."[60] Here, perhaps more than anywhere else, Matthew's "economics" or house-ordering reveals a mutual sharing of relationships and resources, reflecting that just order which results in peace.

The context in which and from which the wandering charismatics were to work was the house church. For this reason, the first thing that those missionaries were to do upon entering any town or village was to "find out who is worthy in it, and stay with him until you depart. As you enter the *oikía*, salute it. If the *oikía* is worthy, let your peace come upon it; but if it is not worthy, let your peace return to you" (10:11–13). Hospitality was to reign.

Judeo-Christian hospitality reflected the ethos of the Greco-Roman world: hospitality was to be shared in the household not only with one's own kin, but with strangers as well. Matthew builds on this concept from Q and indicates that his church's hospitality was to be expressed by sharing both spiritual resources (preaching, healing [and teaching]) and material resources (housing and food). The ordinary place for this resource-sharing would be the household. The house, in chapter 10, thus serves as the basic economic unit for the Christian community and hospitality. At the same time it serves as the origin for the proclamation of the good news. Hans-Josef Klauck has noted this well:

> From the perspective of Q regarding the early Christian missionaries on their travels, the disciples should first seek out to win over for themselves a house and a family. The house mission is the command of the hour. Starting from the house, they can go out into the villages or the city.
> For any such house, the rule holds true: "Remain in this house." This "remaining in the house," however, only makes sense if, apart from the challenge of the salvation offer, there is the solid establishment and continuous caring for a congregation, which we would more precisely call a house congregation.[61]

The foundation and continued ministry of the Matthean church revolved around such house churches. Whoever was blessed with the call, named, and commissioned in the *exousía* of Jesus (10:1 28:18) should expect to be treated like Jesus. Those in the households who received them as ministers commissioned by Jesus would receive their reward (10:40–42).

Given the conflicts existing in his community, which divided family members (see 10:21), as well as the persecution coming from the Jews and wider society (see 10:22), the gift of peace brought by the missionaries to the households might become compromised. Matthew's Jesus warned that this could be expected: their experience would reflect his conflict with the house of Beelzebul (see 9:22–32): "If they have called the master of the house (*oikodespótēs*) Beelzebul, how much more will they malign those of his household [*oikiakós*]?" (10:25). Here Jesus refers to himself as the master of the house, after referring to himself as teacher (in contrast to disciple) and Lord (in contrast to slave). Not only is he Lord, or *paterfamilias*; he is *oikodespótēs*, master of the house; he is its cornerstone (21:42), the Son who inherited the household from the divine householder (21:33). The members of the household (*oikiakoi*) are the members of his house, his church (16:18). Wolfgang Trilling has noted:

> The "master of the house" is Jesus himself. He describes himself only here by this rare word. To understand it properly one must no doubt read it along with the promise to Peter: "On this rock I will build my church" (16:18). The house built by Jesus himself is the community of the faithful which he gathers. In this house, he is the Lord, the *Kýrios* who reigns with fullness of authority.[62]

Though Jesus reigns as "master of the house" with full authority (28:16–20), it will not go unchallenged. In Semitic, "master of the house," *oikodespótēs*, is

"Beelzebul." It refers to a temple or house. Matthew's use of the word on Jesus' lips presents Beelzebul as master over a demonic household of followers in contrast to the household of disciples founded on Jesus.

E. C. B. Maclaurin has shown that in 1 Kings 8:13 and 2 Chronicles 6:2 (and possibly Is. 63:15), *zebul* means *temple* and "this may also represent *oikos—house*" in Matthew 10:25, "the phrase *byt YHWH* being very frequently used for the Hebrew temple (I Kings vii:12 +)."[63] Developing the connection between *zebul* and the new house of the church, Sverre Aalen asks:

> Why did Jesus use this term here? The word used here is *husherren* (houselord)—*husets herre* (lord of the house). This is a play on words. The concept represents a house which stands on a foundation which is the evil territory over which the devil rules. Jesus, on the other hand, represents the other foundation, the church, perceived as the house and sons (cf. 23:38; 17:26). This corresponds to the idea of the housefolk or household. Allegorically Jesus himself is the lord of this house which stands against Satan's house. Jesus himself stands here as a representative of God.[64]

Matthew will have Jesus declare in the later Beelzebul controversy that Jesus is lord of the temple (see 12:28) and that the house of Israel has been abandoned for the church as the new temple (23:38–24:2). Those disciples who belong to the new temple are members of the new house of Israel, the church, founded by Jesus the householder (10:25). In this sense Matthew 10:25 links discipleship to household membership. Those who are faithful to the head of the household will find the pattern of his life in theirs.

The reign of God—which from this context (9:23–32 and 10:25) can be identified with the house[65]—and its gift of peace will endure until the end of this age; they will endure the violence of the household of the powers and principalities in the form of the demonic.

The second discourse concludes with a Matthean triad related to hospitality. This passage—unique to Matthew—revolves around forms of the word *dechesthai*, which means "to welcome" or "to receive." Matthew uses this word related to hospitality twelve times.[66] Since visitors to the house come with the message of the gospel (10:7–13), whoever receives the messenger receives the sender: "He who receives you receives me, and he who receives me receives him who sent me" (10:40). Those wandering charismatics and disciples came in the name of the head of all households (10:25), just as he came in the name of the divine householder (see 20:1, 8, 11; 21:33, 40; 21:42). Those who receive the prophet, the just, and the little ones receive the one in whose name they would come: "A person's messenger is as the person's alter ego." Those who receive the wandering prophet hospitably as a guest in their house are seen as equals to the prophet and will receive the same reward. Those welcoming "the just" will be considered equal in justice as well. If—because they are disciples—they give as little as a cup of cold water to the least ones, they will be properly rewarded.

Thus, hospitality in Matthew's households would manifest a community of people sharing different gifts. Even more, it would reveal a community wherein the welcoming and sharing among the members created a more collegial community.

3. 13:1-53: Parables of God's Reign for Householders

We have already shown that the *third discourse*, like the first, has house references at the beginning (13:1) and the end (13:52-53). In addition, *oikía* serves as a pivotal term in 13:36. Because I have already spent a considerable space on this third narrative, I will merely expand on a few ideas here.

The concluding pericope about the true members of Jesus' family being those who do the will of the heavenly Father was set in the context of the house. This set the context for Matthew's notion of discipleship itself. Elisabeth Schüssler Fiorenza has noted: "The early Christian ethos of coequal discipleship in community could provide a model for the 'new family' as an adult community of equality, mutuality, and responsibility for the home *and* for the world."[67] In this sense, Jesus is offering a new economic by proffering a novel approach to the relations of production: a collegial community sharing in one household under God.[68]

On leaving the *oikía* (13:1) Jesus sat near the lakeshore and told parables about the seed (13:4-8), the weeds (13:24-30), the mustard seed (13:31-32), and the leaven (13:33-35). "Then he left the crowds and went into the *oikía*" (13:36). There he further catechized and formed his disciples in his teaching so that they would *understand*. However, unlike the Markan tendency, this catechesis and instruction were not limited to the house (of Israel?) or a select group within it. Hinting at his universalism, Matthew's Jesus taught and explained his parables not only to an elite group, but to the crowds—an image of the "world," the *oikouménē*. Whoever in the crowds would understand his teachings and put them into practice would be "with him." However, once "with him" the disciples would create a new kind of household. Thus Matthew's use of the Markan image of Jesus returning to "the house" (13:36).

In 13:36, Matthew describes movement into the house with the expression *ēlthen eis tēn oikían* (he went into the house). Such phrasing cannot be found in any of the other gospels; yet it appears in Matthew five other places besides here: *kai elthontes eis tēn oikían* (2:11); *kai elthōn . . . eis tēn oikían* (8:14); *kai elthōn . . . eis tēn oikían* (9:23); *elthonti de eis tēn oikían* (9:28); and *kai hote eisēlthen eis ten oikian* (17:25). One of the six phrases (9:23) seems to indicate that the centurion was the owner of the specific "house." Another (8:14) implies that Peter was the owner of a "house." The uniquely Matthean phraseology may well indicate the equal possibility that the "house" in Bethlehem was owned by Joseph or his kin (2:11), especially since it seems he and his family settled (*katoikein*) in Nazareth *after* the Egyptian exile (2:23). Given the connection between these three passages and possible ownership of the house, and given the same phraseology *ēlthen eis tēn oikían* in the other three verses

(9:28; 13:36; 17:25), all of which take place in Jesus' hometown (*katoikein* [4:13]) of Capernaum (see also 13:1), the very real possibility of Jesus owning "the house" must now move to the realm of probability.

Another linguistic manifestation of the unique function of "house" in this discourse can be found in the first part. Here verses 13:1–36 frame a clear chiasm, with "house" being the beginning and the end:[69]

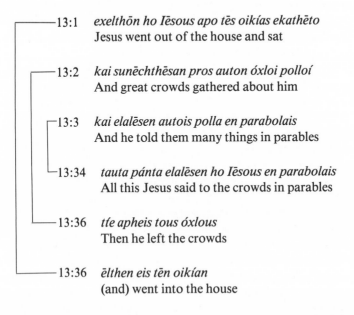

13:1   *exelthōn ho Iēsous apo tēs oikías ekathēto*
Jesus went out of the house and sat

13:2   *kai sunēchthēsan pros auton óxloi polloí*
And great crowds gathered about him

13:3   *kai elalēsen autois polla en parabolais*
And he told them many things in parables

13:34   *tauta pánta elalēsen ho Iēsous en parabolais*
All this Jesus said to the crowds in parables

13:36   *tfe apheis tous óxlous*
Then he left the crowds

13:36   *ēlthen eis tēn oikían*
(and) went into the house

Once Matthew has Jesus inside the house, with his disciples, Matthew followed the Markan tendency to have Jesus explain more fully therein the meaning of the parables and his teaching about the reign of God (13:37–43). There he continues sharing parables: about the treasure and the pearl (13:44–46) and the net which separates the just from the unjust (13:47–50). In concluding, he asks his disciples, in contrast to those who earlier neither saw nor heard (13:10–17): " 'Have you understood all this?' They said to him, 'Yes.' And he said to them, 'Therefore every scribe who has been trained for the kingdom of heaven is like a *oikodespótēs* who brings out of his treasure what is new and what is old' " (13:51–52).

The actual wording in 13:52 is rendered "is like a man [who] is a house-holder." The phrase "is like a man" parallels the openings of the preceding six parables (13:24b, 31b, 44a, 45a, 47a). In 13:24b and 45a Matthew referred to "a man" to designate discipleship. Robert Gundry shows that another favorite word of Matthew related to the householder—*oikodespótēs* (see 20:1, 11; 21:33; 24:43)—"echoes v. 27, where it stands for Jesus. Here it stands for a true disciple of Jesus. Like master, like disciple (cf. 10:25)!"[70]

In ancient usage the house was equated with treasure (*thesaurous*) or possessions. The house of Israel was the personal possession of God (Ex. 19:5).

One variant of Matthew specifically connects houses with possessions (see 23:14). In 13:44 the treasure represents the householder's understanding of the reign of God.

In all likelihood Matthew refers to himself as the scribe who, like a house-holder, goes to the old sources (the Hebrew scriptures and Mark) as well as the new sources (Q and "M"). The resulting gospel invites its hearers to a new way of life. That new way of life will make "every scribe," everyone discipled to Jesus (*mathēteútheis*) who puts the words of Jesus into practice (28:19-20), like Matthew (*Matthaios*). As such they themselves will become true householders, in imitation of the one householder, Jesus.

Earlier, I noted that, immediately before 13:1 when Jesus goes out of the house, Matthew indicates that a new way of life in the house churches was to be shown by a new ordering of relationships, when disciples would live within the church as brothers, sisters, and mother under "my Father in heaven" (12:50). Now, almost immediately after 13:52, Matthew's Jesus repeats his previous reference to mother, brothers, and sisters (13:55-56) in the context of his credibility being called into question and Israel's unbelief: "A prophet is not without honor except in his own country and in his own *oikía*" (13:57).

The united front of Israel imaged in "his own country and in his own house" will not place belief in him. Simultaneously, this lack of faith will lead to the creation of a new household whose members will put their faith in him. Thus just before its beginning and at its end, the third discourse reveals different ways Jesus could be envisioned as relating to the members of his household. One form demands that Jesus adapt to the existing patterns of behavior that reflect membership in the house of Israel (13:57). The other offers a new kind of family relationship that reveals a new community (12:50) that will usher in the new house of Israel, the church. The difference will be the way the faith of the brothers and sisters is put into practice.

4. 17:24-19:1: House Order and Church Discipline

The fourth discourse (17:24-19:12) considers church order and discipline in a divided community.[71] A closer examination of this section of Matthew's gospel suggests that here he is offering his own collegial-type of *haustafel* as a way of dealing with problems in his divided house church.[72]

Contrary to the usual practice, which begins examination of the fourth discourse with 18:1, it seems more appropriate to begin a few lines earlier, with Jesus' entry into the house (17:24-25). In the house the entire discourse or teaching takes place; thus it seems preferable to have everything discussed in the house included in this one discourse. If this is accepted, the discourse would begin with the pericope on taxation (17:24-27). But how, one might ask, does a taxation pericope relate to a household code?

As noted above, New Testament *haustafeln*, or "household codes," often began with some admonition about doing good and the duty for civic obedi-ence. These admonitions did not refer to any specific addressee. After discussing submission to civil authority,[73] they then moved on to discuss more specifically domestic components; these sections usually did contain specific addresses (i.e.: "wives," "children," "slaves"). Thus the question about paying taxes to civil authority at the beginning of this discourse gives even further support to my argument that 17:24–19:1 is a Matthean, collegially-oriented *haustafel*, especially when it is followed by pericopes about the need for all in the households to become like children (18:1–10) and about right house-order (18:11–19).

Matthew begins his household code with Jesus' comments on the tribute or custom paid to the king. Even though the "sons" (members of the household)[74] are free, he suggested payment so as "not to give offense" (17:27). In a society highly influenced by codes regarding honor and shame, giving offense, especially to proper authority, would be considered shameful. Since submission to civil authority was part of the household codes, the payment of taxes, even by the exempt "sons," would not only avoid possible offense; it might be a manifestation of good works that could influence others. However, even here, Matthew shows evidence of a new kind of house-ordering for Jesus' followers in society itself: ultimately "the sons are free" (17:26).

Immediately after the discussion of the payment of taxes to avoid scandal (17:24–27), the next pericope addresses the issue of rank with the disciples' query about who was of greatest importance in the reign of God (18:1). Jesus' response was that they needed to "turn and become like children" or they would "never enter the kingdom of heaven" (18:3). The pericope ends with Jesus' warning to the house churches which seemed to be experiencing conflicts over power: "Whoever humbles himself like this child, he is the greatest in the kingdom of heaven" (18:4).

While submission constituted the heart of secular *haustafeln*, the notion of humility (*tapeinós*) was not invoked. It remained for the Christian household codes to see humility as the unique form of submission.

Philip Carrington was one of the first to note the relationship of submission and *tapeinos*, especially in 1 Peter 5:5–6 and James 4:7, 10 and 1 Clement. He saw it as a minor element in the *haustafeln* tradition.[75] In Matthew it becomes a basic requirement for household membership. Herein all members must give up rank, become like little children, and exercise a new kind of humility (18:1–4).

After the two pericopes containing specific *haustafeln* themes (17:24–18:4), Matthew warns about giving scandal to the "least ones" (18:5–9) and then offers ways to bring about peace in his divided house churches. These include reincorporating the alienated (18:10–14), communal correction (18:15–18), and the power of prayer when a community is united (18:19–20).[76] Then follows the parable about forgiving seventy times seven times (18:21–34), a parable that urges the members of the households to forgive their sisters and brothers from their hearts (18:35).

The text in this chapter that uses the word *ekklēsía* (18:17) does so in the context of the need for reconciliation within the *oikía* (17:25) that begins between individuals (18:15), advances to calling on third parties (18:16), and appeals to the household, the *ekklēsía* itself, as the last resort (18:17). The power of binding and loosing earlier given to Peter upon his confession of faith (16:17-19) is now shared with the local *ekklēsía* as well (18:18). If the keys (to the house/*ekklēsía*) reflect authority and that household authority is to bind and loose, and if the members of the household are to bind and to loose, it follows that they share in the authority (the keys) as well. The two forms of binding and loosing, the two manifestations of the authority of the keys—that of Peter and that of the whole household—were to be united within the *ekklēsía*.

Conflicts with authority were not the only problems dividing Matthew's church. As the twofold mission statements (10:5-6 and 15:24 for the Jews and 28:16-20 for the gentiles) attest, the household churches were experiencing definite division. This alienation was not limited to interpretations of the Law which distinguished Jews and gentiles; it also related to irreconciliation based on problems in relationships (ethnic differences) and the sharing of resources (reciprocity, especially in meeting the demands of justice). Such was inevitable, Filson notes, given the "existence of several house churches in one city [which] goes far to explain the tendency to party strife in the apostolic age." He continues:

> We need not deny the importance of such factors. Nevertheless, the proneness to division which we mark in the apostolic churches was not unconnected with the division of the Christians of a city into house churches. "Birds of a feather flock together." Christians of a certain tendency grouped together and thereby were confirmed in that tendency. Separation from Christians of somewhat different backgrounds, views, and interests must have operated to prevent the growth of mutual understanding. Each group had its feelings of pride and prestige. Such a physically divided church tended almost inevitably to become a mentally divided church. We have thought of each city as a unit. The basic unit, however, was the house church.[77]

From a realization of the divisions within the church, it becomes clearer why Matthew's Jesus would speak about the need for reconciliation with the "brother who sins against you" (18:15). He would necessarily stress the need to go to "others" (assumed to be other brothers and sisters in the household of faith) if reconciliation is still not achieved (18:16). Finally, reflecting a collegial model, the house/*ekklēsía* should serve as the last resort for reconciliation (18:17). Unity among brothers and sisters is so connected to doing God's will (see 12:46-50) that when two or three have become reconciled, Jesus is "in the midst of them" (18:20). Here truly united prayer can be offered to God. By placing Jesus' words about *ekklēsía* (18:17) and discipline in the context of the house (17:24), Matthew was showing how his own house churches should put into practice Jesus' teachings and thus experience his abiding presence.

That abiding presence will be manifest in the forgiveness of debts (material as well as relational) that the members owe each other, indicating their unity within a household which reflects their master's forgiveness as well (18:21-35).

5. 23:1-26:1: Woes to the House of Israel, a Blessing for Just Deeds

In the final discourse (23:1-26:1), the pivotal passage refers to Jesus' final break with Jerusalem and its leaders (23:33-24:2). After scoring the scribes and Pharisees for failing to exercise justice, mercy, and faith in their pursuit of the Law and for killing the just prophets (23:1-36), Jesus, using a feminine image to refer to himself, declared: "O Jerusalem, Jerusalem, killing the prophets and stoning those who are sent to you! How often would I have gathered (*episynágein*) your children together as a hen gathers her brood under her wings, and you would not! Behold, your *oikos* is forsaken and desolate" (23:37-38). As with wisdom (23:34), the presence of Jesus-Emmanuel will be withdrawn from Israel not to be seen again until he returns (23:39). Thus the pivotal passage of Matthew's last discourse of Jesus is expressed from the perspective of the *oikos* of Jerusalem, the center of the people's familial and social life. Possibly building on Jeremiah (Jer. 12:7; 26:6), Matthew portrays the desolation of the temple without the presence of Emmanuel.

Matthew's reference to *oikos* in this context connects the house of Jerusalem with its temple, especially, as we shall see, when this passage (23:37-39) is recognized as inseparable from the next sentence about Jesus' actually leaving the temple (*hierón* [24:1]). "While 'house' could signify Jerusalem or even the whole of Israel, the fact that Jesus is speaking in the temple favors the common OT image of the temple as the house of God," John Meier notes. He adds:

As in Ezek 10:1-22; 11:22-25, the Lord will leave his temple. While the full acting out of this threat was accomplished in A.D. 70, the prophecy already begins to be fulfilled in 24:1, when Jesus leaves the temple, and more fully in 27:51, when the curtain of the temple is rent at the death of Christ. Christians must seek the presence of God in Jesus the Emmanuel (1:23) who is with us all days (28:20) in the midst of the church at prayer (18:20).[78]

While Meier seems to limit the meaning of "house" here to the temple, it would seem, from the specific mention of Jerusalem (23:37), that "house" also refers to the people of the *city* who rejected the person and message of Jesus, as in: "Every kingdom divided against itself is laid waste, and no city (*pólis*) or house (*oikía*) divided against itself will stand" (12:25). In this sense (as in 10:11-14) *oikía* serves as a substitute for *pólis*, the people.[79] In the same connection, the house also refers to a gathered people (23:37), as Jesus indicated: "He who is not with me is against me, and he who does not gather with me scatters" (12:30).

Jesus' declaration about Israel's house (*oikos*) being deserted (23:38) cannot be divorced from Jesus-Emmanuel's actual departure from the temple (*hierón* [24:1]). By omitting the pericope of the widow's mite, which Mark places between the statement about desertion of the house and Jesus' departure from the temple (Mk. 12:41–44; cf. Lk. 21:1–4), Matthew directly links *oikos* (23:38) and *hierón* (24:1). J. Lambrecht notes: "It seems that this omission is not without purpose. Matthew obviously wants to connect the announcement of XXIV, 2 with that of XXIII, 38."[80] Similarly, Fred W. Burnett insists: " . . . even though *hierón* means the temple complex in 24:1, the relation of *hierón* to *oikos* in 23:38 makes Jesus' act of leaving the temple equivalent to his departure from the whole nation."[81] The "Israel" chapter will be closed (see 8:10–13; 21:40–45; 22:1–14; 27:23–26). Douglas R. A. Hare also comments that 23:37–39, as it is placed by Matthew, illustrates his doctrine of the rejection of the house of Israel for the new household of faith:

> While Matthew takes the Jerusalem-saying (23:37–39) from Q and makes no major alteration in it, the position he gives it illuminates his doctrine of the rejection of Israel. It is made the final word in Jesus' valedictory to the Jewish nation. Placed between the promise of judgment upon "this generation" and the subsequent prediction of the destruction of the temple (24:1f.), the Jerusalem-saying declares that Israel's "house" has been abandoned. Not the temple but the commonwealth of Israel is meant by *ho oikos humon*. Not the desolation of the city but the rejection of the rejecting nation is here predicted.[82]

The mention of the temple of Jerusalem hearkened back to the image in Daniel in which the new house of Israel and its temple arose from the ashes of idols because "the stone that struck the image became a great mountain and filled the whole earth" (Dan. 2:35). But now, Matthew's Jesus shows, this temple, this city, and this people will also be toppled. As Ezekiel prophesied earlier, not one stone will stand on another. In their place another temple will be housed in the person of Jesus and his community (26:61). This new temple will be housed in a new household: a house founded on rock (7:24–27; 16:17–19). Those who have gone to the mountain for baptism and now go throughout the whole earth with the message of the gospel (28:16–20) will be part of this new house.[83]

After making the link between the abandoned house (23:38) and Jesus leaving the temple (24:1), the last discourse continues chapter 24 with the narration of the beginning of the calamities and the need for watchfulness. It concludes with Jesus warning: "But know this, that if the *oikodespótēs* had known in what part of the night the thief was coming, he would have watched and would not have let his *oikía* be broken into. Therefore you also must be ready; for the Son of man is coming at an hour you do not expect" (24:43–44).

Matthew has Jesus expand his reflections on the temple by comparing the members of the household churches (who had been entrusted with his *exousía* of preaching, teaching, and healing, all of which called for the reordering of relationships and resources) to responsible stewards entrusted with the property (household) of the master: "Who then is the faithful and wise servant, whom his master has set over his household, to give them their food at the proper time? Blessed is that servant whom his master when he comes will find so doing. Truly, I say to you, he will set him over all his possessions" (24:45–47). But what will be the expectation of the master when "he comes"?

As the final section of the discourse makes clear in the separation of the just from the unjust, when the master "comes in his glory" (25:31), the possession of the reign of God will depend on how members of the household communities shared their resources with the least of their brothers and sisters and, indeed, how the resources of "all the nations" (25:32; see 28:19) would be shared not only with the disciples, but with all those in need (25:33–46).[84] Those to be blessed will be those called "just." Because justice refers to rightly-ordered relationships and resources, at the end of the age those who have lived in fidelity to the ordering of the house will be called "just." The king will call them "blessed of my Father" (25:34) because they did the Father's will.

3

The Presence and Power of *Exousía* in Matthew's Gospel

THE NATURE OF AUTHORITY

Whenever human beings try to live together for extended periods, tensions seem inevitable. Often these problems have to do with the coordination of the group. Barrington Moore has divided issues related to group coordination around what persons will do what work (division of labor) and how resources and services will be distributed. However, the preliminary problem to be resolved, according to Moore, revolves around authority.[1] Where will it lie? Who will exercise it? Over whom will it be exercised?

According to Moore, authority refers to the coordination and control of "the activities of a large number of people. It reaches into all spheres of social life and exists to some degree in all known societies, even in those primitive ones that lack regular chiefs."[2] Authority involves the power and right to command, to enforce a code of living, to exact obedience, to decide and declare, to influence and judge.

Because of historical and geographical differences, people of different epochs and cultures differ in the way they view and grant authority. Since the time of Max Weber, whose seminal analysis of authority has adherents even today, many social scientists have insisted that, in order to be effective, authority demands a legitimation by those over whom it is exercised.[3]

Since all relationships among humans imply forms of authority, Matthew's day and age, like all eras, had its own structures of authority. It affected the lives of individuals and households at every level. Consequently to grasp Matthew's understanding of authority, we should consider its social context.

1. The Historical Setting for House-Based Authority

In his discussion of social relationships within the household, Aristotle linked the exercise of authority with the realization of justice.[4] The three groupings of husbands and wives, parents and children, masters and slaves ultimately dealt with authority and submission.[5] These same groupings and relations formed the dynamics for the historically accepted *haustafeln*.[6] Thus both the nature of Aristotle's household itself, as well the more specific Hellenistic *haustafeln* which evolved from social relations within the household, involve notions of authority and submission.

Aristotle's notion of justice arose from his perspective on hierarchical relationships within the three groupings. For Aristotle justice did not apply to those over whom authority was exercised—to one's chattel (slaves) and to one's children before coming of age—but only to those who were considered more or less equals: "Hence justice can more truly be manifested towards a wife than towards children and chattels, for the former is household justice; but even this is different from political justice."[7]

The world Aristotle described was patriarchal and hierarchical at its core. Social coordination and authority existed within specific forms of social stratification. In any stratified society such as Aristotle's and that of the first century—including the world of Jesus and Matthew—authority operates within a certain set of assumptions. According to Moore these assumptions provide

> a set of limits on what both rulers and subjects, dominant and subordinate groups can do. There is also a set of mutual obligations that bind the two together. Such limits and obligations are not set down in formal written constitutions or contracts, though in societies that have such paraphernalia, some of the provisions—not necessarily the most important ones—may be set down in this fashion.[8]

Although authority in the *pólis* was considered a function of rhetoric and persuasion skills, the entire context for the Greek discussion of authority was the household. Max Weber argued that, sociologically speaking, while the size and inclusiveness of households may vary, connections in households can be made between economics and religion as well as between loyalty and authority. As he reflected on traditional, pre-capitalist societies, he discovered that the household

> is the most widespread economic group and involves continuous and intensive social action. It is the fundamental basis of loyalty and authority, which in turn is the basis of many other groups. This "authority" is of two kinds: (1) the authority derived from superior strength; and (2) the authority derived from practical knowledge and experience. It is, thus, the authority of men as against women and children; of the able-bodied as against those of lesser capability; of the adult as against the child; of the old as against the young. The "loyalty" is one of subjects toward the holders of authority and toward one another. As reverence for ancestors, it finds its way into religion. . . .[9]

In first-century Syria-Palestine, house-based religion legitimated Rome's political authority. That political authority resulted from military power and conquest. It maintained itself by military force, client kings, control of some of the clergy, and procurators with military clout. However, an uneasy balance always existed among these various groups. The older aristocratic families as encapsulated in the high priests vied with the new Roman client rulers of Herod's family. Together these two groups jostled for power with the Roman procurator.[10]

2. First-Century Jewish Religious Authority

The tentativeness of Rome's political power made it mandatory that Rome buttress that power through religion and its authorities. In the case of the Jews, religious-political-economic-cultural authority resided in various leaders. Key among these were the chief priests, the Sadducees, the Pharisees, the scribes, and the elders. In varying ways they all reinforced the legitimation of Roman rule; this was especially true during Roman times of the Sanhedrin, the highest native governing body of the Jewish people. The Sanhedrin contained representatives of all the above-mentioned groups.[11]

The group called the "chief priests" was composed of priests and high priests, the latter office being dominated by priestly families. Because the chief priests held their office at the pleasure of the Romans, they were not critical of Roman authority. The Sadducees, a sect within the priestly class, ran the domestic affairs of the Jewish people under the Roman governors; consequently they accommodated themselves to Roman domination. The Pharisees, especially after the rise of Herod the Great, were generally removed from direct political involvement. They seemed to have adopted an indifferent attitude regarding Roman rule. At the most they cooperated with it; at the least they did not oppose it. The scribes, many of whom adhered to the teachings of the Pharisees, composed the Jewish aristocracy along with the chief priests, Sadducees, and Pharisees. The elders were also part of the aristocracy and would have much to lose if they did not at least tolerate Roman authority.

Besides the aristocratic support of Roman authority, the rest of the Jews had different reactions. Better-known groups, like the Zealots, believed the Romans should be gone from their territory: until they were, the Roman rule should be actively resisted. The Essenes saw themselves as removed from politics, waiting for messianic times when they would rule. The vast middle represented the Jewish population as a whole. While ideologically negative toward Rome, they were politically neutral because their subsistence needs made them more concerned with survival than politics.

After the first Jewish rebellion (66–70 CE), the Sanhedrin ceased to exist. With its aristocratic members generally discredited, the authority-basis of the Jewish leadership was thrown into turmoil. The only group with some credibility was the Pharisees, who had tended to be removed from the upper classes. Not long after the war, with the temple destroyed, some of them gathered at

Yavneh (also called Jabneh or, more popularly, Jamnia) to form a school for the study of Torah. From their study and deliberations the Pharisees came to envision the households of Judaism as the loci for the most effective practice and transmission of Judaism. The household, then, became central to authority because it was in the house-based synagogues that the Jews gathered to maintain their identity via Torah. This would be done under the authority/leadership of the Pharisees. Consequently, with the Pharisees (as well as other significant groups at this time), religious authority revolved around institutional lines and customs of particular family and kinship practices.[12]

However, when Jesus came into "his own country" to teach Torah "in their synagogue," the Jews were astonished and asked, "Where did this man get this wisdom and these mighty works?" (13:54). Referring to his kinship, Matthew says "they took offense at him" (13:57). According to David Bossman, Jesus was perceived as lacking a legitimate basis for institutional authority from kin or polity. Given this lack, one wonders how a gospel like Matthew "could infer authority within a society already structured in matters religious according to kinship norms and political affiliations."[13] This question makes us probe further the notion of authority in Matthew's gospel. The question addressed to Jesus in Matthew by the chief priests and elders—the authorities of the people—becomes central: "By what authority are you doing these things, and who gave you this authority?" (21:23).

3. The Authority of Jesus in Conflict with the Authorities

Within this setting of house-based authority, Matthew presents Jesus as having one form of authority in conflict with that of his society. According to Matthew's narration, Jesus' authority at his birth challenged the existing form of political authority, which threatened Herod (2:1–12). It continued to his death, which was decided, in part, because of his alleged kingship over the Jews (27:11), a kingship that would have made him Caesar's rival.[14] Even the events surrounding his resurrection forced the authorities to develop an alibi to maintain their position (28:11–15).

According to Moore, systems of authority generally specify why persons holding authority have that status and how they obtain it or are maintained in it.[15] This insight helps illuminate Matthew's interpretation of Jesus and helps clarify the fact that conflict over authority underlies the whole narrative of the first gospel.[16] The Jewish leaders (the scribes, the Pharisees, the Sadducees, the elders, and the chief priests) held authority and had status.[17] They obtained their authority and status over a period of time. They held it because of the people's willingness to submit to them and Rome's political reasons to support this form of social coordination.

Into that world Jesus came as a charismatic figure[18] teaching with authority (7:29), healing with authority (9:6; 10:1), and even forgiving sins with authority (9:6). It will be shown in chapter 8 that Jesus undermined the existing social coordination, controlled by the Jewish leaders, with at least four challenges:

1) to reorder table fellowship; 2) to reorder Torah and temple; 3) to reorder the Sabbath to meet human needs; and 4) to do God's will via a new kind of collegial community. These challenges show that his exercise of authority (21:23–27) brought him into direct conflict with the authority of the Jewish leaders (9:3, 11, 34; 12:2, 10, 15, 24–37, 38–45; 13:10–15; 16:1–4; 19:3; 21:12; 23:39; 26:27). As Kingsbury notes, "They rightly perceive that he stands as a moral threat to their authority and therefore to the religion and society based on that authority (15:13; 21:43)."[19]

The debate between Jesus and the leaders over his exercise of authority (21:23–27) was set by Matthew within reworked material in chapter 21 to highlight the tension over the conflict about the notion of authority to be exercised within his house churches (21:1–46). The chapter begins with Jesus ordering his disciples to go into a village to get "an ass tied, and a colt with her"[20] for the subsequent entry into Jerusalem (21:1–11). In the following pericope (21:12–17), Matthew rearranged the Markan material to have Jesus' "cleansing of the temple"—the heart of the nation and center of the cosmos—take place the same day as his triumphal entry into Jerusalem, the center of Jewish authority, the center of its political, economic, religious, and cultural life. These two passages (21:1–11 and 21:12–17) are followed by the cursing of the fig tree for not bearing fruit (an image of Jesus' rejection of the leaders [21:18–22]) and the debate over Jesus' source of authority (21:23–27).

As Matthew sculpted his sources, the entry into Jerusalem (21:1–11) takes Jesus into the source of authority of the scribes and Pharisees; the overturning of the tables in the temple (21:12–17) directly challenged their authority; the cursing of the fig tree (21:18–22) was a rejection of their authority; and the debate with them over the source of his authority (21:23–27) put Jesus' authority in positive contrast to their abuse of authority (23). These four pericopes then connect with the story of the man whose second son obeyed his command (21:28–32) and the parable of the householder (21:33–42), which ends with Jesus declaring: "Therefore I tell you, the kingdom of God will be taken away from you and given to a nation producing the fruits of it" (21:43). The juxtaposition of these pericopes makes it clear that Matthew portrays the chief priests and the Pharisees directly challenged about their authority and the very identification of Israel with God's reign. The result was that, rather than being converted, they tried to arrest Jesus (21:46).

THE MATTHEAN BASIS OF AUTHORITY: THE ABIDING PRESENCE OF JESUS IN *EXOUSÍA*

At the heart of Matthew's understanding of the notion of authority is his understanding of the meaning of God's presence and ultimate authority in the community. Given this understanding, the rest of this chapter will discuss the notion of God's presence and authority in Matthew's house churches. It will try to demonstrate that, from the beginning (Emmanuel/God-with-us) until the end (I will be with you all days), the first gospel reveals how the presence of the risen Christ abides in the church. This abiding presence of Christ in the church is determined by an understanding of *exousía,* or authority. *Exousía* will be shown as the symbol and reality of the abiding power of Jesus at work within his disciples. This authoritative presence of the risen Christ must constitute the foundation for the subsequent exercise of all human authority in the household. Who would exercise that authority, how it would be handled, and through what norms it would be expressed would become key issues.

1. Questions Facing the Matthean Community

Originally Christians believed in the imminent *parousía,* or return of Jesus. Their understanding of God's presence and their effort to experience that presence were influenced by that belief. Consequently, as the Acts of the Apostles and 1 Corinthians show, a significant number of disciples chose to live radical lives, expectantly waiting Jesus' return. In the meantime they "devoted themselves to the apostles' teaching and fellowship, to the breaking of bread and the prayers" (Acts 2:42). "All who believed were together and had all things in common; and they sold their possessions and goods and distributed them to all, as any had need" (Acts 2:44–45). Non-marriage or singleness was counselled "in view of the impending distress" because "the form of this world is passing away" (1 Cor. 7:26, 31).

Such radical forms of living could be the norm, given the communal expectation of Jesus' imminent return. With this sense of immediacy, people living a more radical economic could be tolerated in a community; they did not constitute a threat. Though written decades later, Matthew's gospel retains strong elements of these attitudes, as seems to be evidenced by his references to the presence of wandering charismatics (8:19ff; 10:5ff; 25:1ff).

As the years wore on and Jesus' second coming did not occur as many expected, Matthew's house churches seemed to be following the normal social tendency of a religious movement to adapt gradually to the society around it. We have already seen how problems related to ethnic, power, and urban-rural differences contained in the wider society affected Matthew's house churches.

Much of chapter 24 seems to highlight some of the consequences of these various tensions that existed within and among Matthew's house churches. Some disciples had grown weary (24:42, 48; 25:5, 19) of radical ways of living. Others began to apostatize (24:10) and were in conflict with those who remained (see 11:6; 13:21, 41, 57; 15:12; 16:23; 17:27; 18:6–7; 26:31, 33). Many members who remained connected to the households were betraying and hating one another (10:35–37; 24:10). Others were led astray by the teachings of false prophets (24:4–5, 11), adding to ethnic and status divisions in and among some of the house churches. A sense of the power of evil became strong (24:12a). With the power of evil increasing, a kind of anomie (*anomía*) or disregard for law and authority set in (24:12b; see 7:23; 13:41; 23:28). Because such forms of "wickedness" seemed to be multiplying, the love of "most" in Matthew's households was growing cold (24:10–12).

Within this environment, members of the churches could be easy prey for false prophets who abused their authority by insisting they knew where and how the presence of the Christ could be experienced (24:23–28). As these false prophets were gradually proved wrong, one after another, faithful members understandably asked: "Where is he?"

Such a question about where they could experience God's presence was intensified with the destruction of the temple (CE 70). God's house—the temple—had been traditionally identified with God's presence. With its destruction, the community was forced to reexamine its former theories. If that which represented God's presence was destroyed, where was God? Where could God be found?

With the realization that the temple had become corrupt, the Jamnian Pharisees sought the experience of God's presence by stressing the holiness code and the observance of the Law for the members of the house-synagogues. The Essenes had resolved the question about God's presence by equating themselves with the temple. Paul made the body of the people the new temple. What was Matthew's response going to be?

Matthew had to respond to this tension with words of hope. Sensitive to the people's growing anxiety and disillusionment, Matthew recalled Jesus' words: "Be on guard! Let no one mislead you. . . . Do not be alarmed!" (24:4, 6). Matthew tried to remind the members of his community that Jesus' presence would not be limited to cataclysmic events (24:6–11). His coming-to-be-with-them would never again be limited to an isolated location (24:23–24) such as the desert or even holy shrines (24:26). Matthew asked that his households, rather than being kept in fear by searching for Jesus in empty places (28:5–6), return to their biblical roots by reexamining their genealogy (1:1f).[21]

2. God's Presence in Creation and with the House of Israel

Matthew begins his genealogy—and his whole gospel—with the phrase *bíblos genéseōs Iēsou Christou*, "The book of the genealogy of Jesus Christ, the son of David, the son of Abraham" (1:1). *Bíblos genéseōs* would automatically suggest a connection with the Pentateuch, especially the opening phrase of Genesis. According to W. D. Davies, the evangelist consciously began his gospel with this expression to intimate a parallel with the original creation of the heavens and earth.[22] Somehow, in Jesus and, by extension, in the community of his disciples, God's work of creation was to begin anew; through them creation was to be reordered to reveal God's original plan for the world. Human households came to reflect God's household order for the cosmos.

In many traditions, including that of the Hebrews, God built the world. Creation was pictured as the household of God (Ps. 24:1). By being portrayed as the householder, or manager of the house, God can be considered the divine orderer of all life in the universe. Consequently, all life in every household is responsible to its maker-builder.

From the beginning, the creator of the universe had an economic plan for the world: to bring it from chaos and anomie into reordered relationships and resources (Gen. 1:1ff.). According to Douglas Meeks: "God's economy is fundamentally about God's struggle with the power of death, the *nihil.*" According to Meeks the issue is whether the cosmic household will live or fall victim to God's enemy, death, which seeks in every moment to disrupt the distribution of justice in the household and thus to close out life.[23]

In discussing "Biblical Mandates for Economic Life," the United Church of Christ Study Paper on Christian Faith and Economic Life considered all of our relationships with God from the metaphor of God as the Economist who desires to make a home among us:

> . . . the original meaning of the word economics as household management suggests that "Economist" is an apt metaphor to describe God's work of creation, reconciliation, and redemption. In presenting the Torah and the Gospel, the Old and New Testaments describe the "economy of God."
>
> As Economist, God brings into being and seeks to maintain the household of Israel and the church, the household of the nations, and, ultimately, the household of all creation. These households constantly are threatened by chaos, sin, evil, and death. A great portion of the Bible depicts ways in which God dwells in the creation and works as Housebuilder, Householder, and Homemaker to give all people access to what it takes to live and to live abundantly. God's economy, God's economic work, is to make the creation into a home.[24]

It is not surprising, then, that God's first confrontation with forces denying life takes place at creation. Here, from the nihilism of darkness and disorder, God's *ruah* or Spirit (Gen. 1:2) becomes the means to God's goal of ordering the *oikouménē* in a way that is good.

The first chapter of Genesis outlines God's plan for creation. It stands as a paradigm for the world whenever it experiences being without form, or being in a state of void and darkness, i.e., of being in chaos or *tohû-bohû* (Gen. 1:2a). Experiencing the chaos of the Exile, the Priestly School reflected on its previous chaos in the Exodus and concluded that God's work vis-à-vis the earth/land always involved delivering men and women from *whatever* chaos would create anomie in the form of meaninglessness and alienation, poverty and oppression, enslavement and disenfranchisement. Thus six hundred years after the Exodus, in the upheaval and darkness of the Exile, the Priestly writers described the beginning of the world not so much to express any historical fact as much as to articulate God's perpetual plan for the ongoing liberation of creation accomplished in the Spirit (Gen. 1:2a; cf. Gen. 2:7).

Given the paradigmatic nature of the creation text of the Priestly School, "the Spirit of God" (Gen. 1:2b) was envisioned as continually moving to reorder creation to conform it with God's original plan (Gen. 1:3ff). Thus, from the beginning, the breath of God, God's Spirit (Gen. 1:2a), became identified with the power or authority by which God continues the work of (re)ordering everything in the earth/land, including relationships and resources (Gen. 1:26–28). Since economics involves the ordering of relationships and resources, it can be said that, from the perspective of the writers of the Priestly School writing to an economically deprived people, the Spirit is the liberating principle of economic reordering in creation. Through the Spirit, God's creative work of liberation is communicated to human beings.

The distinctive verse about the role of the Spirit in creation "has long been recognized as having mythological precursors and that is obviously true," Walter Brueggemann has written. But, he adds,

> the verse can also be understood in political-historical terms, without of course denying its mythological antecedents. A political-historical understanding would suggest that chaos (*tohû-bohû*) is the landless situation of exile and the hovering spirit which gives order is Yahweh's act of recovery of land with all its blessing and well-being.[25]

The Priestly School's first chapter of Genesis outlines God's plan for creation or the land.[26] Viewed as God's primordial purpose for the world, it offers a religious paradigm for economics: whenever chaos and disorder reigns, God's Spirit-formed word intervenes (Gen. 1:3ff). However the normal way this intervention will take place is through male and female (Gen. 1:27). As people with dignity who image God, humans must relate to resources in such a God-imaging way that, together, their economics reflects a share in the blessing: "Be fruitful and multiply, and fill the earth and subdue it; and have dominion over the fish of the sea and over the birds of the air and over every living thing that moves upon the earth" (Gen. 1:28).

Genesis 2:4, which links the Priestly and Yahwist versions of the creation accounts, explains: "These are the generations of the heavens and earth when they were created." In Genesis "heavens and earth" refers to the presence of God, as imaged in the dream the fugitive Jacob had of the ladder (Gen. 28:12ff). Here in the dream, the Lord said, "Behold, I am with you" (Gen. 28:15). God's authoritative presence unites heaven and earth.

In his commentary on Genesis, Brueggemann connects Jacob's dream of the ladder with Matthew's interpretation of the abiding presence of God as "I am with you":

> That, of course, is the intent of the ramp-ladder. Heaven has come to be on earth. This promise presents a central thrust of biblical faith. It refutes all the despairing judgments about human existence. A fresh understanding of God is required if we are to be delivered from the hopeless analyses of human possibility made by pessimistic scientists and by the poets of existence. God commits himself to the empty-handed fugitive. The fugitive has not been abandoned. This God will accompany him. It is a promise of royal dimension. In fact, such a promise later is addressed to

another man in jeopardy for God's sake (Jer. 1:19). Then it is reasserted to this whole community called Jacob when the community is in a desperate place of exile (Isa. 43:1-2). It is the name finally assigned to Jesus of Nazareth ("Emmanuel, God with us," Matt. 1:23), who was indeed God with his exiled people: "O come, O come Emmanuel and ransom captive Israel." And this same promise was his last word to the Matthean church (Matt. 28:20), "I am with you always."[27]

Building on the notion of God's presence with "heaven and earth," Matthew refers to God's plan (11:25-26) revealed in the Law and the prophets (5:17-18). This is expressed in the teachings of Jesus (24:35), to whom full authority "in heaven and on earth" has been given (28:18). It cannot be taken lightly that "heaven and earth," which appear as the first and last words of the Priestly creation account (Gen. 1:1; 2:4) and the first words of the Yahwist account (Gen. 2:4), are alluded to in Matthew's first verse (1:1) and used specifically in the last section of his gospel (28:18). It seems Matthew is saying to his community, which shares in Jesus' authority by baptism "in the name of the Father and of the Son and of the Holy Spirit" (20:19), that his gospel is "the book of the generation of Jesus Christ, to whom all authority in heaven and earth is given."

3. God's Presence in Male and Female: Extending the Genealogy

While Matthew's book of genealogy, like Luke's, is used in the broad sense of "household history" (see Gen. 6:9; 37:2), it reveals a theological statement more than a biological report. Without the notion of household and kinship relations, the names he notes would simply constitute a list rather than a genealogy.[28] Matthew's genealogy shows that Jesus' origin lies not only in a people, but in a specific household of people, the family of Abraham and David. In order for Matthew's genealogy to outline the story of a family begetting a household he makes Joseph the vehicle through whom the household will be consummated in Jesus. All is oriented to the birth of the Messiah and how the presence of that Messiah will continue in successive generations.

Matthew's genealogy—offered for his house churches in an urbanized setting—also gives further support to the theory that Matthew's house churches were quite prosperous. According to Robert Smith, genealogies were safeguarded as the historical records of the urban elites: "They served to record a family's pedigree and defended its prestige."[29] However, far from merely supporting the established order of patriarchy and prestige, Matthew's genealogy will show that God's work can be accomplished by rich and poor and not only by men, especially Jewish men, but also by women. By the inclusion of Tamar (1:3), Rahab and Ruth (1:5), and the "wife of Uriah" (Bathsheba [1:6]), Matthew remains faithful to the original vision of Genesis: male *and* female will be the blessed instruments of God's good work on earth (Gen. 1:26-31).

Matthew's reversal of traditional, patriarchal genealogies contradicted the established order. What challenged this "order" was his inclusion of outsiders in God's ordering of the household of Israel. The inclusion of outsiders—women—undermined the traditional patriarchal model and the exclusiveness of the accepted pattern of life. Once these women would not have been considered part of human plans. Now, as Raymond Brown notes, they were a key element in God's designs: ". . . they played an important role in God's plan and were instruments of His providence (or of the Holy Spirit). If to outsiders their lives seemed scandalous (as in the case of Tamar), it was through them that the blessed lineage of the Messiah was continued."[30]

Matthew summarizes his genealogical approach by using a concept with messianic overtones: there are three sets of fourteen generations up to the Christ (1:17). The number "fourteen" may have significance here because the consonants in the Hebrew name David add up to fourteen (D = 4 + V = 6 + D = 4). Since three is a perfect number and Matthew had three sets of fourteen figures, the genealogy of David's house is only perfected in Jesus Christ. His household will be the new Israel of men and women through whom God will continue to be present in creation.

4. House of David through Joseph; Son of God through Mary

The Messiah's lineage had to reach through the generations (i.e., households) of Abraham and David (1:17). It had to come to its climax in the next dramatic way God would reorder creation. It would involve Mary, who "had been betrothed to Joseph" (1:18) and whose subsequent pregnancy and birth of a child was foreshadowed by the previous women mentioned in the genealogy.

"Before they came together she was found to be with child" (1:18). In first-century Judaism, marriage revolved around two legal steps. The first was a formal exchange of consent before witnesses (Mal. 2:14). This exchange constituted a legal tie; the man had rights over the woman even though she still lived with her father. This exchange was followed about a year later by the second step, when the groom took the bride from her father's household to his own (25:1-13). This exchange constituted the formal transfer ("taking" [as of a possession], or *nisuin*) to the husband's household where he assumed her support.

It was during this interim period that Mary was discovered pregnant. Because he was already betrothed to Mary, Joseph was legally her husband and had legal rights over her. If found pregnant by another man, the strict letter of the law said a woman could be put to death. However, Joseph, "being a just man and unwilling to put her to shame, resolved to divorce her quietly" (1:19).

Here Matthew uses the word for "just," *díkaios,* for the first time. Joseph is just in the fullest Hebrew meaning of the word: one who respects the Law as well as one who is full of mercy. *Because* he is just and compassionate Joseph decides to divorce Mary privately. As he considered this way of handling the situation, "an angel of the Lord appeared to him in a dream, saying, 'Joseph, son of David, do not fear to take Mary your wife' " (1:20). Joseph was told to "take" Mary to his household. Joseph, the son of David, was to take Mary into his house both to protect her as well as to confer Davidic paternity on her child so that the scriptures might be fulfilled in him.

While some might see Matthew's genealogy as well as his stress on the angel's annunciation to Joseph rather than to Mary (as in Luke) as manifestations of Matthew's androcentrism, two factors must be remembered. First, Matthew wants to show continuity—how Jesus is part of the house of David; the genealogy through Joseph ensures this. Second, he wants to show discontinuity: that by having Mary conceive the child without her husband, God has acted in a radically new way in history—outside the patriarchal norm. In this sense, Janice Anderson concludes: "Although Jesus is Son of David through Joseph, he is Son of God through Mary."[31]

While the realization of their betrotheds' pregnancy might find other men initiating a divorce, Joseph need not worry: "for that which is conceived in her is of the Holy Spirit" (1:20). Thus through Joseph the patriarchal line continued. But through the woman, Mary, a new house-ordering would be established in the life and work of Jesus.

5. God Is with Us through the Spirit

As in the beginning—the Spirit of God "was moving over the face of the waters" (Gen. 1:2)—the Spirit had hovered over Mary making new life appear before she and Joseph came together. Now what had been conceived in her is "of the Holy Spirit (*Pneumatos Hagious*)" (1:20). As this first use in Matthew of the word "Spirit" implies, the Holy Spirit is the agent of God's creative power in the world.

In these passages Matthew remains true to creation theology, which demonstrates that the life-principle in Jesus comes from the Spirit.[32] Thus, in the passage about God present through the Spirit over Mary, we find Matthew's first response to his house churches questioning where they could find God. Just as God could be found in the Spirit which hovered over Mary, so God could be found through the Spirit which gave life and power to the child in her womb. Through her son and his church, creation would be brought to a new level. As Eduard Schweizer notes in his volume on Matthew:

> In the Old Testament the Spirit of God is already associated with God's creative force, which produces life. . . . In the New Testament the Spirit refers to the presence of God, which characterizes Jesus throughout his entire life and ministry. Thus the Christian community adopted the Old Testament notion of God as the actual creator of all life, who alone can give children. . . . This explains why Matthew 1:18 is so restrained about the miracle of this birth.[33]

Almost immediately Matthew gives another response to those questioning where they could find God: "she will bear a son, and you shall call his name

Jesus, for he will save his people from their sins" (1:21). This son, miraculously conceived by the Holy Spirit, was destined to establish a new presence of God, a new household, with all people. Thus, "All this took place to fulfil what the Lord had spoken by the prophet: 'Behold a virgin shall conceive and bear a son, and his name shall be called Emmanuel' (which means, God with us)" (1:22-23).

The title "Emmanuel" first appeared in Isaiah 7:14, which envisioned a messianic king who would rule in a newly ordered royal household. Through this Emmanuel opposing forces would be reconciled. Relationships and the allocation of resources would again reflect and promote God's original plan. However, where Isaiah had said the "virgin" would call her son "Emmanuel," Matthew says that "they" will call him by that name. The "they" refers to those who become his disciples in faith.

The importance of this verse is attested by the fact that here Matthew uses a Hebrew word and then interprets it. The quote from Isaiah indicates that in the narrative to be unfolded God's presence would be discovered among the people ("they") through the person and ministry of Jesus, who would be the manifestation of God's presence and authority in the world.[34] According to Eugene LaVerdiere:

> The name Emmanuel is a summary of the entire Gospel of Matthew, which can be read as the story of what it means for God to be with us in the person of Jesus. It is as Emmanuel that Jesus saves his people from their sins. His whole mission, his preaching, teaching, healing, and exorcising, as well as the events of his final days, his passion, death and resurrection, all are an expression of Jesus' saving work and of God's being with us. To know what Emmanuel means we must read the Gospel from beginning to end.[35]

After the infancy narrative, the first pericope of Matthew discusses Jesus' commitment to the fulfillment of justice (3:15) that is possible because of God's presence and empowerment. "When you pass through the waters," Yahweh had promised through Isaiah, "I will be with you" (Is. 43:2). Thus, after Jesus was baptized, "he went up immediately from the water, and behold, the heavens were opened, and he saw the Spirit of God descending like a dove, and alighting on him; and lo, a voice from heaven, saying, 'This is my beloved Son, with whom i am well pleased' " (3:16-17). Truly, in Jesus, God was with humanity—through that Son—to establish a lasting household where his presence and authority would be manifest forever.

6. Jesus' Death: Yielding the Spirit to Be with Us

The uniquely Matthean redaction of Jesus' death-resurrection shows how God's power and work extended into the church through the Spirit of Jesus. On the cross, at the moment of his death, Jesus "yielded up his spirit" (27:50). A good many commentators pay scant attention to this phrase, thinking Matthew's use of the words *aphēken to pneuma* refers only to Jesus' act of dying. However, the phrase is unique to Matthew. And where Matthew uses original phrasing, one must go beyond its face-value to its context. What does the context of this text reveal?

Immediately following the deliverance of Jesus' spirit the temple's curtain tears, the earth shakes, tombs open from which "many bodies of the saints who had fallen asleep were raised" (27:51–52). This phraseology clearly alludes to Ezekiel's prophetic vision:

> Behold, I will open your graves, and raise you from your graves, O my people; and I will bring you home into the land of Israel. And you shall know that I am the Lord, when I open your graves, and raise you from your graves, O my people. And I will put my Spirit within you, and you shall live [Ezek. 37:12–14].

For anyone familiar with Jewish thought, this vision typified messianic salvation, the inbreaking of God's reign into a new household. The allusion to Ezekiel's prophetic vision existed in the pre-Matthean text, but Matthew heightened it by further redacting the text to include a reference to Ezekiel 37. According to Rafael Aguirre, this invites "us to see expressed in verse 50 the giving-over of the Spirit of God. The Spirit acts in the irruption of eschatological time which means the end of the old economy of salvation (19:51a). This Spirit now acts in the congregation of the new people of God via their faith in the Messiah."[36] The curtain of the temple being rent symbolizes the creation of another household in whom Jesus' spirit and presence will dwell.

Since Matthew, like John,[37] makes no separation between the death and resurrection of Jesus and the continuation of his presence in the church, the post-resurrection extension of Jesus' spirit now can be found in those members of the house churches baptized "in the name of the Father and of the Son and of the Holy Spirit" (28:16–20). Participating in the spirit-presence of Jesus, the members of the house churches now share in the power and authority (*exousía*) of Jesus (28:18): "I am with you always, to the close of the age" (28:20). In the gathering of the disciples in the house church (see 17:24) the abiding presence of Jesus will be experienced (18:20).

THE ABIDING PRESENCE AND POWER OF JESUS WITH THE DISCIPLES IN THE HOUSE CHURCHES: "FULL AUTHORITY HAS BEEN GIVEN ME . . . I AM WITH YOU ALWAYS"

The last chapter noted that Matthew perceived membership in the house churches from the perspective of the disciples and Jesus being *with* each other. The Greek preposition translated as "with" (*meta* + genitive case) is often used to indicate companionship. For instance, Matthew's Jesus referred to David "and those who were *with* him" (12:3) to indicate the band of David's followers.

Hubert Frankemölle has argued that, as the Deuteronomist and the Chronicler interpreted Old Testament covenant theology (God *with* the house of Israel), so Matthew's use of "with us"/"with you" reveals a covenantal formula expressing Jesus' bond with the church.[38] Besides featuring the uniquely Matthean passages we have already discussed (1:23; 18:20; and 28:20), he discusses where Matthew shared the phrase with his sources (17:17 ["How long am I to bear with you?"] and 26:18 ["I will keep the passover at your house with my disciples"]), and where he adapted his sources to add the phrase, as at the last supper where Jesus discussed drinking the cup "with you in my Father's kingdom" (26:29) and his twice-given request of his disciples to pray with him in Gethsemane (26:38, 40). In at least two other places "with us" is assumed. The first is in the key passage in 11:2-6 where John's disciples ask: "Are you he who is to come [to be 'with us']?" and at the entrance into Jerusalem when the crowds shouted: "Blessed be he who comes [to be 'with us'] in the name of the Lord!" (21:9).

Jack Dean Kingsbury comments on the noteworthiness of the way Matthew carefully restricted the circle of those sharing "with" Jesus and how all revolves around a critical principle: "he who is not *with me* is against me, and he who does not gather *with me* scatters" (12:30). Kingsbury concludes:

> In Matthew's story, then, Jesus grants the privilege of his company almost without exception only to his own. Before the resurrection, these are his disciples. After the resurrection, they are his church (16:18). The disciples before the resurrection follow along "with Jesus" as he leads them to the cross (16:21; 20:17-19). The church after the resurrection makes its way toward the consummation of the age and the Parousia on the promise of the exalted Jesus that he will surely be "with them [you]" (28:20).[39]

The risen Jesus will remain "with" his disciples through rightly-ordered house churches. The disciples will remain with him by sharing in his very authority (28:18) at baptism (28:19). This sharing in Jesus' own authority will no longer reflect hierarchical modes, but a more egalitarian community wherein all share the same "identity as Jesus' true relatives, his real mother, brothers and sisters."[40] This makes them members of a new family, a new household. It also will bring the members of these new households into conflict with the authorities, even those within the church.

1. Two Houses in Conflict

In the previous chapter, I noted connections between Jesus, the head of the household, and the disciples of his household (10:25) who were *his* church

(16:18). In 10:24–25—which is unique to Matthew—as well as chapter 12:25–37—which is primarily from Q, with some from Mark—Matthew portrays Jesus and the house churches in confrontation with Beelzebul. The reign or authority of God and evil conflict. Such a confrontation between the two "authorities" is essential for the mission of proclaiming the reign of God. In 10:24–25, Matthew's Jesus declares:

> A disciple [*mathētēs*] is not above his teacher [*didáskalos*], nor a servant [*doulos*] above his master [*kýrios*]; it is enough for the disciple [*mathētēs*] to be like his teacher [*didáskalos*], and the servant [*doulos*] like his master [*kýrios*]. If they have called the master of the house [*oikodespótēs*] Beelzebul, how much more will they malign those of his household [*oikiakós*].

This uniquely Matthean passage, so included because of those situations unique to Matthew's house-based community, includes key concepts that reveal his economics as well as his ecclesiology. Using the title "head of the household," Jesus also refers to himself as teacher and lord in an authoritative relationship with his disciples and servants/sons who are members of the household. Jesus functioned within the house churches as teacher of the disciples and head of a new family, under God the heavenly Father (12:46–50). *Mathētēs* and *didaskalos* are correlative terms, as are *kýrios* and *doulos/paidion*, as well as *oikodespótēs* and *oikiakós*. The relationship can be diagramed as follows:

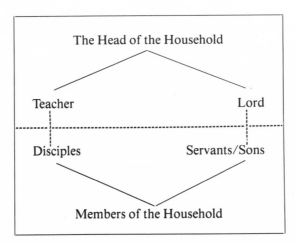

No "insider" calls Jesus "teacher" in Matthew. Only Jesus refers to himself by that title (23:8; 26:18); otherwise, those who use it indicate their lack of commitment to him (8:19; 9:11; 12:38; 17:24; 19:16; 22:16; 22:24, 36). As Günther Bornkamm notes:

Discipleship of Jesus does not arise on the basis of a free attachment to a teacher, but on the basis of a call to follow him which issues from Jesus. Jesus does not exercise authority over his disciples on account of his knowledge of the Torah, nor is he a means to the end of gaining a similar wisdom in the law. Further, the position of a *mathētēs* is not a preliminary stage, with the intention that the disciple himself shall become a *didaskalos* (23:8ff), but signifies a lasting relationship to Jesus.[41]

Recent studies have begun to uncover the implications surrounding the title *Kýrios*. In contrast to Mark, who uses it of Jesus only seven times, Matthew and Luke use it regularly. Qumran evidence shows that the Palestinian Jews used the absolute title "Lord" of Yahweh. It seems quite likely that its application to the risen Christ first occurred among Palestinian Christians themselves and extended throughout the house churches who became aware of the abiding, authoritative presence of the *Kýrios* in their midst.[42] In discussing the socio-political setting of the household, the first chapter noted that *Kýrios* meant *paterfamilias* or head of a household. Those calling Jesus "Lord" submitted, like sons and daughters and servants, to his authority. Bornkamm concludes: "Those who do not belong to the disciples say to the disciples 'your master' (9.2; 17.24); likewise, over against the Jews he is designated by the disciples as 'the Master' (26.10), but among the disciples themselves this title is not adequate for him, but only the Lord-title will do."[43] Matthew alone shows an intimate connection between Jesus as Lord (24:42) and Jesus as Householder (24:43).

The healing of a blind and dumb demoniac sets the context for the next Beelzebul controversy (12:22–32). While the people saw the possibility of Jesus being a true member of the house of David (see 12:23), the Pharisees said, "It is only by Beelzebul, the prince of demons, that this man casts out demons" (12:24). Responding to their "thought," Matthew couches Jesus' power of exorcism as a confrontation between two authorities or reigns: "Every kingdom divided against itself is laid waste, and no city or house divided against itself will stand" (12:25). Matthew here uses the Markan metaphor linking kingdom (*basileía*), city (*pólis*), and house (*oikía*). Jesus is the Lord, the head of the household constituted of disciples and servants (10:25) who share in his power; the household of Satan contains members influenced by the power of evil (12:43–45).

Although the tradition about the cure of the demoniac and resulting controversy is confused, it seems Matthew grouped five different sayings together in this pericope. Following the cure came: 1) the Beelzebul charge and Jesus' reply (from Mark and its Q parallel [12:24–26]), 2) the attribution of his healing to the Spirit of God (from Q [12:27–28]), 3) the strong man's *oikía* (from Mark [12:29]), 4) an independent saying about loyalty (12:30), 5) the blasphemy against the Spirit (from Mark [12:31–32]).

Matthew's Jesus makes it clear: his ability to exorcise the demoniac was grounded in the Spirit. Matthew's gospel thus links Jesus' healing work of God with the Spirit.[44] This power of God at work in Jesus confronted any authority, including economic and political forces, that stood in the way of God's reign and will. How the Householder exercised that authority must be continued by the householders. As it brought him into conflict with injustice and other abuses of authority, so it will bring disciples of Jesus today into conflict with their leaders for the same reasons. In the words of Donald Senior:

> The political dimension of the Kingdom motif means that God's saving activity challenges every structure and system of values which threaten human life and the beauty of creation. Jesus' healing activity and his exorcisms mean precisely this. The text of 12:28 is decisive: "But if it is by the Spirit of God that I cast out demons, then the kingdom of God has come upon you."[45]

God's reign stands against any abuse of authority. Where authority is abused, there the image of the demonic is present; it must be exorcised. Thus Matthew's Jesus cast out demons by "the Spirit of God."

Other places identify Jesus' healing with *exousía* (9:6; 10:1; 21:23-27). Matthew and the early Christians claimed that Jesus' authority came from God. Thus, through the Spirit of God and *exousía*, the authority of God's reign and presence was revealed in Jesus. Today we would make the function of *exousía* and the Spirit the same. Since *exousía* reveals Matthew's notion of God's presence and power at work in Jesus (and in the church as well), it will be important to understand more exactly its meaning and function.

2. Exousía *in the House Churches and the Gathered Disciples*

Returning to the question of how Matthew could infer Jesus' authority within a society which structured authority in religious matters according to kinship norms and political affiliations, we find an answer in the notion of *exousía*. An understanding of *exousía* as Matthew's source within the house churches for all authority—including the power of the keys—makes its central role in Matthew clearer.

Exousía as used in Mark means God's power at work in Jesus.[46] Yet an investigation of the way Matthew included, adapted, and added to the use of the term reveals not only the singular way Matthew portrays Jesus' authority but also how it continues in the church.

Matthew first uses the word at the end of the Sermon on the Mount. Jesus spoke with *exousía* (7:29), not like "their scribes."[47] But the power to speak with this authority came from God's authority (11:27) through the Spirit (see 22:43), and it would be through the power of this same Spirit that the disciples would be able to speak, especially in the face of persecution (10:20).

The power of the Spirit (12:28) constituted the foundation of Jesus' healing.

Its expression in *exousía* was part of the "all things" delivered "to me by my Father" (11:27). The centurion compared his own authority (8:9) to Jesus'. Its exercise brought Jesus into conflict with the high priests and elders who challenged him regarding the source of his authority (21:23-27). Matthew followed the story of their confrontation with Jesus over his authority (21:23-27) with three more confrontational pericopes showing Jesus' power over that of the leaders (21:28-22:14). He gave his power to heal "every disease and every infirmity among the people" (4:33) to the disciples (9:35). The apostles shared in his *exousía* for their mission (to the house of Israel [10:1ff]).

Matthew shared the eight uses of *exousía* mentioned above (7:29; 8:9; 9:6; 10:1; 21:23 [2x], 24, 27) with Mark and Luke (except 8:9, which is not in Mark). However, by inserting two unique uses of *exousía* (28:18 and 9:8), Matthew shows how Jesus' authority was entrusted to the church to be exercised until the end of the age. These two uniquely Matthean texts clearly show that, through *exousía*, the church is to continue God's creative work of reordering relationships and resources to their original purposes.

We have already seen that the deliverance of Jesus' Spirit at his death/ resurrection was the source of the church's *exousía* (27:50). This is followed with the uniquely Matthean universal mission mandate where the "full authority" given to Jesus is shared with the baptized disciples to whom Jesus promises: "I will be with you" (28:18-20).

The identity between the historical Jesus and the church through a sharing in his authority can best be understood by examining the other place in which Matthew uniquely uses the word *exousía*. In the story of the cure of the paralytic, which occasioned blasphemy in the hearts of some of the scribes, Jesus linked his ability to heal the body and the soul (through forgiveness of sins) to *exousía*: " 'But that you may know that the Son of man has *exousía* on earth to forgive sins'—he then said to the paralytic—'Rise, take up your bed and go home.' And he rose and went home" (9:6-7). However, according to Matthew, the crowds did not understand this *exousía* as being limited to Jesus alone: "When the crowds saw it, they were afraid, and they glorified God, who had given such *exousía* to men" (9:8). The *exousía* given by God to Jesus now was the *exousía* of the baptized. Thus both uniquely Matthean uses of the word *exousía* (9:8; 28:18) refer to the sharing of this power with the church. In an extended passage, James Reese asks:

> Why do the crowds praise God for giving "such authority to *men*? Jesus alone displayed the power. The comment of Matthew focuses attention not on the physical cure but on an ongoing expression of the authority of Jesus that was not limited to his earthly existence. The display of authority is exemplary. . . .
>
> It is true that Matthew does not explicitly state the transfer of authority until the final scene of his Gospel. Yet the organization and dynamism of his presentation tells readers that this transfer is uppermost in the intention of Matthew. He sees the function of the earthly life of Jesus as

bestowing the transcendent authority of Jesus Immanuel to the believing community.[48]

It seems quite evident that by the unique inclusion of the phrase "God, who had given such authority to men" (9:8) Matthew did not intend to limit God's *exousía* to Jesus alone. Rather that authority must be exercised in the whole world "until the end of the age" (28:20) in the lives of the members of the church without exception. With Bossman we can conclude: "The continuing influence of his teaching and the manifestation of his presence within the early Christian communities bears witness to a manifestation of authority implicit in his life and teaching but expressed in early households of faith."[49] Not only in households of faith, but in gatherings as small as two or three, that *exousía* is to be exercised by baptized disciples. The experience of Jesus' *exousía*—in the house churches and wherever two or three gather in "my name" (which make him present in the midst of the church)—was the experience of lived faith. All those among the baptized who put into practice everything that had been commanded by Jesus would do so because of their share in that *exousía*.

THE EVOLUTION OF AUTHORITY FROM THE FOUNDER TO ITS INSTITUTIONALIZATION: THEOLOGICAL *EXOUSÍA* AND SOCIOLOGICAL CHARISMATA

Edward Blair writes that "Matthew's portrait of Jesus centers in his representation of Jesus' authority."[50] Matthew and the early Christians had to face and solve the problem of authority behind their deviation from Jewish norms as well as the problem of abuses of authority among the leaders in their own households. According to Fred Burnett, *exousía* was part of the "all things" that were given Jesus by God (11:27). He contrasts this phrase with Jesus' statement about "full authority" (*exousía* [28:18]) being given him.[51]

Like theologians, sociologists have reflected on the nature and exercise of Jesus' authority and how it was exercised in the church. Chief among these has been Max Weber. He identified three types of authority: 1) traditional authority (i.e., status); 2) rational-legal authority (i.e., office); and 3) charismatic authority.[52] In connection with the latter, Weber found a strong relationship among vocation, discipleship, and charism (which he connected to *exousía*). He wrote that those who are the bearers of the charisma—the master and his disciples and followers—must, if they are to do justice to their mission, "stand outside the ties of this world, outside the everyday vocations and also outside the everyday family duties."[53]

Matthew's gospel reveals evidence of this kind of charismatic activity of prophets (5:12; 10:41; 13:17, 57; 23:34, 37) and false prophets (7:21-23; 24:4-28). However, tensions in Matthew's community were not circumscribed by debates over the expression of charismatic authority; the conflicts revolved around whether that charismatic activity that once earmarked the early community would remain as it was tempted to become more institutionalized. The tensions around which mode of authority (noted above from Weber) would prevail were definitely at work in Matthew's community. These tensions, Wayne Meeks notes, affected Matthew's narrative:

> There is dissension within Matthew's communities over different sources and modes of authority. On the one hand, we see clear signs of the development of formal— institutional and legal—kinds of authority; on the other, the "charismatic" power of prophets is still acknowledged, though with some ambivalence. Traditions of Jesus, both stories about his life and his pronouncements and parables, play an important role in these discussions.[54]

While any evidence from earliest Christianity fitting Weber's model of the charismatic leader to Jesus and the Jesus movement has been called into question recently,[55] the *exousía* which Jesus received from the Father (11:27) and shared with the disciples (10:1; 28:18) has definite parallels in Weber's model. He writes that "it must not be forgotten for an instant that the entire basis of Jesus' own legitimation, as well as his claim that he and only he knew the Father and that the way to God led through faith in him alone, was the magical charisma he felt within himself."[56]

According to Weber, because of the charisma of the one holding this power, others who had been experiencing *anomie* (normlessness or meaninglessness)[57] began to gather around that charismatic figure. By identifying with the bearer of the charisma they "also possess some special charismatic qualification. . . . These may, on occasion, group themselves into a congregation for a particular temporary activity or on a continuous basis."[58] In Matthew this "charismatic qualification" involved the call to discipleship which originated with their share in Jesus' *exousía* given at baptism (28:18-20).

Weber showed that, in the early stages of religious movements, a basic equality often exists among the members. It is my thesis—to be elaborated in the next chapter—that Matthew's gospel, while depicting leaders within the community, envisions that leadership being exercised within a spirit of greater egalitarianism grounded in the equal sharing of Jesus' *exousía* by the disciples. Despite efforts by some to show that Matthew adapted the traditional authority model and the rational-legal authority model, it is clear that Matthew presents Jesus arguing against those forms. Matthew envisioned a more charismatic model—a community of disciples equally sharing in Jesus' *exousía*.

Bossman concludes: "If one were to look for organizational structure it would be a vain search, for none is suggested in the teaching of Jesus and little is expected in the family setting."[59] The hermeneutical conclusion reached by Bossman as well as the conclusions I have stated thus far are supported by Leland J. White's examination of authority in Matthew's community. It reveals

> the lack of a formal power structure and the prohibition against recognizing rank or achievement within the community. Only one type of

leadership role appears to be recognized within this community, namely teaching and/or prophesying. The one who teaches (*didáxē*) all the commandments will be called great, and the one who relaxes any will be called least (5:19). But this ranking is "in the kingdom of heaven." Moreover, this rank is dependent on observing the norms. The link between "doing" and "teaching" binds the teacher to the same obligations as all other members of the community.[60]

At the time Matthew wrote his gospel, the tensions already discussed indicate that specific house churches exhibited patriarchal forms while others reflected the *collegia* or more egalitarian model. Yet, although some local house churches may have been patriarchal and though leadership would arise naturally even in egalitarian households (which often depended on patrons), no formal hierarchical functions can be found as such in the Matthean church. Rather Matthew's vision for his households was that they witness to the shared charismatic dimension of *exousía* distributed equally among all the baptized members. Baptism in Jesus' *exousía* empowers all house members equally.

Max Weber also showed that if a religious movement is not to remain a purely transitory phenomenon and desires to "take on the character of a permanent relationship forming a stable community of disciples or band of followers or a party organization, [it is] necessary for the character of charismatic authority to become radically changed."[61] The community of disciples that begins as a community of relative equality under the charisma of the founder begins to become institutionalized with distinctions (between ministries [offices] and services [works]), rank (the greatest and the least), titles, and hierarchy, even though the original vision abrogated them all. This "routinization of the charism" of the founder's *exousía* sooner or later gives way to the legal-rational model, which stresses certain clericalized ways to imitate the founder as being the only ways. This is called the "praebendal provision." "When a charismatic movement develops in the direction of praebendal provision, the 'laity' become differentiated from the 'clergy'; that is, [from] the participating members of the charismatic administrative staff which has not become routinized. These are the priests of the developing 'church.' "[62] Once priests achieve control, the temptation to abuse their power becomes even greater. The teaching that once represented *exousía* (7:29) becomes like that of scribes or Pharisees whose goal is primarily the preservation of that order which ensures the continuation of their power. As Martin Hengel notes:

> The free, prophetic *exousía* becomes increasingly petrified as the "authority" of the head of a school or of an office-bearer, legitimated by virtue of the "succession" (*diadoche*), and in this way the living process of following the master becomes the formally defined *imitatio*.[63]

Even though Matthew's vision of community reflected a more egalitarian composition and while there were no "priests" in the house churches when

Matthew wrote his gospel, Matthew's community had leaders nonetheless. As with any humans with personal power, they were tempted to use it for their own self-interests. This could have detrimental effects on the community. In addition to Matthew's warnings that his community's leaders should not abuse their authority (*katexousiázein* [20:25]), the repeated challenges about abuses of the scribes and Pharisees, culminating in chapter 23, indicate Matthew's paradigmatic way of dealing with the abuse of power already arising in leaders of his own house churches. The conflict Jesus may have had with the authorities of his day had become the conflict Matthew had with church leaders fifty years later. This helps explain why Matthew would modify his sources to put the Jewish leaders in a negative light (3:7 with Lk. 3:7 and 6:39; and 12:33–35 with Lk. 6:43–45), especially during the 80s and 90s when the tensions with the Jews seemed to be waning.

David Garland has argued convincingly that the intention of Matthew in highlighting Jesus' challenges to the leaders of his day—which reached their zenith in chapter 23—was to challenge the same forms of behavior in his house churches and, for that matter, in the church of any day.[64] According to Garland, the verses about not having titles and functions that Matthew includes in 23:8–12 "are specifically directed to 'you', the disciples, who may be seen as paradigms for the community; consequently, vv. 8–12 comprise regulations for the community."[65] Any teaching, leadership, title, or role that elevated anyone above the rest of the brothers and sisters in the believing community was to be rejected as undermining the way *exousía* was to be lived by the brotherhood and sisterhood in the house churches. While there would always be leaders within a group that shared authority equally, the exercise of that leadership was to be so structured that the great would be the servant and the first the slave (20:26–27).

Another major difference between Jesus' and the disciples' ways of exercising the same *exousía* would be Jesus' conviction about its power and the disciples' little or great faith regarding it. The challenge to Jesus' church was to deepen its faith to let the presence of God's power flow through it. Even though a lack of faith in God's presence and authority might be reflected in Jesus' followers, Matthew invited his readers to abandon their doubt and to worship and live in God's abiding presence under the authority of Jesus' Spirit (28:16–20).

4

The Household Churches:
Rightly-Ordered Relationships
and Resources

The previous chapter focused on authority, one of the three elements of social coordination, and discussed how it functioned in Matthew's households. This chapter will be concerned with the way household relations were ordered through the division of labor and how resources were allocated.

REORDERING RELATIONSHIPS

1. The Division of Labor and the Household

Adam Smith showed that human acquisitiveness gave rise to the division of labor. Every known society has manifested some form of relationship- and resource-ordering centered around production; this is known as the division of labor. As with the first dimension of social coordination, authority, the division of labor involves implicit social assumptions or a kind of social contract which determines productive roles and activities. According to Barrington Moore, this social contract acts to regulate potential conflicts among the various economic actors in three specific areas: "(1) the demands and requirements of the individual worker or household for food, clothing, shelter and a share in the amenities and pleasures of life; (2) the needs of the society as a whole; (3) the demands and requirements of the dominant individuals or groups."[1]

Since Matthew's households served as the basic unit of production, some kind of a division of labor took place within them. What specific form this took is not clear. However the productive unit of the house in the wider environment which gave rise to Matthew's gospel broke down the division of labor along male-female roles. To believe that Matthew would not be affected by these patterns and their accompanying assumptions would be naive as well as ahistorical. Thus men built houses (7:24), women made bread (13:33), and children played (11:16). Bruce Malina has shown clearly how, in fact, the

division of labor in the wider world was reflected in the images of Matthew's
Jesus as well:

> The preindustrial Mediterranean world is marked by families which are
> producing units. However, men's and women's work is sharply segre-
> gated (for example, note that the parable on anxiety in Matt. 6:25:31 has
> birds compared with men's work, while the lilies of the field are com-
> pared with women's work). As producing unit, the family was the focus
> of the activities of each family member, and potentially disruptive extra-
> familial associations were taken care of by the head of the family.
> Similarly, membership in the craftsmen's guilds of the preindustrial city
> was normally based on kinship, just as membership in the elite classes
> derived from birth.[2]

Malina's comments seem oriented to the patriarchal family. It is not as clear
whether kinship played as strong a role in the voluntary associations. The
possibility of a fictive kinship which united people with similar values, common work, or shared interests cannot be discounted. However, whether patriarchal or collegial, Matthew's households had definite divisions of labor.

2. Status and Patriarchy

Chapter 2 discussed how social relations in the Greco-Roman world were
divided into two kinds of households, the patriarchal form and the voluntary
associations or *collegia*. Not surprisingly, the patriarchal form predominated. I
have already shown how, in the case of the Roman Empire, the patriarchal
oikía/oikos was the microcosm of the *pólis* and the *basileía*. According to
Derek Tidball:

> The Romans did not invent the household system, the Greeks had it too,
> but subordinated it to the *politeía*. Under the Romans a number of
> economic and sociological changes took place which made the household
> the primary structure of the Empire. The old senatorial families of the
> republic declined whilst, at the same time, the increased distribution of
> wealth led to the founding of many more household communities. In
> addition to the extension in the number of households a further step
> elevated the importance of the structure. Augustus, needing to secure his
> authority, strengthened the personal links between himself and his ser-
> vants and citizens. To do this he exploited the paternalism which was
> implicit in the household system and, using the emotional ties which it
> involved, he became the *pater familias* of the Empire. Consequently the
> Empire became on a macrocosmic scale what the household was in
> microcosm. The Empire was a complex network of households which all
> loyally interlocked into one grand system under the authority and protec-
> tion of the Emperor.[3]

In chapter 1, I noted that the primary concepts which have been used in microsociology to study how people tend to organize themselves into social groups involve *status, role,* and *act.*[4] Status was the determining factor that separated the various groups. Status refers to a person's social position in relationship to others in the same social system. Based mainly in birth and symbolized by the honor and prestige (as well as shame) already accumulated and preserved by one's household family, it benefited some and kept others in permanent margination. Status was inherited; as such it was connected to familial position or households. It preceded possessions in importance; however it was identified in possessions and households. Thus status determined one's possessions, while possessions constituted an essential component of the household (see 23:14).

Every individual had a given status and role within a well-defined and highly organized, determinate system of status and roles. The key structure at each level and within this hierarchical system was the family (kinship) constituting the household.

While the Jews had their own internal levels of classification,[5] at the time of Jesus the social order in Syria-Palestine itself structured people into various groups.[6] The two most distinguishing differentiations determined whether people were free, freedmen, or slaves, and whether people were Roman citizens or not. These orders of people crossed the basic status determinations which ranked people into the upper and lower classes. As to the upper class, the first group was made up of the members of the household of Caesar, then came senators, *equites,* and other urban elites who owned large tracts of land and flocks. The commercial bourgeoisie constituted the second sphere. This group was constituted of those involved in local and international trade. If any members of this group were slaves, they gradually acquired autonomy as time passed. The third part of the triad of power, under the royal household, was the religious oligarchy of Jewish Palestine. It fits under the term "chief priests"[7] and was composed, on the one hand, by Herod and his household, and, on the other hand, by the priests who formed the high clergy who administrated the temple and its treasury. These three poles created the dominant classes of society, after the royal family.[8] The lower class began with lesser officials such as local judges, official administrators, lesser tax collectors, and stewards of absentee landlords. Then came the rural proletariat composed of wandering day laborers and craftspeople. Below these classes were the peasants and city people who usually lived in one- or two-room apartment-type housing. Fifty years later, when Matthew wrote his gospel, the same stratification remained in the agrarian society and its urbanized setting, except for the fact that the "chief priests" were no longer part of the system.[9]

An economic key related to the stratification in the society of that time can be found in the anthropological concept of the "perception of the limited good." Ninety-eight percent of the people unquestionably accepted the authoritative domination of the 2 percent who directly or indirectly controlled the conditions of their lives. According to Bruce Malina, this meant that, for the most part,

> the people presented in the pages of the New Testament would see their existence as determined and limited by the natural and social resources of their village, their preindustrial city, their immediate area and world, both vertically and horizontally. Such socially limited and determined existence could be verified by experience and lead to the perception that all goods available to a person are, in fact, limited.[10]

The notion of limited goods allocated among individuals lays the foundation for any economics; thus a composite definition of economics taught in "Economics 101" in capitalist societies is the "allocation of limited resources among competing individuals to meet their limitless wants." However, as has been demonstrated above, at the time of Jesus and Matthew's gospel, the economic system was neither capitalistic nor communistic. It was a traditional society in which a pre-feudal cottage industry or house-based economic system existed. Here status determined the ordering of relationships and resource allocation and, thus, the ultimate distinctions of position and roles between powerful and powerless, between rich and poor. "Since all goods exist in limited amounts which cannot be increased or expanded, it follows that an individual, alone or with his family, can improve his social position only at the expense of others," Malina writes. His words about that era are echoed in the concept of a "zero-sum economics," which has been articulated by the contemporary economist Lester Thurow.[11] Malina continues:

> Hence any apparent relative improvement in someone's position with respect to any good in life is viewed as a threat to the entire community. Obviously, someone is being deprived and denied something that is his, whether he knows it or not. And since there is often uncertainty as to who is losing—it may be me and my family—any significant improvement is perceived not simply as a threat to other single individuals or families alone, but as a threat to all individuals and families within the community, be it village or city quarter.[12]

Despite continual tensions between individuals of differing ranks on the day-to-day level, people unquestionably accepted their family and household *status*. Rank was accepted as part of the social order and, indeed, ordained by the gods (for the Romans) and by God (for the Jews). Insofar as culture reflects basic values that guide people's behavior,[13] rank was culturally reinforced. One was born, not only physically, but ideologically, into conditions that denied the possibility of any real structural change. The uncritical acceptance of this order, sanctioned by religion and/or social ideology, is what Marxists call "mystification."[14] Since status always reflects the value a culture places on various groups of people in terms of power, and since the world of the New

Testament contained the above-mentioned levels or ranks of people, how the gospels would deal with power in the form of status is key to understanding the way the ordering of relationships among people and the allocation of limited resources would be further mystified or demystified.

The household served as the basic economic unit of production/consumption. Within this arrangement the division of labor was characterized by the informal principle of reciprocity. Consequently reciprocity was perhaps the most significant form of social interaction in the limited-good world of the first century.[15] At the heart of reciprocity in a subsistence-based, ranked, and patriarchal culture stand two dominant principles: normative reciprocity and the right of subsistence. Within this system peasants gave up certain resources (especially food and work) in exchange for protection from their overlings. Those who were over the peasants needed to ensure their security and subsistence needs would be met in times of difficulty. Within this system a "moral economy" regarding economic justice and exploitation was ordered. This moral economy determined which claims by members of the dominant group and especially by peasants were tolerable and which were intolerable.[16] According to James C. Scott, these claims were "firmly embedded in both the social patterns and injunctions of peasant life."[17] Peasants were born into society and culture realizing that they were to supply surplus products to the landlord; on the other hand the landlord was expected to ensure their protection and subsistence needs in times of economic hardship. This dynamic undergirded the notion of reciprocity which was normative between peasant and landlord. Only when the landlord did not meet subsistence needs in difficult times would a challenge to that order be made in the name of justice.

According to Malina, it is likely that "the most significant form of social interaction in the limited-good world of the first century is an informal principle of reciprocity, a sort of implicit, non-legal contractual obligation, unenforceable by any authority apart from one's sense of honor and shame."[18] According to Marshall Sahlins, there were essentially three types of reciprocity:[19] 1) negative reciprocity—doing to others what you would *not* have them do to you (hostility and warfare toward non-kin or enemies); 2) balanced reciprocity—*quid pro quo* exchanges; and 3) general reciprocity—the giving of gifts (especially to household members) without expecting return.[20] These forms of reciprocity characterized the entire social order. They can be charted as a continuum in the following way:[21]

1. General reciprocity, extreme solidarity: A ◄------► B
2. Balanced reciprocity, the middle: A ◄-----► B
3. Negative reciprocity, extreme unsociability: A ══════► B

The closer one related to household, family, and kin, the more likely general reciprocity would characterize social relations; the further away, negative reciprocity would be the order of relations. To think of any other kind of ordering would be out of the question. The moral claims of individual A or group A paralleled the moral obligations of individual B or group B. Only if these claims were violated through forms of injustice, especially exploitation on the part of the dominant group, would challenges to the system be justified. Otherwise the basic order would stay in place.

Within such a tightly organized structure of pre-capitalist, house-based economy, only religion could undermine ideologies which perpetuated class systems and debilitating forms of negative and balanced reciprocity. In fact, it seems that *only* religion could undermine such a system of economic rank and reciprocity as it existed in the first century because the latter's moral principles about justice were rooted in religion. Stephen Charles Mott points to this power of religion as legitimator or delegitimator of the social system when he notes:

> Any system of stratification requires a system of belief to explain, justify, and propagate the inequalities and persuade people to accept as legiti-mate the fact of their inequality. In a traditional society religion provides the ideological basis for status in the system. When this base is removed, the whole system is shaken.[22]

The ramifications of this insight are extremely important for those who wish to respond to the challenge of Matthew's gospel. Besides redistribution, which was Rome's way of collecting from the households and funneling back social services, the wider, urbanized setting that was the environment in which Matthew wrote perpetuated stratification and operated on the *quid pro quo* moral principle of balanced reciprocity. As the constitution of his house churches increasingly reflected greater prosperity and cosmopolitan attitudes, the house churches were tempted to reflect the reciprocity values of the wider community.

Since first-century society viewed an increase in one's wealth as quite possi-bly based on the exploitation of another and because a large part of Matthew's community seems to have become powerful and prosperous, while the bottom levels remained dependent and poor, tensions were bound to be generated. Religious tensions about the Law and the experience of God's presence were aggravated by the stratification of the surrounding society and its balanced and negative reciprocity forms which gradually crept into the households. This opposed Jesus' vision of a community-reflecting-God's-reign. Thus Matthew wrote to help the disciples in his house churches return to Jesus' original vision of general reciprocity, especially toward the outsider, the poor, and the marginated.

3. The House Churches and Collegiality

The first chapter discussed how, in contrast to the predominant, patriarchal model of household, recent scholarship has highlighted parallel kinds of *collegia* and *koina* as voluntary associations. This section will demonstrate that these nonpatriarchal models are a clearer reflection of the house church envisioned by Matthew.[23]

The sociologist Rodney Stark considers the house churches of Matthew's day reflective of cults that not only were affected by their culture, but adapted to it.[24] Gerd Theissen argues that the early Christian missionary movement outside Palestine did not conflict with its society but was well integrated into its structures. However Theissen's view has been challenged by John Elliott, who considers his "functionalist preoccupation with the issue of societal stability and the elimination of tension" unsupported by facts.[25] A more egalitarian constitution of the house churches would be one case wherein a direct challenge to the wider patriarchal system existed since egalitarianism, by definition, supports political and social equality.

That women like Mary functioned as leaders of the households from which the Antiochan ministry may have been launched (see Acts 12:12) contributes to the claim about Matthew's vision for his house church being more egalitarian. However my thesis about the more egalitarian nature of Matthew's vision must be grounded on stronger claims. One way to establish those claims is to apply the historical-critical method to his text. Another way is to apply models from sociology and anthropology to the first gospel. That I did, using Weber, in the previous chapter.

To begin to apply the historical-critical method, one must first consider the overall context of the early world of the New Testament. An increasing number of writers are finding elements of the collegial form dominant in the post-resurrection period of the house churches. Elisabeth Schüssler Fiorenza claims that Gerd Theissen "overlooks the fact . . . that the egalitarian community structures of private collegia or cultic associations provided the model for the early Christian movement in the Greco-Roman world, not the patriarchal family."[26] More recently she has asserted that the "house church presents an institutional structure which was patterned after the collegia rather than the patriarchal household."[27] In fact, she argues, a critical evaluation of the household code trajectory has found that its patriarchal ethics was "asserted in contrast to an 'egalitarian' ethos" found in the earlier gospels.[28]

Edward Schillebeeckx has shown that the *collegia* form of house church stood opposite the patriarchal mode:

> In the Roman Hellenistic household the *paterfamilias,* the father of the house, was the unspoken authority, and the structure of the family in antiquity was markedly hierarchical, with a patriarchal order, and in this respect was also the basis of the welfare of the whole of Greek and Roman society. By contrast, initially in the Christian household or house community this hierarchical model was radically broken up (we find a difference in the post-Pauline developments to which the Pastoral Epistles bear witness . . .). Early Christianity was a brotherhood and sisterhood of equal partners: theologically on the basis of the baptism of the Spirit, and sociologically in accordance with the Roman Hellenistic

model of free societies, called *collegia,* who also assembled "at the house of NN." Therefore it was not the Graeco-Roman codes of the *oikos* but the form of organization of the more democratic or egalitarian (religious and non-religious) *collegia* or associations which lent itself as a model for the earlier Christian house communities.[29]

Wayne Meeks goes so far as to argue that the Christian communities were not just reflective of the *koina* or *collegia* forms but were "much more inclusive in terms of social stratification and other social categories than were voluntary associations."[30]

If the voluntary associations constituted a potential threat to the status quo of patriarchy,[31] how were these Christian groups—which Meeks says were "more inclusive" (than the patriarchal forms)—constituted?[32] While patronage represents one way, those who promote patronage as the model for the voluntary association seem less secure in getting internal Matthean support than those seeing a more egalitarian collegial form as the alternative.

The very call of Jesus involved leaving "father" (4:22; 8:21) to follow Jesus freely (4:22). The collegial model represented a free association of people who came together in contrast to patriarchal models. Furthermore, Matthew 18:18–20 implies not only a house-based church but a church that can be constituted whenever two or three gather (*synágein*) in Jesus' name. *Ekklēsía* was a political concept which involved a gathering of free individuals. In that stratified society, these may not have been "equal" in the same sense as that proffered in theoretical democracy; however nowhere in Matthew's gospel does Jesus canonize forms of social stratification. On the contrary, as we will show, the very reality of the poor and marginated demands reordering by those claiming to be his disciples.

A historical-critical approach reveals Matthew articulating a more egalitarian household by the way he treats the notion of *exousía* or authority within the households. Among the Hebrews, as all communities in the empire, patriarchal family patterns existed long before Jesus and during his lifetime as well. However, reading deeper into the covenantal implications of relationship between God and Israel, Matthew's Jesus stressed *exousía*. As indicated in the previous chapter, *exousía* was linked to baptism (28:18–20). Baptism thus conferred on *all* household members a new kind of being—an equal participation in the authority of the risen Jesus. Given this equal sharing of *exousía,* Matthew's vision of *exousía* undermined the domination of patriarchal blood ties and became the most important determinant of the family of the new age (19:28–30).[33] While members of the household might remain in patriarchal households, when they became the *ekklēsía* their exercise of authority was not to imitate that of society (20:25); it was not to be that way among them (20:26).

Letty Russell has shown that Jesus' "authority (*exousía*) and power (*dýnamis*) represented gifts of God for the work of ushering in the New Age."[34] Because the *oikía* was the basis of the *politeía* and the *basileía,* the new age of God's reign would be eschatologically realized in the dynamics of the household. Since Matthew apocalyptically collapsed God's reign in heaven to its inauguration on earth, the household was the social location for its realization. This understanding makes it all the more imperative that we investigate the implications of the statement of Matthew's Jesus—addressed within a society of patriarchy—to "call no man your Father on earth, for you have one Father, who is in heaven" (23:9).

In distinction from Mark and Luke, Matthew stressed the fact of God not just being "Father,"[35] but "your" Father, the "your" referring to his audience. At least thirteen times Matthew's Jesus refers to God in terms related to being "your" heavenly Father (5:16, 45, 48; 6:1, 8, 14, 15, 26, 32; 7:11; 10:20, 29; 23:9; see 6:9). God is to be addressed as "our" Father (6:9).

Insisting that no human on earth should be called "Father" (for only God is to be called by that title) does not transfer an earthly patriarchal form to a heavenly form.[36] First of all, it can be argued with Joachim Jeremias: "From the earliest time the word 'Father' when applied to God included for the Orientals something of what 'mother' means to us."[37] Jesus was one such Oriental. Next, Sandra Schneiders rightly distinguishes between a God who is "paternal" and one who is "patriarchal" and concludes: "It is possible for God to be experienced as paternal without being experienced as a patriarch. And a father-God who is not experienced as a patriarch can equally well be experienced as a mother-God without loss of status."[38] These reflections must be kept in mind when dealing with Matthew, who uses the term "Father" of God much more than Mark and Luke.[39]

Returning to our passage about calling no one on earth "Father," and connecting it to our previously discussed central passage of 12:46–50 about being mothers, brothers, and sisters of Jesus doing the will of the "heavenly Father," we can concur with Gerhard Lohfink that:

> Fathers are deliberately not mentioned in the second part of the saying because in the new family there are to be no "fathers." They are too symbolic of patriarchal domination. Jesus' community of disciples and together with it the true Israel are to have only a single father, the One in heaven. This is shown by Matt. 23:9.[40]

The whole context of 12:46–50 and 23:8 puts the stress on the members of the family who are to shun patriarchal modes of leadership in favor of a style wherein members of the households are treated more egalitarianly. In this sense Rosemary Ruether maintains that "the fatherhood of God could not have been understood as establishing male ruling class power over subjugated groups in the Church or Christian society, but as that equal fatherhood that makes all Christians equals, brothers and sisters."[41] Matthew's unique understanding about the important implications of God's "Fatherhood" in the households is reinforced by his references to God's reign which envision God as a householder (13:27, 52; 20:1, 11; 21:33; 24:43) with Jesus calling himself the head of the house (10:25). Among the Synoptics, only Matthew (who used the term

"Father" in reference to God 45 times, more than Mark [4 times] and Luke [17 times]) tells the members of his house churches to call no one on earth "Father." Indeed, in a society dominated by codes of honor and shame, there are to be no titles indicating status or role at all (23:6–12).

The Matthean statement about calling no one on earth "Father" (23:9) cannot be separated from the previous statement about calling all *adelphoi* (23:8), a term which can be an inclusive for all brothers *and* sisters. Commenting on this statement, Gerhard Lohfink writes:

> The structure of the new, open family, which transcended its own boundaries in openness to the community, is exemplified in the families of those who placed their homes at its disposal. It was in the realm of "house churches" that brotherhood and sisterhood were lived concretely. When Matthew told his community, "Do not let yourselves be called Rabbi, for only one is your teacher and you are all brothers" (23:8), "brother" was not only an ecclesiological hallmark of the community (church as brotherhood). Behind the saying stands the totally concrete practice in the communities of one addressing each other as "brother" and "sister." What with us today remains restricted to sects, religious orders, and "brothers in spiritual offices" was obviously in the early church a standard form of address within its communities. One's comrades in the Christian faith were "brothers" and "sisters."[42]

In addition, Matthew's use of the terms "brother" and "sister" 18 times, in comparison with Luke's 4 times and Mark's 3 times, argues to a new kind of egalitarian relationship based in voluntary associations. The children of God are the sons and daughters of the divine *paterfamilias*. Through the new bond of baptism and by doing the Father's will (12:50) they are "sisters" (*adelphai*) and "brothers" (*adelphoi*) of Jesus and brethren (*adelphoi*) of each other (23:8). After the resurrection Matthew does not have Jesus refer to his closest associates as apostles, "the twelve," or disciples; they are "my brothers" (28:12). The resurrection creates a new family of disciples who are brothers and sisters. These brothers and sisters are not even to reflect society's separation between the two, which favored the males; in God's reign all share in the authority (28:16–20).

Adelphai and *adelphoi,* in Judeo-Christian as well as secular usage, referred to those bound not only by blood ties or kinship, but also by such close association and common commitment as would occur in household churches.[43] Here the ideal would be a greater egalitarianism based on a new kind of general reciprocity of sharing faith and resources to meet the needs of all. In his article, "The Egalitarian Church of Matthew," Edgar Krentz writes that, in such a community, the "least"[44] among the Christians is to be of major concern:

> The neophyte Christian . . . is of as much significance as a Peter. It is not the will of the Father in heaven that one of them perish. Therefore one

must forgive (the parable of the ungrateful servant, 18:23–35) and not calculate value on the length or nature of the service (the parable of the laborers in the vineyard, 20:1–16).

> The church is inclusive. . . . In the present time, before the consummation of the age, the church is a mixed group, embracing all who confess Jesus, no matter what their past, their race, or their social position.[45]

In Matthew's gospel, as in the other Synoptics, Jesus' call to discipleship demands *leaving* one's *oikía* and patriarchal family (19:29). However, Matthew adapted Mark to have James and John leave "the boat *and* their father" (4:22). No longer is Matthew's *ekklēsía* to be constituted by blood or patriarchal relationships; discipleship demands that they be left behind (8:21–22; 10:37). The bond to Jesus demands a total and radical reordering of old patriarchal bonds. Following Mark, those doing the will of the Father will now be bonded to Jesus' true family as his mother, brothers, and sisters (12:46–50). As Q declares, this will of God, the mystery of the Father's plan, will be communicated to receptive disciples who come to Jesus (11:27). Not only does the call to discipleship demand possible separation from family; it means accepting the very possibility of being rejected by members of one's "own *oikía*" (13:57). Furthermore, as Matthew's Jesus alone warns, adherence to Jesus' way of life within households may demand being in situations that pit members of the family against each other (10:21). The assumption is that not all in the traditional, patriarchal households were members of the church. The constitutive values of the more egalitarian church would be the basis of conflict, even in the patriarchal house churches.

Another bit of evidence that supports the claim that Matthew envisioned his house church as more egalitarian than patriarchal can be deduced from his approach to the traditionally patriarchal form of *haustafeln* or household codes. New Testament studies have shown that *haustafeln* in Paul and Peter tended to reflect the traditional, patriarchal model which linked the household to the *pólis* and, ultimately, to the patriarchal *basileía*. We have seen that one of the models of *haustafeln* dealt with two forms of submission: that of a household to civic authority and that of wives, children, and slaves to their husbands, parents, and masters respectively. The other dealt with the three dyads and followed with instructions about wealth and acquiring money.

Later in this chapter I will discuss Matthew's unique kind of *haustafel* in 17:24–20:16. In the first section of this *haustafel* (17:24–18:35), Matthew follows the basic format of civic and domestic duties; yet nowhere does he speak about traditional domestic forms of submission for wives, children, and slaves. And although he begins with a discussion "in the house" (17:24) about tribute paid the ruler, the children "are free" (17:26). Furthermore, he goes on to outline a new order for the household wherein all must become children (18:1–6) and where submission is given ultimately to the household, the *ekklēsía,* itself (18:17–18). Here nonretaliation and reconciliation constitute a new kind of reciprocity.

The next modified *haustafel* (19:3-20:16)[46] is based on the second model, which discusses human relations and ends with comments about wealth and making money. In Matthew's approach, a new relationship between husbands and wives will be ordered (19:3-11). And again, all must become as children (19:13-15). Here Matthew offers his version of a *haustafel* that reflects a new, more egalitarian order (19:28) wherein "everyone" subscribing to it will be rewarded (19:29). Here distribution of wealth will be equalized; the first will be last and the last will be first (19:30; 20:16).

In summary it can be said that Matthew's vision for a new community, aware of the existence of patriarchal forms, even in some of the house churches, called for a radical reordering of all relationships into a greater egalitarianism under the one Householder, God (see 20:1,11). This vision stood counter to the all-pervasive cultural pattern. Consequently, when Jesus prescribed this reordering, in effect he called into question the underpinnings of social order itself, because it was based on patriarchy and stratification. If the household, the basic unity of society, would no longer receive religious justification for its stratification, but be organized on a new kind of justice (20:14-16), a new social order would prevail. A general reciprocity would become normative for all.

Jesus' threat to the social ordering of his day went further by undermining his culture's approach to reciprocity. In the ranked society of Jesus' and Matthew's day, all persons knew their place. Many people's place was at the bottom of society. These were the "least," and the marginalized. They were the "sinners" and "enemies." The seventh chapter will show how, by means of the "antithesis statements" (5:20-48), Matthew portrays a model of inclusion for his community that set it apart from the traditionally-received attitudes and behaviors that justified separation. In the last two "antitheses" Jesus demanded that his followers "not resist one who is evil," go the extra mile, "give to him who begs from you" (5:38-42), and love the enemy (5:43-45).[47] In opposition to his society's kind of reciprocity and retaliation, Matthew's Jesus offered a new approach to submission, especially to those outside household and kin: "For if you love those who love you, what reward have you? Do not even the tax collectors do the same? And if you salute only your brethren, what more are you doing than others? Do not even the Gentiles do the same? You, therefore, must be perfect, as your heavenly Father is perfect" (5:46-48).

Until now I have offered an interpretation of Matthean texts that supports the notion that Matthew took a more egalitarian approach to his house churches which contrasted with the patriarchal and negative reciprocity forms of his wider society. At this point I turn to an anthropological analysis of the text itself to support my thesis that Matthew's approach reflects a greater egalitarianism for his audience.

Bruce Malina has used the tools of cultural anthropology to investigate how the scriptural texts reveal the constitution of the early Christian community.[48] In his *Christian Origins and Cultural Anthropology,* the main tool he uses is that pioneered by Mary Douglas about high/low "grid" and strong/weak "group."[49] By "grid" Douglas means the degree of socially constrained adherence that persons in a given group usually give to the community's symbol system—the system of classifications, definitions, and evaluations—through which the society enables its members to bring order and intelligibility to their experiences. By "group" she means the degree of social pressure exerted upon an individual or some subgroup to conform to the demands of the larger society to stay within the "we" lines marking off group boundaries.

In his book Malina notes that the Matthean community reflected a strong group, low grid constitution.[50] Strong group characteristics involve clear group identity with pressure to conform, definite "insiders" and "outsiders" with clear division of their boundaries, along with normative symbols which define, express, and continue the group identity. Low grid indicates a low degree of fit or match between an individual's experiences and societal patterns of perception and evaluation.[51]

Using the grid/group model proposed by Mary Douglas and applied by Malina, Leland J. White demonstrates that the insistence of Matthew's Jesus in the Sermon on the Mount on good works and justice as well as settling with opponents and nonretaliation (which deal with shame and honor codes) reveals a "strong group" sense. Other texts in the Sermon reveal a "low grid" in Matthew's community, showing it to be one "of equals" insofar as in it authority was shared, titles were eschewed, and human leadership imitated, through service, the example of its founder.[52]

Thus the historical-critical approach combined with the sociological insights of Weber discussed in the last chapter and the anthropological findings noted above show Matthew presenting Jesus effectively challenging the existing norms supporting negative reciprocity, retaliation, and social stratification. In their stead Matthew's community should be characterized by mutual sharing, forgiving love, and greater egalitarianism reflecting the perfection, the holiness, of God. In this sense, François Houtart sees Matthew's Jesus calling for a classless social ordering.[53]

The new covenant to be sealed in Jesus' blood for all (26:28) dramatically called the household churches (26:18) to live in more egalitarian, mutual relations as children of the same Father. Such children do not betray their tablemates (see 26:20–25). In texts unique to his gospel, Matthew shows that a certain kind of equality must predominate because of the dignity of each member of the community, including the "littlest" (18:10–14). Each member is of special value (12:12); distinctions and titles are to be minimized (23:8–10).[54]

a. Were Women Equal in Matthew's Gospel?

Having considered Matthew's vision of a more collegial and, therefore, more egalitarian model of house church, we can now ask if women were viewed as equals in his gospel.

Traditional historical-critical methods have tended to preserve an androcentric or male bias, and a narrative approach can be equally frustrating. Consid-

ering the functions of the "implied author" and "implied reader,"[55] Janice
Capel Anderson has concluded that: "There is no doubt that the author of the
Gospel of Matthew wrote from an androcentric perspective. Whether the
author was male or female, the story world embodies patriarchal assumptions."[56] Anderson's comments should not be surprising. Except possibly for
some feminists, few writers today remain totally free of androcentrism. However, trying to develop an interactive interpretation, we can conclude that,
while the *Matthaios* of the first century manifested androcentrism, it is not to
be that way for the twentieth-century *mathētaí.* Given this goal, it can be asked:
While most traditional exegetical approaches based in the historical-critical
method as well as the literary-critical method of narrative have been locked
into an androcentric mode that keeps women in submissive situations, can any
mitigation be offered when an interactive reader-reaction method is used?

In her *What Are They Saying about the Social Setting of the New Testament,*
Carolyn Osiek concludes her discussion of the household codes with a section
on "Social Science Becomes Social Critique."[57] In it she shows that, while Balch
and Elliott have opened up new possibilities for situating New Testament
writings within their social contexts and early Christian history and theology,
their approach—as indicated in their treatment of the *haustafeln,* for
instance—has canonized the male-dominated household structure, "and with
it the patriarchal pattern of dominance and submission which it implies."[58] In
contrast to Balch and Elliott, I have just argued that Matthew's adaptation of
the wider structure of the *haustafeln* in 17:24–20:16—an adaptation that does
not keep the traditional order of submission (he calls on *all* to become least)—
reveals his more egalitarian vision.

Next Osiek comments on Gerd Theissen, who makes "love-patriarchalism"
the foundational ethic of early Christian communities. Theissen argues that
while equality of status in Christ belongs to all in Christ, the class-specific
differences were essentially accepted, affirmed, and even religiously legitimated in the political and social realm.[59] We have already seen clearly that the
household was the foundation of the *pólis* and the *basileía.* If a household
changes, so will the *basileía;* thus the continual fear by the Principate that the
patriarchal system would be undermined by the *collegia* that worshiped a
goddess and promoted equality.[60] I will be arguing later in this chapter that
Matthew's unique use of the word *paliggenesía,* meaning a rebirth in a new
world (19:28), implies a reordering of the entire world back to the "original
world" intended by God wherein male and female equally have access to the
resources they need (Gen. 1:26–28). Here, as Matthew said, "the two shall
become one" (19:5).[61] In this text, the maleness and femaleness of the Divine
are implicit in the creation of the human person.[62] If God's unity is to be a
model of human community between male and female, there can be no
inequality.

In the context of this same passage, two elements need to be noted regarding
Jesus' approach to issues of equality. The first deals with the levirate in the
Bible which demanded that it was a man's duty to marry the childless widow of

his brother[63] and with how Matthew's Jesus reacted to it (22:23-33). That women were considered property is clear from the verb used about the seven brothers who "had" (*échein*) the woman (22:28).[64] While Jewish society saw the levirate as necessary to continue the patriarchal line, Jesus interpreted it in light of the final reign of God where patriarchy and its marriages would cease (22:30). Since that heavenly reign was to be realized on earth, the interpretation of Matthew's Jesus provided "a revolutionary concept of family."[65]

The second deals with Jesus' own teachings on divorce (5:31-32; 19:3-9). In certain ways patriarchalism in Jewish households was more pronounced than in those of Greece and Rome. According to rabbinical and Mishnaic tradition a man could divorce his wife for any reason, although rabbinical leaders like Hillel and Shammai—basing their opinions on differing interpretations of Deuteronomy 24:4—debated what constituted the grounds for divorce. At any rate, a wife could not divorce her husband at all. While she could bring charges against him in the court, the court would decide to force him to divorce her.[66] Jesus interpreted such norms on divorce as an expression of "hardness of heart" (19:8). As John Meier comments:

This phrase refers not to lack of feelings or a low cultural level, but to Israel's unwillingness to be taught and guided by God's word, a sin excoriated by the prophets. The divorce provisions of the Torah thus reflect the rebellious will of fallen man, not the gracious will of the Creator. Since Jesus is bringing in the kingdom, which is paradise regained, he also reestablishes the original will of the Creator for marriage in paradise.[67]

By refusing divorce on any grounds save adultery Matthew presents Jesus offering a new ordering for households. In this way, Jesus moved "toward equalizing the dignity of women with that of men by making the married male subject to charges of adultery even if he had relations with an unmarried female, just as the married woman who had sexual relations with an unmarried man was guilty of adultery."[68]

Finally, Osiek discusses the liberation critique of Elisabeth Schüssler Fiorenza. Schüssler Fiorenza has attempted to show that the private associations and minority religious groups which became the foundation for Christian assemblies—in contrast to the traditional patriarchal households—gave women the experience of freedom and respect that they had tasted but that was officially denied to them elsewhere. Schüssler Fiorenza posits an early Christian community of egalitarianism which later was adapted to "love-patriarchalism" in the Pauline churches and later Pauline teaching. Much of this patriarchalism became enshrined in the *haustafeln*. She has concluded that "Western misogynism has its root in the rules for the household as the model of the state."[69] Beside these conclusions about the patriarchal basis for the Pauline epistles, Schüssler Fiorenza tries to use a broader approach to justify women as disciples. However, given her method, it appears to me that her approach overlooks an essential element about discipleship and women that can be gained not by looking to Mark, as she does, but to Matthew.

b. Were Women "Disciples" in Matthew Gospel?

Arguing that because discipleship in Mark is understood as a literal following of Jesus and of his example, Schüssler Fiorenza concludes from Mark 15:41 that women were disciples because "they *followed* him in Galilee, they *ministered* to him, and they *'came up with him'* to Jerusalem."[70] I believe her approach here is overly controlled by the historical-critical method. A reader-reactor approach, on the contrary, demands an interaction of our present "horizons" about women with that of Matthew to determine how the heart of his message can be applied today. The task this implies is best summarized by David Balch, who has begun to offer a revisionistic approach to the *haustafeln:* "Let us democrats and/or Christians imitate Jesus' relational ethics by presenting a successful, politically effective critique of Aristotle's repressive view of patriarchal, hierarchical, family relationships."[71] Given Balch's ideal, as well as the shadow of Matthew's underlying androcentrism, we can now address the question of whether women were disciples in the first gospel.

A purely historical-critical method generates a negative answer if one would ask if any specific woman is called a "disciple" as such. Applying such a method to Matthew it would be shown that he distinguishes among the crowds, the disciples, and the twelve (disciples)—whom he calls apostles only once (10:2). While the twelve disciples are named, and Joseph of Arimathea is called "a disciple of Jesus" (from *mathēteútheis*), no woman receives the appellation. A narrative approach argues basically the same way. Anderson says that women "are never pictured as members of 'the disciples' as a character group."[72] However, it would be wrong totally to characterize Anderson's argument in this vein. As a narrative interpreter she does distinguish between two different evaluative points of view: "The difference in evaluation depends on whether 'discipleship' is viewed as membership in the character group 'the disciples' or as the proper response to belief in Jesus."[73] It is this second interpretation that helps me conclude that, indeed, women are disciples in Matthew's gospel.

First of all we reiterate the one text in Matthew where he has Jesus describe the function of a disciple. In response to the man who noted the presence of Jesus' mother and his brothers "outside," Jesus stretched out "his hand toward his disciples" who were "inside" and said, "Here are my mother and my brothers! For whoever does the will of my Father in heaven is my brother, and sister, and mother" (12:46–50). In Matthew function determines discipleship more than any specific appellation. *Whoever* does the will of Jesus' heavenly Father becomes identified as a disciple in his new family, in his house church.

I have already shown how God's will is linked to bearing fruits of justice. In a society where women and children did not count (14:21; 15:38), whoever

(19:29) does God's will now is an equal disciple in whom God's work of establishing the new creation (19:19-28) can be realized.

What God began in the beginning, in creating the heavens and earth (Gen. 1:1-2), is to continue in male and female. Thus, in indicating that all authority both in heaven and earth had been given him, Jesus said all nations were to be discipled (28:20). In this passage, in his reference to Joseph of Arimathea, and in 13:52, Matthew is alone in using this word. In 13:52, which concludes the apex of Matthew's gospel,[74] Matthew's Jesus asks, "Have you understood all this?" Understanding is at the heart of discipleship; practicing what has been understood by doing the heavenly Father's will represents the body of discipleship. Thus Jesus responded, "Therefore *every* scribe who has been trained [*mathēteútheis*] for the kingdom of heaven is like a householder who brings out of his treasure what is new and what is old" (13:52).

Matthew's vision of being discipled is inclusionary. This is clear from Matthew's inclusion of women in his genealogy. All four women were used by God in the process of fulfilling his/her will. All four were outside the patriarchal family structure, were wronged or thwarted by the male world, and risked damage to the social order. Though, as Susan Niditch shows, they were returned to the patriarchal status quo,[75] Matthew does not choose to highlight that dimension, but rather how they were used by God to bring about the presence of Jesus Christ. This reached its culmination through the obedience— or openness to God's will—of another male (*anēr* [1:16,19]), Joseph, and female (*gunē*), Mary. Through their coming together to form a household, with their child, Jesus, they represented a serious challenge to things the way they really were (2:1-18).[76]

The seldom used term for male (*anēr*) is used in the context of a man's relationship to a women via household relations. The pairing is used alone by Matthew twice. At the conclusion of both accounts of the multiplication of the loaves (14:13-21 and 15:32-39) he keeps the word *anēr* used in Mark 6:30-44 and 8:1-10, but adds the word for woman/wife (*gunē*) and little children (*paidíon* [14:21 and 15:38]). By using familial terms for male, female, and little child, Matthew gives a household connotation to the gathering of the crowds. Noting Matthew's connection of the family with the church, Robert H. Gundry concludes: "Thus Matthew portrays the crowds as the church, a gathering of Christian families."[77] However, in this gathering, something different happens than in traditional patriarchal families. From Jesus, women and children receive equal treatment with men. All can be fed the miraculous food because all are children of his heavenly Father, who wants to meet the needs of all (see 6:32-33; 7:11).

REORDERING RESOURCES

1. Household Allocation and Resource Sharing

After authority and the division of labor, the third dimension of social coordination involves the allocation of goods and services. Goods and services constitute what we call here "resources." In all societies the methods in use for the allocation of resources in the forms of goods and services closely relate to the prevailing division of labor and methods of production. Although the division of labor defined the ordering of household relationships, within traditional methods of resource allocation two contradictory principles tend to co-function. One is a general notion of equality based on what consumer units need: a sense that every person or household should receive "enough."[78] The other is a principle of inequality based upon some ranking of the value of different tasks and social functions.[79]

Throughout his gospel, Matthew makes strong connections between "house" and rightly-ordered relationships. However, while this connection can be found between "house" and *relationships,* one can ask if Matthew offers a strong connection between "house" and reordered *resources.* If such a connection can be discovered, one can rightly say that his gospel reveals an ethos that calls for an economics of justice (since economics deals with the ordering of relationships vis-à-vis resources, with justice as its goal).

Matthew's first use of the word *oikía* appears in the infancy narrative. Within the *pólis,* Bethlehem, a certain house became more significant than all the rest. In fact, what happened in that *oikía* affected not only the local *pólis,* but the *basileía* as well: "When Herod the king heard this, he was troubled, and all Jerusalem with him" (2:3).

The wise men followed a star "till it came to rest over the place where the child was. When they saw the star, they rejoiced exceedingly with great joy; and going into the house [*oikía*] they saw the child with Mary his mother, and they fell down and worshiped him" (2:9–11a). "Going into the house," we have seen in the second chapter, is one of the unique Matthean formulae that includes the use of the word "*oikía.*"[80] Its first use occurs here.

Interesting differences arise when one compares Matthew's infancy narrative with that of Luke, at least from the perspective of which "outsiders" first discover Jesus and where they find him. In Luke, the shepherds, members of the under class, discover "the babe lying in a manger" (Lk. 2:16); in Matthew, the wise men, of the upper class, discover Jesus upon "going into the house." As I have stated above, where gospel accounts differ, one must consider the community to which they were addressed. Because Luke's community seems to have had a significant number of poor within its midst, he represents Jesus born in a condition that reflected their reality, which needed salvation—thus the "manger." However, since Matthew's community seems overall to have been considerably more well-off, with many living in prosperous houses, Matthew contextualizes the birth of Jesus in that social location within which they were to work out their salvation—the house (1:11).

The wise men come into the *oikía.* They come into the presence of "Emmanuel (which means, God with us)" (1:18). Jesus in Bethlehem is also of the house of David (see 1:17). He will become the new house of Israel (see 19:25; 23:37–24:2), the house of living bread that will be broken not just for one group, but for the many (26:26). Jesus in Bethlehem is the new temple of God's presence. The closer those in the house come into this presence of God, experiencing the power of that presence, the more willing they are to share their resources. Within the house the wise men knew how their resources should be reordered.[81] Matthew uses liturgical words to refer to the wise men's next actions: "they fell down and worshiped him" (2:11b). Such gestures as falling down to kneel or worship (*proskunein*) contained religious overtones, for they were gestures made to God alone or to those acting as God's surrogates, like the king. But Jesus is not only a king (2:2); he is "God-with-us" (1:18). Except for one place in Mark 5:6 and twice in Luke's parallel version of Matthew's depiction of the temptation in the desert (Lk. 4:7, 8), only Matthew uses the word *proskunein* to describe the religious act of worship (see 2:2,8,11; 4:9, 10; 8:2; 9:18; 14:33; 15:25; 20:20; 28:9, 17). All of these except 4:9 (about worshiping the devil) refer to Jesus.

In Matthew, religion in the house is also connected to justice. Thus, in the house, this act of the wise men's worship combined an act of religion with an economic act. Both reflected justice or a reordering of resources: "Then, opening their treasures, they offered him gifts, gold and frankincense and myrrh" (2:11b). Being in the presence of Emmanuel and worshiping properly, as the prophets before insisted, demands justice, the reordering of resources (Is. 58; Mic. 6:6–8).

I do not propose here to discuss the possible meanings of the various gifts; I want to show only that they were "gifts"—resources people have but are willing to share with someone who has become significant in their lives. With such an offertory Matthew seems eager to show his house churches that the more significant the risen Lord's *exousía* would be in their lives, the more willing they would be to reorder their resources. The same theme is developed by Matthew later in the gospel: general reciprocity is to be the norm toward all.

2. "What She Has Done Will Be Told in Memory of Her"

The story of the woman who anoints Jesus in anticipation of his burial (26:6–13) is at the beginning of Matthew's passion narrative.[82] With Mark, Matthew locates Jesus at Bethany "in the *oikía* of Simon the leper" (26:6). There, in the house, someone with resources that reflected wealth and extravagance performed a religious ritual of anointing: "a woman . . . with an alabaster jar of very expensive ointment . . . poured it on his head, as he sat at table" (26:7). Again, like the wise men, the woman had a resource of great value. Experiencing the presence of Jesus-Emmanuel in that house, she was empowered to reorder her resources on behalf of him to meet his anticipated need.

After the woman poured the perfume on Jesus' head, the disciples "were indignant, saying 'Why this waste? For this ointment might have been sold for a large sum, and given to the poor' " (26:8–9). Here it goes without saying that resources that a group or person doesn't need should be reordered on behalf of the poor. Matthew assumes that sharing with the poor was an essential part of the household ethos; thus the comment of the disciples. But, this passage is not what should be remembered about the text.

Jesus' response to his critics underscores my basic thesis. "Why do you trouble the woman? For she has done a[n] *érgon kalon* to me" (26:10), he said. *Érgon kalon* is "good work." The good work that God began in the beginning, that was part of some general traditional instruction for all Christians (Rom. 12:17–21; 13:2–4) as well as part of Peter's *haustafel* (1 Pet. 2:12; 3:8–12), is performed now by this disciple. Her "good work" was to respond to Jesus' projected *need*: to "prepare me for burial" (26:12). In Jesus' eyes, according to Matthew, good works are those which meet the needs of others (11:2, 5). People are blessed (11:6) when their work imitates Jesus' works (11:2) by being directed to resource the needs of others (25:31–46).

Furthermore, Jesus said, "For you always have the poor with you, but you will not always have me" (26:11). The reference recalls Deuteronomy 15:11, where it is clear that the fact that "the poor will never cease out of the land" demands a sabbath (Dt. 15:9) and a regular openness to the needy and poor in the land (Dt. 15:11). By referring to the abiding presence of the poor, Jesus is not prophesying or affirming the fact of their presence any more than he did when he commented on the abiding presence of the weather (16:2). Besides the Deuteronomic base, his comments must be seen in light of the way he related to those in need who came to him (11:2–6).

When the poor were with him, even though he might have tried to avoid doing so (15:21–28), Jesus always shared his resources with them (15:28). He directly linked his entire life (11:2–6) and the legitimation of discipleship with the way the poor would be resourced (19:21ff). Now she has done the same; she has put into practice the heart of his teaching which he came to proclaim (11:2–5; 19:21f).

At the end of the pericope, Matthew follows Mark in explaining that this woman personified that discipleship which is modeled on the pattern of Jesus in the gospel. He has Jesus conclude, "Truly, I say to you, wherever this gospel is preached in the whole world, what she has done will be told in memory of her" (26:13). "What she has done" was to continue the good work of creation which God began (Gen. 1:28) and which Jesus and the church were to continue (11:2) by way of reordering relationships and resources in order to bring light out of darkness in the house (5:15). Through the woman's good work of reordering her resources in this household, people could see her "good works" done in the house (5:15–16). By sharing her resources with Jesus in light of his projected need, i.e., his burial, she modeled the heart of discipleship, the fulfillment of God's will.

What she did was to be proclaimed throughout the whole world precisely because her deed of reordering her resources revealed the core of that teaching of the gospel that was to be shared with "all nations . . . to the close of the age" by those who shared in Jesus' authority or *exousía* (28:16–20). As a result of living under that authority, as did Jesus (11:3–6), good news will now come to the poor.

With the same *exousía* in them which impelled Jesus to minister to the poor, the disciples for all time are to continue performing the works Jesus did (11:2). The presence of the poor in the disciples' midst is a continual invitation, a kind of sacrament, inviting all followers of Jesus, especially those with appropriate resources, to continue the work of Jesus by meeting the needs of others. This demands an ongoing reciprocal responsibility to bring good news to them in imitation of Jesus. Consequently, interpreting "the poor you will always have with you" (26:11) in the context of Jesus' whole ministry, we conclude that—in light of the call to perfection which demands a reordering of resources on behalf of the poor (19:21)—the reality of the poor becomes the environment in which those with resources can experience the reign of God. Their very presence is a continual reminder that the work of creation and reordering relationships and resources is not yet complete in God's household. Good news comes to the poor when those with resources experience the reign of God. But that experience of God's reign is predicated on a life oriented to meeting the poor's needs (25:31–45).

Jesus could have said: "I assure you, wherever the good news is proclaimed throughout the world, its first recipients will be the poor; they will recognize in my disciples those who share in my *exousía* by calling for a reversal of ideas and institutions, a reversal which will restore the poor to wholeness!" To interpret 26:11 in any other way (especially to legitimize non-involvement on behalf of the poor) is to manipulate the text so that it becomes an ideological reinforcement of the social arrangements of injustice that exploit the poor and keep them in misery.[83]

"Wherever this gospel is preached in the whole world, what she has done will be told in memory of her" (26:13). What she *did* in sharing her resources with one in need, for Matthew, was central to the observance of the gospel. To whatever nation (28:18-20) the gospel would be preached, her good deed was to be memorialized as representative of the essence of its message (see 11:2-6; 19:21-22).

MATTHEW'S *HAUSTAFEL* IN 19:3–20:16: A HOUSEHOLD OF RIGHTLY-ORDERED RELATIONSHIPS AND RESOURCES

It would seem, from the above discussions of the wise men (2:10-11) and the woman (26:6-13) who shared their resources in the house, that our earlier question asking if Matthew promotes *rightly-ordered resources as well as relations* within his house churches has been answered affirmatively. But if this is so, can we find any passages wherein he seems to link the two and call for a new order of relationships and resources in his household?

Recalling the two main formats for *haustafeln* discussed earlier, a closer look at 19:3–20:16, immediately following the former *haustafel* in 17:24–19:1-2,[84] suggests that, in 19:3–20:16, Matthew offered a new approach to *haustafeln* with his unique kind of house code that promotes right-ordering of relationships and allocation of resources.

The foundation for that statement is not just that Matthew's Markan source (Mk. 10:2-45) has been labeled a "kind of *haustafel.*"[85] Another foundation for that statement can be uncovered through an analysis of the structure of 19:3-20:16. The characteristic feature of one kind of *haustafel,* which can be traced back to Aristotle, involved two dimensions. The first considered relationships among persons (husband-wife, parent-children, master-slave). The second considered suggestions dealing with resources or "the so-called art of getting wealth." This form was carried over to New Testament *haustafeln.*[86] However, rather than reinforcing a patriarchal husband-wife, parent-child, and master-slave dynamic, the first part of this section in Matthew's gospel addresses other issues related to household members such as divorce, celibacy, and the treatment of children within the house churches.

Matthew has Jesus begin with a discussion on divorce (19:3-9), adapted from Mark (Mk. 10:1-10).[87] Within households at that time, women were generally dependent on their husbands. Divorce would often cut them off from any source of livelihood, unless they had their own source of income. Matthew's Jesus thus supports the indissolubility of marriage as part of God's plan for all in the household of creation (19:4-8). Jesus rescinds the right of a man to marry more than one woman. The only exception he gives relates to adultery (19:9).[88] According to Phillip Sigal, with this teaching Jesus not only elevated "the status of women in sexual matters and forbids men their wanton power to abuse them"; he also expanded the meaning of adultery to "include sexual relations of a married man with a woman not his wife, whether or not she is anyone else's wife."[89] One more blow against patriarchal order!

The next section on celibacy (19:10-12) is unique to Matthew. Jesus' time was marked by great population density, with consequent suffering and deprivation, especially for the marginated. Partly in reaction, according to David Bakan, "some of the people had dedicated themselves to chastity in order to bring no further human beings onto the earth. The Essenes, for example, abstained from sexual relations."[90] Within a wider culture that placed little value on celibacy (19:10), Matthew's Jesus raises up celibacy in the house churches as a gift (19:11) for those who have dedicated their very bodies to God's kingdom or reign (19:12). In that reign people will neither marry nor be given in marriage (22:30). Matthew's house churches were to be prefigurements of that reign.

In a world too often manifesting negative reciprocity, the next pericope's invitation—which was extended to all in the churches to become like little children (19:13-15)—reflected a desire for a new kind of house-ordering.[91] In the Law, children had neither independent status nor rights. They were dependent. In Matthew's ideal community, a new kind of status was envisioned in which all would depend on one another. Within this household all would be treated in the same way.

An examination of the next two passages, both ending with a phrase related to reordering (the "first will be last, and the last first" [19:30; see 20:16]), reveals a new model for sharing and allocating resources. That model contrasts with the traditional *haustafeln* which discussed ways of acquiring wealth.

The first passage or pericope builds on the Markan story of the man who came to Jesus and called him "Teacher[92]"; only Matthew has him asking what "good" (*agathon*) he might do to inherit eternal life (19:16f). "Doing good" was part of *haustafeln* (1 Pet. 3:8–12; Titus 2:11–14; see Rom. 12:17–21). In the beginning, when God ordered creation aright, it was called "good" (Gen. 1:31). Jesus explained that only God was good. Continuing, Jesus added that entrance into eternal life was predicated on doing good—specifically through observance of the Law's commandments. Besides those commandments articulated by other evangelists in response to the man, Matthew puts on Jesus' lips the last part of the first and greatest commandment (22:30): "You shall love your neighbor as yourself" (19:19). Doing good, in Matthew, was a sign of love of neighbor (see 5:43–47). If persons, especially those whose possessions guaranteed them status and wealth, would love their neighbors as themselves, individual needs would be balanced with communal needs. In fact, meeting communal needs would be the sign of proper self-love. Justice would reign. Good would be done. God's goal for creation would be realized. A new *haustafel* uniting doing good, love, and submission to God's will would be realized.

The rich young man with many possessions said he had kept all these commandments and asked, "What do I need to do to go further?" (19:20). Jesus explained that following *him* demanded walking in the way of goodness (see Dt. 18:13) or perfection (*téleios* [19:21]). For Matthew's Jesus, being perfect, whole, or integral paralleled the "wish to enter eternal life" (19:16).

In Matthew, salvation involved entering eternal life or the reign of God; this represented perfection. In the language of the Essenes, their community was the "house of perfection" (1 QS, xi,11,17). Reflecting perfection (in the way God was perfect [5:48]) demanded that the young man (i.e., the prosperous Matthean house churches) "go sell what you possess and give to the poor" as the essential requirement for experiencing God's reign. But "the young man . . . went away sorrowful; for he had great possessions" (19:21–22).

According to Otto Michel, possessions (*hypárchonta* [19:22; 24:47; 25:14]) can also mean *oikía,* "as shown by a striking expression which is not uncommon in Greek; namely 'you devour the houses of widows' (23:14)."[93] "Possessions" did not merely represent material goods. Since material property, especially for someone young, was inherited, "possessions" reflected one's status and household position in life. To be young and wealthy meant to have been part of an elite family in society. Thus Jesus' invitation to discipleship demanded a change in house-ordering, in economics, in family status as well as material goods. Jesus' invitation to discipleship involved the need for a total reordering of relationships and resources on behalf of the poor. Thus the young man's chagrin. Possession of "eternal life" and entrance into the reign of God as a disciple are predicated on the reordering of possessions in the form of relationships (status) and resources (wealth).

When the disciples expressed their sense of inadequacy about being able to reorder their own lives, as well as the wonderment that anyone could (see 19:23–26), Matthew shows how it can be done: "With men this is impossible, but with God all things are possible" (19:26). *Exousía* can accomplish a total reordering of life. He continues the pericope by having Jesus say that "in the new world [*paliggenesía*]," the new creation, God's reign would be constituted of those who, in the present world, reorder their relationships and resources "for my name's sake." This reordering demanded leaving *oikías,* whether relations with others (brothers or sisters or father or mother or children) or resources (land).

Paliggenesía—the "new genesis" (from *palin* and *genesis*)[94] spoken of by Jesus—is used only here by Matthew (19:28); it is not found in any of the other gospels. The word refers to a total reordering of individual and social life. Using Genesis overtones, Matthew's Jesus spoke of a new way of relating for all, male and female, for those with possessions and those without. Elaborating on the implications of Matthew's choice of this word, Fred Burnett comments:

> I would like to suggest that Matthew has inserted 19:28 as part of his overall effort to minimize distinctions between disciples in his community. . . . The theological function of *paliggenesía,* then, is to minimize the tendency of community members to exalt one disciple over another. The Evangelist's redaction here is consistent with his overall effort to temper in an egalitarian manner the proclivity of his community towards hierarchical distinctions (cf. 23:8–12).[95]

Inheriting the "new world" will be contingent on the degree that other inheritances and relationships in the present world are reordered to reflect the "original world" intended by God wherein male and female equally have access to the resources they need (Gen. 1:26–28). This demands a reordering, especially of any present relationships based on distinctions and prejudice. This demands a change in relationships whereby those "many that are first will be last, and the last first" (19:30). In the present age, those who are first lord it over others and make their authority felt. In the new age, which begins with immediate reordering, it cannot be so among brothers and sisters in Matthew's house churches (20:20–28).

Matthew's vision of *paliggenesía* demanded a new kind of household. In this sense it must also be seen along with his other references to the "new" as part of a social reordering that is to begin making God's reign come on earth as it is in heaven. For Matthew, the end time of this "new age" was inaugurated by the life and activity, the death and resurrection, of Jesus.[96] But the narrative about Jesus is to be realized in the church in which the new age is to be revealed and continued. Even if Jesus and the primitive community expected an apocalyptic inbreaking, the values of the new age are to be made operable now if one will be considered faithful later. Thus it was incumbent upon Matthew's house churches so to light their lamps that all in the house could see their new way of living (5:15).

In a study of the social world of early Christianity, John G. Gager asserts that when new religions are geared toward the creation of new worlds,

> old symbols are given new meanings and new symbols come to life; new communities define themselves in opposition to previous traditions; a new order of the sacred is brought into being and perceived by the community as the source of all power and meaning; new rituals emerge to remind the community of this sacred order by creating it anew in the act of ritual celebration.[97]

Whether it be symbolized by new wine in fresh wineskins (9:17), the householder bringing out the new and old (13:52), or the ritual celebration of the breaking of the bread which prefigures the new table fellowship (26:28, 29), a new age or *paliggenesía* is predicated on a restructuring of old relationships that do not reflect God's reign: "many that are first will be last, and the last first" (19:30).

Having identified the reign of God and the new age with those who reordered resources (house and land) as well as relationships (brother and sister, mother and father), Matthew inserts a parable (20:1–16) instead of continuing with the third prediction of the passover (as do Mark and Luke). This parable shows the need for disciples to restructure not only their activities but even their ideology, or way of thinking, about the meaning of the just order of God's reign.

Matthew places on Jesus' lips a parable using images that reflected a daily economic occurrence of that era: the visit of a householder to the marketplace where people waited for work. In the process of framing the parable by placing the same phrase about the first being last and the last first both before (19:30) and at the end (20:16) of the pericope, Matthew reveals a deeper meaning of "households" within an entirely reordered economic system in the "new age": "For the kingdom of heaven is like a *oikodespótēs* who went out early in the morning to hire laborers for his vineyard . . . for a denarius a day" (20:1–2).

Oikodespótēs (householder) is a favored word in Matthew. He uses it eight times.[98] At the time of Jesus, according to Bernhard Lang, three main forms of relations between householders and workers existed: patronage, exploitation, and cooperation.[99] In the first, patrons controlled access to key economic resources. In return for being able to extract the surplus product of tenants and workers, the landlord reciprocated by promising protection and to meet subsistence needs when the occasion demanded.[100] Exploitative relationships often happened when a landowner/householder lived in a city. Here the owner was chiefly interested in extracting surplus from the tenant with as little reciprocity as possible. This gave rise to tension. Douglas Oakman has shown that both the patronage and the exploitation "types of relationships were undergirded by the self-sufficient ethos of the household economy."[101] However, the third type of economic relationship between the householder and workers—that which stressed cooperation—seems to be the moral reminder behind this parable. God's economic reveals that activity of a householder upon which all households in Matthew's community must be measured. The largesse of God, the ultimate householder (20:1), must be the ultimate criterion for economic relations on earth—if those relationships are to be perfect in the way God is perfect (5:48), i.e., just (5:20; 20:13).[102]

While this parable primarily reveals a dimension of God's reign, rather than strictly economic problems like (un)employment and just wages, the experience of entering into God's house, into God's economics (salvation), is predicated on human economics or house-reordering in "the new age." "Not everyone who says to me, 'Lord, Lord,' shall enter the kingdom of heaven, but he who does the will of my Father in heaven" (7:21). By having the householder pay the workers hired at the fifth round the same as those who bore the burden of the heat, Jesus shows that the ordering of the house (i.e., economics) of God's reign involves certain characteristics: 1) the land is God's; 2) God gives resources to every person who is open; 3) God resources all people equally no matter how much or how hard they work (20:12); 4) the goal of resource-sharing is not "more to those who do more" or "less to those who do less," but justice (20:13); 5) God's generosity (*hagathós*) stands opposed to the niggardliness (*ponerós*) of humans (20:15); and 6) in contrast to that mentality that seems to legitimate "more" for some, in God's reign there is enough for everyone. The parable not only reveals that everyone's needs will be met with a living wage when human justice reflects the justice of the divine Householder; it reveals an entirely new kind of general reciprocity based on the model of God's gracious mercy toward all, especially the least ones.

The generosity of the householder upsets the prevailing expectations, especially for those assuming society's balanced reciprocity—who bore "the burden of the day and the scorching heat" (20:12). So, like the Israelites in the desert, they too grumbled (Dt. 6:1ff; 8:1ff). They forgot to remember that earlier they too had been without resources (20:1-2).

Despite its economic overtones, this passage primarily reveals a message about the mercy and generosity of God that are given without distinctions and shine equally on the just and unjust (5:45). Here one discovers a Matthean Jesus whose goal was to establish, on earth, a proximation of God's reign in heaven (see 6:10). Discipleship is not for one group only; it exists especially on behalf of those still outside the system—any system (28:18-20). It is directed toward the marginated. It demands bringing good news to them in the fullnes of that salvation which includes participation in the "land." In this sense, experiencing God's reign now is predicated on reordered relationships and resources, on reordered forms of status and class, where the last will be first and the first last.

Stephen Charles Mott makes a strong case that the New Testament notion of poverty or need was not as much class-oriented (economic-based) as status-oriented (power-based). This follows good economic historical theory. Robert L. Heilbroner, for instance, has said that "in pre-market societies, wealth tends to follow power; not until the market society will power tend to follow wealth."[103] Thus Mott explains:

The contrast between class and status is important and helpful for our purposes, although it is a simplification because there are many forms of each. Class deals with the economic opportunities that an individual can expect in life by virtue of the group to which he or she belongs. It is related to property relations and economic power. It is objective. Status is subjective. It is based on the value the culture places on various groups of people. On account of certain characteristics, prestige and respect (or its lack) are granted by custom or law. . . . Both class (economic position) and status (social position) are power resources.[104]

In applying distinctions such as these to Matthew's presentation of Jesus,[105] it is clear that his form of *haustafeln* outlined a code of house-ordering which undermined both the status (relationships) and class (resources) reciprocity structures of his era. Both would have to be reordered for the "new world"; both demanded a reversal of the system so that "the last will be first, and the first last" (20:16). Thus, in this uniquely Matthean pericope (20:1–16), as in the story of the rich man with many possessions (19:16–30), the new age of God's reign begins in the present.

5

Ethos/Ethics: Jesus/Church

REVIEWING PREVIOUS CHAPTERS

This chapter serves as a pivot in my argument about the need to fuse Matthew's horizon—especially the heart of his ethics—with that of twentieth-century interpreters. For this reason a brief summary of the chapters thus far may be in order.

The first chapter established the setting of Matthew's gospel and discussed how his gospel addressed various conflictual issues facing his community. Besides ethnic differences, a major concern was the issue of wealth in a world of the poor. The second chapter showed how the major theme of Matthew, as well as the structure of his five books, revolve around the pivotal pericope in 12:46–50. His five discourses, viewed from the perspective of the "assumed primary metaphor of house," were shown to offer a way of discipleship. Chapters three and four discussed how Matthew treated the three main areas involved in social coordination: authority, the division of labor, and the allocation of scarce resources. The third chapter dealt with Matthew's notion of authority as *exousía*. It showed Jesus sharing his God-given *exousía* with the disciples in the house churches and those who gathered in his name (as well as the name of the Father and the Spirit [28:16–20]). The fourth chapter discussed how the division of labor (based on status) in Matthew's gospel reflected a less patriarchal style and a more egalitarian set of social relationships. It then investigated how Matthew's vision of resource-sharing subverted existing forms of negative and balanced reciprocity in its call for an economy or house-ordering based on justice and general reciprocity.

Chapter 4 discussed reciprocity within the framework of the notion of a "moral economy."[1] Since reciprocity was house-based, and since economy means the "ordering of the house," a "moral economy" implies a certain moral code for the household. However, the household also constituted the basic unit of the whole social order. Therefore, since this chapter will treat Matthew's ethics, it must take into account the notion of "moral economy" *and* the implications for ethics of a number of key notions about the "moral world of the first Christians."[2] Given a house-based morality as well as a "moral world," how did Matthew's "moral economy" for his households offer a way of taking the teachings of Jesus into the whole world? What can we learn from it for today?

CHRISTOLOGY, ECCLESIOLOGY, AND MORALITY IN MATTHEW

Matthew's gospel identifies the personal presence of Jesus Christ with the church he founded. Raymond Brown writes that, "for Matthew . . . there is no time of the church separated from the time of Jesus."[3] But if the person of Jesus Christ and the church he founded are inseparable in Matthew, what connection can be made among Jesus Christ, the church he founded, and morality or ethics?

John Meier states unequivocally that the nexus among Christ, church, and morality can be called *the* specific characteristic of Matthew's gospel.[4] Disciple-ship involves sharing in the life of the master and walking in the master's footsteps. If, by *exousía*, Jesus shared his life with the church, what form of morality will evidence walking in his footsteps?

Since Matthew's ecclesiology is essentially house-based, it can be stated clearly that his gospel would have to present a morality that appeals to a social ordering of life. His morality would have to be essentially communitarian. Matthew frequently has Jesus address not individuals but "the crowds," "the disciples," and "the eleven." His concern is that the community manifest those dynamics that would usher in God's reign. While each member of the house was important, the significance of each was always considered in light of the right functioning of the entire household. The right-ordering of the household would depend on whether all the teachings of Jesus would be observed not only by individuals, but by the communities themselves (28:20).

New Testament morality involves the way relations should be ordered and resources should be shared among members of the church. However, given the background about the economy or ordering of the house in the Christian community discussed thus far, we now can ask: What was the image of Jesus in Matthew's narrative that portrayed a model of morality for his church? Since this book deals with Matthew's "house" as church and economics, we can go further with our questions. If Jesus Christ, the church, and morality must be considered together, we can ask: Does Matthew go beyond general norms about morality to a specific ethic regarding church life and economics? If Jesus identified his life and presence in the world with bringing good news to the poor (11:2-6) and if discipleship in the church was articulated by him as being inseparably linked with re-allocation of resources to the poor (19:21ff), do these values have any bearing on a specific ethic about economics outlined in the teachings of Matthew's Jesus for his house churches? Furthermore, if Matthew's church can be classified as prosperous, and if we allow for the differences between our age and Matthew's, we can also question: Does his gospel reveal any economic ethic for middle-class Christians today whose baptism demands that they put into practice the teachings of Jesus until the end of time (28:18-20)? In conclusion, we can ask: What image of Jesus did Matthew offer his house churches to emulate in their moral life? How did he see the members of his house churches implementing Jesus' way of life in theirs? In other words, reiterating Meier's connection among Christ, church, and morality, the basic question is: How will the pattern of Jesus' life and teachings be witnessed by the church through its morality?

CONTEXTUALIZING MATTHEAN MORALITY
THROUGH THE METAPHOR OF HOUSE

The approach this book has taken to understand the dynamics of Matthew's gospel has been that of the "assumed primary metaphor" of the house. House as assumed primary metaphor also involves moral economy and ecclesiology—or overall house-ordering. In using this same device to contextualize Matthean morality, I have preferred some approaches over others. The choices I use to explore the connection between ethics and Matthew's gospel are supported by those presented by Wayne A. Meeks in his "Understanding Early Christian Ethics."[5] Meeks's comments are important for our consideration because of his expertise regarding first-century urban Christians and their house churches.

According to Meeks, in determining options for approaching Christian ethics, the first choice must be whether simply to make a socio-historical description of early Christian ethics or to apply the gospel normatively to our contemporary reality. Given my understanding of the need to understand the "horizon" of Matthew as well as my own and, from this, to seek some sort of fusion of horizons, I have chosen to see how the ethics presented by Matthew might be applied to church and economics today.

The second option is whether I choose to describe history as a chronology of ideas or in terms of a community and its moral formation. It should be quite evident that I have tried to show how the members of Matthew's house churches manifested a moral understanding of what Meeks calls the "world of meaning and of relationships, special to that group in its own time and place, within which behavior is evaluated."[6]

The third option involves understanding rather than explaining the moral universe of those first Christian groups. Meeks's meaning of "understanding" demands consideration of "the early Christian movement as a cultural entity and [adopting] that mode of cultural analysis, Weberian in its roots, which construes culture as a system of communication."[7] Recognizing the cultural grounding for all communication patterns, it is not necessary to create a chasm between Meeks's notion of "understanding" and "explanation." Following the cross-cultural and multi-variate models, I have tried to understand *and* explain how the subculture of Matthew's households and their "moral economy" functioned within a wider "moral world of meaning." These functioned as part of, yet distinct from, the wider socio-economic and political-legal as well as the cultural (belief systems and mores) elements of society. As the basic unit of society, the households could not remain unaffected by the mores of that society. The consequences of society's influence on morality for a community like Matthew's is quite evident to Meeks:

> The first Christians had to deal with their cousins and inlaws in their villages, and the concern for honor or shame of their extended families was as much a part of their world as the smell of the village dung heap. Such ties were weaker in the cities, no doubt, but one has only to consider the plan of residential streets excavated in places . . . to see that most people, living in small spaces chockablock with their neighbors, would not have much choice about sharing those neighbors' world, metaphorically as well as physically.
> Understanding the ethics of the early Christians must therefore begin with a rigorous attempt to describe the ethos of the larger culture—with its various local permutations—within which the Christian movement began and spread.[8]

Meeks's approach to morality—as I am applying it to Matthew's gospel—demands a deeper understanding of the ethos of the larger culture—with its various local adaptations—within which the Matthean house churches lived and ministered.[9] Having examined this "wider world of meaning" of the overall system in previous chapters,[10] I can now analyze the fundamental character of the moral life of Matthew's communities.[11]

MATTHEW'S ETHOS AND/OR ETHICS?

Since the ethos of a group reflects its culture, before considering the meaning of "ethos," we should recall what we have identified as "culture." Culture is an integrated system of beliefs, values, and traditions which influence the relationships of people and resource-allocation within institutions which express those beliefs, values, and traditions; thus, culture binds society together to give it a sense of identity, meaning, cohesion, security, and continuity. For our purposes, the household characterizes the basic "institution" of the first century. A community's ethos involves those styles of operating, customs, and practices which become acceptable and even normative, having taken on religious and ideological legitimation. An ethos reflects a network of habits, values, expectations, and the like which gives communities their unique character. The ethos of a community expresses a group's mores more than its specific morals or ethics. It does not describe what "ought to be"—a specific task of ethics; rather it reflects what the lifestyle of a group actually is. In this sense, ethos and culture are quite parallel.

Leander Keck has been among the contemporary pioneers in distinguishing New Testament ethics from ethos. Given our discussions about religion and economics in Matthew's house churches, his distinctions bear consideration. For him, a community's ethos refers to its lifestyle; it reflects certain beliefs, values, and traditions such as those that we have identified as the subculture of

Matthew's households. This subculture represents an ethos within the wider culture. In contrast, Keck considers ethics as the systematic reflection on the nature of the good or the right. With its specification of the ethos, it further nuances and defines those beliefs, values, and traditions as they are to be concretely practiced.[12]

Keck shows how both ethos and ethics functioned in Matthew:

> Every community develops a style, a set of customs and practices which are regarded as acceptable, and perhaps even mandatory. We may call that the ethos of the community—a network of habits, values, expectations and the like which give the community a profile. Most of the time the community's ethos is taken for granted. In this light the ethics of a community would be the rationale for the ethos, the reason people would give for the way they behaved and what they valued.[13]

Given the unique tensions and problems facing his community, precisely because of ethos- or cultural-conflicts, Matthew set out to outline a distinct ethic. As such he addressed a specific community with an unique call for ethical responsibility rather than merely echoing the ethical codes of the wider, patriarchal society. Because Matthew distinguishes his ethics from the codes of the wider culture, Keck concludes:

> To begin with, the ethics of the Gospel of Matthew is not general ethics but specifically Christian ethics. To be more precise, the ethics of this gospel is not ethics as advocated by one who happens to be a Christian. Rather, Matthew's ethics is the ethics of a Christian who stands within the Christian community and who addresses the Christian community. Matthew did not write a story about Jesus for anyone whom it may concern nor did he write for the so-called religious readership in Antioch. He wrote within and for a particular Christian community.[14]

Given some of the problems facing Matthew's house churches, the ethos of his house churches—with their "network of habits, values, and expectations"—was the context for Matthew's decision to add three more teachings (5:1–7:29; 10:1–42;[15] 17:24–18:35) to the two extended teachings offered by Mark (Mk. 4:1–33 [par. Mt. 13:1–58] and Mk. 13:1–37 [par. Mt. 24:1–44]). He rearranged these sources so that the members of his house churches might better understand the values and norms which would bear fruit worthy of the daughters and sons of a heavenly parent (see 12:45–50 with 13:51–52).

When members of a community disagree on their values and norms for behavior, the community experiences conflict. Tension results. Inevitably the ethos of the community itself is called into question. In light of our previous discussion regarding tension in Matthew's house churches, Keck's insights about what happened with the ethos of Matthew's house churches when tensions arose are particularly relevant here:

An ethos becomes problematic when someone deviates enough from what is customary to generate a debate over what is the right thing to do. Then people begin giving reasons for their behavior, values, or expectations. Matthew's Gospel does not, in other words, deal with all aspects of behavior in Matthew's church, but only with those matters which have become problems.[16]

Among various problems facing the church around the time Matthew wrote his gospel, a major source of tensions involved differing interpretations regarding the Mosaic Law. One group—"Judaizers"—said the whole Law applied, including circumcision. The other group—"Antinomians" (*a* + *nomos* = anti-law [see 7:23; 13:41; 23:28; 24:12])—said that none of it applied. Much of this dispute revolved around ethnic-based interpretations of the Mosaic Law and the sharing of resources in the community. Another source of tensions seems to have been possible injustice in resource-sharing in the community. To address these problems, especially the sociological, religious, and economic dimensions that dealt with the relationship of people and resources, Matthew told stories of Jesus which would suggest a certain ethos. In addition he adapted his sources to share certain teachings of Jesus and to suggest a certain ethic. Thus, while there can be no clear-cut separation, the narratives of Matthew offer a kind of ethos for his households, while the discourses present a type of ethical instruction that can be called "paraenetic," since paraenesis is merely a kind of moral instruction with a dash of exhortation.[17]

1. Matthew's Ethos

While Matthew's ethos for his community—as well as his ethics—can be found throughout the gospel, an examination of the infancy narrative, the death-resurrection narrative, and the other five narratives reveals a certain ethos about Jesus that Matthew seems to have sculpted to impress upon his audience in the house churches. The next section will discuss how, through his narratives, Matthew outlined that ethos. The story of Jesus' response to his temptation in the wilderness will be shown as offering Matthew's households a certain way of responding in similar fidelity.

a. Matthew's Household Ethos Shaped by His Narrative

Metaphors are often employed in narratives. By telling the story of Jesus, Matthew demonstrated how the pattern of Jesus' life could be reflected in the lifestyle or ethos of his house churches. An investigation of the dynamics Matthew envisioned taking place within his house of disciples reveals an assumed primary metaphor for house-ordering (ecclesial and economic) which reflects Matthew's system of "attitudes, beliefs, values, and norms." He articulated more clearly the implications of his assumed primary metaphor through the vehicle of story.

In analyzing a story one not only looks at the words themselves but at the images and symbols behind them. In reading Matthew's narration about Jesus one must always be aware that at front and center of the story is the primary assumption that church is figuratively described or imaged as parallel to house; church-order parallels house-order; house-order parallels economics and all involve a certain house-culture or ethos. Jack Dean Kingsbury, a contemporary Matthean expert, has highlighted the role of story in the first gospel by describing how Matthew's narrative created a world composed not only of events, but one which also reflected an ethos filled with values:

> Specifically, Matthew imbues his story with an "ideological (evaluative) point of view" (i.e., with a particular way of construing reality; a system of attitudes, beliefs, values, and norms), which the reader, in order to involve himself in Matthew's story, contracts to adopt. By the same token, Matthew develops his story in such a fashion that the evaluative point of view of Jesus, the protagonist of his story, will be in alignment with his own. Hence, as Matthew describes it there is only one correct way in which to view things: the way of Jesus, which is likewise Matthew's own way.[18]

Following the way of Jesus' response to God and God's reign was to become the model of discipleship for Matthew's house church. This "story behind the story" must be continually remembered. In this sense we need to be particularly mindful, for our purposes, of how Matthew treated economic elements (or the "ordering of the house"). Matthew's discussion reveals, in story form, the kind of religious order and economics that should order the life of increasingly secure and prospering house churches. Matthew "handles the Jesus tradition as a whole in such a way as to adapt it to his wealthier, urban community," Keck writes. He continues: "Thereby he affirmed the importance of being a committed community while at the same time he showed that this did not mean simply repeating Jesus. As a whole, Matthew's Gospel showed the church how to be faithful disciples in new situations."[19]

The new situation facing Matthew's house church reflected a changed religious perspective and an economic situation different from that of the time of Jesus and, indeed, of the generations immediately after his death and resurrection. The latter period had been influenced by the absolutist ethics of the wandering charismatics, who depended on the generosity of households they visited (10:11–12; see 8:18–22; 24:4–28). These groups of itinerants had left their patriarchal structures, families, and possessions to gather into alternative communities which seem to have been more collegial.[20] While a small number of wandering charismatics seem to have remained, times had changed and so had the religious viewpoints and economic condition of Jesus' followers. Whereas earlier the church was constituted of the marginated, those at the bottom of society, a good proportion of the members of the church now were at the upper levels. In the highly stratified society of Matthew's day, being a beneficiary of the system often meant having rights and resources at the expense of others.[21] How could those whose lifestyle benefited at the expense of the poor still call themselves faithful followers of Jesus, who said he came to bring good news to the poor (11:2-6)? How could their life reflect authentic discipleship when Jesus said that those who followed him should equally reorder their lives on behalf of the poor (19:21ff)?

Through the vehicle of story, then, Matthew offered his struggling church another ethos, a way to order its relationships and resources that would reflect a just ecclesial and economic order patterned on the model of Jesus' example and teaching. By making *exousía,* or authority, so central, he not only offered a way of life; he also showed how a share in that life through *exousía* itself would empower others to follow the way.

Some of these stories have already been reflected upon; others will be elaborated in the next chapters. But here it may be good to consider just one such story which the Matthean scribe took, like a householder, from the storehouse (13:52). While its meaning can have different levels, the level I want to consider is its effort to create an ethos for Matthew's community, which was tempted to be unconcerned about the poor who were always with it (26:11). This is the story of Jesus' temptation in the desert. It is a story in which Matthew united both the new and the old: quotations from the Hebrew scriptures, Mark, as well as Q.

b. The Test in the Desert: To Choose God or Mammon

The testing of Jesus in the desert immediately follows the opening pericope about his baptism. After Jesus has committed himself to the fulfillment of justice (= the fulfillment of the Law and the prophets = fulfillment of God's will) and after he has undergone baptism by John, the voice from heaven declares of him: "This is my beloved Son, with whom I am well pleased" (3:17). This declaration of Jesus as "beloved Son" recalls Isaiah 42:1 and Psalm 2 from the house of David (= son of David) whom God decrees as "my son" (Ps. 2:7) and who also is called God's "king" (Ps. 2:6) and anointed one (*Christos*— messiah) (Ps. 2:2). Immediately after this Jesus puts his commitment to justice to practice by allowing the devil to tempt him in the desert (4:1-11). He who was called "beloved son" manifests his fidelity to his heavenly Father by choosing God's will rather than that of society.

The whole conflict in the wilderness revolves around the exercise of two kinds of authority related to the notion of sonship. If Jesus would follow a patriarchal model he would seek power, possessions, and prestige for himself (and probably at the expense of others). On the contrary, if he would be faithful to God's order for the household and sonship, his response would shape a more collegial, egalitarian model based on trust in God and openness to God's will that expressed itself in sharing power, possessions, and prestige with others in the household. These notions deserve greater investigation, for they reveal the Matthean character of Jesus and a good part of his responsibility ethic for disciples.

Jesus is portrayed as experiencing in the wilderness (4:1) the testing of Israel in the desert. Commenting on the image of wilderness, Walter Brueggemann draws upon the Genesis image of being void and without form (Gen. 1:2):

The wilderness tradition is the most radical memory Israel has about landlessness. Wilderness is not simply an in-between place which makes the journey longer. It is not simply a sandy place demanding more stamina. It is space far away from ordered land.[22]

Ordered land means ordered economics because, at that time, all economics was house- and land-based. Ordered economics involves justice. Where there is no justice there is disorder and where disorder exists, chaos reigns. Thus Brueggemann continues:

Wilderness is the historical form of chaos and is Israel's memory of how it was before it was created a people. Displacement, in that time and our time, is experienced like the empty dread of primordial chaos, and so Israel testifies about itself.

Wilderness is formless and therefore lifeless. To be placed in the wilderness is to be cast into the land of the enemy—cosmic, natural, historical—without any of the props or resources that give life order and meaning. To be in the wilderness is landlessness par excellence, being not merely a resident alien, as were the fathers, but in a context hostile and destructive.[23]

Following Mark, Matthew's Jesus was placed or "led up by the Spirit into the wilderness" (4:1). However, recalling the insight that "there is no time of the church separated from the time of Jesus," as well as the Christ-church-morality connection, when Matthew says that "Jesus was led up by the Spirit into the wilderness to be tempted by the devil" (4:1), one must not separate this statement from the Matthean community's experience of temptations in its wilderness fifty years later. The question facing them was how they, as church patterned on Jesus, would adjust their ethos in accord with Jesus' response to the primordial temptations of life. By calling on the central image of Israel's wilderness experience, Matthew not only recalled Jesus' experience but the situation of his church: a place of trials and persecution, of darkness and tension.

The desert/wilderness image evoked the idea of the "void" and "darkness" which covered the earth/land in the beginning (Gen. 1:2). Over this the Spirit hovered to bring order out of disorder (Gen. 1:2ff). Matthew wanted to remind his readers that this same Spirit which also hovered over Mary (1:20) to give life to Jesus now was in the community (27:50; 28:16–20) to help it be faithful to God's word during its time of trial. If the community would be open, as was Jesus, this Spirit would give the community the power to come through its testing in fidelity.

The basic issue presented by Matthew's adaptation of the abbreviated Markan narrative and Q about the wilderness trial scene is whether Jesus will be true son and the disciples will be true mothers, brothers, and sisters of Jesus by putting all resources at the service of God's plan for creation.

The image of testing (*peirasthai*) refers to a time of trial between opposing forces which vie to achieve adherents. The place of testing is the wilderness, the land. The purpose of the testing is to determine if one will be just in adversity (see Wis. 2:1ff; 5:1ff).

In the scriptures, the land is regularly understood as the place for testing and conflict. Matthew's church had to be reminded how its scriptures should be read as a story of conflict about the land and how those conflicts could be repeated in its own increasingly prosperous and urbanized "land."

Brueggemann says that "land is a central, if not *the central theme* of biblical faith."[24] Further, W. D. Davies has made the connection between the Hebrew and Christian scriptures by declaring: "To overlook the emphasis on the land in Judaism is to overlook one of the most persistent and passionately held doctrines with which the Early Church had to come to terms."[25] The land, in the form of possessions, power, and prestige, can easily dominate one's loyalties; thus the necessity continually to bring it under submission to the service of God. Only from this land-perspective can one understand the ethos articulated in Matthew's version of Jesus' testing in the wilderness. The conflict between the two reigns is one of two households, of two economics: one Spirit-formed, the other controlled by Satan (see 12:22-32). If Jesus is the Son of God (see 3:17; 17:5), the way he relates to the land/wealth/economics will determine his authenticity, and the way his followers relate to land/wealth/economics will determine their authenticity also.

After he had fasted forty days and nights, Jesus underwent his first test. What lay behind it was the invitation to make possessions an end in themselves:

And the tempter came and said to him, "If you are the Son of God, command these stones to become loaves of bread." But he answered, "It is written, 'Man shall not live by bread alone, but by every word that proceeds from the mouth of God' "[4:3-4].

The quotation used by Matthew was drawn from Deuteronomy (8:3) and goes further than Luke, who speaks only about not living by bread alone (Lk. 4:4). When Israel came to the promised land, it was about to move from the state of dependent sojourner to independent possessor; this in itself would be a great temptation to take unto itself the control of God's economy. Thus it paused to hear Moses speak God's word about the impending temptation to allow the land and its wealth (i.e., economics for its own sake) to dominate. Once there, Yahweh warned, the land in its various forms could easily become the dominant force in the ethos or values, ideals, and lifestyle of the people unless the people continually considered it as gift: "And you shall remember all the way which the Lord your God has led you these forty years in the wilderness

. . . that he might make you know that man does not live by bread alone, but that man lives by everything that proceeds out of the mouth of the Lord" (Dt. 8:2, 3). Life is not to be rooted in the land but in God's word.

If Israel would not make the experience of Yahweh in its midst the source of its life, the land would become an end in itself. Thus, after Israel had eaten its fill, built goodly houses and lived in them, multiplied its herds and flocks, as well as its silver and gold, it forgot the Lord who brought it "out of the land of Egypt, out of the house of bondage" (Dt. 8:12–14).

The temptation facing the house of Israel, once freed from its "house of bondage" and in the land, was the temptation now facing Matthew's house church: to let its security be grounded in its possessions rather than in its experience of God. The specific temptation facing the community was to equate God's reign with economic security itself, the possession of bread. Matthew wanted to show that the mark of true discipleship was to remain in union with the Spirit in the wilderness and be surrendered to God's word, which sustains humanity in all its needs even to the point of giving bread on a daily basis (6:11). The lived expression of this trust, for Matthew, lies in sharing with others. According to Donald Gelpi,

> In Matthew's gospel, this expectant faith in the day-to-day providence of God must also find practical expression in the freedom to share one's bread, one's possessions with others, especially with the dispossessed. The sharing born of faith expresses the determination to look to God rather than to one's worldly goods as the ultimate source of life. It therefore guarantees membership in God's kingdom in the life to come.[26]

Matthew's description of Jesus' second test (Luke's third) involved the element of land-seduction connected with the abuse of power. In a society based on status and class, power is an especially common determinant. Thus the temptation to make power serve one's own ego rather than its author (see Dt. 8:18):

> Then the devil took him to the holy city, and set him on the pinnacle of the temple, and said to him, "If you are the Son of God, throw yourself down; for it is written, 'He will give his angels charge of you,' and 'On their hands they will bear you up, lest you strike your foot against a stone.' " Jesus said to him, "Again it is written, 'You shall not tempt the Lord your God' " [4:5–7].

The second temptation shows the devil's effort to turn the tables on the Spirit. If the Spirit led Jesus (and the Matthean households) into the wilderness to be tested, then to be given over to the wilderness and seduced by it is to test the Spirit's presence. In the second test, Jesus asserts that faith in God's providence must be unconditional. Yet, it becomes conditional when people make the land an end in itself. Thus Matthew's Jesus interpreted this testing again from that part of Deuteronomy which recalled the house of Israel's temptation to make the land and its resources so dominant that these stood in opposition to the one whose power made them available to Israel:

When the Lord your God brings you into the land . . . with great and goodly cities, which you did not build, and houses full of all good things, which you did not fill, and cisterns hewn out, which you did not hew, and vineyards and olive trees, which you did not plant, and when you eat and are full, then take heed lest you forget the Lord, who brought you out of the land of Egypt, out of the house of bondage. . . . You shall not put the Lord your God to the test [Dt. 6:10–12, 16].

Putting God to the test meant that Israel would begin to let the land, in the form of the power to acquire wealth, so dominate its values, ideals, and decisions that it would not share it with others. As in the desert with the bread which it tried to hoard and which then turned wormy and rotten (Ex. 16:19–20), so, once in the land, Israel would try to acquire more. As a result Matthew's community had to "remember" this fact as well, especially as it became more secure in its "land." It had to refrain from storing up earthly treasure lest it rust or be stolen away (6:19). Only by such "remembering" could it place its unconditional trust in God rather than in its power and possessions. Only by such "remembering" would it be willing to share its resources unconditionally, aware that God, who knew what it truly needed, would meet those needs as a loving parent (6:32; 7:11)—as long as it shared with God's other children, especially the least ones. Not to do so would be to imitate the Israelites at Massah: to test God.

Testing God is to attempt to set the terms determining to what degree one will trust God. With this in mind, Donald Gelpi asks a question that brings the issue of economics and ethics to bear upon this part of the testing story:

Does the moral message of Matthew's Jesus cast any light on the ethical consequences of trusting in God unconditionally? If for Matthew's Jesus, the sharing of one's goods with others is a practical test of faith, one would anticipate that in His teaching the practice of faith-sharing would reflect in some way the unconditioned character of the faith in God it expresses. And such indeed is the case. For Matthew's Jesus demands that His followers set no conditions in principle upon the scope of their sharing. Anyone is to be eligible, especially the needy.[27]

If the final judgment would be based on the degree one's resources were shared with the needy (25:31–46), it is understandable that Matthew would incorporate the Deuteronomic text about testing the Lord in his version of Jesus' testing.

The third test (Luke's second) changes the scene. As Moses was led up a high mountain to see "all the land"—which according to rabbinic interpretation meant the whole earth (Dt. 34:1-4)—so the devil took Jesus

> to a very high mountain, and showed him all the kingdoms of the world and the glory of them; and he said to him, "All these I will give you, if you will fall down and worship me." Then Jesus said to him, "Begone, Satan! for it is written, 'You shall worship the Lord your God and him only shall you serve.' " Then the devil left him, and behold, angels came and ministered to him [4:8-11].

The first commandment ordered Israel to worship God alone and to avoid all false worship, especially of mammon in its various forms. The most common form of idolatry in the Hebrew scriptures involved mammon-worship or forms of greed. Again, the allusion on the lips of Matthew's Jesus was to address an ethos that was beginning to invade Matthew's house churches: the idolatry of letting their resources and prestige become ends in themselves rather than to be put at the service of God. "Ask of me," Yahweh said to Israel, "and I will make the nations your heritage, and the ends of the earth your possession" (Ps. 2:8). Now Matthew's Jesus, again quoting Deuteronomy, demanded that his landed community, like Israel, must worship and serve God alone (Dt. 6:13). It was that creator of the earth, the divine Householder, and that one alone who Matthew insisted must be adored.

2. Matthew's Ethic

Having considered how Matthew used his narrative to outline an ethos of sharing for his households, we can now examine how his presentation of Jesus' teachings offers a distinct ethic of responsibility for the disciples in his house churches as well. As Jesus proved his fidelity as "beloved son" of the divine Householder, so those disciples will be his mother, brother, and sisters who manifest a similar fidelity by fulfilling their heavenly Father's will. They will fulfill the Father's will if their households reflect the ethos of Jesus' response to it, and that will be accomplished through an ethics of responsibility which puts into practice his teachings.

a. An "Interim Ethic"?

For some, Jesus' teaching and life cannot be considered a concrete answer for contemporary ethical questions, even less so as a basis for a specific economic ethic. In his *The Quest for the Historical Jesus*, Albert Schweitzer argued that "modernizing" Jesus' teaching was impossible. He contended that Jesus preached an "interim ethic," given his expectation of his imminent *"parousía,"* or second coming. Since the *parousía* did not materialize, Jesus' ethic, spoken for the "interim," no longer applies.[28]

Since Matthew alone used the word *"parousía"* (24:3, 7), the notion of "interim ethic" should apply particularly to his gospel if Schweitzer's argument convinces. But is it as simple as Schweitzer would make it?

We have seen that an exegesis of the context for the *"parousía"* in 24:3 must be connected with 23:38, four verses earlier. Matthew presents Jesus as concluding his castigation of the scribes and Pharisees by speaking of his rejection by Jerusalem: " 'Behold your *oikos* is forsaken and desolate.' For I tell you, you will not see me again, until you say, 'Blessed is he who comes in the name of the Lord' "(23:38-39). Having said these words, Jesus "left the temple," and spoke of its destruction (24:1-2). Then, "As he sat on the Mount of Olives, the disciples came to him privately, saying, 'Tell us, when will this be, and what will be the sign of your *parousía* and of the close of the age' "(24:3).

First of all, chapter 2, above, showed that this passage (23:38-24:2) reveals the transfer of God's authoritative presence from the old *oikos*, the temple, to the new *oikos* of the church. Second, in 24:3 the *parousía* is connected to "the close of the age." From what I have already written, it is clear that the "close of the age" (a uniquely Matthean phrase used in 13:39, 40, and at the end of the gospel, 28:20) cannot be separated from the *paliggenesía*, or beginning of the new age (19:28). Third, this passage sets the stage in the last discourse for the "apocalyptic testament" (23:38-26:1).

The apocalyptic testament can be divided into two parts. The first half (24:3-36) adapts material from Mark: the birth pangs (24:3-8), outside persecution and inside tensions (24:9-14), the "great tribulation" and the *parousía* itself (24:15-31), with the concluding parable about the fig tree (24:32-36). The second half (24:37-26:1) exhorts the church to vigilance. From this perspective we can more clearly address the question about the "interim ethic" of Schweitzer.

Schweitzer's notions of apocalyptic[29] and eschatology[30] gave rise to his concept of an "interim ethic." Yet, far from being irrelevant fifty years after Jesus' physical departure from the community, the apocalyptic perspective which frames these pericopes calls for a style of life within the church that reveals *now* the presence of the householder and bridegroom who has gone but will return.

An essential element of apocalyptic thought is that its stories about the coming judgment ("kingdom") disclose those transcendent and perennial values that should be realized *in* the period before the judgment, whether that period is "interim" or extended. John Donahue notes, "Apocalyptic affirms that the sufferings and injustice which mar this world will be bearable because the order of justice will be restored. Sin and evil will be unmasked and goodness rewarded. Simply put, the world will be made 'right' again."[31] Those who try to make the world "right again" in the "now" will be rewarded in the "then."

Since apocalyptic calls for the world to be reordered, the restoration of justice is at the heart of its stories because justice deals with right order. Adela Collins has noted that apocalyptic reminds us that the love command (22:37-40) must always be accompanied by the implementation of justice.[32] In this light we can now say that this section of Matthew (24:37-26:1), based on Q and material unique to the first gospel, seems to have been written for a community struggling to live a moral life faithful to the teachings of its master who went away and, like a bridegroom, delayed his return (25:5). For such house churches, Matthew compared the end of time to that faithful householder (*oikodespótēs*) who allocated his resources among the members of the household (see 24:43–51) to be *used* by them as responsible stewards (*douloi*) until his return.

From the back-to-back stories in the "apocalyptic testament" about the servant who ordered the household (24:43–51) and the ten virgins (25:1–13), as well as the following parable of the silver pieces (25:14–30), Matthew's ethic hardly can be called "interim" in Schweitzer's sense. The same can be said of the final "parable" about the last judgment (25:31–46). Rather, Matthew's ethic reflects the realization that the community did not know at what hour Jesus would return. Its moral life would have to be colored by this conclusion. Whether it be good works symbolized by the property entrusted the servant by the householder (24:45), the oil for the lamps of the virgins (25:3–4), the silver pieces given the servants of the master who went on a journey (25:14–15), or the works of justice by those called the sheep in the last judgment (25:31–46), all these works were to bear fruit; they were to manifest the disciples' response to the Father's will.

If Schweitzer is wrong about his "interim ethic," what is the alternative?

b. Toward a Matthean Ethic of Responsibility

Traditionally, moral philosophers have considered ethics from three main perspectives. The first views humans as creators who are oriented to some end. This approach is called teleological ethics. Because it is goal-oriented, it asks: What are the consequences of my/our actions? Because Matthew's gospel places so much stress on entrance requirements for the "kingdom," some people, like Leander Keck, think Matthew's gospel reveals a teleological ethic or moral code.[33] Thus the parables would be seen as outlining qualities which call for a reordering of life in order to meet the goals of the "kingdom." A second approach considers human beings as members of a corporate body, or citizens. This stresses moral commandments, rules, and principles and their applicability to particular moral actions. This approach is called deontological ethics because it stresses duties, obligations, and imperatives. An example of this would be a *haustafel* as it was traditionally used, even by 1 Peter and Paul. It asks, What ought I/we to do? In Matthew, the "antithesis" statements must be considered examples of deontological ethics.

The third main approach to ethics stresses the manner in which the scriptures relate to the identity of the moral person and community. It asks: What sort of person or community do I/we want to become? Here the stress is not on the impact of moral precepts on particular acts stressing obligation (deontology). Neither does it emphasize the consequences of action via emphasis on values (teleology).[34] Rather than stressing particular acts or the consequences of acts, the thrust of this model is the *character* of the actor, the agent. According to H. Richard Niebuhr, the image of the person as a person capable of response leads to an ethic of *character* or *responsibility*. Contrasting a character/responsibility ethic with teleological and deontological ethics, he noted that each of the three has different answers to the question: "What shall I do?" First, teleology raises as prior to that question another question:

"What is my goal, ideal, or telos?" Deontology tries to answer the moral query by asking first of all: "What is the law and what is the first law of my life?" Responsibility, however, proceeds in every moment of decision and choice to inquire: "What is going on?" If we use value terms then the difference among the three approaches may be indicated by the terms, the *good*, the *right*, and the *fitting*; for teleology is concerned always with the highest good to which it subordinates the right; consistent deontology is concerned with the right, no matter what may happen to our goods; but for the ethics of responsibility the *fitting* action, the one that fits into a total interaction as response and as anticipation of further response, is alone conducive to the good and alone is right.[35]

When *responsibility* is viewed as the key element of the morality of individuals and groups, the stress is on their *character*. In this ethic they are seen as agents who, in relation to each other and their communities, interact with other communities and the world. Such responsibility is both a response to God's word and a response to make that word bear fruit in the world.

The core of Matthean morality revolves around a responsibility ethic for disciples based on the model of Jesus' own loving and obedient response to his "heavenly Father." The character of Jesus in Matthew's narrative is shown, from the beginning (2:15; 3:17; 4:1-11) to the end (27:40, 43, 54), to be that of the faithful son (21:37) of the divine Householder (*oikodespótēs* [21:33]) whose response to the Householder finds him rejected by the tenants because he was the heir, the alter ego of the one who sent him (see 10:40). Consequently, since the Householder who sent him is the "heavenly Father," and since he came to announce that God's reign was at hand for the tenants—who did not prove fruitful—Matthew's Jesus assured "them" that "the kingdom of God will be taken away from you and given to a nation producing the fruits of it" (21:43).

The fruits of God's reign are born in justice. Disciples who respond to the presence of the son of the divine Householder will manifest their responsibility in deeds of justice. Making the link between justice and that morality to be lived in the church "all days" which best re-presents the character of Matthew's Jesus, the words of Donald Senior make it strikingly clear that Matthew's morality is basically a responsibility ethic. After commenting on the "faithful and wise" servant as the one whom the *oikodespótēs* (24:43) finds busy giving food to the members of the household (24:45-46), Senior concludes:

Matthew insists, therefore, on responsible action. Christian life is not a matter of mere aspiration or good intentions; faith must be translated into just and compassionate acts. This emphasis on responsibility may reflect Matthew's strong Jewish heritage in which obedience to the Torah was always the touchstone of authentic faith. His concern with judgment is the corollary of the concern for responsible action. The judgment texts are exhortations, warning the disciple that the experience of God's grace brings with it a responsibility to act graciously. Justice is not an "option" but an urgent demand flowing from the reality of the gospel.[36]

Just as Matthew's ethos reveals Jesus as the obedient son, always responding in love to his Father and to his neighbor, so that ethos becomes concretized in the ethical life of disciples by a similar response in loving fidelity. In Matthew, the way individuals and the household churches were to experience God's reign or presence in their midst and act "responsibly" together to fulfill God's will through justice constitutes the basis for ethics. Responsibility grounds Matthew's ethics; it is the essence of discipleship. And at the heart of this responsibility is the response of love realized in the first and greatest commandment and in the second commandment—which only Matthew repeats twice: "You shall love your neighbor as yourself" (19:19; 22:39). This love, which fulfills the Law and the prophets (22:40), unites justice with responsible action.

MAKING MATTHEAN MORALITY CONTEMPORARY

Having adapted stories of Jesus such as his experience in the wilderness to reveal an ethos of obedience and having recalled more specific teachings of Jesus, Matthew was, in fact, outlining an ethic of responsibility for the disciples in his house churches which would show how they were called to deal with their tensions and the tendency to make their possessions idols. For instance, in recalling from his "story-house" (see 13:51–52) the pericope about Jesus' trial in the wilderness, Matthew invited his church to develop a similar ethos.

Matthew's specific morality is oriented within and from what he considered to be the natural order realized in and through the household. This implies a Matthean ethic that is social insofar as it is essentially oriented to the other, to the neighbor, but also only insofar as this neighbor is related to one's self and household (19:19; 22:39).

Building on the connection between the individual and community realized in the household of Matthew's day, Stanley Hauerwas correctly calls the church itself "a social ethic" which should be modeling authentic moral life through the way its individual members interrelated not only for their own good and interests but as an example for society. Thus the conclusion of the first of Jesus' teachings according to Matthew—the Beatitudes—urges the members of his house church to be a light for each other in the house and an example before all. People do not "light a lamp and put it under a bushel, but on a stand, and it gives light to all *in* the house. Let your light so shine before *men*, that they may see your good works and give glory to *your* Father in heaven" (5:15–16).

This modeling flows from the community's perception of Jesus and is expressed in the way it observes all that it has learned of Jesus (see 28:20); thus the Christ-church-morality triad. Just as Matthew saw Jesus as the fulfillment of Isaiah's vision of the servant (8:17; 12:18–21), so we can conclude about "that" church what Hauerwas says about the church "now":

> The first social ethical task of the church is to be the church—the servant community. Such a claim may well sound self-serving until we remember that what makes the church the church is its faithful manifestation of the peaceable kingdom in the world. As such the church does not have a social ethic; the church is a social ethic.[37]

The church is a community of people—faithful, responsible people—who are trying to let their lives reflect their beliefs. In this process they are nourished by the life of the tradition. Hauerwas continues:

> The church is where the stories of Israel and Jesus are told, enacted, and heard, and it is our conviction that as a Christian people there is literally nothing more important we can do. But the telling of that story requires that we be a particular kind of people if we and the world are to hear the story truthfully. . . . By being that kind of community we see that the church helps the world understand what it means to be the world. For the world has no way of knowing it is world without the church pointing to the reality of God's kingdom.[38]

No one wrote more about the kingdom of God and the kingdom of heaven than Matthew. Jesus' parables in Matthew revolve around the kind of characteristics membership in that reign requires. Membership in the reign-to-come depends on creating the conditions for that reign to be realized on earth as those conditions are and will be realized in heaven (see 6:10). This membership in God's reign will be realized through house churches of dedicated disciples (now as then) who act responsibly.

The household theoretically remains today the basic unit of the church. The family is the "domestic church."[39] However the household that once was the basic unit of the economy has been displaced in the industrial, technological, and information revolutions. While making connections between Matthew's church and church order today may be more apropos, to make any direct parallels to the current economic situation can be misleading. While I have noted this at various times, especially in the Introduction, it deserves greater emphasis here as we struggle with making Matthew's ethic contemporary for ourselves.

In the first section of this chapter where I summarized the previous chapters which lay the foundation for our ethical response, I recalled the need to understand the "horizon" of Matthew so that we, with the twentieth-century horizon of our post-industrial societies and our particular "horizons" within this, might better find some way of fusing Matthew's moral vision with our own. This demands what Max Stackhouse has called a "double hermeneutic."

Such a "double hermeneutic" involves "a hermeneutic of texts, one alert to the contexts in which they were composed, and to the contexts into which they are transposed, but seeking above all else for those thematic possibilities in the texts which are trans-contextual in importance and able to evaluate, effect, and transform contexts."[40]

Part of the resolution of this need for fusion can come if we recall the ethos of Matthew—the values, ideals, and style of life he raised up (consciously and unconsciously). For Matthew, this "ethos" revolves around doing God's will— which makes us one family. This notion offers an insight that is applicable to today's ecclesiastical and economic problems, especially those related to the dignity of persons in the church and economy and to the distribution of resources—be that distribution in the form of roles or material goods. Leander Keck writes:

> Once the dialectical relation between the writers of the NT and the ethos of their communities and their traditions comes into focus, the task of interpreting the NT and articulating it into the church and into society today becomes significantly enriched and infinitely more exciting. No longer will the interpretive task center in the effort to locate theological ideas (including the kerygma) which, in demythologized form, are tenable today—though it is not to be ruled out. Rather, the interpreter's task would be to liberate the text so that it could accost today's church as critically as it originally did.[41]

The text is not to "accost today's church as critically as it originally did" for its own sake, but in order to make the message of the gospel as relevant to our age as it was for the age of the 80s and 90s. From the perspective of faith, the story of Jesus and his teachings written for Matthew's era must have some relevance for all times because this story and his teachings are to be observed by "all nations . . . to the close of the age" (28:19, 20).

Given these reflections, the answer to earlier questions about how Matthew approached ethics and its applicability to us should be clearer. A viable approach linking scripture and ethics, particularly Matthew's gospel and ethics today, can be found in probing Matthew for his understanding of justice and how our responsibility is to ensure an abundant justice. Here "universally valid claims about the implications of a Godly justice, known in Jesus Christ," enable us to "apply them to quite distinct contexts."[42] By continually contextualizing Matthew's gospel narratives in the social environment of his day, the underlying attitudes and virtues they contain can be applied to today's followers of Christ as they confront social problems in their church and economics. This is what Stackhouse calls "transcontextualization."

Despite the changed situation, the underlying ethos related to church-ordering and economics in the 80s and 90s cannot be totally isolated from ecclesiastical life and economics 1900 years later. Through his narrative Matthew offered his urbanized, middle-class house churches the pattern of Jesus' responsibility to be fulfilled, and that narrative must be applicable to the present if the church is to be alive in these last years of the second millennium. "The first-century house-churches were alive—alive to Christ, the reality of Christian fellowship, and the responsibilities for world conquest," Morris A. Inch has written. He continues: "They were rejoicing in the blessedness which transcended their circumstances, coloured their ministry, and whetted their anticipation. In Matthew's gospel they found a text remarkably applicable to their situation."[43] Twentieth-century and twenty-first-century disciples of Jesus must be equally challenged to make Matthew's gospel "remarkably applicable" to our day. As Max Stackhouse implies, this challenge must address some critical issues facing our *oikoi*, the *oikouméne*, and the ecological balance of life itself:

Is it possible to identify any fundamental patterns of truth and justice behind the pluralism of the texts and contexts which can guide economic systems? Is it possible to identify how these can provide ecumenical guidance to structure the common life in a global civilization to which we are moving? Is it possible to argue convincingly that concerns of justice are not a matter of "preferential option" but a matter of universal truth which no one has the right to deny and which must become prudently built into modern economic systems?[44]

HOUSEHOLD JUSTICE AS THE CENTER OF MATTHEAN MORALITY

The situation, then, is clear: the issue is not "an option for the poor" but a decision to be made to bring justice to the poor *if* one chooses to follow Jesus. The option is discipleship. But, if one chooses discipleship, following Jesus is predicated on responding to the heavenly Father's will by bearing fruit in justice. Thus Matthew's morality reflects a justice-oriented ethic equally applicable today as then, even though the implementation of that will differ because of changed economic and ecclesial situations.

Matthew's entire gospel, but especially his Beatitudes (5:1–16) and the entire Sermon on the Mount, can be considered the evangelist's attempt to outline a way of justice for his prosperous house churches. This way of justice, or bearing fruit, will characterize the ethical stance in the house of disciples who do their heavenly Father's will.

Matthew uses two main words for justice: *krísis* and *dikaiosýne*. *Krísis* tends to reflect eschatological judgment based on people's deeds (5:21, 22, 10:15; 11:22, 24; 12:18, 20, 36, 42; 23:23, 33). The eschatological dimension is clear in the references from Q which Matthew shares with Luke;[45] otherwise neither Mark nor Luke ever uses the word. Matthew uses *dikaiosýne* seven times (3:15; 5:6, 10, 20; 6:1, 33; 21:32), whereas the only other Synoptic use is Luke 1:75. From this quick overview it is evident that words related to justice dominate the first gospel when compared to their use by the other Synoptics. Because justice, especially in the five uses of *dikaiosýnē* in the Sermon on the Mount (5:6, 10, 20; 6:1, 33), is a central theme in Matthew, his gospel has been rightly called the "Gospel of Justice."

The first words of Jesus in Matthew revolve around the notion of *dikaiosýnē*: "Let it be so now; for thus it is fitting for us to fulfill all *dikaiosýnē*" (3:15). These words indicate that his life (and, thus, the life of his house churches) must be centered around justice as the fulfillment of God's plan (3:15). Justice involves right-ordering of relationships among people (toward each other) and among their resources. At the heart of this right-ordering is fidelity to household relationships. What John Donahue has written about justice-as-relational in the Hebrew scriptures has equal application to Matthew's gospel, since the author of the first gospel envisioned justice as the former's fulfillment:

> In general terms the biblical idea of justice can be described as *fidelity to the demands of a relationship*. In contrast to modern individualism the Israelite is in a world where "to live" is to be united with others in a social context either by bonds of family or by covenant relationships. This web of relationships—king with people, judge with complainants, family with tribe and kinfolk, the community with the resident alien and suffering in their midst and all with the covenant God—constitutes the world in which life is played out.[46]

The new covenant to be sealed in Jesus' blood for all (26:28) represented a dramatic call to the household churches (see 26:18) to live an ethical life that would manifest relations of fidelity among equal children of the same Father. Therefore, just as the notion of house is inseparably linked with the concept of the family as the basic social unit, with its religious and economic relations, so the notion of justice also should be considered as a relational and social concept as well as an ethical norm, whether it refers to one's dealings with God or others. In this sense Hans-Hartmut Schroeder has written:

> If we apply the word "justice" to the house, it obviously results that the individualistic conception of justice no longer applies. We need more. We need to refer to a group of people or an institution constituted or represented by various persons.
>
> The term justice refers to a mutual relation. We affirm in this case that where justice is found, peace will reign. Furthermore if the relations in a house are regulated by justice, peace will predominate in that house. We thus can ask if such a concept of justice is found in the New Testament and if so, if it is possibly related to the term *oikos*.[47]

The next two chapters, the sixth on the Beatitudes and the seventh on the rest of the Sermon on the Mount, will probe the moral implications of Matthew's use of the notion of justice.

6

The Beatitudes: Building Blocks
for a House of Wisdom

WISDOM BUILDING HERSELF A HOME

According to wisdom literature, each person is destined for an orderly role in an orderly cosmos. All people must discern that order and responsibly accept their role in its perpetuation. Since much of wisdom literature discusses household order, much of its ethics gives consideration to the way officials and others ought to order relationships and resources in their households.[1] Justice is the goal.

The theme of blessedness or blessings is woven throughout wisdom literature as well. The blessed person (*makários*) reflects a life conducted according to the norms of wisdom. Beatitudes (i.e., blessings) flow throughout the Old Testament. Male and female are blessed (Gen. 1:28; 5:2). The final work of creation is blessed (Gen. 2:3). The blessing for Noah and his descendants (Gen. 9:1) reaches its peak in the promise made to Abram, who was called from his father's house (*bayith, oikos* [Gen. 12:1]):

Now the Lord said to Abram, "Go from your country and your kindred and your father's *oikos* to the land that I will show you. And I will make of you a great nation, and I will bless you, and make your name great, so that you will be a blessing. I will bless those who bless you, and him who curses you I will curse; and by you all the families of the earth will bless themselves" [Gen. 12:1-3].

The blessing of God to Abraham and Sarah reached its culmination in the formation of a new *oikos* through the covenant God made with them (Gen. 15:3-6; 17:12-13). The land they would enter would be blessed as well as their seed—their entire household. This house would be the nation of Israel, their offspring. In them not only this household but all the households of the earth would be blessed (Gen. 12:3). However, no matter how humans were involved in the process of becoming a household and being blessed in the land, Israel was never to forget the Lord said "I will build you a house". Consequently Israel was to be submissive to Yahweh and to no other god.

John F. A. Sawyer has noted that, while "house" is a frequent figure throughout the biblical tradition, wisdom literature gives it special prominence.[2] Proverbs urged obedience to the king (see Prov. 24:21–22) and often invited the children or pupils to "hear" (obey) the instruction of the parents or teacher (Prov. 1:8; 4:11; 7:24; 8:23; 19:20, 27; 22:17; 23:19, 22). Wisdom and house have some definite connections (Ps. 127; Prov. 12:7; 14:11; 15:6, 25; 24:30–31; Job 8:15; Sir. 21:4, 8, 18; 22:16–18). While wisdom cannot be *equated* with house, or with religion, justice, or economics, some parallels exist. It will be helpful for us to examine what connections may be uncovered.

Earlier we saw that Matthew's Beatitudes—which open the Sermon on the Mount—end with a reference to showing the light of good works within the house. The Sermon comes to a close with the following house-image:

> Everyone then who hears these words of mine and does them will be like a wise man who built his house upon the rock; and the rain fell, and floods came, and the winds blew and beat upon that house, but it did not fall, because it had been founded on the rock. And everyone who hears these words of mine and does not do them will be like a foolish man who built his house upon the sand; and the rain fell, and the floods came, and the winds blew and beat against that house, and it fell; and great was the fall of it [7:24–27].

Matthew's image of wisdom and foolishness and house-building from the Q source merely echoed a parallel idea found in Proverbs: "Wisdom builds her house, but folly with her own hands tears it down" (Prov. 9:1; 14:1; 24:3). The conclusion of chapter thirty-one of Proverbs praises the woman of the household who provides food, buys a field, spins and sells her merchandise, yet opens her hands to the poor and needy (Prov. 31:15–25): "She opens her mouth with wisdom, and the teaching of kindness is on her tongue. She looks well to the ways of her household . . . " (Prov. 31:26–27).[3]

At the time of Jesus, Jewish teachers, like Hillel and Shammai, were invited in pairs into the houses of people who wanted to learn their wisdom. "Let thy house be a place of meeting for the wise," Jose ben Joezer (c. 175 BCE) said, "and dust thyself with the dust of their feet and drink their words with thirst" (Abot. 1:4). Following Mark, Matthew locates many of Jesus' wisdom sayings (especially those found in his parables and teaching) "in the house." Jesus' disciples too are to use the house as their base to explain the wisdom of Jesus' teaching and to launch their missionary activity (10:11–15).

The wisdom literature extant today can be traced to two schools, or, to be more precise, to a main school having various expressions. Proverbs and Ben Sira represent the main school. In a passage that shows parallels between the urbanized and prosperous context of Matthew's gospel, which reflects a way of wisdom, and the context of wisdom literature, Robert Gordis contends that wisdom literature

> reached its apogee during the earlier centuries of the Second Temple, roughly between the sixth and the first half of the second centuries, B.C.E., [and] was fundamentally the product of the upper classes in society, who lived principally in the capital, Jerusalem. Some were engaged in large-scale foreign trade, or were taxfarmers, like the Tobiades. Most of them were supported by the income of their country estates, which were tilled either by slaves, or by tenant farmers, who might have once owned the very fields they now worked as tenants.[4]

Wisdom was handed on to young men in a special school, or house (*bet*), of study (*hamidras*). *Bet hamidras* is the technical term used by Sirach in his plea: "Draw near to me, you who are untaught, and lodge in my *bet hamidras*." The kind of instruction taught in such houses of study was to be implemented in domestic households. Household wisdom revealed proper ordering of relationships and resources, as did the wisdom literature; thus the parallels between wisdom and house. Since wisdom went hand-in-hand with justice in the scriptures (see Wis. 1:1f),[5] their ordering within the household should not be overlooked (see Prov. 14:1-2).

Of the Synoptics, Matthew's gospel has been identified as most influenced by wisdom themes. Certainly the economic of his increasingly wealthy community paralleled that earlier situation of the fifth and sixth centuries which gave rise to much wisdom literature.

We have already seen that Matthew himself may have etched a self-portrait when he noted that "every scribe who has been trained for the kingdom of heaven is like a householder who brings out of his treasure what is new and what is old" (13:52). According to Krister Stendahl, Matthew was a converted rabbi and was not working entirely alone. Rather "there was a school at work in the church of Matthew."[6] While I have shown that Matthew seems to have been a gentile, Stendahl's ideas are provocative, especially if one would make the connections between wisdom and house, teaching and discipleship, as noted above.[7] Jesus could have been identified as the teacher of wisdom, the disciples who put his words into practice via justice as the members of his school or household.

Walter Brueggemann has shown that the theology of the wisdom teachers is consistent with underlying themes in Matthew's gospel. He adds that Matthew's Jesus proclaimed the reign of God as

> a realm of wholeness, freedom, responsibility, and security where men can be the men God intends them to be. Indeed, to affirm that we do live in that kind of world is a close approximation of the world in which the wise said we lived. Jesus' teaching, particularly in Matthew, has remarkable confidence in man's capacity to be free, safe, whole, and responsi-

ble. He affirms that men are responsible for the future they choose (cf. Matt. 25:31-46). He celebrates man as one who is especially precious and loved (Matt. 6:25-33). His teaching has the same buoyancy, confidence, and openness as that which characterizes wisdom teaching at its best.[8]

Matthew portrayed Jesus not only as the personification of the ideal foundation of the house of Israel and as a teacher of wisdom, but as incarnate wisdom extending its blessing to his followers. The first of Jesus' teachings highlights blessings or beatitudes (5:1-16). The last of his teachings does the same (25:34). The key passage indicating Jesus' messianic role and the community's need to continue this work culminates in a blessing (11:2-6).

An important example of the wisdom motif in Matthew can be found in Jesus' lament over Jerusalem (the house of Israel) for not putting his teachings into practice: "O Jerusalem, Jerusalem, killing the prophets and stoning those who are *sent* to you" (23:37). Earlier Matthew's Jesus said that *he* sent prophets and wise men (23:34). Only one possessing wisdom could send "wise men." So, as the wise one, Jesus continued:

> How often would I have gathered your children together as a hen gathers her brood under her wings, and you would not! Behold, your house is forsaken and desolate. For I tell you, you will not see me again, until you say, "Blessed is he who comes in the name of the Lord" [23:37-39].

"Blessed is he" is a *makarism*, or a blessing-phrase used frequently in the scriptures. By performing a blessed activity, one would become blessed. The one receiving a blessed person in hospitality would be blessed as well.

This passage about the rejection of Jesus by Jerusalem (i.e., the house of Israel) reveals that Jesus not only taught wisdom, but came to be identified with it. By rejecting Jesus' teachings, Israel rejected his wisdom. In rejecting his wisdom, Israel rejected Jesus. M. Jack Suggs declares:

> Matthew successfully transfers a Wisdom saying to Jesus because for him Jesus is identified with Sophia. It is in Wisdom's person that Jesus can speak of "how often" in relation to Jerusalem, for the call of Wisdom had been heard again and again in "the prophets and those sent"; the "how often" has nothing to do with the number of trips made to Jerusalem by the historical Jesus, but with how Wisdom in every generation has appealed to men through her prophets and has not been heeded. As this figure, Jesus can say—as no merely historical individual might— "I would have gathered your children under my wings." Jesus is Wisdom incarnate.[9]

Another part of Jesus' lament over Jerusalem contained the prediction: "Behold, your house is forsaken and desolate" (23:38). Earlier Baruch lamented over Jerusalem for its rejection of wisdom. He placed in Jerusalem's mouth the words, "Let no one gloat over me, a widow, bereft of many: For the sins of my children I am left desolate, because they turned from the law of God" (Bar. 4:12). By speaking about the desolation of Jerusalem's "house," Matthew's Jesus forewarns that the house of Israel will be abandoned; as in Ezekiel, a new house will be established. In Matthew the new house of Israel becomes the church (see 23:38–24:2). *Their* synagogues will be replaced by *his* church (16:18).

If the first evangelist portrayed Jesus as personified Wisdom and if the house is an assumed primary metaphor in Matthew's gospel, it would follow that wisdom themes should play a significant part in Jesus' teachings for his house-based followers. Consequently, Matthew portrays wisdom as the way members of the house built on Peter should reflect and promote the order promoted by Jesus. If wisdom built herself a house, those house churches whose members put into practice the teachings of Jesus are like wise ones who have built their house on rock (7:24–27).

The Beatitudes of Matthew represent, in eight (or nine) short sentences, the outline of an entire ethos of wisdom which Matthew offered his households which were stumbling because of their divisions.

THE BEATITUDES IN MATTHEW AND LUKE: DIFFERENT NARRATIVES FOR DIFFERENT HOUSEHOLDS

In examining the Beatitudes of Matthew and Luke it becomes clear that both adapted their sources in a way that would respond to their varied social locations. From a cursory examination, it would seem that, while definite similarities existed, the contexts of the two communities for which Matthew and Luke wrote their beatitudes and their sermons (one on the mount, the other on the plain) were quite different. They adapted their sources to fit the unique situations of their particular communities: the one relatively prosperous and the other less so, with larger numbers of the poor.

We have already seen that, on the whole, Matthew's house churches were relatively prosperous. Despite the existence of significant numbers of the poor (status-wise [power] and money-wise [wealth]), the poor did not seem to be as dominant and pervasive as in Luke's community. The poor could be hidden from the prosperous.

A major reason the poor do not seem to dominate in Matthew is that nowhere does the first gospel canonize poverty or the poor. However, Luke's gospel does. The differing approaches to "the poor" are especially evident in two key beatitudes. In the first, Luke has "Blessed are you poor, for yours is the kingdom of God" (Lk. 6:20) while Matthew has "Blessed are the poor in spirit, for theirs is the kingdom of heaven" (5:3). Luke's second beatitude is "Blessed are you that hunger now, for you shall be satisfied" (Lk. 6:21). Besides including two more beatitudes (for the meek and those who mourn) before his parallel to Luke, Matthew has another version: "Blessed are those who hunger and thirst for righteousness, for they shall be satisfied" (5:6).

Matthew adds "in spirit," whereas Luke simply has "Blessed are you poor."

He also adds "for *dikaiosýnē*," whereas Luke baldly declares: "Blessed are you that hunger now." In trying to find a rationale for these differences, various commentators[10] have said that the first evangelist has "spiritualized" his sources as a way of addressing the prosperity of his house churches. For instance, Raymond Brown has written:

> The end product of Mt's collection is a moral instruction on the spiritual needs of the Gospel message—the classical guide to the newness of the spiritual life preached by Jesus.
>   Lk's beatitudes are emphatically not primarily on the spiritual plane. His poor are the real have-nots of this world; his hungry know the misery of an empty stomach; his unfortunate are weeping. And just so that we do not miss the realism of his beatitudes, Luke narrates a series of corresponding "woes"; stark anathemas hurled against the rich and the content who do not know the meaning of need.[11]

Brown's explanation seems to make a dichotomy between economic involvement and religious activity. However, we have seen that, within the households of Matthew, both economics and religion were imbedded. In this sense Matthew could not have "spiritualized" the Q source. Indeed, the very idea of "spiritualizing" stood alien to that Hebrew mentality with which Matthew seems to have been so familiar. On the contrary, a truly "spiritual" approach involved a total commitment of one's life to whatever was "spiritualized," in this case the poor themselves. In this sense I find Donald Senior's comments apropos: "These phrases [added by Matthew] are not meant to blunt the reality of Jesus' mission of justice to the poor. Instead, they amplify an essential dimension of God's kingdom: to be gifted by God demands a change of heart."[12] Only those who have interiorized the Beatitudes in the deepest level of their being, in their "spirit" (26:41), can live up to their demand for a total conversion in their own lives as well as the commitment this demands to transform all social life through responsible action.

THE BEATITUDES AS WISDOM'S WAY

In Matthew, the mountain symbolizes God's presence (4:8; 14:23; 15:29; 17:1-9; 24:3-4). The disciples are those who have been to the mountain (28:16) to be baptized (28:19). Thus, at the beginning of the first of Jesus' discourses, Matthew narrates: "Seeing the crowds, he went up on the mountain, and when he sat down his disciples came to him" (5:1). In the past, disciples had come to their wisdom teachers who would sit dispensing their *makarisms* and teachings. On the mountain that is what Jesus did: "He opened his mouth and taught them" (5:2). What Matthew's Jesus taught in the Beatitudes[13] and the Sermon on the Mount which followed created a powerful impression on his listeners. When Jesus finished his teaching the crowd was astounded, "for he taught with authority (*exousía*)" (7:29). This is the first use of *exousía* in Matthew.

The last use of *exousía* is in the final commissioning of the gospel (28:18–20), again on a mountain (28:16), where Jesus ordered that his teachings be put into practice by his disciples "always, to the close of the age" (28:20). True disciples, authentic members of Jesus' household, are not those who have simply been to the mountain and read the words of Matthew's Jesus. Rather they are those who allow the horizon of their lives to interact with the horizon represented in those words. It does not suffice to have heard the teachings of Jesus; Matthew wants to make it clear that his house churches were to put them into practice if Jesus' wisdom would be reflected in their own (7:24–27). According to Dom Jacques Dupont:

> The spirit which animated their work was the spirit of the primitive Church. The Gospel tradition is not to be conceived as a mechanically exact repetition of the words of Jesus; it is a question of witness, of testimony. The words of Jesus are living, life-giving words; the early Church passed them on clothed also with its own life.[14]

The Beatitudes, which summarize the teachings of Matthew's Jesus, will make sense only if they come alive in the house church. Because the members of the house church are blessed (with *exousía*), they can live the Beatitudes. Living the blessings, the members become blessed. This blessing is grounded in the abiding presence of Jesus; it is expressed in continual fidelity to his teaching.

1. God's Reign for the Poor in Spirit

Matthew's favorite phrase indicating the reign of God was "kingdom of heaven" (*hē basileía tōn ouranōn*). Both John (3:2) and Jesus (4:17) said that it was "at hand" (*éggiken* [3:2; 4:17; 10:7]). While the meaning of the reign of God will be discussed more fully in the last chapter, we can say here that it exists personally in Jesus (3:1–17; 4:17; 10:7; 11:2–6; 13:16–17) and his message (4:23; 9:25) as well as spatially in the community gathered in his name (18:20; 28:20). Since the reign represents participation in the authority of the heavenly Father, those who are "poor in spirit" already share in the reality. In them the eschatological promise is fulfilled.

Matthew added "in spirit" (*tō pneúmati*) to Q to have his first beatitude read: "Blessed are the poor in spirit, for theirs is the kingdom of heaven" (5:3). On the one hand, we have rejected the notion that Matthew's is a "spiritualization"—in contrast to an embodiment—of the beatitude. However, another interpretation suggests the possibility that, in part, its wording meant to "water down" the original so as to avoid challenging his prospering house churches. This possibility has been put forward by Thomas Hoyt, Jr.:

> Matthew could have easily added "in spirit" in order to spiritualize the understanding of poverty so as not to offend his more affluent readers. Such a view becomes even more credible when we consider that "nowhere

does Matthew reveal any emphasis on poverty and ascetic rejection of wealth. . . ." If we take this view along with that of Professor Jeremias, who contends that "the Matthean tradition of the beatitudes was formulated in a church which was fighting against the Pharisaic temptation to self-righteousness," we may conclude the following: For Matthew's Church we are probably correct to detect that the source of his use of "in spirit" is entwined with his purpose, namely to set forth the requirements of discipleship to an affluent Church fighting against the Pharisaic temptation to self-righteousness.[15]

But are Hoyt and Jeremias correct in connecting Matthew's addition of "in spirit" to a rejection of Pharisaic self-righteousness? They are correct only if that self-righteousness is taken in the sense of 9:13, where Matthew's Jesus stressed mercy over sacrifice and concluded that his message about God's reign was not for the self-righteous but those who are sinners.

I have already shown that nowhere does Matthew canonize poverty. Instead his economic is one of household sharing of resources. Thus it would be contradictory for Matthew's Jesus to say (as does Luke), "blessed are the poor." Furthermore, since Matthew of all the gospel writers seems most versed in the Hebrew scriptures, it would be safe to say he knew the Hebrew mentality quite well, even if it is debated whether he was a Jew or a gentile. The Hebrew mentality did not "spiritualize" or "materialize"; it united the two. While one might be stressed at various times, the body and spirit in a person were not in opposition but somehow brought together in a unified whole.

If this is what "poor in spirit" does not imply, what is its meaning? While the exact phrase does not occur in the Old Testament, it can be found in Qumran's War Scroll. In the context of Qumran, as well as Isaiah 61:1ff, those who are poor or broken in spirit are the just. They are the *anawim*,[16] a community of individuals dedicated to realize God's will in their lives. In this sense Matthew's *"ptōchoi tō pneúmati"* are neither a particular social or economic class nor people suffering from actual physical want, but those disciples who hear Jesus' teachings about the will of God, understand them in the depths of their being, and obey them with their lives through justice.[17] Those who realize their own need to be reordered to God and who dedicate their lives to work for a reordering of God's creation are the poor in spirit. In the depth of their being, at the core of their lives, they proclaim whole-hearted dedication to God, to God's will, and to God's work. Matthew's vision of the reign of God given to the "poor in spirit" is predicated on relationships and resources being ordered in a holistic way that fulfills God's plan. Any group of persons dedicated to that will of God will inherit God's reign (6:10; 7:21).

From an understanding of the mentality behind Matthew's gospel, we can say, then, that the poor in spirit are those who work for the fulfillment of justice on behalf of those who are poor. Thus, the phrase "the poor in spirit" is a means neither of "spiritualizing" nor "watering down" the Beatitudes.

Matthew is not trying to avoid challenging his prospering house churches—rather he is challenging them to bring all aspects of their lives to bear upon the need to reorder their relationships and resources.

As early as Isaiah 61, the terms "poor" and "justice" were interconnected. With the Spirit of the Lord upon the Servant, the poor would be liberated and justice would reign. The Psalms of Solomon noted the connection between the reality of the poor and the demand for justice (Pss. Sol. 5:2, 11; 10:7; 15:1; 18:2). By the time of Qumran, the poor in spirit were described as those with knowledge of God who were committed to support the weak and broken.[18] They were the just.

Thus we discover two significant factors related to being "poor in spirit." First, by their knowledge of God, the "poor in spirit" recognize their own need for God. Recognizing their dependence on God, they become abandoned; they trust in God's loving care to meet their needs. Second, by their awareness of the Spirit of the Lord given over to them (see 27:50), they recognize their responsibility to image God by working to reorder creation. They abandon themselves to cooperate with God in renewing God's household on the earth. The passive dimension of abandonment or being "poor in spirit" involves the admission of one's need before God; the active dimension recognizes God's need to use humans to continue the divine creative activity of bringing about the original order envisioned by God.

These dimensions of being poor in spirit—recognizing one's need before God but also working to make the mystery of God's reign "take place" in one's world—have been clearly described as beatitudinal by Eduard Schweizer:

> Only to one who can hear the Beatitudes and hear in them his own lack do they make sense: such a person knows very well that being poor necessarily means being "poor in spirit." By his amendment of the phrase Matthew has made a most significant change—his version points out the danger of thinking that poverty is an honor. Poverty is not a virtue; it should no more be boasted about by the poor than despised (and upheld) by the rich. Matthew has been more insightful about what Jesus said than Luke, who merely translated Jesus' dictum literally into Greek. In Luke the statement becomes simply the legalism that in heaven all conditions are reversed, so that the poor become rich and the rich poor. Matthew, by contrast, has retained the point that this saying becomes true only when the mystery takes place that the Old Testament calls an event of the "Spirit."[19]

As the "Spirit" hovered over the waters in the beginning (Gen. 1:2), over Mary to bring forth Emmanuel (1:18), and over Jesus as he committed himself to God's will by fulfilling all justice (3:15), so now the poor in spirit let the Spirit guide them in *exousía* to heal and preach and teach in such a way that the new age (19:28) of God's reign can be proclaimed in word and deed.

2. Comfort to Those Who Mourn

The Old Testament context for the Beatitudes of Matthew is most fully articulated in Isaiah 61. Its underlying themes are expressed probably nowhere more clearly than in the wisdom offered in the second beatitude. Isaiah 61 touches the core of the human experience of bringing comfort to those who mourn, healing to the afflicted, glory over suffering, and resurrection in place of death:

> The Spirit of the Lord God is upon me, because the Lord has anointed me to bring good tidings to the afflicted; he has sent me to bind up the broken-hearted, to proclaim liberty to the captives, and the opening of the prison to those who are bound; to proclaim the year of the Lord's favor, and the day of vengeance of our God; to comfort all who mourn; to grant to those who mourn in Zion—to give them a garland instead of ashes, the oil of gladness instead of mourning, the mantle of praise instead of a faint spirit; that they may be called oaks of righteousness, the planting of the Lord, that he may be glorified [Is. 61:1-3].

In this passage parallels of "mourning" (*penthein* [5:4; 9:15]) and comfort (*parakalein* [2:18; 5:4]) reveal the depth of the human condition of brokenness and the eschatological promise of restoration. According to Bruce Malina the mourning/weeping correlation refers to behavior that recognizes and protests evil and injustice and the need to work for a reversal of some present form of status which oppresses: "Matthew discovers the evil requiring mourning behavior as the lack of righteousness, that is, proper interpersonal relations in the social body. Mourning/weeping behavior points to evil within the boundaries of the social body. . . ."[20] Thus an image of Jesus continually presented by Matthew is that of the person who fulfilled this beatitude of bringing comfort to those who mourned, healing to those who were afflicted in a generation gone astray.

At the end of the first narrative (3:1-4:25) Matthew adapted his Markan text to say: "And he went about all Galilee . . . healing every disease and every infirmity among the people. So his fame spread throughout all Syria, and they brought him all the sick, those afflicted with various diseases and pains, demoniacs, epileptics, and paralytics, and he healed them" (4:23-24).

The second narrative (8:1-9:38), which serves to prepare Matthew's readers for the subsequent discourse (10:1-11:1), chiastically arranges three miracle stories (8:1-17), three discipleship stories (8:18-27), two more miracle stories (8:28-9:8), three more discipleship stories (9:9-18), a final set of four miracle stories (9:20-34).[21] The narrative ends with almost the same phraseology used to conclude the first narrative. However Matthew unites Mark and Q to explain: "When he saw the crowds, he had compassion for them, because they were harassed and helpless, like sheep without a shepherd. Then he said to his disciples, 'The harvest is plentiful, but the laborers are few; pray therefore the

Lord of the harvest to send out laborers into his harvest' " (9:36–38). With God's *exousía* in him, Matthew's Jesus was able to proclaim jubilee, the reordering of a broken world. He "healed all who were sick" (8:16), thus fulfilling Isaiah's prophecy "he took our infirmities and bore our diseases" (8:17 [Is. 53:4]). Now, realizing the sheep without a shepherd needed restoration, he, the "Lord of the harvest,"[22] the head of the household (which included the harvest), shared his *exousía* with the disciples (10:1).

The expectation of comfort to those in mourning nourished the hopes of the Israelites in exile. Restoration of broken relationships and alienated resources was envisioned as a messianic blessing. Until that restoration would occur (which included moving from landlessness to landedness as much as from other forms of brokenness to a place of consolation), Israel would not be "comforted"; instead it would be in mourning or lamentation.

In the Lamentations of Jeremiah, the mourning of Israel was likened to that of a lonely city and to a widow with none to comfort her (Lam. 1:1–2). "Judah has gone into exile because of affliction" (Lam. 1:3). Even the "roads to Zion mourn" (Lam. 1:4); her children have gone away (Lam. 1:5). Jerusalem remembers "in the days of her affliction and bitterness" (Lam. 1:7) and has no comforter (Lam. 1:9).

While landless Israel in its sixth-century exile was "not comforted," prophets like Hosea envisioned a day of restoration. Second Isaiah expressed the reversal of Israel's exile from its land in terms of comfort coming to the people (Is. 40:1–2). "For the Lord has comforted his people, and will have compassion on his afflicted" (Is. 49:13).

Continually Matthew presents Jesus as the one who had compassion on the crowds (9:36; 14:14; 15:32; 18:27; 20:34), especially when they experienced need and forms of brokenness (i.e., "mourning"). This compassion of Jesus— a prefiguring of the reign of God—was also to be the pattern in the life of the disciple as well (18:33). Matthew envisioned Jesus and his community healing sickness and disease of "every kind" with *exousía*. By entering into the mourning to the point of death (26:38; 27:46–50), Jesus was able to empower the new Israel to restoration. The members of the house churches were to confront the power of sin and death by doing as Jesus had done.

3. The Land for the Meek

Before discussing what Matthew meant by "the meek" in the third beatitude, it is necessary to discuss what the terms "land" and "earth" meant in Matthew's context. In this beatitude, which is unique to Matthew (and which may have been a later addition), *gē* (for the Hebrew *'erets*) is used to speak of the "earth." He uses it in the same sense as "heaven and earth," the two places where God's reign must be manifest.

Scripturally speaking, "earth" is another word for "land."[23] While "earth" and "land" may be the same scripturally, at the time of Jesus as well as our own, they had different social implications. When people talked about "earth," they were not speaking about something that was owned; all was God's. The earth was the Lord's; it was God's possession,[24] part of God's household. Consequently it was to be under the authority of the divine House-holder. As Walter Brueggemann notes, "In affirming that the earth belongs only to God, Israel's faith means to deny ultimate ownership to any other."[25] Brueggemann's whole thrust implies that, while God might be acknowledged as the House-orderer who controlled the earth (Ps. 24:1), the Israelites, especially after the Exodus, gradually came to distinguish between the earth as God's and the land as theirs.

By the time of Jesus, under the Roman occupation, the possession of land in its figurative sense and material sense was a key source of conflict. To be sheltered from taxes, liquid assets were quickly converted into land. As a result riches were often identified with land. In a stratified society where wealth was not accumulated, people were rich because they had inherited land and amassed it. I noted in chapter 1 that, with urbanization at the time of Mat-thew's Jesus, these landowners were often absent from their households (21:33–46; 22:5; 25:14–30; see 20:1–16).

Most household land was passed from one family generation to the next. Land constituted the basis of one's "possessions," as in the case of the young man who "had great possessions" (19:22). "Since land was ancestrally owned," Walter Wink has noted, "the wealthy had to find powerful means by which to pry tracts loose from their owners. One way was cash; the more frequent was the foreclosure for debt."[26] Not surprisingly, because the records for such foreclosures and other forms of indebtedness were kept in the temple treasury, the first act of the Zealots at the outbreak of the Jewish War in 66 CE, according to Josephus, was to burn the temple treasury to destroy the records. Since Brueggemann has noted that "every settlement of the land question must be a conflictive one,"[27] it is not surprising that much violence during the Jewish-Roman War was based on conflicting land claims.

Possessions, however, not only pertained to land or property; ultimately in this stratified society, they were grounded in power and prestige. Thus, when Jesus came into Jerusalem, the center of the world, he was "entering" into a constellation of possible personal and political conflicts related to power, possessions, and prestige. While he came in a spirit of meekness (21:5; Zech. 9:9), those with economic and religious power (the "landed") perceived it as a threat to their power base. They became indignant (21:15). Consequently, they concluded, force would have to be used to silence him (see 21:45–46). Jesus' teachings threatened all their land arrangements—their possessions, power, and prestige—for they owed their possession of much of their "land" to the Roman occupiers, and Jesus' words and ministry were perceived to be undermining that Roman system from which they benefited.

In his book *The Land*, Walter Brueggemann explains how Jesus called into question the traditional house-ordering of that system, along with those norms and values which served to enfranchise and disenfranchise. He writes:

Jesus and his gospel are rightly received as a threat. The new enlandment is a threat to the old arrangements. And he evokes resistance from those who wish to preserve how it had been. A proper understanding requires that we discern the socio-political, economic issues in the religious resistance which forms against him. A threat to landholders mobilizes his opponents, land here understood both in literal and symbolic senses.[28]

Land in its forms of power, possessions, and prestige can be approached in one of two ways: meekness, which grounds all life in God, or violence, which bases all life in greed and obsession for more power. In a society whose great ones made their authority felt (*katexousiázein* [20:25]) through control of the literal and symbolic land, the *exousía* of heaven and earth given Jesus' followers (28:18) was to be exercised differently. Rather than maintaining the existing order, a new order was to be proclaimed.

Rather than in greed or violence, the new order would be grounded in an attitude of *praüs* or meekness (5:5; 11:29; 21:5; see 18:1-10; 19:13-15; 20:20-28; 23:8-12). Of all the gospel writers only Matthew used the Greek term *praüs*. It expresses an attitude which moves people to desire to order their lives and all reality not according to individualistic and self-seeking human plans but according to God's will.[29] Those who appropriated the teachings of the Wisdom figure would come to learn the way of meekness (11:29) and use the authority over the land given them (28:18) in the same way as their master (21:5). Thus, according to Bauer, *praüs* was to be a quality "required of church leaders."[30] This attitude of meekness would not prompt them to seek to be first or to be served but to serve, even to the point of laying down their own lives (20:27-28).

The attitude of *praüs* toward the *gē* envisioned by Matthew's Jesus disrupted the accepted ideology of society that was beginning to penetrate Matthew's households.[31] What had happened to Israel throughout its history was now occurring in Matthew's house churches: the land was becoming an end in itself. The ordering of the house, its economics, was being used to give more to those who already had. Consequently the landless were being kept out. While some houses were prosperous, many people were homeless. The landed and the housed lived in the midst of landlessness and homelessness. We have already seen that the first century, like ours, had its share of street people. Malina has shown that much of this division between the wealthy and the poor involved exploitàtion and injustice.[32] Thus in a situation wherein some were landed and housed at the expense of others, reciprocity was violated. In contrast to this violence, Matthew's Jesus offered another vision: a reordering of such violence to create households of the *praüs* which would be open to all.

Psalm 37:11, the foundation for this beatitude, said the meek would inherit the land. The Didache, which some believe first appeared in house churches in Antioch between 50-70,[33] urged the disciples: "Be meek, since the meek will inherit the earth (land)." While it may be debated about how this passage reached the redaction of Matthew as we have it now,[34] the fact that Matthew wrote to his house churches less than a score of years later and quite probably at the same place—Antioch—makes this beatitude all the more relevant to conflictual situations, especially those related to various claims about power, possessions, and prestige, i.e., "wealth."

4. Satisfaction from Hungering and Thirsting for Justice

"What characterizes all the wealthy," Bruce Malina has written, "is their lack of contentment, of satisfaction—and this at the expense of others."[35] An understanding of this condition of human experience is at the heart of this fourth beatitude.

Wealth was often seen in terms of exploitation or acquiring resources at the expense of others. This indicates something significant about the human appetite for more. It also indicates something about justice and injustice.

From an economic perspective, hunger and thirst constitute the basic needs or appetites of the human race. In the desert, without productive land, Israel depended on Yahweh to meet all of its basic needs, especially food and water. Despite its dependence on God in the desert, Israel was not satisfied with the provisions offered. Wanting to control the land rather than depend on Yahweh who had promised always to be with it (Ex. 3:12), Israel grumbled. "Would that we had died by the hand of the Lord in the land of Egypt, when we sat by the fleshpots and ate bread to the full," they said to Moses and Aaron, "for you have brought us out into this wilderness to kill this whole assembly with hunger" (Ex. 16:3).

As was stated above, the desert and wilderness symbolized places of conflict, testing, and trial. Led by Yahweh into the desert to make Israel aware of its need for God to provide all resources, the people sought their security in resources even if they were identified with enslavement. Despite the people's grumbling, God showed fidelity to the promise to be with them not only spiritually but economically as well. Life's basic resource of food would be provided: "Behold, I will rain bread from heaven for you; and the people shall go out and gather a day's portion every day, that I may prove them, whether they will walk in my law or not" (Ex. 16:4).

During the period when Israel was homeless it was invited to trust that Yahweh would meet its basic need for daily bread. The sign of its trust would be a concrete manifestation of its response to God's word; Israel would not hoard what was given: "And Moses said to them, 'Let no man leave any of it till the morning' " (Ex. 16:19). Called to be satisfied that it was resourced in its needs rather than its wants, Israel failed the test. It was not satisfied with enough (Ex. 16:17); it wanted more: "But they did not listen to Moses; some left part of it till the morning, and it bred worms and became foul" (Ex. 16:20).

The Deuteronomist's recalling of Israel's experience in the desert (especially in chapters 6 and 8) was used as a figure for the temptation facing Matthew's house churches: the tendency to store up for themselves rather than to prove their trust in God by sharing with others in need. They were tempted to forget then the basic moral principle which the development economist Denis Goulet has articulated so well today: to seek just enough in order to be more; to seek just enough resources in order to be more human in relationships.[36] Thus Matthew's Jesus warned his households as Yahweh earlier warned the Israelites (Ex. 16:20): "Do not lay up for yourselves treasures on earth, where moth and rust consume and where thieves break in and steal, but lay up for yourselves treasures in heaven, where neither moth nor rust consumes and where thieves do not break in and steal" (6:19-20).

Another basic need every economic system must meet is that for water. In the desert—a symbol of land that is needed—Israel experienced thirst: "there was no water for the people to drink" (Ex. 17:1). Rather than being meek in this kind of "land," secure in Yahweh's presence, the people let the land control them; they became violent: "Therefore the people found fault with Moses, and said, 'Give us water to drink' " (Ex. 17:2). Again, the Israelites' "treasure" was in trying to resource themselves rather than in trusting God's promise to be with them in their need. Despite their violence, the mercy of God again was revealed:

And the Lord said to Moses, "Pass on before the people, taking with you some of the elders of Israel; and take in your hand the rod with which you struck the Nile, and . . . strike the rock, and water will come out of it, that the people may drink." And Moses did so, in the sight of the elders of Israel. And he called the name of the place Massah and Meribah, because of the faultfinding of the children of Israel, and because they put the Lord to the proof by saying, "Is the Lord among us or not?" [Ex. 17: 5-7].

The presence of the Lord is revealed in the provision of resources. When people find their satisfaction in sharing rather than hoarding, when they trust in God's promised salvific presence, they will discover their needs being met. Thus Matthew adapted the Q source to have Jesus invite the members of his house churches to hunger and thirst for the ultimate justice of God—salvation—and to live out that salvation—if ever their satisfaction would be realized. They were to stop running after material things (especially things related to drink and food) and were to satisfy their hunger and thirst by seeking first God's justice, God's saving power, which alone could satisfy (6:33). Along with this they were to make certain that their search for God did not involve the exploitation of the poor around them. In their never-ending search for God, they would never be satisfied until they came to know God; however this knowledge of God would be inseparable from the promotion of justice within the household. The connection between knowing God and doing justice could not be made better anywhere than in the oracle of Jeremiah:

Woe to him who builds his house by unrighteousess,
   and his upper rooms by injustice;

who makes his neighbor serve him for nothing,
and does not give him his wages;
who says, "I will build myself a great house
with spacious rooms,"
and cuts out windows for it,
paneling it with cedar,
and painting it with vermilion.
Do you think you are a king
because you compete in cedar?
Did not your father eat and drink
and do justice and righteousness?
Then it went well with him.
He judged the cause of the poor and needy;
then it was well.
Is not this to know me?
says the Lord [Jer. 22:13-16].

In this sense of knowing God as the fulfillment of justice on behalf of the poor, the fourth beatitude summarizes the previous three. The first four beatitudes form a distinct unit. Like the second unit of four beatitudes, these also end with *dikaiosýnē* or justice.[37] Matthew's Jesus proclaims those blessed who hunger and thirst for justice, who order their relationships with God and each other according to God's saving plan. This justice demands that one's ultimate concern must rest in that trust which finds all needs resourced by maintaining a relationship with the divine House-orderer. Only in God and the treasured experience of God's saving reign will one's deepest satisfaction be realized. That salvation, that justice, must be sought before all else. When found, it is expressed in mercy.

5. A New Reciprocity in Mercy

Like the first four beatitudes, each *makarism* in the second group reveals dimensions of justice. While the first four underscore the justice which is based on "knowing" God, these four beatitudes revolve around non-exploitation of the poor, or "doing" justice. This holds true especially for the fifth beatitude: "Blessed are the merciful, for they shall obtain mercy" (5:7). Its rendition here is unique to Matthew.

Especially in the Septuagint (the Greek Old Testament) there are strong links between justice and mercy. C. H. Dodd noted that, in the Septuagint, two aspects of justice or *tsedeq* "are polarized into *dikaiosýnē* and *eleēmosýnē*. In place of the comprehensive virtue of *tsedâqâh*, we have justice on the one hand, mercy on the other."[38] In the Hebrew scriptures there are 115 occurrences of the noun *tsedeq* (justice), 158 of another noun, *tsedâqâh* (almsgiving), and 208 of the adjective *tsâdaq* (just). In the Septuagint *tsedeq* was translated as *dikaiosýnē* (justice), *tsedâqâh* as *eleēmosýnē* or *éleos* (mercy), and *tsaddiq* as *díkaios* (just). Although frequently used in the Septuagint, the Greek word *eleēmōn*, or merciful, occurs only once in the gospels—here in Matthew's fifth beatitude.

The Greek word for mercy (*éleos*) corresponds to the Aramaic *hisda*, which means an integrated or holistic state of mind characterized by understanding, compassion, and justice. Merciful people act out of their own integrity by being open to the needs of those around them.

According to Eduard Schweizer, "For Matthew, mercy is the focal point of Jesus' message, which shows what it means to fulfill the Law (see the discussion of 5:17-20; 9:13; 12:7; 25:31-46). Mercy has been forgotten by the Pharisees (23:23; unique to Matthew)."[39] Jesus' way of fulfilling the Law and the prophets (5:17-20) was the way of justice (3:15); but mercy fulfills justice (9:13; 12:7). Psalm 37, which considers the meek and violent ways people deal with their resources, says that the just show mercy (see Ps. 37:21).

Householders basing their lives on justice manifest compassion and mercy (see 18:21-35). The First Book of Kings declared: "Behold now, we have heard that the kings of the house of Israel are merciful" (1 Kgs. 20:31). The new house of Israel and all its members in the household churches must be equally merciful. According to Marcus Borg, mercy was so central to Jesus' teaching that it represented a totally reordered structure and way of holiness.[40]

When Matthew uses *éleos* in 9:13 (the meal at Jesus' house) and 12:7 (the disciples eating the needed grain on the Sabbath) he quotes Hosea 6:6: "For I desire steadfast love [*hesed* in Hebrew; *éleos* in Greek] and not sacrifice, the knowledge of God, rather than burnt offerings." In the previous section I discussed the Jeremiah passage that links "knowing" God and "doing" justice; Matthew's use of the Hosea passage makes the link even stronger. Earlier Hosea had bemoaned the fact that there was no compassion (*hesed*) or knowledge in the land (4:1). According to José Miranda, "The synonymy between to-know-Yahweh and interhuman justice is here so taken for granted that this prophet of the early eighth century B.C. includes in his testimony all the previous centuries of Israelite tradition."[41] Mercy and compassion are the Matthean response to meeting needs (*chreía* [9:12; see 25:31-46]).

In Matthew mercy and compassion are invariably used in the context of basic needs being met and in the context of a meal (which, in turn, has eucharistic overtones). Mercy is revealed when Jesus includes outsiders at table (9:13) and when the hunger of the disciples is satisfied by sharing in the grain resources available by the roadside (12:7). Similarly, in both accounts of the multiplication of the loaves (14:14; 15:32), the realization of the needs of the crowds triggered compassion in Jesus. The depths of his heart—his "guts"— were moved with mercy or pity (*splagchnízomai*) and he fed them, just as it moved him to heal the sick (9:36; 20:34).

Social anthropologist Marshall Sahlins has shown that, in a traditional society, compassion was required of people in the household or the village inasmuch as kinsfolk were expected to show mercy in face of needs. But, he adds, "the quality of mercy is strained in peripheral sectors, strained by kinship distance, so is less likely" with those beyond one's *oikía* or village.[42] For Matthew's Jesus, the house churches were to be filled with people showing the same compassion (18:27). However, this compassion was not to be limited to the members of the house church or the gathering; it was to be universally ordered to the *oikouméne*, to the crowds.

At the sight of the crowds in need of bread, Matthew shows Jesus' heart moved, *splachnízomai*. However, rather than responding to their needs directly; Matthew's Jesus says to the disciples, "you give them something to eat" (14:16). This phrase was not an invitation; it expressed a command to meet evident needs. Giving food to the hungry (25:35, 42) and to those who asked (see 5:42) was a specific application of Jesus' command. Jesus' command to the disciples to feed the crowd implied that they had the power to do so. This power was given the apostles earlier (10:1). Thus Matthew's Jesus was not out of order in expecting them to feed the masses, just as had been done in the desert. Joseph A. Grassi notes:

> This is an authentic command of Jesus, and was interpreted as such by the early church. The words "you gave me to eat" in 25:35 are an exact counterpart of Jesus' command. The only difference is the substitution of "me" for "them." In Matthew 25:44, lack of response to the hungry, thirsty, naked, stranger, sick and prisoner is all put together as "not serving you."[43]

The meal at Jesus' house, the eating of the grain, and the multiplication of loaves seem to indicate that mercy in the form of serving needs reveals the heart of table fellowship. Table fellowship, Matthew's Jesus wanted to remind his divided community of Hellenists and Judaizers, demanded reconciliation. The sign of this reconciliation and union of tablemates within the house churches would find its peak expression in the eucharistic meal itself.

The early community was divided in its interpretation of the Law and these tensions would naturally arise in the households when the members came to celebrate eucharist. Jerome Murphy-O'Connor reminds us, in discussing "House Churches and the Eucharist," that private houses were the first centers for church life:

> Christianity in the first century A.D. and for long afterwards, did not have the status of recognized religion, so there was no question of a public meeting place, such as Jewish synagogues. Hence, use had to be made of the only facilities available, namely, the dwellings of families that had become Christian.[44]

The situation among the Matthean house churches reflected tensions between Judaizers and Hellenizers as well as the rich and the poor. Household relations often fell short of mercy. Not surprisingly, therefore, Matthew discusses the eucharist in the context of both mercy to tablemates and the household: "He said, 'Go into the city to such a one, and say to him, "The Teacher says, My time is at hand; I will keep the passover at your house with my disciples" ' " (26:18).[45] Furthermore, he adapts Mark to link the eucharist (not baptism) to the forgiveness of sins (26:28). The eucharist in Matthew's house churches must reflect reconciliation and forgiveness among brothers and sisters, not tension and betrayal among estranged tablemates.

For Matthew, the eucharist shared in house churches must fulfill mercy and justice. There can be no repetition of the rejection of tablemates as Judas betrayed Jesus (26:20–25). Rather table companionship should be celebrated by those who have compassion: who invite the stranger, who do not betray each other, who have been reconciled, and who share their resources with those in need, whether those resources are material, spiritual, or relational. In the eucharist, those who are full of this mercy will receive it.

6. The Vision of God Grounded in Purity of Heart

So far, scripture scholars have been able to offer little satisfactory interpretation for this uniquely Matthean beatitude. The purity of heart leading to the vision of God seems more akin to an ethical attitude than an interior disposition (although the two can never be entirely separated). The generation with pure hearts, sinless hands, truth on their lips, and free of deceit can ascend the Lord's mountain and stand in the holy place. There, Psalm 24 says, they can seek the face of the God of Jacob (Ps. 24:3–6).

Whether a generation or a household has purity of heart can be determined from discovering the source of their priorities and preoccupations. These represent the biblical meaning of "treasures"—as in "where your treasure is, there will your heart be also" (6:21). If the priorities and preoccupations are earth-bound, seeing God will be impossible. If life on earth is ultimately preoccupied with God, then the search for the face of God will be blessed.

This beatitude is not the only reference connecting the "heart" with "seeing." In the phrase immediately following the treasure verse (6:22–23) indicating where one's heart will be (6:21), Matthew's Jesus speaks of the eye being good, sound, or single (*haplous*) rather than evil (the "evil eye"), unsound, or divided (*ponerós*). While *haplous* has traditionally been translated as simple or whole, it has an ethical connotation meaning to be generous or ready for sacrifice.[46] In the same way, *ponerós* has not only been translated as one who is wicked or does evil, but also is a social and political term with an ethical meaning indicating covetousness or avariciousness.[47] Thus, given the social dimension of the gospel and Matthew's Beatitudes, it would seem that purity of heart can be determined negatively as the absence of stinginess or greed and positively as the presence of generosity and openness to those in need. Whether the members of Matthew's house churches will see God will be contingent on whether their economic or ordering of the house alleviates the needs of others.

This meaning for purity of heart becomes clearer when one realizes that, immediately after distinguishing between the eye that is *haplous* or *ponerós*, Matthew's Jesus says, "No one can serve two masters; for either he will hate the one and love the other, or he will be devoted to the one and despise the other. You cannot serve God and mammon" (6:24). Mammon represented the peak of idolatry; it was the essence of greed and stinginess (i.e., *ponerós*). Those with hearts centered on themselves and their mammon serve (are "given over" to) avariciousness and covetousness. Conversely, people whose hearts are centered on God reflect openness and generosity in the way they relate to each other.

In the Old Testament, besides Psalm 24, several passages treating purity or cleanness of heart do so in the context of just behavior toward one's neighbor (Gen. 20:5; Dt. 6:5–19; Ps. 15:2; Is. 33:15). The last two of the ten commandments (Ex. 20:17) address intentions or attitudes that undermine the neighbor: "coveting" or being given over to the neighbor's spouse and/or possessions.

Matthew made the conventional association between "seeing" and "heart" not only in this beatitude, and in the section from the sermon on "treasure," but also when he noted Jesus saying that all those who *looked* lustfully at a woman coveted her and thereby committed adultery in their *hearts* (5:28).[48] Equally, from the original connection between the ninth and tenth commandments, as well as the context of this pericope from Matthew's gospel, it becomes clear that those who looked upon their neighbor's possessions covetously possessed divided hearts; they could not see God.[49]

In contrast, those experiencing God's presence (i.e., "seeing God") would manifest the authenticity of that experience in their generosity toward those in need. Meeting the needs of others reveals integrity of heart. In the final judgment, those who have demonstrated this kind of integrity—which is justice toward those in need—will see God (25:31–46).

7. Peacemakers Called God's Children

Matthew's Jesus summarized the content of his gospel's message in the gift-word of peace that should be shared with all houses which hear the gospel and from which the gospel is preached (10:12, 13). This peace, however, was not a passive peace which accepted disorder. Rather it resulted from reordering relationships and resources within the households in a manner that reflected that eschatological condition where justice and peace would meet (Ps. 85:11). Because Jesus' message of peace was the expression of justice in unjust situations, it brought both reconciliation (18:1–35) and division (10:34) in households.

Peace-making would create a new kind of household wherein people, acting as sisters and brothers, would be called God's children. Peacemakers not only proclaim peace with their lips; they put into practice Jesus' teachings. Since the heart of that message reveals Jesus' commitment to the fulfillment of the Law and the prophets, or the covenant of justice (3:15; 5:17–20), those imitating Jesus in this way also will receive the beatitude of being called children of God as was he (3:17; 17:5). The resources of one's whole household should be made available to those who come with the gift of peace (10:11–15).

The seventh beatitude is the only place in the entire Bible where the word "peacemaker" appears. It refers to those who not only possess peace, but "make peace" (a rabbinic expression). According to Eduard Schweizer:

In the Judaism of the period, the call to make peace is as important as the law of love in the New Testament. Shortly after the destruction of the Temple, Johanan ben Zakkai, the foremost rabbi of that period, promised the salvation that could formerly be obtained only by a sacrifice at the altar to whoever made peace.[50]

Matthew's Jesus reflects this rabbinic teaching to the members of Matthew's households when he predicates altar sacrifice on making peace with one's enemies: "So if you are offering your gift at the altar, and there remember that your brother has something against you, leave your gift there before the altar and go; first be reconciled to your brother, and then come and offer your gift" (5:23-24).

The passage in Matthew—which is unique to him—is another indication of division within Matthew's audience. Filson has noted that irreconciliation within "the apostolic churches was not unconnected with the division of the Christians of a city into house churches."[51] Matthew's community, like that of Paul at Corinth, argued about the interpretation of the Law as well as about the right-ordering of relationships and resources. An analysis of chapter 18, which has been called Matthew's advice to his divided community,[52] indicates causes and manifestations of this irreconciliation. Greed and power were at play as house members vied with each other about being the greatest (18:1-4). Poor example was being given converts, while others were misled (18:5-9). Some were lost to the church, like straying sheep (18:10-14). This "going astray" might not have been limited to this or that slave or house member joining another *koina* and converting to its gods. Since entire households may have converted, Abraham J. Malherbe notes that not only individuals or groups but entire congregations "could also be led astray."[53] All these divisive realities appear between the lines of Matthew's chapter 18. Given such a situation of conflict, a new way of making peace was necessary.

As I showed elsewhere,[54] the rest of chapter 18 outlines a uniquely Matthean way of working for peace within his house churches. However, given what I have said thus far about this section being part of Matthew's unique *haustafel* (17:24-18:35), we can call this the peace-plank for Matthew's *haustafel*:

I. Avoid the situations that create tensions
and scandal (18:1-10:11).

II. Make peace by the following steps:
   A. Affirm the significance of each member (18:12-14)
   in a way wherein the least will feel equally
   important.
   B. Follow a model for settling confrontation:
      1. Correction among members one-on-one (18:15).
      2. Correction with "one or two others" (18:16).
      3. Correction within the house church (18:17).

III. The power of prayer among gathered, united people (18:19-20).

According to Leland White, Matthew's threefold approach to settling conflicts within the house church indicates the lack of a formal, hierarchical/ patriarchal power structure and the prohibition against recognizing rank or achievement within the community. The Matthean peace-procedures

reflect a pattern of organization that places minimal reliance on formally distinguished roles. *When we ask who governs Matthew's community, who enforces its norms, we find no evidence that such functions have been assigned to any individual or group.* The community apparently functions in the ad hoc fashion of an extended family.[55]

This extended family is no longer one reflecting a patriarchal order of domination but a collegial model of greater egalitarianism.

Immediately following his stating the steps to correction within the community, Matthew's Jesus indicated that the extended family constituting the house churches themselves had the very power of heaven to bind and to loose that had been given Peter (16:19): "Truly, I say to you, whatever you bind on earth shall be bound in heaven, and whatever you loose on earth shall be loosed in heaven" (18:18). The goal of reconciliation and peace demands that opposing factions come to agreement. Thus, Matthew's Jesus added, "Again I say to you, if two of you agree on earth about anything they ask, it will be done for them by my Father in heaven. For where two or three are gathered in my name, there am I in the midst of them" (18:19-20).

The final section of chapter 18 declares that unity and peace within the community will be achieved when forgiveness is extended on all levels (18:21-35). Forgiveness involves the relief of material as well as relational indebtedness. Debt-forgiveness (6:12) and peace-making both are demands for entrance as children into God's household. That entrance into the reign of God is contingent on debt-forgiveness and peace-making efforts made on earth.

8. God's Reign for Those Persecuted for Justice' Sake

Matthew's last beatitude actually contains two *makarisms*, while Luke's contains only one. The first part, following the pattern of the previous seven beatitudes, refers to "*those* who are persecuted" for justice' sake (5:10). The last part (actually a ninth beatitude) is addressed to "*you* when men revile you and persecute you and utter all kinds of evil against you falsely on my account" (5:11). The "you" refers to Matthew's house church. This "you" also must be connected to the following verses about being the salt of the earth and the light of the world (5:13-14) which must shine in the house. Those verses conclude with the admonition: "Let your light so shine before men, that they may see your good works and give glory to your Father who is in in heaven" (5:15).

We saw earlier, in chapter 2, that this passage urges good works to be the form of submission the Christians would manifest in face of their persecutors.

Since this passage implies the community's incorporation of the other beatitudes in their lives, all the beatitudes might be considered an extended moral commentary on the need for good works, i.e., justice, that must be practiced in Matthew's house churches for all, especially persecutors and nonbelievers, to see.

The earlier persecution of the Christians by the Jews was continuing after their expulsion from the house-synagogues. But now the persecution was not felt from Jews alone; it came from members of the community and from wider society. Matthew changed the person from "them" to "you" to address the concrete reality of persecution being realized in his community. As Jesus, the just one (27:43), was persecuted for justice' sake and was blessed in the resurrection, so a blessing will come to those who are persecuted in the cause of justice. Whenever there are unjust situations, working for reordered relationships by practicing mercy, purity of heart, and peace-making can lead to rejection and persecution.

For many years scholars have noted the images related to tensions and persecution in the first gospel. Both Christian and non-Christian sources indicate that, at the time of its writing, various forms of persecution were used against religious enemies: death, floggings, imprisonment, exclusion from the synagogues, as well as social and economic reprisals such as boycotts of goods, the imposition of fines, and refusal to hire those professing other beliefs.[56]

Douglas Hare has shown that the the Jewish persecution of Christians underlies many of the passages in Matthew's gospel (10:16–33; 22:6; 23:29–39), including this beatitude (5:10–12). He lists the following as causes for the persecution: Christians lived in a manner which reflected justice (5:10); they were advocating the cause of Jesus (5:11); and they were living the lifestyle of the prophet (5:12).[57] However, even though the pain of past harsh rejection remained, Hare may be making too much of the Jewish persecution, which had generally subsided by the time of the final redaction of the first gospel. While definitely alluding to this persecution, Matthew does not limit his narrative to the past, but seems to be using this passage for *any* persecution that results from preaching the gospel of justice.

In Matthew's approach justice, the cause of Jesus, and prophecy intertwine: "for so men persecuted the prophets who were before you" (5:12). The themes underlie Jesus' diatribe against the scribes and Pharisees where Jesus scores them for killing and crucifying, scourging and persecuting those just prophets whom he sent (23:34–36). Such persecution, John Meier writes, should be expected by Christians:

> The Christians of Mt's church probably saw themselves symbolized in the suffering just man of the OT (cf. Ps 22; Wis 5). The disciples of Jesus who practice justice, mercy, and peacemaking must expect the same fate, the fate of the persecuted prophets. This is made explicit in the last beatitude . . . by switching to the second person plural. . . .[58]

Justice was at the heart of the prophets' message. The United Church of Christ *Working Paper on the Economy* saw the prophets evaluating justice in institutions according to God's household rules.[59] Since Jesus came to fulfill the Law and the prophets (5:17), justice was at the heart of his message as well. Jesus not only fulfilled the role of the prophets who proclaimed justice; he also sent prophets to promote justice. Identifying with his cause of justice they too could expect persecution. Rather than being threatened by its possibility, they could rejoice that persecution itself would reveal their fulfillment, with Jesus, of the heavenly Father's will. Those receiving these disciples and their message would receive Jesus; those receiving a prophet would receive a prophet's reward; those receiving the just would receive the reward of the just. Finally, "whoever gives to one of these little ones even a cup of cold water because he is a disciple, truly, I say to you, he shall not lose his reward" (10:40-43).

The reward promised to those who reorder their relationships to each other and their resources (19:29a-b) and who live the Beatitudes (5:1-15) will be "a hundredfold, [and they] will inherit eternal life" (19:29c). While Matthew's Jesus does not assure this reward for this life (as Mark promised [Mk. 10:30]), he does assure his house churches: " . . . your reward is great in heaven" (5:12).

When one's spirituality manifests adherence to the ethical posture outlined in the first seven beatitudes, two things are assured by Matthew's Jesus: persecution in this life and a reward in heaven. But the Beatitudes manifest those good works (5:15) that hopefully will be the form of submission that will even win over persecutors so that they too can begin to experience this reign of God.

In summary we can say that those who justly reorder their relationships and resources are those whose households will ultimately be blessed. The ultimate reward or blessing for such justice will be the reign of God itself (5:10).

7

The Sermon on the Mount:
Building a House on the Rock of Justice

THE DIVINE HOUSEHOLDER AND THE HOUSE OF ISRAEL

This chapter will discuss Matthew's connection between *oikía/oikos* and *krísis/dikaiosýnē*, especially as Matthew uses these words for "house" and "justice" in the Sermon on the Mount.[1] However, before we investigate the Matthean New Testament linkage of these terms it will be good to review how these two themes can be found throughout the entire Old Testament.

Psalm 24 begins, "The earth is the Lord's and the fullness thereof, the world and those who dwell therein; for he has founded it upon the seas, and established it upon the rivers" (Ps. 24:1-2). As Psalm 24 indicates, the Hebrews envisioned God's role in creating the world to be like that of a builder of a house (see Ps. 127:1) in possession of the entire world (Ex. 19:5; Ps. 89:12; 95:5), which contained all households. In this sense, the Hebrews considered themselves God's special household within the household of the universe—all ordered religiously and economically by the divine Householder. Indeed, more than any of the Synoptics, when describing God's reign in parable form, Matthew has Jesus refer to God's reign as that of a householder (13:27, 52; 20:1, 11; 21:33; 24:43). This metaphor of God as divine Householder (Douglas Meeks and the United Church of Christ document on the U.S. economy use the term "Divine Economist") can be considered a primary metaphor throughout the scriptures. As the early United Church of Christ study paper stated:

> As Economist, God brings into being and seeks to maintain the house-
> hold of Israel and the church, the household of the nations, and, ulti-
> mately, the household of all creation. These households constantly are
> threatened by chaos, sin, evil, and death. A great portion of the Bible
> depicts ways in which God dwells in the creation and works as House-
> builder, Householder, and Homemaker to give all people access to what it
> takes to live and to live abundantly. God's economy, God's economic
> work, is to make the creation into a home.[2]

In the Septuagint, the Greek word for the "inhabited world" of creation used by the psalmist is *oikouméné*, a word linked with *oikos/oikía* or house (see Ps. 19:4). *Oikouméné* referred to the inhabited world of creation (a geographic reference) in extra-biblical Greek sources also. Gradually it took on cultural as well as political and economic overtones by being equated with the Roman Empire itself. By the time of the Principate, *oikouméné* referred to the entire socio-economic structure of the Roman Empire.[3] This was the "whole world" which Matthew alone uses in the context of where the gospel must be preached (24:14) by those of Jesus' household (10:25), those of *his* church (16:18).

Until the seventeenth century any discussion of "economics" presupposed God to be the householder or ultimate owner of the world. Humans acted merely as stewards (*economoi*). Since order characterized God's creation, humans were not to deviate from that order. "Justice" determined that orderly relationship of humans to God and to each other vis-à-vis the resources of the earth.

This divine ordering or justice underlies the entire creation myth. Persons, resources, and their interrelations are to reflect God and God's plan for the world. *Persons* made in the divine image (Gen. 1:26, 27) as male and female enter into *relationship* with God and each other by being blessed (Gen. 1:28). This blessing empowered male and female to have access to all the *resources* so that they could "be fruitful and multiply, and fill the earth and subdue it; and have dominion over the fish of the sea and over the birds of the air and over every living thing that moves upon the earth" (Gen. 1:28).

Male and female were created to be in relation to the resources of the earth (*'erets* [Gen. 1:2]) in such a way that their co-creative activity would be blessed (Gen. 1:26–28). This blessed way would be called good (Gen. 1:31) for human beings (God's images) insofar as they reinforced God's original economic or ordering of the house. Created as *'âdâm*, male and female were to be earthly representatives of God the Householder, just as offspring represented the parent of a household.[4] As Douglas Meeks notes:

> . . . in God's economy the only thing that ultimately separates the human being from the rest of the animals is that the human being is called into being in order to keep God's household. This is what constitutes being a human being. Being human is an economic commission: to join God the Economist in distributing righteousness so that the world may live.[5]

The "righteousness" needed for the world's livelihood is justice. Again, God's economic cannot be separated from the human ordering of the world in justice.

The root word for justice in Greek is *díkē*,[6] which means an ethical norm valid for all social relationships. Hugh Lloyd-Jones has noted: "*Díkē* means basically the order of the universe."[7] The just person (*díkaios*) is the one who respects and does not violate this universal order. If male and female will be images of God, they must relate to each other and the goods of the earth in a just manner. However, as the narrators of the story of the transition from Genesis to the foundation of Israel as a household tell it, God's people proved to be lacking.

As stewards of God's household, male and female proved unfaithful and, therefore, unjust. They let human householders set idolatrous terms for their resource-sharing and relationships rather than the divine Householder. Because some appropriated God's earth to themselves and in the process oppressed the poor, justice was denied.[8] Consequently, over a period of time, jubilee legislation was detailed to forestall human greed and chicanery from being institutionalized in a way that kept the poor permanently from having access to resources.

The process of composing jubilee legislation covered three periods: Exodus 21–23 was the first stage; Deuteronomy 12–26 the second; and Leviticus 1–27, written in the context of the Exile, the third.[9] Jubilee legislation envisioned a kind of economic restructuring to return the world (*oikouméné*) to its original purposes: "The land shall not be sold in perpetuity, for the land is mine; for you are strangers and sojourners with me. And in all the country you possess, you shall grant a redemption of the land" (Lev. 25:23–24). The redemption of the land would return the whole *oikouméné* to the original plan for the *oikos/oikía* (a central theme of the legislation [Lev. 25:29–34]). The redemption of the land would also create an ecological (*oikos/oikía*) order (Lev. 25:11). Furthermore, the jubilee invited the people—images of God the Creator/Householder—to share the world's resources in a manner that reflected God's original economic or ordering of the house (Gen. 1:26–28). Thus every fifty years "a comprehensive scenario for economic reform [which] encompassed slave release, interest free loans, debt release and the restoration of land to the original owners"[10] was to take place throughout the house of Israel.

THE HOUSE OF ISRAEL, THE LAND, AND THE COVENANT

In the Hebrew scriptures, the earth is called '*erets*. The word can be translated as "earth" or "land." In the beginning God created male and female, who lived (to use Adam Smith's term for the first stage of economics) as hunters on the earth/land. Even though Smith envisioned our early ancestors as peaceloving food grubbers making no claims on each other for earth, the first chapters of Genesis teach an anthropology which demonstrates how conflicting land-claims constituted the basis for alienation almost from the beginning.

If a dichotomy between the "earth" and the "land" can be effected, God can own the earth while humans will control the land. Disputes over land will thus be the cause of conflicting claims. Walter Brueggemann has noted:

"Land," as contrasted with "earth," is always assigned, owned, and occupied. When one talks about "earth," everything is not owned, except by God. But when one talks about "land," everything is owned according to legal legitimation. That makes a very great difference in social reality and social possibility.[11]

From the beginning the temptation has faced humans to change the language about economics or house-ordering in ways that serve not God but their interests (i.e., wealth). Given human anthropology and the nature of language, it was inevitable that, sooner or later, the ideology about God as owner of the land would be transferred to humans.[12]

The relationship of Israel to the land was not only spiritual and religious; it had specific political and economic implications. If he would leave his father's *oikos* Abraham was promised the land (Gen. 12:1–2) as a blessing for "all the families of the earth" (Gen. 12:3). Although named for him, Abraham's new household would become part of Yahweh's possession. So, leaving with Sarah and their household, Abraham came "to the land of Canaan" where "the Lord appeared to Abram and said, 'To your descendants I will give this land' " (Gen. 12:5,7). This claim to the land reveals how a shift had been made from Adam Smith's second stage of economic life—the shepherd/nomadic model—to the third stage of agriculture. When people move to the agricultural stage, specific land-claims are made. With land-claims staked, disagreement among varying claimants cannot be far behind (see Gen. 13:6). Thus resulted the conflict by opposing "house-holders" over land and property that has typified divided societies ever since, especially in Smith's fourth stage of economic development—"industry"—which now seems to have evolved to post-industrial corporate capitalism.[13]

Once constituted as a house "there was a famine in the land" (Gen. 26:1). Consequently the descendants of Abraham and Sarah went to Egypt. In the process, their household lost its land and entered into the "house of bondage" in Egypt (Ex. 13:3, 14; 20:2; Dt. 5:6; 6:12; 8:14; 13:5, 10; Jos. 24:17). The people came under the domination of Pharaoh (a term coming from the Egyptian *per-aa*, which means "the great house").

Following the Exodus experience, the original inhabitants of the households and city-states of Canaan and the followers of the God of Abraham and Sarah began to interact. In time the Israelites emerged from being marginated groups that had revolted against the dominant economic system. By coming together the Canaanite-Israelite peasantry gradually created an anti-authoritarian and more egalitarian society.[14]

During the process of achieving their identity, a common abhorrence of the patriarchal cultic images and household gods that surrounded them became a rallying point. Since religion and economics were embedded in socio-political structures, Israel's struggle against the idols was not just a religious or even economic activity, it represented a rejection of the patriarchal structures around it as well. Building on the ideas of Norman Gottwald, James M. Kennedy has concluded:

Early Israel's rejection of the cultic image stems from the social revolt by which Canaanite-Israelite peasantry overthrew a hierarchical social structure. In its place it attempted to form a society marked by decentralized power and an even distribution of material goods. At the social level, the idol functioned as a legitimating device for Canaanite social hierarchies. Through sacrifice to the idol, large amounts of material productivity were funneled into the control of the Canaanite priestly and royal classes. The idol was therefore a kind of tax or tribute gathering device. In this context, Israelite hostility to cultic images yields to a possible twofold interpretation. First, by repudiating the cultic image, Israel rid itself of an important source of wealth for the ruling classes, thereby thwarting possible internal programs seeking to re-establish political hierarchy. Second, frontier Israel was insuring that agricultural goods used in cultic sacrifice would be circulated back into the producing community. An imageless cult was one way of enhancing political and economic self-sufficiency.[15]

According to Gottwald, the formation of this self-sufficient entity, now called Israel, along with its tribal confederacy, which battled the Canaanites, began at the "grass-roots," in the *bayith/oikos*, or household.[16] From independent households, autonomous extended families grouped themselves into local protective associations to give mutual socio-economic aid and to levy troops. These autonomous, protective associations joined as regional tribes— according to common migration and struggles as well as geographical and economic conditions—to extend mutual and group aid to field effective fighting forces against such claimants to their "land" as the Canaanites. The autonomous tribes associated in a national confederacy or league called the house of Israel, which had cultic, military, and juridical functions. Thus the final encompassing confederacy, co-terminus with the socio-economic system, resulted from the aggregated or pyramided smaller households. In this sense, the formation of the house of Israel evolved from *oikos* to *pólis* to *basileía*.

In contrast to the "bottom-up" theory noted above, the formation of the house of Israel can also be viewed from a "top-down" approach. According to this theory, groups of people who were once unorganized or loosely organized joined together and committed themselves to perform certain cultic, military, and juridical functions within a confederacy or league called the house of Israel. This confederacy segmented itself into tribes to address regional needs. The segmented tribes were further divided into local protective associations of several households. These groups of households served neighborhood needs, supplied troops to the tribal levy, and insured socio-economic security to the households. The already-segmented protective associations were further segmented into extended families or groups as economically self-sufficient households. Thus the final subdivision—the local house—existed as the basic economic unit.

I agree with Gottwald who thinks "it seems wisest to view 'bottom-up' and 'top-down' analyses as complementary approaches to a single process in which complicated forces are working in both directions simultaneously."[17] Whether one follows the top-down or bottom-up theory, both demonstrate that Israel's realization of itself as a unified body, as one household, was essential to its self-understanding. This metaphor of the "house" of Israel (or Jacob) gradually became a vehicle for translating that self-understanding into a body of scriptures.

Almost 6 percent (146) of the references to Israel in the Old Testament refer to it as a "house." Twenty-one refer to the "house of Jacob." Daniel I. Block has categorized the frequency, distribution, and genre of *byt* Israel and *byt* Jacob in the Hebrew scriptures as follows[18]:

	byt Israel (146)		byt Jacob (21)	
Book	Narrative	Poetry	Narrative	Poetry
Genesis	–	–	1	–
Exodus	2	–	1	–
Leviticus	5	–	–	–
Numbers	1	–	–	–
Subtotals	8	–	2	–
Joshua	1	–	–	–
1 Samuel	2	–	–	–
2 Samuel	5	–	–	–
1 Kings	2	–	–	–
Subtotals	10	–	–	–
Isaiah	1	3	–	9
Jeremiah	15	5	–	2
Ezekiel	82	1	1	–
Amos	2	6	–	2
Obadiah	–	–	–	2
Micah	–	3	–	2
Zechariah	1	–	–	–
Subtotals	103	21	1	17
Psalms	–	3	–	1
Ruth	1	–	–	–
Grand Totals	122	24	3	18

Israel's process of being liberated from Pharaoh's house of bondage-economics and being reordered as one house united with the divine Householder took place in the context of the covenant. Covenants were created when representatives of different households formed a bond of mutual obligation.[19] One of the parties was Yahweh, the liberating Householder, who had proved faithful to basic religious and economic promises by meeting Israel's needs.

God's justice had been revealed in the giving of manna and the flowing of water from the rock. For its part of the covenant, the house of Israel was also to be just. This justice would serve as a reflection of God's justice. It would be accomplished by Israel's observance of the covenant. The means to accomplish this would be the Torah. The study paper on the U.S. economy of the United Church of Christ puts it this way:

> After God led the people out of slavery, God created a new economy or household of freedom. God made a covenant with "household rules" in order to keep Israel from falling again into an economy of slavery. The terms of the covenant, embodied in the Torah (the first five books of the Old Testament), had many provisions for economic life, with special emphasis on the needs of the poor. As guidelines for household management, the Torah provided Israel with the way to live faithfully to God and responsibly to the community.[20]

Covenanted with Yahweh, the paradigmatic Householder and Economist, Israel would act as God-images by becoming house-orderers or economists. Douglas Meeks shows that this would be accomplished to the degree Israel kept the Torah: "The Torah is essentially God's economy, that is, God's way of distributing righteousness, God's power for life. Life in God's household of freedom, then, means living in obedience to God's way of distributing righteousness."[21] The issue is not the law but the quality of relationships.

As a means of reminding the house of Israel of its early sojourn under the power of the divine presence housed in the ark, and as a means of recalling its covenantal obligations to Yahweh, a symbol of this covenant with God was built. This was the temple; it would be called the house of God. In time, although God's presence would remain "everywhere," the perception of many localized that presence within the temple. Access to the temple, and therefore to God, also gradually became restricted to the temple leaders. This would prove beneficial to those leaders who would give Yahweh the "earth," but wanted to control the "land" for themselves. Israel might be Yahweh's house or possession, along with the earth and its fullness; but the land was Israel's, the possession of its leaders and its rich. By housing the householder of the earth in a small place, the temple, Israel could control the land for its own purposes. Thus Israel, especially its leaders, became idolatrous by misusing people and resources to serve human purposes rather than God's.

By the eighth century BCE economic and commercial ventures flourished. Israel was now divided into two kingdoms. The prosperous upper strata in both Israel and Judah increasingly depended on the poor through all-too-frequent exploitation. The more covetous and idolatrous the two kingdoms became, the more prophets arose with a covenantal call to conversion. They continually challenged Israel and Judah to responsible obedience to the divine Householder by fidelity to the Torah. Amos, Hosea, Isaiah, and Jeremiah were the strongest in their call for a reordering of the house of Israel—a conversion to a covenantal life based on reordered relationships and resources, or justice. For them a temple of the Lord that did not serve the needs of the people by the promotion of justice made the notion "house of God" a sham. As Jeremiah noted (in words Matthew would recall from Mark about Jesus cleansing the temple [21:13]):

> Thus says the Lord of hosts, the God of Israel, Amend your ways and your doings, and I will let you dwell in this place. Do not trust in these deceptive words: "This is the temple of the Lord, the temple of the Lord, the temple of the Lord."
> For if you truly amend your ways and your doings, if you truly execute justice one with another, if you do not oppress the alien, the fatherless or the widow, or shed innocent blood in this place, and if you do not go after other gods to your own hurt, then I will let you dwell in this place, in the land that I gave of old to your fathers for ever.
> Behold, you trust in deceptive words to no avail. Will you steal, murder, commit adultery, swear falsely, burn incense to Baal, and go after other gods that you have not known, and then come and stand before me in this house, which is called by my name, and say, "We are delivered!"—only to go on doing all these abominations? Has this house, which is called by my name, become a den of robbers in your eyes? [Jer. 7:3–11].

In the midst of the early, post-exilic Jewish community (518 BCE), as Zechariah reflected on the reasons for the fall of Jerusalem and the exile, he recapitulated words of the pre-exilic prophets as a challenge to shape a new way of household order: "Render true judgments, show kindness and mercy each to his brother, do not oppress the widow, the fatherless, the sojourner, or the poor; and let none of you devise evil against his brother in your heart" (Zech. 7:9–10). Justice, kindness, and compassion shown to the widow, the orphan, the sojourner, and the poor were to characterize a healthy household.

Donald Gowan has shown that, while the kind of economics or house-ordering regarding wealth and power envisioned in the Old Testament cannot be taken as prescriptive for any modern society, its description of right-order in a household has relevance today:

> The Old Testament's final criterion for determining how adequately wealth was distributed in the land and how much opportunity was offered the poor to better their position was diagnostic, and it can still be used that way. That is, no matter what the economic system may be, no matter whether the region is relatively poor or relatively prosperous, one can judge how good that system is and how well it is administered by considering what becomes of people like the widow, people who experience a sudden, involuntary change of fortune for the worse. One can observe what happens to people like orphans, physically and mentally unable to take care of themselves and dependent on others for all their needs. One can study what it is like to be a foreigner in that society, how

many opportunities there are, and just how unpleasant it may be to be foreign. Then it is up to "the righteous" in that society to find ways, institutional or otherwise, to correct that which does not measure up to the Old Testament vision of people where the widow, orphan, immigrant, and their counterparts do not have to cry out to the Lord because of those who afflict them.[22]

Recalling with Jeremiah that "to know" God is "to do justice" (Jer. 22:15–16), Gowan's conclusions about justice to the marginated and oppressed now bring us to see how Matthew tried to build his redaction around these underlying notions of justice as rightly-ordered resources and relationships— with God, self, and neighbor.

THE SERMON ON THE MOUNT:
JUSTICE IN MATTHEW'S HOUSE CHURCHES

Except for one verse in Luke's infancy narrative (Lk. 1:75) Matthew is the only Synoptic who uses the word *dikaiosýnē* or justice. Because all his uses appear to be redactional, his use of the term must be considered "important."[23] Before examining its meaning as a word, an understanding of its communal context is equally important.

The last chapter discussed how Leland White's word analysis of Matthew's Sermon on the Mount demonstrates that the community for which it was written evidences qualities of "strong group" (pressure to conform to socially held values, a strong corporate identity, and a clear distinction between "insiders" and "outsiders") and "low grid" (a low degree of links between someone's experiences and his/her society's patterns of perception, evaluation, horizon, or paradigm). The "strong group" characteristic is found in Matthew's view of the community as a household of the just in a world of the unjust (5:45; 13:47–50; 23:28; 25:31–46). The teachings of Jesus were "norms that serve to set Matthew's community apart from its environment as the righteous from the unrighteous. Establishing sharp boundaries, these norms mark the community as a strong group." The low grid of Matthew's house church is characterized by its egalitarian approach to status, roles, and behavior. As a result the community failed "to articulate procedures for [its] internal structure as well as its concern to defend the group's honor."[24] The community's concern about its honor would be defined by codes other than those of society.

Honor and shame were key factors related to grid-group insofar as honor and shame constituted cultural norms within and among pre-industrial households. Because wealth was not accumulated (systemic accumulation being a sign of capitalism), power dominated in such pre-capitalist, traditional societies as that of Matthew. With power defining society, rank and status determined relationships among members in that society. Roles and behavior were determined accordingly. Bruce Malina has shown that, at the heart of these relationships ordered around rank and status, shame and honor were central moral values.[25]

For Malina, honor can be described as socially proper activities and behavior in the arena where the three lines of power, rank for women and men, and religion intersect. For instance, according to Malina, it was "considered highly dishonorable and against the rules of honor to go to court and seek legal justice from one's equal."[26] To go to court would be to violate the code of honor and bring shame to one's self and one's household. This helps in understanding Matthew's adaptation of Q to speak about the need to be reconciled with one's "brother" and make friends with one's accuser *before* going to court (5:24–25). Indeed, only in Matthew, the *ekklēsía* is offered as the last resort for settling disputes among "brothers" (18:17). Matthew envisioned a community of brothers and sisters whose style of life imaged the coming of God's reign. It would be dishonorable and shameful to take disputes meant to be settled within the house church outside, to unbelievers.

When grid-group and honor-shame characteristics are brought to bear upon the Sermon on the Mount's meaning of *dikaiosýnē*, we discover a definite and unique code of conduct revealing "rules to govern the way of life of the community to which it was preached. The norms elaborated in this code provide significant insight into how Matthew's community understood itself."[27]

Strong-group cultures that make shame and honor part of their codes also incorporate the influence of reciprocity. In these cultures reciprocity determines an ethos of justice. Justice reflects the underlying assumptions related to the moral code of reciprocity. Consistent with this pattern, Matthew seems to have highlighted *dikaiosýnē* as a goal for his community against the so-called righteous ones (*hypocritēs*) in Judaism as well as in wider gentile society, especially the leaders (5:20).

Because of Matthew's unique use of the term *dikaiosýnē*, no one doubts its significance in his gospel; yet much debate has revolved around how he actually used the word and its consequent meanings.[28] Unfortunately much of the debate has been over-influenced by the post-Reformation debate over *dikaiosýnē* as "righteousness." This Pauline image has colored all other paradigms. However, since Matthew envisioned justice as Jesus' fulfillment of the Law and the prophets, the better way to understand Matthew's meaning of justice is in the context of the Hebrew scriptures. This approach, I noted in the previous chapter, rejects the "non-justice" approach toward house building (Jer. 22:13) and instead concludes that "to know" God was "to do justice" (Jer. 22:15–16). Matthean notions of justice imply this understanding.

Within this understanding, as well as the understanding of justice as rightly-ordered relationships of persons with each other and their resources, I follow the position that 5:6 and 6:33 stress *dikaiosýnē* as the saving gift of God's presence and order in humans' lives (i.e., "to know" God), while 5:10, 20, and 6:1 highlight humans' response to others as their sign of fidelity to the saving gift of God's presence and order (i.e., "to do justice"). These five uses, besides the first words of Jesus about fulfilling all *dikaiosýnē* (3:15) and John's preaching *dikaiosýnē* (21:32), must be seen as the fulfillment of the Torah and the Old Testament covenant.[29]

Five of the seven uses of *dikaiosýnē* appear in the Sermon on the Mount. Two are beatitudes (5:6, 10). In 5:20 Matthew's Jesus warns about having a *dikaiosýnē* that exceeded "that of the scribes and Pharisees" even though in 5:17-19 Jesus talked about fulfilling the Law and the prophets. This "fulfillment" must be understood in the context of his fulfillment of all *dikaiosýnē* in 3:15. The location of the other two uses of the word in the Sermon, in 6:1 and 6:33, suggests that Matthew arranged the main body of the Sermon around key passages related to justice. In the process, Matthew seems to be saying that experiencing the saving power of God's *dikaiosýnē* (5:6, 6:33) brings about the blessing, the fulfillment, of God's plan of salvation. Members of the community are to witness to this saving act of God's justice by their own acts of justice (5:10, 20; 6:1).[30]

With this as background, we now can consider the Sermon on the Mount as articulating variations on a basic structure of justice. This structure can be outlined according to the following schema[31]:

5:1-5:16: Introduction: The Beatitudes revolving around justice/good works in the house
5:17-5:48: Fulfilling the Law and prophets fulfills that justice which exceeds that of the scribes and Pharisees
5:17-5:20: The Law and prophets as prophesying
5:20-5:47: The "antithesis" statements
5:48: Achieving the way of perfection/*téleios*
6:1-6:32: Realizing justice through observance of deeds performed for God to see
6:1-4: Almsgiving
6:5-15: Prayer (with implications for debt-forgiveness and the jubilee).
6:16-18: Fasting
6:19-32: Choosing between God and mammon
6:33-7:12: Justice as right relations with others and God
7:13-23: Conclusion: The triad of contrasts about doing good and putting words into deeds which build the house on rock

With the above as a framework for our reflections, and having already reflected on the Beatitudes, we can now consider the rest of the Sermon, beginning with the controversial part dealing with the respectful approach to the Law.

1. Fulfilling the Law and Prophets Fulfills Justice Which Exceeds That of the Scribes and Pharisees

a. The Law and the Prophets Prophesying

After declaring he has come to fulfill the Law and the prophets (5:17), Matthew's Jesus says: "not an iota, not a dot, will pass from the law until all is accomplished. Whoever then relaxes one of the least of these commandments and teaches men so, shall be called least in the kingdom of heaven" (5:18-19). Yet at the end of the Sermon he says that entrance into God's reign will be contingent on keeping *his* words and practicing them (7:21-27). Do not the two contradict each other? They do not if we recall the opening statement about Jesus' coming not to abolish and Law and the prophets, "but to fulfill them" (5:17). If Jesus fulfills the Law and prophets (through justice [3:15]), he is the image of the divine Torah, which "is essentially God's economy, that is God's way of distributing" justice.[32] His approach to religion and economics is salvific, the fulfillment of justice. And since justice is the basis of both the Law and prophetic utterance, his way of Law-observance outlined in the Sermon reveals the way of justice. Justice, then, is salvation and reveals the way to salvation. Households that fulfill the salvific and economic elements of justice fulfill the Torah. Following the example of Jesus, they are to fulfill what all the prophets and the Law *prophesied* until John (11:13).[33]

The first words Matthew places in Jesus' mouth make a connection between fulfillment and justice (3:15). Since the heart of the prophets' message was an interpretation of the Law that would promote justice, Matthew's use of the references to the Law and "prophets prophesying" reflects his conviction of the need for their fulfillment through justice. Consequently, the way the members of his house churches would continue to fulfill those scriptures would be different from the way practiced by the scribes and Pharisees of Jesus' day.

Immediately after the statements about the fulfillment of the Law (5:18-19), Matthew has Jesus say that unless his followers' justice (*dikaiosýnē*) exceeds that of the scribes and Pharisees they will never be able to enter God's kingdom (5:20). The experience of God's salvation or reign in heaven is contingent on the exercise of justice on earth, and the reordering of life on behalf of the poor is the *sine qua non* for entrance into heaven for those wanting to be perfect (19:21). With its increasing prosperity, Matthew's community was tempted to adapt to the surrounding culture. These words (5:20) and what follows (5:21-58) call it to express a justice that set it apart from its society's norms for justice. According to John Meier all of Christ's moral teaching demands of the disciples of Jesus justice that expresses that moral activity which fulfills God's will. He writes:

> In the life of a true disciple justice must overflow ("exceeds") with an abundance befitting the definitive salvation Jesus brings. This abundance is not a bigger and better Pharisaism, an ever more precise observance of legal niceties. It is radical gift of self to God and neighbor in both inner thought and outward action. It pursues the Law to its ultimate intention, even if that means abrogation of the letter. This justice far surpasses the legalistic approach of "the scribes and Pharisees" (Mt's stock phrase for official Judaism).[34]

Because Matthew took "from his storehouse" incidents in Jesus' life that would serve as a model for his own community, one cannot limit an understanding of the "scribes and Pharisees" in 5:20 to those leaders in conflict with Jesus fifty years before. As Jesus was the model for discipleship, so the scribes and Pharisees served in Matthew's narrative as household (church, economic, or political) leaders of any day whose behavior does not reflect their words (23:3–4).

b. The "Antithesis" Statements

The theoretical statements about the Law in 5:17–19 imply one practical concern: justice as the condition for membership in God's reign. To show how justice, the basis of the Law and the ordering of the house, should be exercised, Matthew places on Jesus' lips six unique statements, traditionally called the "antithesis" statements (5:21–47) because they have been translated, "You have heard it said . . . *but* I say to you." These six reflections can be desribed as radical in the way they call for a reordering of many current practices; yet, as Pinchas Lapide has stated, none stands outside elements of the tradition itself. That Matthew's Jesus demanded of his disciples the practice of justice (*krísis*), mercy (*éleos*), and faith (*pístis*) as the foundation of the Law, without neglecting the minutiae (23:23), also supports Lapide's retranslation of the "antithesis" statements to read: "You have heard it said *and* I say to you."[35]

Building on our previous discussion about the relational dimension of justice, we can say that the six statements are not primarily concerned with the validity of the Torah or its tradition of interpretation or even Jesus' position regarding the two, but rather they are concerned with the nature of the disciples' relationship with God and each other, again in light of the advent of God's reign.[36]

The first,[37] second, and fourth statements are proper to Matthew. He makes significant changes from the material shared with Luke in the third, fifth, and sixth, especially when he wants to give stress to familial relationships (5:24, 45). In response to traditional legalisms, if not to the Law itself, the antitheses offer a justice-as-love approach to anger (5:21–26), to exploitative sexual relationships (5:27–30), to divorce (often based on an economic rationale related to dowries [5:31–32]), to swearing to the Lord or heaven (5:33–37), to exploitative enemies (5:38–42), and to enemies who hate (5:43–47).

In the fifth (5:38–42) statement—the law regarding retaliation—Matthew's Jesus offers a vivid example of his vision for restructured ethics and house-ordering. In a society influenced by honor-shame codes, the Law clearly reinforced retaliation (Ex. 21:24; Lev. 24:20; Dt. 19:21) as a form of reciprocation in order to avoid continuous antagonisms among households and families. Retaliation was grounded on traditional, patriarchal models of reciprocity and submission. Jesus challenged these mores with his statements about nonresistance. In contrast to those *haustafeln* which reinforced patriarchal house patterns with submission, a new kind of submission would be the order for his household members—the doing of good even to enemies and persecutors: "Do not resist one who is evil. But if any one strikes you on the right cheek, turn to him the other also; and if any one would sue you and take your coat, let him have your cloak as well; and if any one forces you to go one mile, go with him two miles" (5:39–41).

When Matthew wrote the gospel, relations between those in power and the powerless, the landlord and the tenant, were guided by negative reciprocity, balanced reciprocity, and general reciprocity. Since negative reciprocity involved doing to others what one would *not* have done to one's self and balanced reciprocity involved exchange on a *quid pro quo* basis, in this passage (5:38–42), Matthew shows Jesus turning the traditional approach to the law of reciprocity upside down again by requiring general reciprocity in his demands about doing good. Good must be done to all because all are to be part of God's household.

A traditional interpretation of the admonition to offer no resistance to injury, to give the extra clothes, to go the extra mile, and to give to those in need identified these actions with nonviolence, specifically toward enemies. For instance, at that time—Josephus notes in his *Antiquities*—Roman representatives had the right to requisition civilians into service. One kind of service involved carrying the gear of Roman soldiers for one mile. This civic requirement seems to constitute the argument for the radicality of Jesus' approach.

While this specific connection seems applicable here, the context seems broader than how Roman troops should be treated or what reaction should be given to being forced to work by an oppressor. The context reinforces the concept that, rather than the *lex talionis* of balanced reciprocity, all of the Sermon talks about "doing good" and "bearing fruit." Here this is specified in nonretaliation and sharing resources—clothing, time, or whatever else—with the generosity indicative of general reciprocity.[38] Matthew's Jesus was inviting disciples to create a new household order no longer based on traditional structures of negative or even balanced reciprocity but the third form, general reciprocity. While its ultimate grounding would be knowledge of that God who knows all that is truly needed (6:32; 7:11),[39] its expression would be manifest in nonretaliatory attitudes toward the enemy and in sharing with those in need.

Such a knowledge of God expressed in a new justice of general reciprocity undermines all approaches to law based on balancing needs and ensuring mutual rights. "The 'otherness' of the kingdom and of its justice could not be clearer," Meier writes. "In the sermon on the mount, Jesus is not presenting a new program for human society; he is announcing the end of human society, the end of the world"[40] as it was legally, politically, and economically ordered. A new age (19:28) of sharing freely rather than legally was being inaugurated: "Give to him who begs from you, and do not refuse him who would borrow from you" (5:42). People could share with those in need if they trusted in God's provident care to provide for their own needs. This realization had earlier enabled the psalmist to declare about those whose lives reflected such justice: "I have been young, and now am old; yet I have not seen the righteous forsaken or his children begging bread. He is ever giving liberally and lending, and his children become a blessing" (Ps. 37:25).

With the sixth challenge (5:43-47), societal norms about justice and reciprocity are turned upside down another time. The members of Matthew's house churches are to "love your enemies and pray for those who persecute you, so that you may be sons of your Father who is in heaven" (5:44-45a). Because Jesus manifested his sonship by loving his enemies and praying for his persecutors he overcame death and created a new relationship with his followers. Where before they were called "disciples," he now called them "brothers" (28:10). As brothers and sisters of Jesus in the household of God, submission to God's will now demands an equal love of enemies as well as prayer and good words for persecutors.

At the time of Jesus, love of neighbor meant love of "insiders," those of one's extended family or religion—in this case, the Jews. "Outsiders" were real or possible enemies. However, given the tensions inside as well as outside his house churches, Matthew's Jesus realized that enemies could be everywhere, including one's own household (10:36) and city.

When Jesus said to love enemies, he was expanding the traditional practice beyond the doors of the *oikía* to the *oikouménē*, saying: love those within and beyond your household. Let your love be nonexclusive. However, this love was not merely to be a matter of affection; it was to be a manifestation of justice (5:20). This justice had to manifest a reordering of the whole household. Moreover, from the household, it had to extend to the village or city around. Thus Richard Horsley writes of this admonition to love enemies:

> These sayings of Jesus rather call people in local village communities to take economic responsibility for each other in their desperate circumstances. Those addressed may have little or nothing themselves. But they are called upon to share what they have willingly with others in the community, even with their enemies or those who hate them. . . . The message seems to be: take responsibility for helping each other willingly, even our enemies, in the local village community.[41]

Nowhere in the Old Testament was hate of enemies condoned (see 1 Sam. 24:19). However, again, the practice of retaliation against enemies then (as now) happened so often that people easily developed enmity toward their enemies and felt justified in those feelings before God.[42] It was not to be that way in the new order. If the members of the house churches would love their enemies and pray for their persecutors (5:44), they would become children of the heavenly Father (5:45a).

For the Jews, becoming a child of God was not a privilege of birth as it was for the Greeks. Rather it was achieved by one's deeds. Matthew's Jesus shows that these deeds must now be expressed in love of the enemy as well as doing good and praying for persecutors. These good deeds, again fulfilling the heavenly Father's will, would constitute a new household of the just ones living among the unjust (5:45b, c; see 10:41; 13:43, 49; 25:37, 46). Love could not be

limited to members of the house churches alone ("brothers" referring not just
to members of the same family, but especially to those belonging to the same
household). Its universality had to be extended to all in creation (5:46–47).
Reflecting an economic as well as religious interpretation of the saying,
Douglas Oakman notes: "Such kinship is not, however, restricted to the
narrow horizon of the village or tribe. There seems to be implied in the Jesus
tradition a genuine quest for universal love for enemies as an ethical corollary
of indiscriminate economic exchanges based upon general reciprocity."[43]

When considered together the themes of the last two "antitheses"—loving
submission and nonresistance, doing good and prayer for persecutors—offer a
striking resemblance to themes connected with *haustafeln* elsewhere in the New
Testament. In his study of *haustafeln* in the New Testament, Kenneth Dupar
identifies submission with "doing good" and finds this articulated in Matthew's gospel in particular. He concludes that the rationale for submission as
doing good involves three dimensions: 1) first of all it involved nonretaliation;
2) the nonretaliation is not passive but actively works to influence change (in
potential antagonists); that is done so that 3) social obligations in that society
might be influenced by Christian witness.[44]

c. Achieving the Way of Wholeness/*Teléios*

The conclusion of the "antithesis statements" sums up their purpose and
goal: "You, therefore, must be perfect [*téleios*], as your heavenly Father is
perfect [*téleios*]" (5:48). God's perfection or wholeness has been revealed in
making friends of enemies. Consequently, by breaking down barriers within
and beyond the household of faith—by embracing the poor, including the
marginated, and even loving the enemy—the members of Matthew's house
church would mirror the very pattern of God's integrity (see 19:21).

Jesus' concluding call to a similar integrity (5:48) returns Matthew's reader
to the beginning demand for an all-embracing justice that exceeded that of the
scribes and Pharisees (5:20). Thus the link between justice (5:20) and integrity
or wholeness (5:48). Here justice is identified with "perfection"; its salvific
expression becomes the goal of an ethical life of love. Just as the Essenes
considered their community the "house of perfection and truth in Israel to
establish the covenant according to everlasting precepts" (1 QS xi, 11, 17), so
Matthew's language in 5:48 suggests his households must live up to the demands of the new covenant through a similar justice.[45]

In the Old Testament justice and perfection were often equated (Gen. 6:9;
Dt. 25:15; Job 1:1, 8; 2:3; Prov. 11:5). Yahweh was called perfect (see 2 Sam.
22:31; Ps. 18:30) as well as "our justice" (Jer. 23:6). To know Yahweh was to do
justice (Jer. 22:15–16) by fidelity to God and by meeting the needs of others.
Such was the way of integrity, of walking blamelessly (*téleios*) before Yahweh
(Dt. 18:13).

In contrast to the scribes and Pharisees, the disciples of Jesus were to be and
do more; they were to be just and perfect in ways that reflected Yahweh's
dealings with all people, the just and the unjust, the good and the evil. Leopold

Sabourin declares that the greater justice of Jesus' disciples demands an entirely new ethic for life among the members of Matthew's house churches:

> The "more" demanded of the disciples, in respect of the lower ideal of "the scribes and Pharisees" (5:20), does not consist in the observing of a larger number of precepts, but mainly in an intensifying of the love of God and of neighbor. Such a radicalizing of Christian ethics finds a paradigm, a normative example, in God's own perfection. . . . In other words, Christ says in Mt that perfection is the mark of discipleship, therefore the mark of Christian ethics, which are an ethics of obedience to God's law, a total commitment to do his will.[46]

2. Realizing Justice through Deeds Performed for God to See

"Beware of practicing your *dikaiosýnē* before men in order to be seen by them," Matthew notes Jesus saying: "for then you will have no reward from your Father who is in heaven" (6:1). The Father who is in heaven demands of the members of Matthew's household another kind of justice expressed in almsgiving (6:2-4), prayer (especially expressed in forgiveness of debts [6:4-15]), and fasting (6:16-18). These represented specific ways of fulfilling the Law and the prophets, since, in the Old Testament, almsgiving, prayer, and fasting (see Tob. 12:8) manifested justice.

a. Almsgiving

In the world of Matthew's households there existed a huge gap between the powerful and powerless, the rich and the poor, those with status and the marginated. Hebrew scriptures called the responsibility of the upper social classes toward meeting the needs of the underclasses in reciprocity *sedaqa* and *sedek*. *Sedaqa* and *sedek*, not charity, demanded that those with greater resources use them responsibly on behalf of those poorer because the poor often had helped create those resources.

After the exile, *sedek* and *sedaqa* took on the meaning of almsgiving. The Septuagint translated the words as *dikaiosýnē* and *eleēmosýnē*. *Eleēmosýnē* was translated as almsgiving. Not surprisingly, therefore, the first manifestation of *dikaiosýnē* (6:1) for Matthew's Jesus was *eleēmosýnē* (6:2). However, as with the manifestation of perfection (5:48), the implications for an economic ethic based on almsgiving in the Matthean sense went further than the Law demanded (19:16-19). In contrast to a society whose approach to the poor often was based on exploitative forms of redistribution, Matthew's Jesus demanded of his disciples a general reordering of possessions and status on behalf of those without possessions or status, namely the poor (19:21). The concrete expression of this mercy or almsgiving was to go further in meeting the requests of those who ask or in responding to those who take (5:40-42).[47] Again, almsgiving was not so much a matter of charity as an essential demand of justice.

b. Prayer

The second of the three specifications of *dikaiosýnē* stresses prayer as a way of making God's reign come on earth as in heaven. The ways to translate the prayer into action are outlined in the Lord's Prayer.

The opening petitions about God's name being holy, the kingdom coming, and God's will being done on earth as it is in heaven (6:9c–10) should be considered as a triad. Here, as in 19:29, Matthew identifies *name* and *kingdom* with the *will* of God. Thus God's name must be made holy, God's reign must come, and God's will must be done "on earth as it is in heaven." This prayer is to be offered and struggled to be realized though the good works of the members of Matthew's households.

We have already seen that "heaven and earth" refer to God's presence. By working for conditions on earth that give praise to God's name, the reign of God's will is continued in the work of Jesus and the church (11:2–6). The order in the heavenly household is imaged in the earthly order. These petitions call for a reordering of relationships and resources to manifest on earth the fulfillment of God's plan. These petitions stand as subversive to whatever keeps the world in darkness rather than light, in chaos rather than order.[48]

The name, the reign, and the will of God represented desired conditions not always found in the house churches. Neither, Joachim Jeremias indicates, were they found in the wider society:

> These petitions are a cry out of the depths of distress. Out of a world which is enslaved under the rule of evil and in which Christ and Antichrist are locked in conflict, Jesus' disciples, seemingly a prey of evil and death and Satan, lift their eyes to the Father and cry out for the revelation of God's glory. But at the same time these petitions are an expression of absolute certainty. He who prays thus, takes seriously God's promise, in spite of all the demonic powers, and puts himself completely in God's hands, with imperturbable trust: "Thou wilt complete Thy glorious work, *abba*, Father."[49]

The next petition addresses the most basic economic need on earth: "Give us this day our daily bread" (6:11). I have already noted that the need for bread ultimately involves an abandonment to God to satisfy needs. This inner abandonment is expressed externally by sharing bread as a sign of trust in that providence. In this sense I want to note the word "daily" (*epioúsios*), which has a unique meaning in this gospel.

Recalling the Jews in the desert who depended on God each day for their resource of bread, the word has both economic and eucharistic overtones. R. ten Kate has noted that the request for daily bread has various implications: all are in need, God gives us what we need, God gives us only enough.[50] One way of keeping the request to God for bread from becoming a mere babbling (6:7) was that the members of the house churches were to work to create those economic conditions, or the ordering of their houses, that met the needs of others. Not only were they to seek only enough for themselves, they were to forgive each others' debts.

(1) Implications for Debt Forgiveness. The demand for an economic reordering in the household and among the members of various households is even more clearly articulated in the next petition: "Forgive us our debts, as we also have forgiven our debtors" (6:12).

The problem of debt contributed to tensions between the propertied class and tenants and laborers of Jesus' and Matthew's day.[51] Debt, then as now, was a major mechanism whereby the rich became richer and the poor poorer and more dependent. Because they had the power in making bargains, the rich could set terms and extract the surplus product of their workers to their own advantage.

In contrast to the Lukan version of the Lord's Prayer, which uses *hamarita* or "sin" for debt, Matthew used the term *opheilēma*. According to Eugene LaVerdiere this word encompassed three levels of debt: debts of justice, debts of gratitude, and debts of offense. "Debts of justice" referred to a kind of commutative justice wherein employers were obliged to pay for employees' work. "Debts of gratitude" included repayment expected in unique situations, such as that expected of the steward who had his huge debts forgiven (18:32–33). "Debts of offense" dealt with acts which violated a relationship and which demanded reconciliation (5:23). While each has a different object, according to LaVerdiere, "all result from the fact that someone has done something to or for someone else. All express a relationship of dependence between the parties concerned. And all require further action or behavior which flows from this relationship."[52]

While "debts of offense" were included in the phrase "forgive us our debts," it cannot be easily discounted that Matthew alone used the word that expresses the justice-form of economic debt forgiveness (18:21–35).

The cancellation of economic debts figured centrally in the dynamics of the jubilee year, which envisioned a restructuring of land tenure according to its original state every fiftieth year. Jesus came to announce this jubilee (see 11:2–6)[53] and said that the mark of discipleship would be whether his followers reordered their possessions toward the dispossesed (19:21). In light of this, the phrase about debt in the Lord's Prayer involves a petition that individual and group deeds of economic reordering be viewed as a commitment to a reordering, not only of relational debts (as in Luke's redaction), but of material and economic debts as well. John Howard Yoder makes this connection between a material form of debt forgiveness and the jubilee when he writes:

The Lord's prayer, which summarizes the thought of Jesus concerning prayer, includes the following request: "remit us our debts as we forgive those who have offended us." Accurately, the word *opheiléma* of the Greek text signifies precisely a monetary debt, in the most material sense of the term. In the "Our Father," then, Jesus is not simply recommending vaguely that we might pardon those who have bothered us or made us trouble, but tells us purely and simply to erase the debts of those who owe us money; which is to say, practice the jubilee.[54]

Yoder's contention makes all the more sense when we realize that *áphesis*, the noun form of the verb *aphíenai*, "to forgive," is the term used by the Septuagint for the jubilee year which called for the forgiveness of debts (Lev. 25:23ff). *Aphíenai* and its cognates mean both debt cancellation and metaphorical forgiveness. Thus Matthew's Jesus makes it clear that authentic prayer must involve working for the jubilee.

(2) Implications for the Jubilee. Past scholarship has highlighted Luke's overtones of the Sabbath-jubilee (especially in Luke 4:18–19). However, more recent studies have noted that the metaphors and images underlying the actual words and actions of Matthew's Jesus increasingly reveal strong notions of a Sabbath-jubilee societal conversion which reflect those based in Leviticus 25 and parallels in Second Isaiah.[55]

Leviticus 25 outlined conditions that would convert society to its more egalitarian origins. The original covenant, intended to preserve the honor of Yahweh and Israel, would be recalled in an effort to proclaim liberty to all inhabitants, to restore property to rightful heirs, and to cease agricultural activity for one year (Lev. 25:10–12). The Sabbath-jubilee insisted on insuring that the needs of the poor be met in order to offset Israel's anticipated break of the covenant and the dishonor Israelites would show each other and Yahweh by their exploitation of the poor who were always in need.

According to Paul Hollenbach, the needs of the poor were "to be met generally in three time frames—their immediate need for food and clothing, their short-term need for family restoration, and their long-term need for total social reconstruction."[56] While basic, immediate needs were to be continually met through familial *care*, and short-term needs should be met as situations demanded through *redemption*, long-term needs were to be resolved every fifty years through structural *release*. Kinship ties expressed in care and redemption were to address individual needs within households. If households (*oikía/oikos*) would be reformed, it would lead to structural release which would meet the needs of the wider community (*pólis*) and the entire society (*basileía*). Hollenbach's insights can be charted as follows:

Conversion
of households
(*oikía/oikos*)
through
{
A. Kinship (*oikeion*) ties providing
  1. Care: Immediate response to human needs
    (hunger, thirst, etc.)
  2. Redemption: Short-term response to material needs (esp. landlessness)
B. Political (*politeía*) action giving
  3. Release: Long-term response to denial of freedom, exploitation, and landlessness
}

If care, redemption, and release were essential to the Sabbath-jubilee and if these can be shown to be central to Matthew's message, the first gospel would thus reveal a Sabbath-jubilee concern. An application of this Sabbath-jubilee model to Matthew's Jesus makes it clear that *care* or compassion in response to the physical needs of others was a characteristic of his ministry (9:36; 14:4; 15:32; 18:27; 29:34). Consequently, meeting others' immediate needs should characterize Jesus' disciples (19:21; 25:31-46). Because forms of land tenure at that time made the goal of *redemption* merely a dream,[57] the debt forgiveness of the Lord's Prayer (6:12) not only called for spiritual but definite economic notions of redemption.[58] The third dimension—*release* from practices and attitudes that undermined the honor and dignity of people—is clearly evident in Jesus' use of *exousía* which released people from ignorance, suffering, and sin. Other release-images, especially of a more political type, can be found in the works Christ and his disciples do for the poor (11:2-6)—which recalled Isaiah's allusion about the Messiah and the Sabbath-jubilee fulfillment (Is. 61); the reordering of first and last in new households of faith (19:29-30); the rejection of the *póleis* who refused to be reordered (11:20-24; 23:37-39); as well as the acceptance of any group (8:11-12; 32:31) or nation (25:31-46) that responded to God's will by serving those in need.

Thus, because care, redemption, and release were at the heart of the Sabbath-jubilee and because these same characteristics constitute the heart of Matthew's interpretation of Jesus, the first gospel clearly indicates notions of social conversion which reflect the Sabbath-jubilee, and those notions reinforce the phrase about forgiveness of debts in the Lord's Prayer.

c. Fasting

The final phrase, "And lead us not into temptation, but deliver us from evil" (6:13), also should not be divorced from its economic or house-ordering implications. In the first gospel fasting is the third manifestation of justice (6:16-18). Perhaps this underlies the reason why, immediately after announcing that he had come to fulfill all *dikaiosýnē*, Jesus went into the wilderness—to be tempted by the personification of injustice—and started a fast.

The heart of Matthew's Jesus was touched with compassion toward those whose economic situation demanded that they fast because they were exploited; he used his resources to meet their needs (15:32). His ministry to the poor represented a kind of fasting, or a reordering of resources toward the poor (9:14-15). This reordering (see 26:11-13) was to be emulated by the disciples when Jesus would be with them, not physically but in *exousía* (see 28:16-20).

More than any other gospel, Matthew used Second Isaiah. For Matthew, Jesus was the fulfillment of the justice which Second Isaiah preached. Thus it follows that the first gospel's notion of fasting would parallel that economic reordering described by Isaiah in chapter 58 as the essence of fasting. Isaiah railed against those who exercised the ritual of fasting without reordering those economic conditions that exploited people and perpetuated economic dependency. In fact, people were often oppressed and treated unjustly by precisely those practicing the ritual of fasting (Is. 58:1-5). Isaiah's Yahweh called for a new kind of household ordering geared to a deeper form of justice—that which would bring good news to the poor:

> Is not this the fast that I choose: to loose the bonds of wickedness, to undo the thongs of the yoke, to let the oppressed go free, and to break every yoke? Is it not to share your bread with the hungry, and bring the homeless poor into your *oikía*; when you see the naked, to cover him, and not to hide yourself from your own flesh? [Is. 58:6-7].

In his environment of injustice Matthew urged his house churches to manifest justice by clothing the naked and meeting the needs of the least (25:31-45). This was to be part of the Matthean fast which would keep society's injustice from overtaking the members of his house churches. If we keep in mind that Matthew's community evidenced a strong group/low grid composition, this fasting-for-justice makes immediate sense in situations that spell the "death" of the group, notably by having boundaries penetrated by evil.[59] In a world of injustice, fasting would help restoration.

d. Choosing between God and Mammon

The theme of eradication of injustice by the reordering of one's household and wealth on behalf of the needy brings us to the next section, which outlines the way justice should be observed through deeds. This demands a "purity-of-heart" view toward wealth (*mamōnas* [6:19-32]).

In Matthew mammon means something ungodly which entangles (6:19, 21, 24).[60] Entrance into the reign of God demanded a justice greater than that of the scribes and Pharisees (5:20) as well as almsgiving, prayer, and fasting (6:1-18); and the great obstacle to the realization of that justice would be hearts hardened by mammon in all its forms.

Love of God and neighbor is the foundation of the Law and the prophets (22:37-40; see 5:43-46; 19:19). Since justice is the foundation of the Law and the prophets as well, love is at their core. However that love must be realized, like justice, in good works. When the members of the house churches did good they fulfilled the heavenly Father's will. When they did not, they were evil doers, or part of the *anomía* (7:23; see 13:41; 23:28). They also were lacking love. Thus, in his fourth unique use of *anomía* Matthew made the connection between it and the lack of love: "And because *anomía* is multiplied, most men's love will grow cold" (24:12)

When people do not surrender to God's will, their hearts[61] are divided (Dt. 4:29; 10:12; 11:18; 1 Sam. 12:24) because God's law is written in their hearts (Jer. 31:33). When one's will is directed justly (Ps. 119:36; see Job 11:13), this is renewal of heart (Ez. 18:31). Since the heart is the center of life and symbol of love, from it will come either *dikaiosýnē* or *anomía* with all their implications.

3. Justice as Right Relations with Others and God

In 6:33 Matthew's Jesus challenged the members of Matthew's prosperous house churches to ". . . seek first his kingdom and his *dikaiosýnē* [the latter phrase added by Matthew], and all these things shall be yours as well" (6:33). "Seeking his kingdom" involved conversion *toward* God. But conversion *to* necessitates conversion *from*. Thus this phrase, while envisioning God's saving activity in the disciples' lives, demands that an economic reordering take place to bring good news to the poor, and this reordering must occur *in order* to experience the kingdom (19:21). In urging the disciples to seek first God's reign and God's order in their lives (*dikaiosýnē*), Jesus recalled to them God's loving care as a parent. Thus he could say: "Therefore do not be anxious about tomorrow, for tomorrow will be anxious for itself. Let the day's own trouble be sufficient for the day" (6:34).

While some consider these phrases about first seeking God's reign and justice and the need to take one day at a time as the conclusion of the previous section, I view them as the foundation for the two pericopes that follow: that about the need for compassion and prudence in dealing with others (7:1–6) and the one about dependence on God's providential care (7:7–11).

The first pericope comments on a problem endemic to any household: judgment (7:1–6). Harsh judgment of others, according to Matthew, manifests a kind of hypocrisy (*hypokritēs* [7:1–5]). *Hypokritēs* is used by Matthew 13 times (6:2, 5, 16; 7:5; 15:7; 22:18; 23:13, 15, 23, 25, 27, 29; 24:51), while it is used only once in Mark (Mk. 7:6) and 3 times in Luke (Lk. 6:42; 12:56; 13:15). Matthew's use of the term contrasts it to justice and good works. For Matthew, hypocrisy involved a lack of coherence between word and action, the image of one thing versus the reality of another.

Matthew's ethical position for his households can only be understood when its stress on justice is contrasted with its opposite, hypocrisy.[62] The practice of justice (6:1), expressed in almsgiving, prayer, and fasting, is not like the practice of hypocrites (6:2, 5, 16). Through his woes Jesus inveighed against the hypocrisy of the scribes and the Pharisees, especially for violations of justice, mercy, and good faith (23:23). According to Bonnard, "justice" here (the use of *krísis* rather than *dikaiosýnē)* refers to the Old Testament meaning of respect for the rights of every person, just judgments toward others, and fair verdicts for the weak.[63] It means right order in households.

The second pericope in this section invokes a triad of asking and receiving, seeking and finding, knocking and opening (7:7–12). Matthew uses these images related to the household to talk about the approach his readers should take to prayer (7:7–12). He concludes that, if the heads of households, evil as they may be, know "how to give good gifts to your children, how much more will your Father who is in heaven give good things to those who ask him" (7:11). Matthew's prosperous house churches, tempted to a selfish reliance on their own resources, needed to hear this challenge.

Returning to the original use of justice related to the Law and the prophets (5:17–19), Matthew concludes this section with the basic tenet of justice: "So whatever you wish that men would do to you, you do so to them; for this is the law and the prophets" (7:12). The justice that exceeds that of the leaders demands equal treatment for all within the community. It demands love of neighbor as oneself (20:19; 22:36–40).

The Triad of Contrasts

The first part of the triad, which discusses entering by the narrow gate to find life (7:13–14), comes from Q. However Matthew adapted the text to have the wide gate and the easy way lead to *apōleia* or life's destruction. Matthew's only other use of the word *apōleia* expresses the disciples' response to the woman who anointed Jesus in the house of Simon: "Why this waste?" (26:8). The way of sharing leads to life; the other way leads to destruction or waste.

J. Duncan M. Derrett has noted that such terminology about the gates reflected economic overtones. Tolls were collected at gates. The broader the gate, the more likely it was that one would be charged a toll. Thus the need to look for narrow gates to enter, since these were generally used by townspeople who did not need to pay such tolls.

The "narrow gate" also served as image for entrance to eternal life. So "the children of light must strive to find that entry to the Kingdom of Heaven which will admit them to 'life' while it disencumbers them of attachment to their belongings," Derrett observes. That reign of God "strips them of their superfluities, forces them to recognize what are superfluities, and disqualifies them from being true sons of commerce. In that sense the Kingdom of Heaven has no broad gate, except for those who are already redeemed!"[64]

The second part of the triad, again from Q, deals with the image of trees bearing good and bad fruit and their application to eternal life (7:15–23). Here, again, Matthew adapted the text to insist that not those who *said*, "Lord, Lord," but only those who *did* "the will of my Father who is in heaven," by producing the fruit of good works, would have life. Whether this referred to the wandering charismatics of Jesus' day, the Jamnian Pharisees, or the leaders of Matthew's house churches, the point was clear. All those who failed to do good—not only the Jews—would hear the charge: "I never knew you; depart from me, you evildoers" (7:23). By implication, doing good enables one to be known by God and to know God. Thus, to "know" God demands "doing justice." The notion of "bearing fruit" (which is common in Matthew[65]) refers to fruits of *dikaiosýnē*. God's reign in each person is a gift, but moral living (fruit) must involve the reception of that gift.

This pericope about bearing fruit by doing good—which appears at the end of the first discourse—seems best understood by paralleling it to the pericope at the end of the fifth and final discourse. In both pericopes, those separated from God's reign and eternal life are the ones saying "Lord" because they do not accompany their words with good deeds. In the parable of the maidens with the oil of good works (25:1–13), in the parable about the talents (which canonizes good works, not money getting interest or bearing more) (25:14–30), and in the last judgment scene (25:31–46), those kept from the experience of God's reign are those who say "Lord." Matthew makes it clear: when that day comes, entrance into God's reign in heaven will depend on how one's works ushered in that reign on earth to reflect God's original good work in the world

(Gen. 1:31). Doing God's will demands a new kind of submission by all the members of the house churches: the performance of works of justice by doing good.

The final part of the Sermon, again from Q and found in extra-biblical sources as well, discusses the two kinds of houses: the one built on sand (words without works) and the one built on rock (7:24–27). Members of the house churches were to live in that *exousía* received at their baptism (28:18), the same *exousía* which left the crowds spellbound at Jesus' teaching (7:22–29). With that *exousía* they were the ones to put into practice that teaching; they were to observe all that Jesus had commanded (28:16–20).

"House" concludes the last section of the Sermon on the Mount as it concludes the first section of the Sermon (5:15). The entire ethos contained within this first of Jesus' teachings makes it abundantly clear that authentic discipleship is manifested by house members who do their heavenly Father's will by good works manifested in justice.

8

The Call to Conversion
in a Society Resisting Change

LINGUISTIC ANALYSIS

Matthew used three basic words for conversion (*metánoia* = conversion; *metanoein* = to convert; and *stréphein* [with its various prefixes] = to turn).[1] *Metánoia* described conversion or repentance (3:8, 11). *Metanoein* meant to repent (3:2; 4:17; 11:20, 21; 12:41). *Stréphein* involved a literal turning around (5:39; 7:6; 9:22; 16:23), a figurative turning (to be like a child [18:3]), or a theological, relational turning in the form of repentance (27:3). When prefixes are added to -*stréphein,* multiple meanings are involved.[2]

Since Matthew was addressing his house churches as a community, the linguistic form he used for conversion was invariably plural. The house churches and all of the individuals in them were called to conversion. Like the Hebrew word *shûb,* which formed the basis for New Testament words for conversion, Matthew's was a "collective call to individual conversion."[3]

Of all the many times Matthew wrote about conversion, only one Matthean use of words for it reveals individual repentance[4]: "When Judas, his betrayer, saw that he was condemned, he *repented* and *brought back* the thirty pieces of silver to the chief priests and the elders . . . " (27:3). This phrase contains the two different ways "conversion" was used in the scriptures. The latter use refers to the physical motion of "returning" something to its original source; the former has covenantal overtones. In the covenantal sense, repentance or sorrow is the first step in conversion. Because Judas is not reported to have taken the next step—a change based on his acceptance of the grace of forgiveness—"he departed; and he went and hanged himself" (27:5).

Outside this use of the word for an individual's "conversion," when the first gospel mentions the word[5] it usually refers to the need for communal or social reconstruction (3:2, 8, 11; 4:17; 11:20–21; 12:41; 17:17; 23:37). The initial message of John the Baptizer is addressed to the whole people: "Repent, for the kingdom of heaven is at hand" (3:2). For the Baptizer the authenticity of conversion must be expressed in "fruit that befits repentance" (3:8, see 3:10).

"Bearing fruit" for Matthew (who also used the notion in 7:16–20; 12:33; 13:8, 24; 21:18–20, 33–43) involved performing works that helped reorder social life, especially through the practice of justice.

When Jesus came to receive John's baptism he was not performing an act of repentance. Rather his baptism was a commitment to fulfill all justice (3:15), especially that justice which would fulfill the Law and the prophets. Thus Matthew couched Jesus' words about conversion within the Isaiah (Is. 9:1–2), which heralded a new social order for the people:

> "The land of Zebulun and the land of Naphtali, toward the sea, across the Jordan, Galilee of the Gentiles—the people who sat in darkness have seen a great light, and for those who sat in the region and shadow of death light has dawned." From that time Jesus began to preach, saying, "Repent, for the kingdom of heaven is at hand" [4:15–17].

Matthew adapted Mark's ideas of conversion to his own community's situation. His use of *metanoeite* for John's word for conversion (3:2) as well as Jesus' (4:17) frames individual conversion in relation to community or society. Thus the first gospel's concept of conversion, while grounded in individual conversion, was oriented to communal and social reconstruction. This applies to the entire gospel as well. The social dimension outweighs the individual or personal dimensions.

An analysis of Matthew's Sermon on the Mount shows that over 75 percent of the passages deal with internal group relationships (56 percent) or relationships with others (23 percent) while only 21 percent might refer to personal conduct or attitudes. This analysis of the Sermon on the Mount can be applied to the whole gospel, especially its concept of conversion bearing fruit, since the Sermon grounded Matthew's entire ethical code. In fact, throughout the Sermon, according to Leland White, communal implications override individual implications:

> Thus, we find a community code in which community life is the dominant concern, and merely personal conduct clearly subordinated to social obligations. The focus on social relationships reflects an understanding of the person which is primarily social, embedded in the social group, rather than individual. In so far as this text reflects the dispositions present in Matthew's community, we should expect this community to follow a *strong-group* pattern.[6]

This analysis of the Sermon on the Mount also makes it clear that Matthew's portrayal of Jesus' call to conversion and the basic need for moral (re)ordering, while having individual implications, primarily relates to social groups.

To explore this conversion process, this chapter will analyze how Matthew's notion of social conversion is manifested in his depiction of Jesus' work for societal reform through a reordering of social patterns of behavior; how conversion involves the process of seeking-finding-selling-buying; how the rich young man typified the Matthean house churches' struggle to convert their wealth toward the poor in order to experience God's reign; and, finally, how a deeper experience of God's *exousía* enables conversion from the addictive force of mammon to occur. An exegesis of Matthew 11:2-30 will demonstrate how Matthew integrated the above elements.

MATTHEW'S JESUS AND SOCIAL REFORM

Many scholars argue that neither Jesus nor his movement was geared to overthrow structures. They explain that his was a conservative movement that tried to bring about a conversion of Israel in the truest sense: a *return to* its original values and institutions (5:17). Yet a "return to" means a "return from"; a "turning back" to original values and institutional arrangements means a "turning from" existing values and institutional mores. In this sense Matthew presents Jesus as challenging the existing values and institutions that he viewed as subversive of the original covenantal social arrangements. Such a challenge to the existing order of things must be seen as an invitation to bring about a new order of society.

Jesus challenged his "received social order" in at least four calls: 1) to reorder table fellowship; 2) to reorder Torah and temple; 3) to reorder the Sabbath to meet human needs; and 4) to do God's will through the creation of a more egalitarian kind of community. These calls for conversion, in turn, must be considered from Matthew's perspective on *exousía*.

1. The Challenge to Table Fellowship

To the Jew, table fellowship was a microcosm of the ideal society. It mirrored the social order or structure of justice envisioned for the nation. Israel's unique union with God was thus perceived in terms of table fellowship (Ps. 23:5; 78:19; Is. 25:6; Ezek. 39:20). However, for the Pharisees, who were "a table-fellowship sect,"[7] table fellowship demanded exclusion of non-Jews as a sign of covenantal fidelity.

Norman Perrin has written that table fellowship was perhaps "the central feature of Jesus' ministry."[8] However Jesus' form of table fellowship set him apart from the scribes and other reformers like the Pharisees. Jesus' actions show his acceptance of the basic Pharisaic insights. Yet he went further and mirrored the need for a deeper reordering of the basic patterns of table fellowship. By sitting at the same table (in his own house [9:10]) with the excluded and outcasts, called "sinners and tax collectors" (9:11, 12), Jesus challenged his existing social order; he invited it to turn from a model which excluded and to turn to one that was open to all. Sharing a meal with others in that ranked society symbolized equality with them; inviting the marginated to table made them equal. Jesus' approach to table fellowship not only treated people equally, especially those outside the system; it revealed him as their "friend" (11:19). The Pharisees viewed Jesus' approach as subverting their interpretation of Israel's true social order.[9]

The story of the king's wedding feast (22:1-14) from Q makes it clear that, when table fellowship reflects the reign of God, a radical conversion of the social order takes place: there will be no outsiders. Further, if "insiders"—be they the scribes and Pharisees of Jesus' day, the Judaizers of Matthew's day (or those who exclude in any day [28:20])—insist on limiting table fellowship, they will be excluded themselves: "I tell you, many will come from east and west and sit at table with Abraham, Isaac, and Jacob in the kingdom of heaven, while the sons of the kingdom will be thrown into the outer darkness" (8:11-12).

8:11-12 parallels 21:31-43, wherein Matthew's Jesus declares that the very ones whom the chief priests, scribes, and Pharisees wanted to exclude—the justice-practicing tax collectors and the harlots who converted (21:31) and those nations producing fruit (21:43)—would be entering God's reign before them. This statement was seen as undermining the system. It was enough for the chief priests and the Pharisees to try "to arrest him" (21:46).

Law is the glue of structures; by going beyond the Law (at least the leaders' interpretation of it) to reorder relationships to include the excluded, Matthew's Jesus showed that mercy must be at the heart of the new ethic (see 9:13). Yet, in the eyes of the leaders, with their vested interests, Jesus acted illegally; he was undermining the social order from which they benefited. He would have to die.

2. The Challenge to Torah and Temple-Ordering

The second way Matthew shows Jesus calling for a conversion of the social order involved the Torah and the restructuring of economic relations within the temple. According to Marcus J. Borg, the proscriptions of the Torah and temple-ordering constituted the two poles of Israel's post-exilic quest for fidelity to covenantal holiness.[10] Jesus' resistance in the "antithesis" statements to Torah proscriptions as defined by the leaders (5:20-48) is well known as a contributing factor to his being labelled subversive. These arrangements were reinforced by the Law and its interpretations. Thus, when Matthew placed the "antithesis" statements on Jesus' lips—"You have heard it said . . . but I say to you" (5:21-48)—he was calling for a change of the social order. While I have discussed the implications of the "antitheses" in the previous chapter, the deeper implications of Jesus' challenge to temple-ordering need further elaboration. This can be done by setting the story of the cleansing of the temple (21:12-17) in its context.

In 21:12-17 Matthew rearranged the Markan material to have Jesus' "cleansing" of the temple—the heart of the nation—take place the same day as his triumphal entry into Jerusalem, the center of Jewish political, economic, religious, and cultural life (21:1-11). These two pericopes are followed by the cursing of the fig tree for not bearing fruit (an image of Jesus' rejection of the leaders [21:18-22]) and the debate over Jesus' source of authority (21:23-27). As Matthew arranged his sources, the entry into Jerusalem (21:1-11) takes

Jesus into the source of power of the scribes and Pharisees; the overturning of the tables in the temple (21:12–17) was a direct challenge to their power; the cursing of the fig tree (21:18–22) was a rejection of their power; and the debate with them over the source of his authority put Jesus' authority in contrast to theirs (21:23–27). These four pericopes connect with the story of the man whose second son followed his will (21:28–32) and the parable of the house-holder (21:33–42) which ends with the conclusion: "Therefore I tell you, the kingdom of God will be taken away from you and given to a nation producing the fruits of it" (21:43). Matthew arranges these texts so that they end with his portrayal of the chief priests and the Pharisees being challenged as to their authority. The result was that, rather than being converted, they tried to arrest Jesus (21:46).

Having considered the context for Jesus' approach to temple-ordering, we can return to the actual pericope (21:12–17). Jesus' action of turning over the tables (*katastréphein* [21:12]) and the inclusion of the marginated (21:14) were symbolic acts calling for an overturning or conversion of the old order. Turning over the tables was a judgment on the temple that prefigured its destruction (24:2).

The temple hardly represented an innocent religion divorced from reality. Because taxes were funneled through it, it served as a means of economic redistribution. That Jesus paid the annual half-shekel temple tax (17:24) indicates that Jesus and the Jesus movement were not against the temple as such. The temple-structuring they resisted was rather the way the priestly rulers allowed the temple to be part of a redistributive system that exploited the poor and kept them outside this symbol of the Jewish order of life.

Furthermore, the resistance of Matthew's Jesus to the economic activity of "buying" and "selling" (21:12) in the temple—probably controlled by the priestly class—indicated that it was a form of robbing the people (21:13). Jesus' overturning the tables was a symbolic call for them to stop abusing their authority by exploiting pious pilgrims and the poor. However, rather than converting, the leaders became indignant (21:15). Instead of submitting their authority to Jesus' *exousía,* they challenged it (21:23–27) and tried to have him arrested (21:46).

With the temple restored, "the blind and the lame came to him in the temple, and he healed them" (21:14). Again, the lives of rejected ones are now reordered in the presence of the one who will be the true temple (24:2; 26:61; 27:40). Of all four accounts of the "cleansing" of the temple, Matthew's makes it clear that a restored temple finds Jesus at its heart, with those once excluded coming into his presence (21:14). The implications of Jesus' activity were clear to those exercising authority which might exclude the outsiders. According to Letty Russell: "Like Jesus in the temple, those who are 'house revolutionaries' do not wish to destroy the house of authority. Quite the contrary, they wish to build it up again as a new house in which the authority of God's love and care for the outsiders is clearly seen."[11] Those "outside" are received "inside."

Despite Letty Russell's affirmation about "house revolutionaries" and our affirmations about Matthew's identification of the actions of Jesus with his house churches, it still may be argued that table fellowship, challenges about Torah interpretation, and the temple incident were limited to Jesus' time and thus have no subsequent implications for the church and its need for conversion. Challenging this reservation of the gospel to the Jesus of history, Gerd Theissen makes it clear that the community that preserved this material about Jesus did so because that material or the values behind it were applicable to its experience:

> If we presuppose that a tradition is genuine, we may assume that those who handed it down shaped their lives in accordance with the tradition. If we assume that it originated within the Jesus movement in the period after Easter, we can presuppose that those who handed it down shaped the tradition in accordance with their life. In either case the result is the same: there is a correspondence between the social groups which handed down the tradition and the tradition itself. . . . It suggests that we should assume a continuity between Jesus and the Jesus movement. . . .[12]

The need to move to a deeper economic and religious conversion not only touched individuals in house churches; it affected house churches themselves. What Jesus experienced going into the temple, where moneychangers and sellers of pigeons were "selling and buying" (21:12) to the exclusion or exploitation of the poor, was happening in the house churches as well. Too often ordering of the house, or its economic, was not grounded in faith but in mammon. "He said to them, 'It is written, "My *oikos* shall be called a *oikos* of prayer"; but you make it a den of robbers' " (21:13). By not being concerned about the poor in their midst, the house churches were keeping the poor from fully experiencing the good news. They needed conversion. They needed to be converted to the poor by fulfilling all justice (3:15).

Zechariah had prophesied that a sign of a new social restoration would be that "there shall no longer be a trader in the house of the Lord of hosts on that day" (Zech. 14:21). "That day" was the day of the Lord, the jubilee (see 7:22; 25:31), which involved the reordering of the social order on behalf of the poor. Thus, when Jesus drove out those who sold and bought (economic conversions and transactions), the very ones who had been left outside the temple/house-ordering or economic system—"the blind and the lame"—"came to him in the temple, and he healed them" (21:14). The blind and the lame were not to be excluded from Matthew's prosperous houses churches either.

3. The Challenge to Reorder the Sabbath to Meet Human Needs

Matthew's unique word for Jesus' giving rest (11:29) is *anápaüsis*. In the Septuagint, when God finished creation, "he rested [*katapaüsis*] from all his work which he had done. So God blessed the seventh day and hallowed it, because on it God rested [*katapaüsis*] from all his work which he had done in creation" (Gen. 2:2–3). The root word for the rest found in Matthew's Jesus and the rest of God are the same: *paúein*.

The purpose of the Sabbath rest was ideally to reorder one's week in keeping with jubilee principles, the reordering of creation according to God's original plan, so that there could be true biblical rest. However, with some at the time of Jesus, the legal way the Sabbath was to be observed kept the needs of human beings from being met. To challenge this social order, Matthew deviated from Mark and Luke and put two pericopes about the Sabbath after his unique comments about rest. In doing so, Matthew presents Jesus calling for another kind of structural reordering, the third I want to consider.

At the time of Jesus and Matthew, Israel was occupied. It was threatened by persecution for its various resistance movements on the one hand and fearful of assimilation on the other. In such a setting, "observance of the sabbath became, for the Pharisees, the chief way of preserving Jewish communal identity and the Jewish vocation."[13]

According to Matthew, the first sign of the Pharisees' plotting against Jesus occurred in the context of the disciples eating grain on the Sabbath (12:1–7) and the cure of the man with the shriveled hand. The latter occurred—not just on the Sabbath—but *in* "their synagogue" (12:9–14).

Matthew's placement of these two stories about meeting human needs (of food and health) on the Sabbath after Jesus invites his disciples to rest in him (11:29–30) reveals a unique creation-centeredness in Matthew. The God who entrusted the world to humans rested on the seventh day. However, until all God's creatures have their needs met, alleviating these needs takes precedence over Sabbath rest. Coming to Jesus brings about rest, but coming to him involves knowing the will of God. Whenever disordered relationships and resources are present, chaos reigns. This demands reordering to make creation again fulfill God's will (see 7:21–23).

"Jesus went through the grainfields on the sabbath; his disciples were hungry, and they began to . . . eat" (12:1). Jesus' approach to the Law grounded it in justice (5:20), the reordering of relationships and resources to meet needs. But the Pharisees did not view it that way. This is evident in their response: "Look, your disciples are doing what is not lawful to do on the sabbath" (12:2). Replying to them Jesus showed how necessary it was for them to change their way of thinking and behaving: the Sabbath rest must be temporarily lifted in face of needs.

The same idea is contained in the next pericope about Jesus' healing on the Sabbath, which again created controversy with those who interpreted the Law to serve other purposes besides (re)ordered relationships and resources. The first Sabbath controversy showed that the Law could be disregarded to meet one's own need (12:1–8); now in this second instance (12:9–14), the Law's prescriptions were secondary to *doing good* to those in need whom Jesus saw as so "valuable." Doing good, from Genesis on, was to be expressed in all relationships, actions, and laws. All externals were to be based on this funda- mental dynamic.

Knowing that the Pharisees were plotting against him for calling into question their interpretation of externals and the Law, Jesus withdrew. Matthew's subsequent insertion here of the Deutero-Isaian passage about the Suffering Servant being oppressed for obeying God's will and bringing justice to all is most appropriate (12:17–21). It not only reflects Matthew's ethos about Jesus' wholehearted obedience as son of God. It also contrasts with the Pharisees' authority, which allowed alienation to continue. Jesus' use of authority served all, especially those in need.

4. The Challenge to Do God's Will in a New Kind of Collegial Community

Thus far in this chapter I have shown that reordered table fellowship, Torah interpretation, and temple presence, as well as observance of the Sabbath were three important themes Matthew used to show Jesus' effort to bring about conversion of his social order. The fourth indication—which has to do with who constitutes the family of Jesus—offers the final way Matthew shows Jesus calling for a reconstituted social order.

In a ranked, patriarchal society, Matthew's Jesus indicates that, given that society's intransigence and unwillingness to convert (12:44; 13:55; 23:37–39), a new community would be raised up. This would be a more egalitarian community whose members would be united through their common bonds as mother, brother, and sister; their relationships would be based not so much on submission of some humans to others (households to civil authorities, wives to husbands, slaves to masters, "the least" to "the greatest") as on submission of everyone to God's will (12:50). These would be the ones who converted to the reign of God's will by reordering their lives on behalf of the poor (see 19:21):

> Truly, I say to you, in the new world, when the Son of man shall sit on his glorious throne, you who have followed me will also sit on twelve thrones, judging the twelve tribes of Israel. And every one who has left houses or brothers or sisters or father or mother or children or lands, for my name's sake, will receive a hundredfold, and inherit eternal life. But many that are first will be last, and the last first [19:28–30].

In such communities the only requirement would be doing God's will. Accomplishing God's will by treating all equally and justly, for Matthew's Jesus, was the ultimate norm for household ordering (see 6:10; 7:21; 12:50; 18:14; 21:31). Those who convert and make God's cause for the poor their own (19:19–29) will enter into God's reign. They will be the true Israel.

SEEKING-FINDING-SELLING-BUYING: THE PROCESS OF CONVERSION AND THE RICH YOUNG MAN

In the first gospel, conversion and God's reign go together (3:2; 4:17). God's reign comes to those who convert; conversion occurs because individuals and communities come under the universal domination of the household of God.

Matthew made a connection between entering God's reign and entering the house (churches).[14] To the degree that members of the house churches reordered their individual relationships to God, to each other, and to the marginated as well as to the degree these house churches shared their resources to achieve justice (5:10, 20–48; 6:1), they would be bearing the fruit of conversion. Therefore they could enter God's reign.

An intimate connection exists in Matthew among seeking God's reign, conversion, and bearing fruit in justice. As Dom Marc-François Lacan notes:

> The axis of Matthew's gospel is the proclamation of Christian justice which is the fruit of conversion and the requirement of faith. Now, this justice is nothing other than a permanent conversion; Jesus defines the just man in a word: he is the one who "seeks," who has never stopped "seeking the kingdom of God and his justice" (Mt. 6:33).[15]

"Seeking the kingdom" expresses the first step in conversion throughout the Old and New Testaments, including the first gospel. It reveals the first human step in the conversion process.

Seeking also is the first step in the seeking-finding-selling-buying outline of the paradigmatic elements within the various parables which describe the stages or process of entering in and experiencing the kingdom.[16] Some parables are "seeking" parables, others are "finding" parables, etc. Chapter 13 (which contains parables describing one or the other of the different steps) features the story of the merchant and the pearl. This single parable outlines the conversion process in words that include *all* four steps at once: " . . . the kingdom of heaven is like a merchant in *search* of fine pearls, who, on *finding* one pearl of great value, went and *sold* all that he had and *bought* it"(13:45). Seeking, finding, selling, and buying are not only the essence of the conversion process; they represent Matthew's only way to enter God's life and activity.

A parallel to the seeking-finding-selling-buying process of conversion can be found in the story of the rich young man who *sought out* Jesus about what he had to do to enter into eternal life, or the reign of God. (Matthew's adaptation of Mark's version of the story of the rich young man must be seen in light of the increasing "prosperity" of his house churches. These too needed conversion.)

Jesus said that the young man's seeking and finding of him had to progress to the final two stages if he would be perfect: ". . . go, sell what you possess and give to the poor, and you will have treasure in heaven; and come, follow me" (19:21). In an economic sense, Jesus showed the rich young man (as Matthew wanted to show his rich young church) that "buying" into the treasure of heaven was predicated on "selling" possessions and reordering these to the marginated. Earlier he said that either God or mammon would be the ultimate value in peoples' lives. People would serve one or the other; be devoted to the one and abandon the other (6:24). Only if people made it their practice to store up or "buy into" the treasure of heaven could they expect to be in right relationship with God (6:19–21).

Jesus did not stop there. He did not just say that the rich young man who had sought and found him should now sell his possessions as though the mere selling would "purchase" the reign of God. Since Jesus revealed his fidelity to the justice demanded by John's baptism (3:15) by ordering his life on behalf of the poor (11:2–6), the rich young man was to reorder his resources on behalf of those whom Jesus came to bring into the reign of God, namely the possession-less: those without status and material resources. In Matthew, then, the response by the rich to the poor through converted relationships and resources measures how the rich will share in God's reign and eternal life (19:16,21; see 25:31–46). The poor become the opportunity for the wealthy to experience the reign of God.[17] The way the wealthy "buy into" the reign of God is measured by the degree their lives reflect justice: the (re)ordering of their own and their household's relationships and resources on behalf of those in need, the poor. Perfection or wholeness (*téleios*) is predicated on justice (see 5:20–48).

To reorder one's possessions on behalf of the poor involved reordering one's whole household or familial status or life (relationships with persons and resources) on behalf of the poor; it involved being in solidarity with the marginated and dispossessed in imitation of Jesus' understanding of the good news (Is. 61; Mt. 11:2–6). The rich young man of Jesus' day was saddened by this message of conversion because of his "great possessions"(19:22).[18]

In response Jesus "said to his disciples, 'Truly, I say to you, it will be hard for a rich man to enter the kingdom of heaven. Again I tell you, it is easier for a camel to go through the eye of a needle than for a rich man to enter the kingdom of God' " (19:23–24). Whether the eye of the needle is converted to let the rich man in or the rich reorder their lives on behalf of the poor to fit into the needle's eye, the basic image from Mark used by Matthew declares that a radical conversion of life and resources is necessary to experience the reign of God.

"When the disciples heard this they were greatly astonished, saying, 'Who then can be saved?' " (19:25). The response of the wealthy disciples in the house churches was the same. With the material prosperity that came with urbanization, they were finding it increasingly difficult to reorder their relationships and resources on behalf of the poor. Yet salvation and eternal life were contingent on the way their lives brought good news to the poor and made a new order (19:28) occur in the world. Who then could be saved?

Jesus looked at them and said, "With men this is impossible, but with God all things are possible" (19:26). The "possibility" would be the power of God at work in the community through *exousía* (28:18).[19] Only by experiencing God would salvation for the wealthy be possible. Only by first seeking God (6:33 [by hungering and thirsting for God's justice (5:6)]) and then finding God's reign or presence within them—only then would people with riches experience something more powerful than that which formerly drove them and made them anxiously run after "all these things" (6:32). Peter and the other disciples had been touched deeply enough by their experience of Jesus that they had left "their nets and followed him" (4:20).

In response to Jesus, Peter said, "Lo, we have left everything and followed you. What then shall we have?" (19:27). Peter's response implies that he thought conversion—leaving family and fishing boats (see 4:20–22)—could be accomplished but once, for all time. But leaving family and boats merely reflects an initial "selling" of possessions—familial status and (some) resources.[20] For Matthew's Jesus, conversion must be ongoing and continual.

Conversion also had to move beyond possessions to power and prestige as well. Peter also needed to be converted from his anxiety and need for power and prestige ("What then shall we have?"), even though he had left (some of his) possessions. Possessions, as well as power and prestige, are forms of wealth. All three have to be reordered to enter God's reign. Reordering all three is a life-long process of conversion.

The rich young man could not reorder his wealth; Peter at least had begun reordering his possessions (4:20–22). However, like the other apostles, it would take Peter longer to be converted from his need for power and prestige (19:27b; 20:20–28).

Why was Peter able to leave his "everything" while the rich young man was not? The traditional answer from Matthew is that it was because the young man "had great possessions" (19:22). However there is nothing to indicate that Peter the fisherman (1:18), who *after his conversion* still owned a house large enough for a mother-in-law (8:14), did not have significant possessions as well. One needs to go further, to other Matthean sources, to determine why Peter could experience religious—and economic—conversion and not the young man.

Some sources indicate that the conversion process must always be initiated by God. Thus Jesus always sought out and "called" disciples (4:18–19; 9:9); those who initiated the process were put off (8:19–20). While that seems to be the case, a seeking spirit would have to exist in someone to be open to Jesus' invitation. Thus, to this degree, both Peter and the rich young man expressed the first stage in conversion: they sought out Jesus. Both moved to conversion's next step: they "found" in Jesus a source of significant meaning. However, having sought and found Jesus, the troubles began with the third stage of "selling." Why could Peter enter this stage of selling and the rich young man could not?

The traditional response about the possessions of the rich young man being "great" does not suffice to explain why he stopped the conversion process after seeking and finding Jesus (19:22). History has shown many people with great wealth who have reordered it for some other value they considered more significant than their possessions. This brings us to the heart of the rich young man's cessation of the conversion process: the "finding" or experience of Jesus was significant enough for Peter that he could leave "everything"; the rich young man's "finding" or experience of Jesus was not as significant as his riches. His possessions had more authority over him than Jesus' word of invitation. His faith revolved around what he had. His wealth was too consuming and preoccupying; his possessions kept him from experiencing Jesus' *exousía.* The conclusion thus becomes clear: in order truly to begin the process of conversion from wealth/riches/mammon (6:33), it is necessary not only to seek first the experience of God's reign but it is also necessary actually to experience what has been sought (see Ps. 24:3-6).

1. The Addictive Power of Possessions

The degree the young man was influenced by his "riches" must be considered from Matthew's earlier discussion about mammon in the Sermon on the Mount. Gentiles "sought" material forms of mammon in food, drink, and clothing. " 'What shall we eat?' or 'What shall we drink?' or 'What shall we wear?' " (6:31) were preoccupations. Furthermore, forces in society seemed to know then, as now, how to manipulate the insecurities, anxieties, and fears that can be generated by the preoccupation and search for material goods (6:31-32).

An important obstacle to finding one's security in God was the anxiety that surrounded the obsessive seeking and finding of material goods. Bultmann notes that anxiety reflects excessive self-concern for the means of life needed for the future.[21] Q indicated that laying up treasures on earth reveals that one's preoccupation or treasure rests in material goods rather than in God, for "where your treasure is, there will your heart be also" (6:21). Two lines later Matthew's Jesus, again using Q, makes it clear: "No one can serve two masters; for either he will hate the one and love the other, or he will be devoted to the one and despise the other. You cannot serve God and mammon" (6:24).

Mammon was a semitic word for greed for money or riches. *Douloúein,* to serve, is better translated, for our purposes, as "to be given over to." To be "given over to something" suggests an addictive power which controls one's thoughts and behavior.[22] Thus the first-century notions of "being given over to" or being preoccupied exactly reflect what we have termed in the twentieth century as "addictions."

Matthew's community of house churches—symbolized by the rich young man—was constituted of individuals whose lives reflected the addictions of the surrounding culture. These individual addictions were infecting the house churches; they were family or household diseases, eroding the commitments of the whole community (see 24:10-12). Turning to the addictions meant turning from God.

The only way to begin to be freed of the addictive power of material goods is conversion, to turn from by turning to. This process begins by seeking to find God and God's reign (6:32). This demands climbing the mountain with hands that are clean and hearts that are pure (Ps. 24:3-4; Mt. 5:8). Eyes seeking the face of God will be sound (*haplous* [6:22]). A body oriented toward God will be filled with light (6:22).[23] On the other hand, those storing up material goods will have eyes that are unsound (*ponerós*), and "if your eye is not sound, your whole body will be full of darkness" (6:23).

We have seen that *haplous* can imply generosity (to one's neighbor) while *ponerós* can be associated with stinginess, a characteristic of greed (which is addictive). Trust or lack of trust in God is expressed in parallel generosity and niggardliness toward neighbors. In this sense Peter Davids has noted:

> *Haplous* connotes undivided loyalty to God, joining the saying to the either-or alternative in the following saying. Therefore the "single eye" saying means: if one is undividedly devoted to God and thus generous (*i.e.*, puts his treasure in heaven), he is on the right way (*i.e.*, full of light); if however, he is niggardly, he is on the evil way (*i.e.*, full of darkness), despite his claims to be a servant of God. This saying, then, prepares the reader for the either-or (two ways) construction in verse 24. It is either wealth or God; one cannot serve both. Matthew then resolves the practical problems which this uncompromising teaching suggests in his great passage on trust, which follows (6:25–34).[24]

The only way to be free of addictions is to ground one's life in the experience of a power greater than that which has heretofore controlled one's life.

2. Anxiety, Addictions, and Religious Experience

The addiction, or being given over, to mammon in its various forms generates anxiety about getting certain things every day. One's trust is in whatever enables the addiction to be served. In this light it makes sense that the passage that follows the pericope dealing with one's treasure includes the famous words about anxiety and the need to trust in God like the birds of the air and the lilies of the field. This teaching's importance for Matthew's prosperous house churches is further evidenced in his use of a Q-based chiastic structure for 6:25–34 with four concentric rings clustered around verse 29:[25]

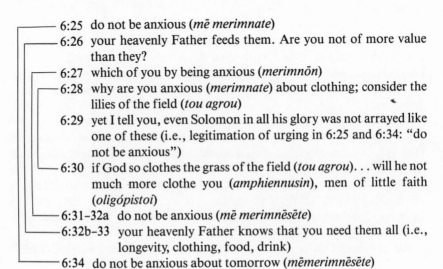

6:25 do not be anxious (*mē merimnate*)

6:26 your heavenly Father feeds them. Are you not of more value than they?

6:27 which of you by being anxious (*merimnōn*)

6:28 why are you anxious (*merimnate*) about clothing; consider the lilies of the field (*tou agrou*)

6:29 yet I tell you, even Solomon in all his glory was not arrayed like one of these (i.e., legitimation of urging in 6:25 and 6:34: "do not be anxious")

6:30 if God so clothes the grass of the field (*tou agrou*). . . will he not much more clothe you (*amphiennusin*), men of little faith (*oligópistoi*)

6:31–32a do not be anxious (*mē merimnēsēte*)

6:32b–33 your heavenly Father knows that you need them all (i.e., longevity, clothing, food, drink)

6:34 do not be anxious about tomorrow (*mēmerimnēsēte*)

The only place where Matthew uses *merimnan* besides the above verses is the mission statement (10:19). There the disciples need not be anxious (*merimnē-sēte*) about what they will say when they will be dragged before officials to give testimony because "the Spirit of your Father" will speak through them (10:19–20). With the same *exousía* in the disciples as was in Jesus, the members of the house church could trust in God's provident care. Their former economic anxiety could be sublimated into trust; their obsession with the goods of the household could be transferred to the God of the household.[26]

By seeking first God's reign and God's justice (6:33) and by hungering and thirsting for that reign of God's justice in their lives (5:6), Matthew's house churches were invited to conversion: they were invited to seek continually the experience of God's reign that alone would satisfy. This would lead them to reorder their lives to God alone. As "seeking" reflects that attitude of those running after or obsessed with material things, so "seeking" God's reign is the first step in the process of conversion.

Only when that sought-after reign revealed in the person of Jesus is found and experienced as *exousía* can the required selling of the addiction, mammon, occur. Only if *exousía* is sought and found—i.e., experienced as a power more significant and having more authority than the addictive forces that the gentiles seek—can its reign begin to have an influence. Thus when Peter exclaimed how impossible it would be for those with riches to enter the kingdom (19:25), Jesus uttered that wisdom that underlies what today is recognized as the first and second steps in dealing with addictions: "With men this is impossible, but with God all things are possible" (19:26).

Humanly speaking, to give up life's addictions is impossible. Only the experience of another, higher power can convert and deliver one from former addictive patterns. Only an experience of God's loving care and presence in the form of *exousía* (28:18) would enable Matthew's economically secure house churches to place their ultimate security and trust in God. Thus the call for an experience of God. If the anxiety connected with "running after" material goods could be replaced by trust in the power of God's spirit within (10:19–20), then freedom *from* anxiety and self-concern would convert to freedom *to* rest in God's reign and concern *for* others.

MT. 11:2-30—A CALL TO COMMUNAL CONVERSION

Probably nowhere do the two themes of the call to conversion and the need to experience God in trusting faith come together so clearly as in Matthew 11:2–30. This narrative is grounded almost exclusively on Q (11:2–27) with some significantly Matthean additions (11:20, 23–24, 28–30). The section begins with the disciples of John, who have witnessed Christ's works (*érga tou Christou*), asking about his legitimacy (11:2–6). This is followed by reflections on John's witness (11:7–15) and allegations of "this generation's" failure to convert (11:16–19); the parallel woes uttered against the *póleis* for not repenting (11:20–24); concluding with the invitation to come to Jesus for contemplative rest (11:25–30).[27]

1. The Deeds of Christ: "Are You He Who Is to Come?"

John in prison heard about "the deeds of the Christ" (*ta érga tou Christou* [11:2]), a phrase unique to Matthew. The term "Christ" is rare in Matthew; before 11:2 it is used only in the genealogy of Jesus Christ (1:1) and in describing how the birth of Jesus Christ took place (1:18). The word for "deeds" or "works" evokes the image of the original good deed and work of creation begun by God. Matthew sees Jesus Christ continuing the work of reordering creation through a reordered religious and economic base, namely the household. This "work" has overtones of an ongoing jubilee.[28]

Specifically the *ta érga tou Christou* in 11:2 refer to the "works" or "deeds" previously discussed in Matthew: Jesus' works of teaching (5:1–7:29) and healing (8:1–9:34) which Jesus shares with the apostles through the gift of *exousía* (9:35–11:1) and which must continue until the end of the age by the baptized who share in the same *exousía* (28:16–20).[29]

John had spoken earlier of Jesus in an allusion to Emmanuel as "he who is coming" (3:11). Now he has his disciples ask, "Are you he who is to come, or shall we look for another?" (11:3). Jesus responds by enumerating his deeds or works. These would determine whether his spirituality indeed reflected characteristics of the expected Messiah, especially as prophesied by Isaiah (Is. 61:1–2). Jesus responds: "Go and tell John what you hear and see: the blind receive their sight and the lame walk, lepers are cleansed and the deaf hear, and the dead are raised up, and the poor have good news preached to them. And blessed is he who takes no offense at me" (11:4–6).

The prophesied year of favor, the jubilee, represented a total reordering or conversion of social relationships and resources so that creation might revert to that original state when God's work brought order out of disorder. In a special way this reordering meant bringing good news to the poor. Commenting on the "work" of Jesus that brought this good news to the poor, Jan Lambrecht notes:

> Six "works" are enumerated in the long sentence. There is in this list certainly a crescendo, a climax. "The dead rise" is a more spectacular event than "the blind see, the lame walk, the lepers are made clean and the deaf hear." But is then the last clause of this list "and the Good News is preached to the poor" not an anti-climax? By no means! Preaching to the poor is the characteristic of the historical Jesus we know. Therefore, we should ask: In this answer and in Jesus' life, what is the inner connection between works and words, between his miracles and his preaching? . . .
>
> One might think that the "poor" in the enumeration constitute a sixth group besides the blind, lame, lepers, deaf and dead. This is not all that certain. Although it is true that by means of the first five terms Jesus undoubtedly refers to his own miracles which he had already worked, these specifications are only examples, specimens of a much larger past

and future activity of Jesus and pointing to more diversified and numerous addressees. Jesus is sent to forgive all sin and heal all human misery. Therefore, it is better not to see in this last term, "the poor", a new category of people. No, the term summarizes and generalizes the previous ones. The "poor" are the blind and lame, the lepers, the deaf and the dead, and also all others in need, be it spiritual or material.[30]

By implication, since Jesus came to resource those in need, and since economics is based on meeting needs, it can be said that Matthew's version of the reordering of creation demands that the needs of all—especially the least of the sisters and brothers (25:31-46)—be met by the wealthier members of the house churches. God's work begun in creation, exemplified in the *érga tou Christou,* and extended to the apostles must be continued in radical economic and religious conversions on behalf of the poor.

Matthew declared to his various household churches that their spirituality would be a countersign to that of Jesus if their relationships and resources were not primarily ordered to bringing good news to the spiritually and materially poor. Good news to the poor must be predicated on the total (re)ordering (religious/economic conversion) of the house on behalf of the poor. Just as Jesus' disciples were overwhelmed upon realizing the need to reorder life on behalf of the poor (19:25), so were the disciples in Matthew's house churches. Jesus' response to John's question thus became Matthew's response to his churches: "And blessed is he who takes no offense" (11:6).

This vision reflects the heart of discipleship; it also reveals a basic ethical requirement. Not only is this reordering of life on behalf of the poor a sign that Jesus is the Messiah; the new age or *paliggenesía* (used only by Matthew [19:28]) is predicated on whether the disciples' lives and resources also will be reordered on behalf of the poor (19:16-30; 25:31-46; 26:6-13).

2. The Witness of John and This Generation's Failure to Convert

Next Matthew takes the section from Q to contrast the committed way of John with the prosperity of society (11:7-15) and his generation's refusal to convert (16-19). The household churches were to have a religion and an economic different from the houses (*oikois*) of kings (11:8); they were to be a sign to all (5:15) of another way of life. As the house would be reordered or converted, so would society. Thus the structural reforms of the new age would be realized if jubilee principles would be applied to the household—the basic religious and economic unit of society.

After speaking of John's message of conversion and reordering which his hearers rejected (11:7-18) and his own message which was rejected (11:19b), Matthew's Jesus gets to the heart of the issue: it does not matter how the message is couched. Whether the message is couched in austere or gentle terms, "this generation" simply will not hear. Consequently, Matthew's Jesus concludes: "Yet wisdom is justified by her deeds" (11:19c). The deeds Christ performed (11:2) are to be the deeds which justify the house churches in every generation (11:19c).[31] These must be the deeds that bear fruit in the reordering of individual and collective life.

Eduard Schweizer views the connection between works and deeds in 11:2 and 11:19c from the perspective of the house or dwelling. He also calls upon the house-image of wisdom when he equates God's wisdom with Jesus' works:

> . . . the statement of Ethiopian Enoch 42:2 applies: "Wisdom came to make her dwelling among the children of men, and found no dwelling place" (similarly Ecclus. 24:6–22). Matthew, however, speaks of "works" or "results," interpreting the saying from the perspective of verse 2. He thus equates the works of God's wisdom with the works of Jesus.[32]

Any house that wisdom would build would have to be a house of justice. The deeds and works that created that building would be works of justice. The place which would evidence this wisdom-building should be the house church (7:24–27): "wisdom is justified by her deeds" (11:19).

3. The Cities' Failure to Repent

"Then he began to upbraid the cities [póleis] where most of his mighty works had been done, because they did not repent" (11:20). Cities do not convert as such; households and individuals within them convert. At the time Matthew wrote his gospel, it was common to make a connection between oikos and pólis.[33] Matthew himself makes the parallel (10:25; 12:5). Thus, from the social context, it would appear that he is speaking of the failure of the households within the cities to convert. Cities, or households within them, that did not convert represented for Matthew any "generation" (11:16) until the end of the age (28:20) that failed to reorder its relationships and resources according to the pattern of the good news.

Although Matthew did not record any miracles worked by Jesus in Chorazin and Bethsaida,[34] he compares them to Tyre and Sidon. These wealthy cities of trade and commerce did not convert from their basic patterns of economic injustice (Is. 23:1–18; Ezek. 26:1–28:26; Joel 4:4–8). His next condemnation deals with Capernaum, Jesus' "own city" (9:1) where he had made his home (katoikein [4:13]). It too refused his message. Its rejection of his message about good news for the poor (11:6) would prompt Matthew's Jesus to say: "A prophet is not without honor except in his own country and in his own oikía" (13:57).

If the mighty works done in houses in Capernaum (11:23; 13:58) had taken place in Sodom (which had failed to convert from its economic injustice), Sodom would have converted. Yet, the mighty works in and among the households of Capernaum had to be limited "because of their unbelief" (13:58). Since Matthew sees no distinction between the time of Jesus and the time of the church, he, in effect, is saying (in light of the miracle of the resurrection and the sharing of *exousía* with the churches) that if the resurrection miracle that took place at Chorazin and Bethsaida and Capernaum had taken place in his house churches (at Antioch?), they would have converted, as Tyre, Sidon, and Sodom would have converted if the miracles worked in Chorazin, Bethsaida, and Capernaum had been worked in them.

The power of God's *exousía* shared by the Spirit in *exousía* demanded a reordering and conversion of relationships and resources in the house churches on behalf of the poor. Thus judgment would be easier on those other cities and households that had not been entrusted with such power. Having said this, Matthew now expands on Q to have Jesus address the source of all his power.

4. Contemplative Rest in Jesus' Yoke

At that time Jesus declared, "I thank thee, Father, Lord of heaven and earth, that thou hast hidden these things [*tautá*] from the wise and understanding and revealed them to babes; yea, Father, for such was thy gracious will. All things have been delivered to me by my Father; and no one knows the Son except the Father, and no one knows the Father except the Son and any one to whom the Son chooses to reveal him. Come to me, all who labor and are heavy laden, and I will give you rest. Take my yoke upon you, and learn from me; for I am gentle and lowly in heart, and you will find rest for your souls. For my yoke is easy, and my burden is light" [11:25–30].

In this section Matthew seems to have added the last part ("Come to me . . ." [11:28–30]) to a Q saying (11:25–27) that had many parallels to the wisdom tradition. Here Matthew links the *tautá* (these things [11:25]), or the content of what had been revealed, to the deeds of Jesus (11:2) and wisdom (11:19c). By coming to Jesus, the wisdom teacher (*Sophía*), the disciples would learn wisdom from him and submit to the yoke of his teachings/law which they could appropriate and express through *exousía*. In a few words, Fred W. Burnett links *sophía*, Torah, Jesus, the disciples, and *exousía* together when he notes:

The evangelist, by his addition of 11:28–30 to 11:25–27, built upon the identification of Wisdom and Torah in order to identify Jesus-Sophia with Torah. In this passage Matthew has identified Jesus with Wisdom-Torah who invites persons to take his "yoke" upon them because he is "gentle" (*praüs*) and lowly (*tapeinós*) in heart (11:29). This pole (*praüs*) of Matthew's *praüs-exousía* christological framework appears clearly in this passage.[35]

Jesus' relationship to God, his Father, was the source of his *exousía* which enabled him to fulfill God's will in his life. *Exousía* was part of the "all things" (*pánta*) that had been "delivered [*paredothē*] to me by my Father" (11:27; 28:18). Burnett notes that the Greek word *paredothē* denotes the *exousía* or authority given the Son by the Father. Consequently, when Jesus adds that "no one knows the Son except the Father, and no one knows the Father except the Son and any one to whom the Son chooses to reveal him" (11:27), he "refers primarily to the mysterious *exousía* of the Son. It is primarily, though not exclusively, the *authority* of the Son which has been hidden from the wise and revealed to babes according to the Father's will" (11:25-26).[36]

In the *haustafeln* tradition, submission to another's will and humility (*tapeinos*) characterized right living. Matthew's Jesus not only submitted to his Father's will in a spirit of *tapeinos* (11:29); he invited the members of his households to develop the same approach. No longer was their submission to reinforce the yoke of oppression coming from an abuse of authority that laid burdens on their shoulders. Jesus' yoke lifted the burden. It created a new way of life that brought rest.

The "all things" delivered Jesus by the Father are the "all authority in heaven and earth" given baptized disciples (28:18-19). By coming to know Jesus, one experiences the power or *exousía* of God's reign. Knowledge in this sense involves an intimate experience of the one known or contemplation; it makes one open to the will of the other.

Seeking is the first step in the process of conversion. But seeking is futile if nothing is found or experienced. Thus seeking and finding begin conversion. In the process, one comes to know Jesus; and, through his *exousía* one comes to know God. In this knowledge one can come to contemplative rest (11:28). In the rest of contemplation there is no more need to be anxious about material goods, as unbelievers are. Resting in God, one can "sell" former ways and stop running after "all these things" (6:32,33). One can "buy" a new way of life. In turning from "these things" and coming to Jesus and knowing him, "you will find rest for your souls" (11:29). Rather than economic yokes that oppressed (see Is. 58:6) or religious yokes that burdened people under the Law, Jesus' "yoke is easy, and my burden is light" (11:30). Contemplation is being given over to the reign of God.

JERUSALEM'S FAILURE TO CONVERT: THE NEW ISRAEL

This brings us to our final consideration of the notion of conversion in Matthew. In the next section of this third narrative, Matthew discusses the disciples and the Sabbath (12:1-8); Jesus' healing on the Sabbath (12:9-14) which evidences his jubilee servanthood (12:16-21); and Jesus' conflict with the Pharisees (12:22-37).[37] Despite Jesus' cures, the scribes and Pharisees asked for a sign (12:38). But because these leaders represented "an evil and adulterous generation," "no sign shall be given to it except the sign of the prophet Jonah" (12:39). Jesus' ministry under the sign of Jonah, as he said in the beginning (4:17), had as its aim a genuine conversion of people to God's reign. Using the Greek *metanoein* for Jonah's *shûb*, Matthew's Jesus said that the "men of Nineveh . . . repented at the preaching of Jonah, and behold, something greater than Jonah is here" (12:41).

By choosing these words and making this connection, Matthew makes a clear parallel between Jonah's mission of turning or converting a social order and that of Jesus. Matthew's Jesus declares that his generation would not convert (12:41; see 11:20). The implications for Matthew's households could not be clearer, and in the next pericope (12:43–45) Jesus speaks of the unclean spirit returning "to my house" and compares the example "with this evil generation" (12:45). The result of the intransigence and lack of conversion in the house of Israel is highlighted in chapter 23 when Matthew has Jesus score the scribes and Pharisees for their oppression of the people and their unwillingness to convert:

> O Jerusalem, Jerusalem, killing the prophets and stoning those who are sent to you! How often would I have gathered your children together as a hen gathers her brood under her wings, and you would not! Behold, your house is forsaken and desolate. For I tell you, you will not see me again, until you say, "Blessed be he who comes in the name of the Lord" [23:37–39].

Jesus' lament over Jerusalem implies that he had made more than token appeals to the authorities to change their ways; but they "would not" convert. These leaders were the symbols of Jerusalem; their corruption and abuse of power was Jerusalem's. Thus the significance of Jerusalem in this part of the diatribe toward the scribes and Pharisees (23). According to Paul Hollenbach:

> *Jerusalem* of course was *the* city of concern for Jesus. It was the locus par excellence of the betrayal of Yahweh's covenant with Israel, the locus par excellence of injustice and impenitence. And in Jerusalem the temple institution was the locus of the core of evil. Some of Jesus' most bitter warnings and threats concern Jerusalem and the temple.[38]

Immediately after Jesus left the temple (24:1), he announced its destruction (24:2). However the conversion or leaving-from the temple was at the same time the creation of another temple; it was a turning to an alternative. By omitting the pericope of the widow's mite, which Mark (Mk. 12:41–44) and Luke (Lk. 21:1–4) place between the desertion of the house statement (23:38) and Jesus' departure from the temple (24:2), Matthew directly links house (or *oikos* [23:38]) and temple (or *hieron* [24:1]).[39]

With Jerusalem's refusal to be converted, the temple is rejected. Matthew's Jesus turns to a new *oikos,* to a new way of relating and sharing life and resources. The old order will be no more. Now Matthew's house church will be the place where God's abiding presence will be experienced.

9

A Sign of the Kingdom
in the House Church

KINGDOM OF GOD = KINGDOM OF HEAVEN = GOD'S REIGN

In this chapter I follow the opinion that equates Matthew's singular use of "kingdom of heaven" (*basileía tōn ouranōn* [32x]) with "the kingdom of God" (*basileía tou theou*).[1] A good example of Matthew's equation of the phrases can be found in Jesus' comments about wealth: " . . . it will be hard for a rich man to enter the *kingdom of heaven*. Again I tell you, it is easier for a camel to go through the eye of a needle than for a rich man to enter the *kingdom of God*" (19:23–24). Eternal life (*aionios zoe*) itself can be equated with both terms as well (19:16).

The gospel of God's reign in Matthew is the good news that, in the person of Jesus (and subsequently in the house churches of Matthew's day and successive house churches for all days in "all nations" [28:19]), God is with us. From giving Jesus' name as Emmanuel (1:23) until the last verse, "I am with you always" (28:20), the whole gospel speaks about the way Jesus established God's reign via preaching, teaching, and healing (4:23) and shared his power (*exousía*) to do so with his followers (9:35–10:1; 28:16–20).

The reign of God, which is announced by Jesus (4:23), is identified with his person (11:2–6; 12:22–28) and will be fully realized at his return (13:41; 24:3; 25:31). Given this centrality of the reign-theme in Matthew, Jack Dean Kingsbury has insisted that the idea of God's reign is the "single most comprehensive concept in the First Gospel. . . . It touches on every major facet of the gospel, whether it be theological, christological, or ecclesiological in nature."[2]

For Matthew, God's reign is a holistic concept covering a wide range of dimensions. It involves salvific-historical perspectives as well as political-economic implications. The salvific-historical dimension refers to God's reign as transcendent and eschatological—something not yet here. In Jesus and his church, that reign is with people now in history, yet it will be fully realized only in the future. However, in the present, God's reign has political-economic consequences. Matthew places in the mouth of John (3:2) and Jesus (4:17) the proclamation that God's reign is "at hand" (*eggike* [3:2; 4:17; 10:7]). Participation in this reign demands conversion, a total reordering of life, a reconstruction of relationships and resources not only by individuals, but by all levels of society up to and including the political-economic center of life, Jerusalem itself (23:34-39; see 11:16-24).

Because the reign of God is at hand it involves both temporal and spatial dimensions. Temporally the final inbreaking of God's reign can be expected at the last day (7:21-23; 25:31-34). However, since Jesus is God-with-us now, in his person and message, God's ultimate reign is imminent (10:23). It exists in the present in Jesus (3:1-17; 4:17; 10:7; 11:2-6; 13:16-17). Therefore, since that reign is present, the "reign of God is less a period of time and more a type of relationship, according to Matthew."[3] The demand for *dikaiosýne* is sanctioned not so much by the nearness of the world to the end of time as by the nearness of humans to God and each other. This "nearness," or the spatial dimension of God's reign, is found in the community gathered in his name (18:20; 28:20). The present can be considered and evaluated only in the light of how it is bringing about the future reign that is already within it as seed. Thus the parables about God's reign envisioned as a seed in the world (13:4-9, 18-23, 24-30, 31-43).

In chapter 2 we saw that the group of parables about God's reign which Matthew gathered in chapter 13 from Mark, Q, and the tradition forms the climax of the two previous chapters wherein the opposition to Jesus' healing is heightened. There Matthew's Jesus makes it clear that the immanence of God's reign—signified by his healing—places the household of faith (see 12:29) against the house of Satan's reign. Furthermore, the expulsion of the demons by *exousía*, by the Spirit of God, represents the evident proclamation that "the kingdom of God has come upon you" (12:28). Here the kingdom (*basileía*), the city (*pólis*), and the house (*oikía*) are viewed in the same context (12:25).

While the parable of the sower (13:3-9) and its explanation (13:18-23) can be found in Mark 4:1-20 and Luke 8:4-8, 11-15, only Matthew calls the seed "the word of the kingdom" (13:19). Despite natural hostility from various sources, God's providence insures that the preaching of the word will help usher in God's reign come on earth as in heaven. God's reign is like a seed among weeds, Matthew uniquely shows (13:24-30, 36-43). No traditional way, based on human expertise, will be able to thwart it. It must exist now among hostile forces (13:24-30) until the householder begins the harvest. Then the just (*dikaioi*), who continue to extend God's creative reign on earth by doing good, will be separated from the children of the evildoers.

Díkaios was used seventeen times by Matthew,[4] more than all the other gospel writers combined.[5] The just will "shine like the sun in the kingdom of their Father" (13:43). At the close of the age (13:49, see 25:31) the just will be separated from the unjust like fish in a net (13:47-52; see 25:37-46). The new order will be predicated on whether people's lives warrant their being called the "just."

In the parables of the mustard seed (13:31–32) and leaven (13:33), the reign of God is signified as a present reality in the process of becoming fully realized. Once experienced, it invites a total reordering of life and all resources (13:44–46). Total reordering of life and resources reflects Matthew's concern about the creation of a new social order within his household churches which images God's reign. This reordering undermines any natural hostility, any political injustice, any unjust economic form of production, or any religious kind of persecution. "Everything" must be sold, "everything" must be reordered to experience this reign (13:43–45).

Possibly because we are used to hearing them, the parables about God's reign have for us lost much of their original sting. However, John Dominic Crossan has said that a parable does not merely convey concepts: "Parable casts fire on the earth."[6] As myths can become the agents of stability, so the parable is meant to overturn "horizons" reinforcing the status quo: "Myth establishes world. Apologue defends world. . . . Satire attacks world. Parable subverts world."[7] Since, in Matthew, the parables were addressed within households or in gatherings of people "with" Jesus (i.e., to the church), they contained an embedded religious and politico-economic dimension. Douglas Oakman points to both religious and economic interpretations when he notes of the parables in chapter 13:

> First, the parables express the theme of providence and lay emphasis upon the ultimate source of sustenance in God. Secondly, these words of Jesus intimate that human labor is devalued, if not abolished, by the reign of God. There is no evident concern with innovations in technology or with changing the means of production. Thirdly, the parables hint in a number of ways that the rule of God undermines the current order of production.[8]

The reign of God's word in the world undermines all disorder, be it religious or economic, spatial or temporal. It creates a new realm of orderly love.

"KINGDOM" AS "MASTER IMAGE" IN MATTHEW'S GOSPEL

Leander E. Keck has noted that the "kingdom of heaven" is a master image in the first gospel. For Keck, a

> master image is an embracing metaphor which overarches all other images and metaphors. It is the controlling term, the hub to which the different spokes are joined. A master image is not a concept, because concepts can be defined. An image does not ask so much for definition as for concretion. A concept toward the abstract, a master image appeals to the whole self because it stimulates the imagination. A concept presses for precision and tries to eliminate ambiguity but a master image incorporates ambiguity and tension. A concept is at home in denotative

discourse, a master image is at home in connotative speech and in evocative language.[9]

Intimately related to the master image of the reign of God, according to Keck, is justice. We have described justice in the household as correctly ordered relationships and resources that image God's original will for creation. According to Keck this has implications for ethics: "When the master image is the Kingdom of Heaven, our attention is shifted to a pattern of right relationships in a field of force, to the Creator's domain in which rightness prevails. The consequence of this shift for ethics deserves to be explored." While I have noted some of the implications of this shift in chapter 5, Keck explores other consequences when he explains:

> Jesus the proclaimer and bearer of the Kingdom appeals to the original order of things in creation. The righteousness of the Kingdom is not what appears to be the equitable thing to do, given conflicting claims to justice in the present, but rather the right state of affairs at the End which corresponds to the beginning. In other words, Matthew's ethics is teleological, not in the sense of human needs and goals but of the telos, the goal and end of God's work—restoration of creation.[10]

We have already seen that Matthew's insertion of the passages about the delay in Jesus' return (24:36–25:30) counters Schweitzer's assumption that his gospel evidences an "interim ethic" and thus is no longer applicable for Matthew's post-Easter church, much less for our era. But what of those who argue that Christianity has nothing to contribute toward a social ethic for society at large? Such people buttress their argument by showing, for instance, that the "house rules" in the New Testament merely repeated the *haustafeln* of the wider society and, indeed, reinforced its negative cultural patterns like patriarchy. The church's *haustafeln*, much less its other "Christian ethics," someone like Jack Sanders indicates, cannot "be truly guides . . . for helping to bring this life into harmony with the life beyond unless the life beyond is really no different from the non-Christian world."[11]

But is Christian morality only what the sociologists say it is—a reflection of the morality of the culture which houses it?[12] If this is not so, then what are the ethical implications for the gospel of God's reign which is to be the epiphany of a *new* age (19:28)?

The Hebrew scriptures' notions about God's reign demonstrate that the primary way of God's relating to humankind was not vis-à-vis individuals, but to house-based social groupings which ultimately constituted the collective house of Israel.[13] Salvation comes not just to individuals, but to the people; liberation is the promise not to this or that person, but for collective jubilee. Personal and social conversion to God's reign is the consequence. In this sense, the conversion Jesus preached was both individual and social. It was personal as well as economic and political. While he preached conversion to God's reign to people in general (4:17), the main thrust of his message, from a linguistic

analysis of *metanoein*, called for social change—or what today can be termed
the conversion of structures and systems (11:20–24; 12:41; see 23:1–39). Central to this moral conversion was the ethos of justice, or right-relations that
manifest love. What Stephen Charles Mott writes of the moral-ethical concept
of justice in the New Testament is especially applicable to Matthew's gospel,
which emphasizes justice more than any of the other gospels:

> Every morally valid political philosophy has a concept of justice. The
> Bible also provides us with one of its own. The New Testament continues
> the Old Testament understanding. There, need is the criterion of distribu-
> tive justice, and justice is the provision of the minimal requirements for
> people to participate in community. The New Testament likewise under-
> stands the principle of justice to be continuous with rather than separate
> from the rest of the value system, particularly with the idea of love.[14]

By his inclusiveness and emphasis on love (5:44; 19:19; 22:39; 24:12),
Matthew shows that morality is relational and social by its very nature. The
church as the city set on a mountain, as the house of light (5:14–16), is the
carrier of the gospel and its ethics about God's reign of justice and love in
the world. In this sense, as Hauerwas says, the church is the ethic.[15] But even
more so, there is an ethos, a style of relating among individuals in this social
grouping called church that should reflect the inbreaking of God's reign on
earth as it is in heaven. In this sense, Charles L. Kammer III writes:

> If the Kingdom of God is the proclamation of God's activity in history
> through social groups and social organization as the Old Testament
> prophets and Jesus proclaimed it to be; then it seems incredulous to say
> that Jesus' teachings are inapplicable because they are too closely tied to
> his expectation of the coming Kingdom. His teachings may not be
> applicable in the direct, literal sense, but . . . by presenting a vision of
> the Kingdom which inspired these teachings, the teachings provide a
> context within which ethical reflection and moral activity can occur.[16]

In presenting Matthew's vision of the kingdom, we have noted Keck declaring that, for Matthew, the "kingdom of heaven" is a "master image."
However, throughout this book I have said that "house" is an assumed primary
metaphor in Matthew. Is the "master image" of the "kingdom of heaven" to
be equated with the "assumed primary image of the house"? How does
"house" as "assumed primary metaphor" relate to "kingdom of heaven" as
"master image" in the first gospel? If, within the *basileía* of his wider world,
the *oikía/oikos* served as its basic component, could Matthew be challenging
the patriarchal assumptions of that order via his "master image" of the *basileía
tou theou* as grounded in the household itself? A resolution of these questions
might be discovered in analyzing what Matthew means by entering God's reign
and entering the house.

ENTERING GOD'S REIGN AND ENTERING THE HOUSE

The announcement of the imminence of God's reign (3:2; 4:17, 23-25) precedes the description of the moral requirements for entrance into the reign contained in the first discourse of Matthew, the Sermon on the Mount. The Beatitudes describe God's reign as present (*estin* = present in a certain sense = already now)[17] to the poor in spirit (5:3) and those persecuted for justice' sake (5:10). Entrance into God's reign demands a unique form of justice (5:20-48; 6:1-7:23) that involves entry through the narrow gate (7:13-14). The other four discourses, which feature house as a central context or theme, also highlight God's reign.

Like the words for house (*oikos/oikía*) and the phrase "entering the house," so the phrase "entering the reign of God" is a key term in all five sections of Matthew. According to G. Todd Wilson: "Entering the kingdom is a major concern of each of the five discourses, and his [Matthew's] references to entering the kingdom or some equivalent expression more than equal the combined total of such references in the other synoptic gospels."[18]

The idea of entering God's reign and eternal life is used widely in other Matthean sayings of Jesus which came from Matthew's sources (8:12; 11:12; 18:3, 8, 19; 19:23; 23:13), in modifications of his sources (7:13-14, 21), and in those statements that were unique to him (5:20; 13:41-43; 21:31). Invariably when Matthew's Jesus used the basic word for entering (*eis* + *erchomai*) it referred to the "kingdom" and "house" and "cities" or "regions."[19]

Heinz Todt says that Jesus' words about entering the reign of God represent "the distinguishing mark of Matthew's theology."[20] Consequently, his narrative has Jesus speaking about people or things being "in the reign of God" (5:19; 8:11; 11:11). In key passages entrance into God's reign depends on a just reordering of one's relationships and resources. Such sayings about "entrance" into the reign of God seem to conceive it in relational-spatial terms, as a kind of territory, a place. Here justice reigns in loving relationships among various persons joined together.

In Judaism God's reign refers to royal notions about God and the people. In contrast to the prevailing Jewish practice, Matthew's Jesus seldom referred to God as a ruler or king, but as "my Father," and to himself as "the Son" (see 7:21; 10:32-33; 11:25-27; 12:50; 15:13; 16:17; 18:10, 14, 19, 35; 20:23; 25:34; 26:29, 39, 42). The disciples were his sisters and brothers, called to live under the will and loving authority of that Father (see 6:9; 23:9). Those remaining united to that will would enter God's reign on earth as in heaven.

Building on the ideas about God's reign as a sphere or locus of authority which one can enter and there enter into familial relationships, Sverre Aalen proffers a good case for concluding that, in the gospels, especially Matthew's, the reign of God should not be limited to a manifestation or revelation of God's royal glory or power. Rather, he argues, it makes more sense to consider God's reign in the spatial sense of a community or household. He notes:

That the New Jerusalem is conceived by means of local categories is quite natural. Here we can in fact observe the use of the word "in" in a Jewish text. All the righteous, also those of earlier generations and of the gentiles, shall assemble "in that house," that is, in the New Jerusalem, prophesies Enoch (I Enoch xc. 33). Into this house, moreover, the holy people is "invited," just as Israel is "invited" to the kingdom (Matt. xxii, 1ff = Luke xiv. 16ff). The entrance of the New Jerusalem is narrow, and one has to strive to enter it (IV Ezra vii. 7ff). It is an "inheritance" (v. 9). Further, it is described as being "full of all good things" (v. 6). The New Jerusalem is, consequently, the sum of all the gifts of salvation and re-creation.[21]

Events usually taking place in a house, such as feasts and meals, are also linked to the reign of God in Matthew. Many will find a place at the banquet in the reign of God while the natural heirs will be driven out (8:11–12). Some "enter" the feast (25:21, 23); others are not allowed through the door (25:11). The eucharist not only takes place in a house (26:18); it anticipates the final reign of God itself: "I tell you I shall not drink again of this fruit of the vine until that day when I drink it new with you in my Father's kingdom" (26:29). That reign will be characterized by God's loving hospitality.

Aalen makes the link among the house, table fellowship, and God's reign clearer when he describes how the reign of God is

> like a room in a house, a hall. The meal feast, on the other hand, stresses the idea of community. This room or house is for men who are in fellowship with God, or with his representative, Jesus, and with each other. Both sides, the room and the fellowship, are included in the idea of the house. A house is a confined area, and it forms a community. The kingdom of God is a house.[22]

The kingdom/house is the "area where the goods of salvation are available and received."[23] The goods of salvation shared in the house are not only spiritual, as in the Pauline sense of the "economy of salvation" (Eph. 3:2; see 1 Cor. 9:17; Eph. 1:10; 3:9; Col. 1:25),[24] but material as well. The reign of God must come on earth as it is in heaven (6:10); this involves reordered resources, both spiritual and material, as in debt-forgiveness (6:12). In Matthew the realization and possession of these "goods of salvation" are contingent on two kinds of reordering: a passive reordering that seeks first God's reign and God's justice (as noted by Aalen [6:33; see 5:6]) and an active reordering of material goods on behalf of the poor (19:23–24) through works of justice (5:20; 6:1). The latter type of reordering prefaces the experience of that reign (5:10).

Table fellowship with the marginated signifies that the reign of God, the new age, has already begun—in the household. John Koenig supports this expansion of Aalen's ideas of spiritual sharing to that of household sharing or hospitality when he writes:

Our own look at Jesus' message tends to confirm this hypothesis [of Aalen] but requires us in addition to highlight particularly that aspect of the kingdom that Jesus presents with images of food, drink, and home. In other words, the kingdom of God is like a movable feast, a roving banquet hall that seeks the people of Israel as guests and hosts. At this table they may find reconciliation with one another, as well as a true home and a plenty that fills them up and propels them toward sharing relationships with their neighbors.[25]

Since God's reign is discovered and celebrated in the house and since the house churches were the places where people gathered—two or three (18:19-20) or twenty or thirty—as a manifestation of God's reign or presence, we can conclude that any ethic of the kingdom in Matthew's gospel must be inseparably linked to an ethic of the house church. The house, as the basic unit of religion and economics and society itself, was the natural order within which ordered relationships would take place. Members justly relating to each other and justly sharing their resources signified the inbreaking on earth of the reign of God in heaven.

In the early house churches, membership was voluntary. One was not usually "born into" a household church; one entered. Thus Matthew, of all the Synoptics (as we saw in chapter 2), has special phraseology about "entering" the house. But he also uses phrases about entering the "kingdom" more than the other Synoptics. Thus, again, one can rightly make the house-reign connection and conclude that Matthew's understanding of discipleship involved freely entering into this new voluntary association based in the house.

During his public life, Jesus seems to have seen his preaching and healing as signs of God's reign to the house of Israel alone (see 10:6; 15:24). These passages might also refer to the continued influence of the Judaizers in Matthew's community. However, with the resurrection, the former house of God, the temple (12:4; 21:13), is deserted (23:38). A new house (7:24-27), a new church (16:16-18), is established in those who hear the word of God, understand it, and practice it (7:24) by observing all that Jesus taught (28:20). This new house is no longer composed of blood family—who are now "outside" the house (12:46-47)—but of those faithful who freely give up blood family (see 7:18-24) and house (19:29) to become mothers, sisters, and brothers to Jesus by doing the will of their heavenly Father (12:48-50).

THE CHURCH NOT TO BE EQUATED WITH GOD'S REIGN

Even though Matthew interpreted God's reign as being withdrawn from the house of Israel and handed over to the church (21:43), and even though the church in its household expression is to be the place where the risen Christ will dwell (16:18; 18:20; 28:20), the church cannot be equated with the reign of God. In fact, those outside the church, from all nations, may be the first to enter the reign because of their faith (8:11-12) and their justice (25:31-46). In this sense, while the "kingdom of God is a house," it cannot be equated with any specific house church.

When any religious institution begins to equate itself with God's reign, its leaders can consciously or unconsciously begin to think that they alone can define who is qualified for that reign and what must be done (or not done) as signs of fidelity to that reign. However, often what they say and what they do can contradict each other (23:3). Consequently, Matthew's Jesus warned the scribes and Pharisees of the house of Israel, and the leaders of Matthew's house church, of that day and subsequent days: "For I tell you, unless your *dikaiosýnē* exceeds that of the scribes and Pharisees, you will never enter the kingdom of heaven [*eiselthete eis ten basileían tōn ouranōn*]" (5:20).

Matthew never identified the church with God's reign, even though he has disciples entering both. Far from being equated with God's reign, the church was to seek first the reign of God and God's justice (6:33). Only those in the house churches and those house churches collectively that seek God's justice (5:6; 6:33) and practice justice (5:20; 6:1) even to the point of persecution (5:10) will experience the reign of God as their own.

Just as the reign of God's presence in the temple, according to Matthew, was taken away, so, he warned his house churches, its wandering charismatics, and its leaders, it could happen to them if they did not put into practice the teachings of Jesus he narrated: "Not every one who says to me, 'Lord, Lord,' shall enter the kingdom of heaven, but he who does the will of my Father who is in heaven" (7:21).

THE WILL OF GOD AS THE DOING OF JUSTICE

In Matthew, God's reign and God's will are often linked to that justice which Jesus faithfully came to fulfill (3:15). Submitting himself to God's plan for creation by being baptized by John, Jesus is called "son" and "favored" (3:17; see 17:5). Since the terms used of Jesus came from Psalm 2 and Isaiah 42 and 61, the baptism of Jesus shows a definite connection among God's will and the fulfillment of all justice, childlike obedience (Ps. 2), and the jubilee restoration of life (Is. 42, 61). The prayer Jesus taught asked that God's will be done on earth and in heaven (6:10). He was faithful to that will from his testing in the desert (4:1–11), through his prayer in Gethsemane (26:36–46), to his death on the cross.

Using the story of the two sons who were asked to do the will of their father (21:28–32), Jesus said to the chief priests and elders (as Matthew said to his household church) that John came in the way of justice "and you did not believe him, but the tax collectors and the harlots believed him; and even when you saw it, you did not afterward repent and believe him" (21:32). Immediately he continued with the parable of the householder and the vineyard. Then he concluded, "Therefore I tell you, the kingdom of God will be taken away from you and given to a nation producing the fruits of it" (21:43). The fruit of God's reign is the product of justice. God's will for the household of faith requires the observance of what is good and just. John Meier explains that the Householder (God) wants the entire produce of justice: "the total and exclusive claim of God is clear. The fruits are the good works which God demands of man, the doing of God's will, justice."[26]

In chapter 7 I commented on Matthew's two uses of justice (*dikaiosýnē*): as God's absolute gift and as God's demand. In all but two instances, which relate to the gift of experiencing God (5:6; 6:33), the emphasis is on the demand, on God's will, which determines what is necessary to enter God's reign (3:15; 5:10, 20; 6:1; 21:32). Writing on "Conditions for Entering the Kingdom according to St. Matthew," G. Todd Wilson comments:

> The demand is most clearly focused in 5:20: "Unless your righteousness exceeds that of the scribes and Pharisees, by no means shall you enter the kingdom of heaven." When considered in the context of 5:17–48 *dikaiosune* can only mean obedience or faithfulness to the will of God as expressed in Jesus' interpretation of the Law. Similarly in 3:15, 5:10, 6:1 and 21:32 it denotes conduct in obedience to God's will. Rather clearly Matthew intended righteousness to refer to the absolute obedience demanded by God. It is "rightness of life, before God, conduct in agreement with his will at the heart of which lies the disposition of obedience and devotion." For Matthew, therefore, *dikaiosune* was the abstract noun which corresponded to the expression *poien to thelema tou patros* (cf. 5:20 with 7:21). Interestingly, in 5:20 Matthew granted to the Pharisees a righteousness; but he added that the "higher righteousness" was required for entrance into the kingdom.[27]

INTERIM TAXES UNTIL THE FINAL INBREAKING OF GOD'S REIGN

No book on "household" from a religious and economic perspective would be complete without some consideration of taxation. Taxation was discussed somewhat in the second chapter, but the approach to the issue in Matthew I want to highlight here revolves around his understanding of the reign of Caesar and the reign of God and how they are to be related.

Matthew has two pericopes about the payment of taxes. One is based on Mark 12:13–17 (22:15–22) and the other is unique (17:24–27). Since taxes then, as today, are a form of economic redistribution, it will be good at this point to investigate how Matthew's church viewed the issue of tax payment or nonpayment.

The fourth discourse begins (17:24) with Matthew's insertion of the pericope about the temple tax (17:24–27). This insertion—dealing with a discussion of civic duties—begins the subsequent *haustafel* (17:24–18:35). This insertion occurs immediately after including Mark's statement about the arrival in Capernaum (Mk. 9:33a). The discussion about the temple tax begins with the question addressed to Peter as to whether Jesus paid the didrachma. Peter answers affirmatively (17:24b–25a). Adapting the Markan theme of special instruction taking place within the house (Mk. 9:33b), Matthew has Peter enter "into the house" (17:25b), where Jesus immediately begins the dialogue about the temple tax. Should the house churches and those in them pay the temple tax?

Exodus 30:11–16 notes the Mosaic prescription about the levying of a census tax of half a sanctuary shekel (in distinction to the common shekel [Gen. 23:15] and the royal shekel [2 Sam. 14:26]).[28] All free males over twenty years old were to pay this tax toward the support of the temple. In varying ways this form of wealth redistribution was still the practice at the time of the writing of Matthew's gospel. However, because our thesis is that Matthew wrote the gospel in the 80s or 90s and because the temple was destroyed at least a decade earlier (70 CE), one must investigate further the meaning behind the words.

There were times when money collected from Asian Jews for the temple was impounded. After the temple's destruction, the temple tax was transferred to the support of Jupiter Capitolinus. Unlike the poll tax mentioned in 22:15–22 (Mk. 12:13–17; Lk. 20:20–26), which was a purely secular tax, this tax was purported to be a religious tax. Whether monies were impounded or religious taxes were transferred, both acts became political forms of economic redistribution. This form of wealth redistribution was being used to reinforce economically the Roman system which oppressed Jews, slaves, and other subjected peoples. From an analysis of the wording of the dialogue with Peter, Richard J. Cassidy shows that Matthew's Jesus viewed the tax as civil rather than religious.[29] Matthew states: "And when he came home [*oikía*], Jesus spoke to him first, saying, 'What do you think, Simon? From whom do kings of the earth take toll or tribute? From their sons or from others?' And when he said, 'From others,' Jesus said to him, 'Then the sons are free' " (17:25–26).

In a more literal and strict sense the "sons" who were not taxed would be members of the ruler's household, including employees, domestics, and other dependents. Yet, in a broader sense, "sons" would be of the *pater familias* and members of *domus Caesari*, the empire. However, since the members of the new household, the church founded on Peter (16:18; see 7:24), are the new temple founded in Jesus' death/resurrection (23:38–24:2), its members, its "sons," were exempt. This reveals Matthew's view of Jesus' power vis-à-vis the emperor's household and the empire itself. But his power is greater still; it has ecological implications: Matthew shows Jesus having authority over all creation. This is revealed in Matthew's description of the manner in which Jesus resolved the payment of the tax: "However, not to give offense to them, go to the sea and cast a hook, and take the first fish that comes up, and when you open its mouth you will find a shekel; take that and give it to them for me and for yourself" (17:27).

This difficult pericope can best be understood, then, not from the perspective of Jesus' paying the temple tax (which he did, it seems), but from the uniquely Matthean redaction which combined economics and ecclesiology. It is obvious that Jesus tells the members of his household, who lived in the reign of the empire (22:15–22), to avoid scandal (17:27) by rendering civil taxes to Caesar. Yet, despite this apparent accommodation to civil authority, it should be remembered where ultimate authority rested. In the two realms of the household of Caesar and that of God-represented-in-Jesus, Emmanuel, the ultimate authority was with Jesus. Paul de Surgy notes of the 22:15–22 pericope that it invites disciples not to look for a messiah who will take actual political power over Caesar and assume the head of that household.[30] Rather, they should live faithfully in society, according to that society's legitimate and just rules, always recognizing Jesus' ultimate primacy over Caesar. All reigns on earth exist under the reign of this God-with-us.

THE LAST JUDGMENT: ENTERING THAT KINGDOM PREPARED FROM THE BEGINNING OF THE WORLD

In Matthew's mind, the reign of God proclaimed in the past was to be proclaimed through the basic unit of society, the household church. Here a living narrative of Jesus' preaching and teaching was to be manifest. In these households, justice would reign, with the preciousness of each member insured (see 18:14) by a sharing of resources which would meet basic needs. While the household churches were to be first witnesses to this ethic, all nations would ultimately be judged by it as well, as the famous "last judgment" scene attests (25:31–46). A. J. Mattil, Jr., argues that, by making 25:31–46 (which refers to the universal or gentile mission of Jesus' followers) a midrash on 10:5–42 (which refers to the Jewish or house of Israel mission), the new house of Israel is now extended to all the nations (28:16–20).[31] The ordering of this new household, religiously and economically speaking, involves the meeting of needs from the perspective of justice. In this new household the just (*díkaios*) will be separated from the others to hear the King say: "Come, O blessed of my Father, inherit the kingdom prepared for you from the foundation of the world" (25:34).

At the foundation of the world (Gen. 1:1–31) God made male and female to be co-creators in bringing light out of darkness, order from disorder, and justice from *tohû-bohû* by reordering relationships and resources (Gen. 1:26–28). The disciples of Jesus, putting into practice his teachings, were to give "light to all in the house," that the light might shine before all who might "see your good works and give glory to your Father who is in heaven" (5:15–16). At the end of the world, those who continued that creation by so imaging God by doing good works in the form of meeting others' needs will be blessed, whether they are Jew or gentile, Christian or non-Christian. David Catchpole notes: "In Matthew, men are divided, not on the basis of whether they belong to the people of God, or their persecutors, but on the basis of whether they have or have not done anything to alleviate human need."[32] Such is God's will.

For Christians, the present time represents the time of testing to determine whether these needs will be met by Christ's disciples in the way he modeled.

Given the unique environment of the prospering house churches for whom Matthew wrote his narrative, Matthew's gospel differs from the other Synoptics in the concretization of the way that modeling must be done. Allen Verhey notes: "It is not, however, testing through *suffering* with Christ, as it is in Mark, but rather through *obedience* to his disclosure of God's kingdom and his righteousness. What is tested is one's response to God's gracious reign."[33] Obedience is submission to another's will. Submission is the heart of any *haustafel*. By their submission to the one will of God, their Father, in the performance of justice, the members of Matthew's house churches become brothers and sisters of each other and heirs of the reign of God.

Verhey's conclusion cuts through the debate about the last judgment regarding exactly who the sheep and goats, the just and unjust, the least Christians and all the nations may be:

> There is here no mention of desert, no claim to a works-righteousness. The surprised question of the saved (25:37–39) stands in opposition to such a reading. The righteousness is not calculating but self-forgetful, responsive to the needs and cares of the neighbor and thus responsive to Christ. Such righteousness is exemplified—but hardly exhausted—in the catalogue of merciful works enumerated here: feeding the hungry, giving drink to the thirsty, practicing hospitality to strangers, clothing the naked, visiting the sick and imprisoned (25:35–36, 42–43). Jeremias's position that Matthew is dealing here merely with the question of the criteria according to which the heathen will be judged has nothing to commend it except the assembly of "all the nations" (Gk. *panta ta ethne*; *ethne* can mean "heathens"). But the judgment on "all nations" proceeds in such a way that the distinction between Jew and gentile is immaterial to the judgment; self-forgetful response to the needs of the neighbor is the single criterion of judgment.[34]

Responding to the needs of the least of the brothers and sisters throughout the *oikouménē*, rather than having the market or the state reinforce the wants of the few, will be the ultimate criteria by which the economic of any nation is critiqued. Such is the responsibility ethic through which Matthew's notion of justice is to be expressed.

10

Matthew's Message for the Third Millennium

SOCIAL INSTITUTIONS AND SOCIAL COORDINATION
THEN AND NOW

New Testament scholar Bruce Malina has distinguished four basic social institutions or structures which people use to realize fundamental human values. These basic social institutions are generally called kinship, economics, politics, and religion. Depending on times and geography one model dominates. The other three are embedded in it, their dynamics determined by way of flows from and to the dominant model:[1]

> Briefly, kinship is about naturing and nurturing people; it is held together by commitment (also called loyalty or solidarity), and forms a structure of human belonging. Economics is about provisioning a group of people; it is held together by inducement, i.e., the exchange of goods and services, and forms the adaptive structure of a society. Politics looks to effective collective action; it is held together by power, and forms the vertical organizational structure of a society. Finally, religion deals with the overarching order of existence, with meaning; it is held together by influence; i.e., it provides reasons for what exists and the models that generate those reasons.[2]

Barrington Moore has shown that in every social institution coordination of social relations is a basic issue.[3] The social coordination within each of the four institutions involves authority, the division of labor or status,[4] and the allocation of resources. These three essential components of society's fundamental institutions are embedded in them in varying ways.

When Moore's ideas of social coordination involving authority, division of labor, and resource-allocation are joined to Malina's insights about kinship, politics, economics, and religion as the basic social institutions, we find an excellent structure within which we can summarize differences between Matthew's first-century environment and our own in the First World. Just as each of the four social institutions (kinship, politics, economics, and religion) deals differently with the issue of social coordination (authority, division of labor, and resource allocation), so each of the four feeds from its base backward and forward into the other three social systems to provide meaning for life. Each reflects a different type of horizon and culture.

In the first century as well as in present peasant economies, *kinship* ultimately determines the functioning of religion, politics, and economics. Survival is oriented around belonging or solidarity. Belonging is ensured by the commitments household members make to each other. While there may be more collegial forms, authority tends to be patriarchal, with status determining the division of labor and covetousness affecting the allocation of resources.

When kinship, politics, and economics are embedded in *religion*, as when Christendom reigned or in present-day Islam, survival revolves around norms for truth and validity which provide meaning. Symbols which provide that meaning are geared around the notion of ideological influence. Authority rests in those who control the ideology; usually these are the religious leaders. All resources are viewed as divine blessings. Those with more are more blessed.

When *politics* embeds kinship, economics, and religion, as is the case in the applied Marxism of the Soviet Union and the People's Republic of China, human beings adapt to reality through political organizations meant to provide collective effectiveness. Power is the ultimate mediating symbol. Authority is determined by membership in the political organization with the control; the control is determined by party leaders, while greed and avarice characterize their way of allocating resources, especially power.

If *economics* represents the dominant social institution, as in the First World, kinship, politics, and religion feed backward and forward into it. People adapt to this form of social institution by production and consumption; its ethos revolves around inducement to buy and sell goods and services. The inducement to buy and sell which facilitates the expropriation of goods does so in a way "which measures usefulness in terms of money."[5] Authority is determined by the ability to buy and sell those goods and services. Here persons owning and/or controlling the wealth ultimately make the laws that determine the social order. Resource-allocation is determined by the "bottom line" or profit motive.

Adapting Moore's three areas of social coordination with Malina's elements in social institutions offers the model shown on page 231.

While the kinship model provided the context for Matthew's horizon, the economic model offers the context for what Peter Berger calls our "economic culture."[6] Having considered how Matthew's horizon—conditioned by the kinship model—dominated his households, we can examine how authority, the division of labor, and the allocation of resources reflect a certain kind of social coordination in the twentieth century. This reveals an economic horizon.

Throughout the previous nine chapters I showed how justice was the underpinning providing the ethos and ethics for Matthew's households. Elements of that same justice are equally needed as the cornerstone for the edifice of today's society as well. In their letter on the economy, the Catholic bishops of the United States stated that "the biblical understanding of justice gives a fundamental perspective to our reflections on social and economic justice."[7] They then go on to "propose an ethical framework that can guide economic life today in ways that are both faithful to the Gospel and shaped by human experience and reason."[8]

KINSHIP/(BELONGING)
Commitment
PATRIARCHY
Hierarchy/
(Covetousness)

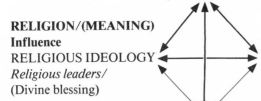

POLITICS/
(ORGANIZATION)
Power
PARTY AUTHORITY
Party leaders/
(Greed/avarice)

RELIGION/(MEANING)
Influence
RELIGIOUS IDEOLOGY
Religious leaders/
(Divine blessing)

ECONOMICS/(PRODUCTION-CONSUMPTION)
Inducement to Buy and Sell
CONTROLLING OF WEALTH
Corporate elites/money managers/
(Profit motive)

Legend: **SOCIAL INSTITUTION/(SOCIETAL BOND)**
Mediating Symbol/Central Value
FORM OF AUTHORITY
Status/
(Resource allocation)

Given the bishops' comments about justice, I want to spend the rest of this chapter examining the nature of authority in today's society, its division of labor, and its allocation of resources. With the bishops, this analysis will show that our society has contributed much to "the present-day situation of the world, marked as it is by the grave sin of injustice" and that, consequently, as citizens of nations whose behavior has helped create and sustain this grave sin of injustice, it is necessary that "we recognize both our responsibility and our inability to overcome it by our own strength."[9]

The language of the above statement from the 1971 Synod of Catholic Bishops indicates a kind of addictiveness in society which undermines the realization of justice. I will show that in order to build a society which grounds all its policies and practices in justice we must understand the obstacles to that justice. The main obstacle will be shown to be contemporary forms of mammon or "cultural consumerism" to which society and all its members have become addicted. I will conclude that only by turning over our lives to a greater power (through the religious experience of God's presence-with-us in *exousía*) and by creating alternative, house-type communities will we be able to provide the necessary environment for a new order of justice in our lives and that of society.

With this as background, we begin now examining the above-mentioned three forms of social coordination: authority, the division of labor or status, and the allocation of resources.

1. The Nature of Authority in Post-Industrial Capitalism

While elements of all four kinds of Malina's social institutions can be found in various places in today's world, the two main models are the political model of the "East"—the Soviet Union and the Warsaw Pact nations and the People's Republic of China—and the economic model of the "West." Except in theory, neither represents a pure "political" or "economic" model; in fact both are "mixed," and, as such, are two different kinds of political economies. That of the "East" is organized through what is called the administered or command system. Our own is called the "market" system.

Whether the market or administered system, each politico-economic system employs certain mechanisms for social control. These are geared to bring the mass of individuals (voluntarily or through coercion) under the authority of that system. In his *Politics and Markets*, Charles E. Lindblom makes authority central to both command and market forms of today's main political economies. With Moore he grounds authority in basic social relationships, especially the effort to control: *"Every specific control can be used either as a method of direct control or as a method for establishing a rule of obedience (authority) which, once established, itself suffices for control as long as it stands."*[10]

Authority is not expressed only in forms of social control. Exchange itself— in the form of the inducement to buy and sell—can be another kind of control, as well as moral codes arising from the ethos of a group. Another significant form of social control, both in command and market economies, is persuasion. According to Lindblom, persuasion is central and fundamental in all social systems:

> In the form of ideological instruction and propaganda, persuasion is a major method of elite control of the masses, much more so in communist systems than in liberal democratic ones. In the form of commercial advertising, it is a major instrument of corporate control of masses of consumers in market societies.[11]

Command and market systems have unique methods of persuasion to bring individuals and groups under their authority. The way those with power within those systems attempt to bring people under the authority of that system has been called "propaganda" by Jacques Ellul. Ellul defines "propaganda" as "a set of methods employed by an organized group that wants to bring about the active or passive participation in its actions of a mass of individuals, psychologically unified through psychological manipulations and incorporated in an organization."[12]

According to Ellul there are two main forms of propaganda: political and sociological. Political propaganda is that which North Americans normally associate with "propaganda" as employed by command or administered political economies, especially as refined by party leaders like Hitler, Stalin, and Mao.

When sociological propaganda dominates a culture, economic, political, and sociological factors progressively create a certain way of thinking (ideology) in people. Through economic and political structures this ideology leads "to the active participation of the masses and the adaptation of individuals" in such a way that individuals participate actively in and adapt to some "specific sociological context."[13] According to Lindblom and Ellul, the "specific sociological context" which acculturates individuals in Western economies is a certain form of materialism which I call cultural consumerism.

The culture of the "West" has not always been oriented around cultural consumerism. Cultural consumerism seems to have begun in the United States toward the end of the nineteenth century, and its roots seem to lie in a device developed to reach widespread markets—the catalogue. What began as a service ended as an enslaver. Rural development and Western expansion, combined with the rise of department stores, gave birth to the catalogue. For pioneers on the move or in out-of-the-way places, products in catalogues from practice-proven department stores became equated with quality and trust. However, over a period of generations, the advertising which began as a method of communication gradually evolved to be a method attempting social control.[14]

a. Social Control and Democracy

In *Democracy in America*, his classic work which examined the psyche of the United States in the nineteenth century, Alexis de Tocqueville predicted that the nation's stress on individualism "could lay itself peculiarly open to the establishment of a despotism."[15] Far from being violent and harsh, as in the case of many kinds of political despots, it would be different: "It would be more widespread and milder; it would degrade men rather than torment them."[16]

Connecting the ideas of de Tocqueville and Lindblom, one can legitimately ask if that contemporary form of "widespread and milder" control over the masses of individuals[17] is not exercised through corporate-controlled advertising that seeks to bring people under the authority of the corporation. Since today's advertising costs constitute a "barrier to entry" for a small business seeking a mass market, this possibility is reinforced by the conclusion of Lindblom's book wherein he states that it is quite "possible that the rise of the corporation has offset or more than offset the decline of class as an instrument of indoctrination" and that, more "than class, the major specific institutional barrier to fuller democracy may therefore be the autonomy of the private corporation."[18]

We are not speaking here of the private corporation that is put forward as a symbol of the core of North American "free market" culture: the small businessperson in the heartland with dedicated hardworking employees. Rather we speak, with church leaders of various denominations, of those large and complex (often multinational) corporations that may be small in number but powerful in the exercise of their authority, especially in their ability to influence governmental policy[19] and to create "barriers to entry" to the masses so that small business people are excluded.[20] It is essential that this distinction between large and small corporations be kept in mind. Even though most job-creation in the United States recently has come from small businesses with less than twenty employees,[21] the companies of the "Fortune 1000" are able to exercise undue influence over the culture and mores of the culture.[22]

Through their advertising, these large businesses play on people's security needs, fears, and increasing individualism in their never-ending pursuit of selling their products. This approach which "exalts possessions," the 1971 Synod of Bishops declared, "encourages narrow individualism."[23]

Individualism and cultural consumerism go together. One of the most discussed books among religious leaders in the 1980s has been *Habits of the Heart: Individualism and Commitment in American Life*, whose authors (Bellah, et al.) insist: "Individualism lies at the very core of American culture."[24] Arguing that people in the United States speak two languages—the primary language of individualism spoken by all and reinforced by the media and economic system coupled with the secondary language of community—the authors declare that the "search for spontaneous community . . . is belied by the strong focus of American individualism on economic success. The rules of the competitive market, not the practices of the town meeting or the fellowship of the church, are the real arbiters of living."[25]

b. The Religious Overtones of Cultural Consumerism

The research of Bellah and his co-workers shows that the "real arbiter" in today's society is no longer the household, as in Matthew's day, or religion, as in centuries past, but the consumeristic-oriented market economy. This can best be contextualized in the words of de Tocqueville, who first studied the "habits of the heart" of the United States in the 1840s. De Tocqueville reasoned that democracy favors the taste for physical pleasures: "This taste, if it becomes excessive, soon disposes men to believe that nothing but matter exists. Materialism, in its turn, spurs them on to such delights with mad impetuosity."[26] To counter such an influence de Tocqueville argued that "at all costs Christianity must be maintained among the new democracies."[27] However, if religion through the church is to provide guidelines and a moral code for discipleship, how effective will its authority be when it seems another authority has the control? Since authority functions in a free society only when people have faith in it, what happens when people do not have faith in religion as the arbiter of ultimate meaning, but place that faith elsewhere?

According to Ellul, propaganda eliminates anxieties stemming from irrational and disproportionate fears; it generates *faith* in the "party" or the "product" which alleviates such fears.[28] In doing so, it gives people the assurances formerly provided by religion. Ellul explains:

> One might go further and say that propaganda tends to give a person a religious personality: his psychological life is organized around an irrational, external, and collective tenet that provides a scale of values, rules of behavior, and a principle of social integration. In a society in the process of secularization, propaganda responds to the religious need, but lends much more vigor and intransigence to the resulting religious personality.[29]

The resulting religious personality comes to identify the good life, or what is good, with consumption and competition for scarce resources rather than community and service. Consumerism thus becomes the religion. Worship consists in participation in the rituals of buying and selling. Thus, following Bellah, while the secondary language is one of (Christian) community, commitment, and care for "the least of the brothers and sisters," the primary language speaks individualism, consumption, and self-interest. The ideology of cultural consumerism has become myth, and the myth is enshrined in a kind of civil religion. Since buying and selling are facilitated through advertising, advertising becomes "the only faith of a secularized consumer culture."[30] According to Ellul, this process is inevitable if sociological propaganda is to be effective in a democracy:

> The creation of the etiological myth leads to an obligation on the part of democracy to become religious. It can no longer be secular but must create its religion. Besides, the creation of a religion is one of the indispensable elements of effective propaganda. The content of this religion is of little importance; what matters is to satisfy the religious feelings of the masses; these feelings are used to integrate the masses into the national collective. We must not delude ourselves: when one speaks to us of "massive democracy" and "democratic participation," these are only veiled terms that mean "religion."[31]

c. The Influence of Religion

When religion is no longer embedded in the household, but is officially separated from economics (although unofficially present through "civil religion"), what are the consequences of this kind of "religion" on organized religion itself, especially the Christian churches? For many years, *U.S. News and World Report* featured the results of a survey called "Who Runs America." Among its sections is one entitled "Institutions That Influence American

Life." Prominent leaders are asked to rank (from a low of "1" to a high of "7") thirty institutions and organizations according to the impact each has "on decisions affecting the nation as a whole." The results indicate where leaders ("authorities") of thirty institutions see the location of authority itself in the United States. The results as of May 1985[32] were:

INSTITUTIONS INFLUENCING AMERICAN LIFE

1. The White House 6.71
2. Big Business 5.92
3. Supreme Court 5.78
4. Television 5.77
5. U.S. Senate 5.53
6. Banks 5.47
7. Wall Street 5.31
8. U.S. House 5.19
9. Cabinet 5.10
10. Lobbyists, pressure groups 5.03
11. Oil industry 4.99
12. Newspapers 4.85
13. Federal bureaucracy 4.82
14. Advertising 4.69
15. Military 4.44
16. Republican Party 4.41
17. Family 4.33
18. State, local government 4.16
19. Radio 4.15
20. Public-opinion polls 4.11
21. Educational institutions 4.10
22. Legal profession 4.09
23. Magazines 4.07
24. Organized religion 4.02
25. Labor unions 3.71
26. Medical profession 3.58
27. Democratic Party 3.45
28. Civil-rights groups 3.25
29. (Tie) Small business and movies 3.22

Big business (#2), television (#4), banks (#6), Wall Street (#7), lobbyists and pressure groups (#10), the oil industry (#11), newspapers (#12), advertising (#14), radio (#19), the legal profession (#22), and magazines (#23): each is considered to have more authority over "American life" than "organized religion." Collectively these institutions exist for one purpose: to get as many benefits as possible from the production-consumption cycle which keeps the First World running.[33] When these institutions are embedded in the cultural consumerism of the political economy itself, the possibility of religion offering an alternative vision becomes extremely difficult, especially since it is perceived as having very little influence over people's lives.

2. The Division of Labor in Post-Industrial Capitalism

The second way social institutions coordinate their activities is through the division of labor, which determines status and rank in society. Matthew's gospel was written in a world (*oikouménē*) and for a world (24:14) controlled by elites who were reinforced by an ideology that never called their status into question. In today's culture of corporate capitalism,[34] a new ruling class of elites has replaced the emperor and patriarchs of the kinship institutions and the religious leaders of those social institutions dominated by religion. In the Marxist world the new elites are often the leaders of the "Party" or the "Vanguard" of the revolution. In Western corporate capitalism the new group of elites consists of businesspeople and managers, especially those connected to the global banks and corporations.[35] As early as 1980 *Business Week* pointed to their growing influence when it declared: "For the most part, today's corporate leaders are 'professional managers'—business mercenaries who ply their skills for a salary and bonus but rarely for a vision. . . . They become more concerned with buying and selling companies than with selling improved products to customers."[36]

The corporate culture within which these bureaucrats function has been called a "corpocracy" by Richard G. Darman, Deputy Secretary of the U.S. Treasury Department under Ronald Reagan.[37] However, rather than isolate it as an exception to the values of wider society, Darman sees it mirroring the culture: "The corporate culture is a reflection of the larger culture in which it resides. And problems in one suggest the likelihood of problems in the other."[38]

Today's corporate culture or "corpocracy" stresses four elements—all geared to the fastest, highest, and most extensive rates of return: short-term profits, rapid money movement, the buying and selling of other corporations,[39] all contextualized within the need to think globally. Thus, the profit motive underlies the rationale of resource allocation.[40]

Today's global banker or businessperson must be truly universal in order to survive, for in this age of technology and vast flows of information, everything is interconnected. The ultimate vehicle for this global interconnection revolves around money and its flow between East and West, North and South. Thus a panic in the money markets of Wall Street feeds that in Hong Kong. The world is the market. This market is reinforced with an ideology affecting every nation and its politics. Today's culture, especially in the West, is, at its core, controlled ideologically by the economic imperative of growth but practically by the movement of money for the greatest return. This process effectively controls politics. According to Howard Wachtel, economics professor at American University in Washington, D.C.:

> The supranational economy, by definition, erodes the importance of the economic role of the nation-state while elevating the influence of private economic values. As the economic functions of the nation-state are weakened in the supranational era, the political system cannot advocate its values of equality as effectively as before. The result is a retreat from social welfare policies, an assertion of economic values over political values, and a privatization of what had previously been public obligations.[41]

One of the greatest signs of this trend, having an extremely negative effect on the division of labor, has been taking place in the transition from a manufacturing-based economy to one that is based on the flow of money, electronics, and computers, on the one hand, and the rise of the service-sector on the other. Business analyst Peter Drucker projects that by the year 2000, blue collar/manufacturing jobs, which were once the backbone of the unparalleled economic growth of the United States, will follow the pattern of agricultural jobs and shrink to an extremely small percentage of the work force:

> And now it is suddenly all over. There also is no parallel in history to the abrupt decline of the blue-collar worker during the past 15 years. As a proportion of the working population, blue-collar workers in manufacturing have already decreased to less than a fifth of the American labor force from more than a third. By the year 2010—less than 25 years away—they will constitute no larger a proportion of the labor force of every developed country than farmers do today—that is, a 20th of the total.[42]

While some point to statistics showing that the U.S. economy has created millions of jobs, they do not count the hundreds of thousands of jobs lost by mergers and deindustrialization. Neither do they mention that the majority of the jobs created, as Drucker notes, are not in the higher-paying manufacturing sector, but in the low-paying, nonunionized service sector.

The conflict between the above-mentioned activities of the existing corporate culture and values such as those outlined in the gospel of Matthew seems clear. The conflict is further clarified when one considers an October 9, 1987, feature in *The Wall Street Journal* which noted an analysis of ten academic studies dealing with corporate virtue and ethics codes. It concluded that there is a vast difference between the ethical statements of businesses in "corpocracy" and their actual behavior. Despite stated values and codes of conduct, the article notes:

> These actions merely pay lip service to a larger—and clearly unmet—problem: a business climate that condones malfeasance. Indeed, the studies together indicate that even the most upright people are apt to become dishonest and unmindful of their civic responsibilities when placed in a typical corporate environment.[43]

The studies discussed indicate that corporations with codes of ethics are actually cited by federal agencies for infractions more often than those that lack such standards because the codes themselves typically emphasize improving the companies' balance sheets rather than their social responsibilities as well as because "the codes are really dealing with infractions against the corporation, rather than illegalities on behalf of the corporation."[44]

3. Disparity in the Allocation of Resources

Despite their radical differences, if one views the "economy" of first-century Palestine and that of Matthew's house churches alongside the economy of the world today and that of certain churches in the First World, two areas of similarity seem clear: (1) the growing disparity between rich and poor; and (2) the increase in prosperity among the members of certain Christian communities. If the challenge of Matthew's gospel is going to bring good news to the poor of our day (11:6; 19:21), the disparity between rich and poor in our time cannot be left uncritiqued.

a. Disparity between Rich and Poor

For most people in the developed world, the standard of living has advanced dramatically since the end of World War II. In the United States the average per family income almost doubled between 1950 and 1984, even after adjusting for inflation. Between 1979 and 1986 in England real incomes increased more than 6 percent while inflation decreased, to about 3 percent annually. However, while many have benefited, others have been hurt.

The Catholic bishops of Canada noted in 1983 that within that nation itself "the top 20 percent of the population receive 42.5 percent of total personal income while the bottom 20 percent receive 4.1 percent."[45] In their letter on the U.S. economy, the U.S. Catholic bishops noted their concern about "the fact that poverty has increased dramatically during the last decade. Since 1973 the poverty rate has increased by nearly a third."[46] In the United States during the late 1980s, the separation between the rich and the poor reached the greatest level since the Depression. Whereas Census Bureau statistics showed that the most affluent 20 percent of U.S. families averaged 7 times more after-tax income than the poorest 20 percent in 1974, the gap was over 9 to 1 in 1985.[47] The realization that almost four million English people were out of work or in official training programs for the unemployed prompted the authors of a 1986 report from the Church of England to conclude that, despite economic success for some, "there are some developments today which Christians cannot approve."[48]

Despite such figures, the majority of Christians go about business as usual. In commenting on "A Have and Have-Not America," Hodding Carter III wrote: "Even as the evidence grows steadily stronger that we are building a class-ridden society of ever-sharper contrasts between haves and have-nots, we are treated to long treatises on the triumph of capitalism and the American dream."[49]

Besides creating terrible hardships for the poorest, this gap is increasingly ominous for the middle class. Some economists interpret statistics in a way that indicates that the middle class is not decreasing.[50] However an increasing number of economists and economic journals show quite convincingly that it is shrinking.[51] According to one calculation, a middle-class household is defined as one with an income between 75 percent and 125 percent of the median household income. If so, according to a 1986 Federal Reserve Bank of Boston report, the middle class—which ranged from 20,000–49,999 in 1984 dollars—declined 5.1 percent between 1973 and 1984. In the same period over five times as many households moved from the middle class to the bottom fifth than moved from the middle class to the top fifth (4.3 percent to 0.8 percent).[52] Reflecting on such statistics, Lester C. Thurow concluded: "Even when slightly different definitions of income factors constituting a middle class are applied to the statistics, the trend is not reversed. The American middle class is disappearing."[53]

Most seriously affected in the transition from an industrial economy to a service economy are racial minorities. In 1985, black per capita income in the United States was $6,840, less than 60 percent of the per capita income of whites, who made $4,831 a year more. In the top 50 cities, the number of whites living below the poverty line declined by 18 percent between 1970 and 1980; the number of blacks increased by the same 18 percent.[54] When jobs are cut black blue-collar workers, as well as black managers, are the first to be fired.[55]

Although women and racial minorities have achieved their "freedom" via rights within the last century and a half, the economic system still keeps them unequal with white males. A special report on "The Corporate Woman" in *The Wall Street Journal* discussed the sexist corpocracy that represents "the invisible barrier that blocks [women] from the top jobs."[56] According to a 1987 Census Bureau study, women in comparable jobs still earn but 68 percent of the salaries of men.

The reality of the income gap within developed nations, like the United States, is greatly magnified in the world economy. Commenting on global poverty, the United Church of Christ paper *Christian Faith and Economic Life* noted:

> In a world whose technology has made it possible to eliminate poverty, the overwhelming majority of the members of the human family still live on the margin of economic survival. The situation is particularly bleak in the 35 countries classified as low-income economies, whose citizens have average incomes of only $260 a year; but levels of poverty and suffering also remain unacceptably high among broad sectors of the population in the 37 middle-income countries whose per capita incomes fall between $400 and $1,500.[57]

It can be shown that the unprecedented surge in world trade and economic growth after World War II materially improved the lives of most people around the globe. However, contrary to the expectations of some economic theorists, this growth has failed to narrow the gap between industrialized and developing nations. *Business Week* noted in 1987 that "real average per capita income in 1984—calculated in 1981 dollars and at 1981 exchange rates—was about 14 times higher in the advanced nations than in the developing world. That's about the same ratio that existed 15 and 25 years earlier."[58]

b. Prosperity in Christian Communities

Matthew's gospel was written to deal with the horizon created by greater prosperity. So too the prosperity of many Christians in the First World has grown. White, ethnic Catholics are one example of this. With the transplantation of England's industrial revolution in the United States in the first half of the nineteenth century, a wave of Catholic immigrants came to the shores of the United States. When they arrived, most were penniless and powerless with no one to lead them except the leaders of their church.

Building schools and hospitals, organizing unions, fighting for economic and political rights, these Catholic immigrants and their descendants strove to adapt to the dominant culture. Between the end of World War II and the early 1960s the ethnic Catholics, like Matthew's house churches, had moved from a condition of poverty to relative affluence. By 1975 it became clear that the goal of integration into the mainstream of the economy had taken place. A study by the National Opinion Research Center in Chicago showed that many Catholics, whose ancestors were immigrants to the once predominantly Protestant United States, now outclass Protestants in wealth and education, having become "more successful than the American Protestants, which constitute the host culture."[59] The study, which did not include nonwhites and Spanish-speaking groups, indicated to what extent strong, ethnically supportive institutions were able to help meet the goal of participation in the American dream. In fact, four of the ethnic groups—the Irish, Italian, German, and Polish Catholics—surpassed all but the Jews in family income:[60]

DENOMINATIONS/ ETHNIC GROUPS	HOUSEHOLD INCOME
Jews	42,047
Irish Catholics	39,187
Italian Catholics	37,132
German Catholics	36,985
Polish Catholics	36,621
Episcopalians	35,602
Presbyterians	34,587
Slavic Catholics	34,083
British Protestants	32,597
French Catholics	32,103
Methodists	31,837
Median Family Income	31,505
German Protestants	30,750
Lutherans	30,573
Scandinavian Protestants	30,241
"American" Protestants	29,224
Irish Protestants	29,183
Baptists	28,825

As Matthew's house churches reflected greater prosperity and became more assimilated into the dominant culture, they also were tempted to become alienated from the poor and outcast around them and in their midst. The process has been similar for many ethnic Catholics in the United States: the dynamic of assimilation has been accompanied by a gradual alienation from the alien and the poor. Reflecting on the acculturation to the consumer society that now has become endemic to ethnic North American Catholics, the Catholic bishops wrote in the first draft of their *Pastoral Letter on Catholic Social Teaching and the U.S. Economy*:

Our sense of community is also fostered by the memories we share as descendants of immigrants who came often as aliens to a strange land. The stories of our past remind us of the times when our Church was a defender of the defenseless and a voice for the voiceless. Today as many Catholics achieve greater economic prosperity, we are tempted like the people of the Exodus to forget the powerless and the stranger in our midst.[61]

One of the main reasons why we forget is that not-remembering can serve as a defense mechanism to keep from changing. This realization helps us understand why we can call our society addictive, since denial is at the heart of addictions. The fact that almost everyone is fervently pursuing money supports the connection to addiction theory. This societal addiction to money was underscored in a special issue of *Business Week* called "The Casino Society." The basic point of the article, published in 1985—over two years before the crash of October 1987—was that the nation had become "obsessively devoted to high-stakes financial maneuvering as a shortcut to wealth."[62] With everyone running after money in its various forms, its addictive influence keeps us from being concerned about the other members of the human family who suffer from our disease.

CONCRETIZING AN ETHIC OF JUSTICE FOR PUBLIC HOUSEHOLDING

This book has tried to show that justice in the form of (re)ordered relationships and resources was a central image in Matthew. His unique use of the image indicated the special need for the practice of justice in his house churches if their economics or house-ordering was to reflect the pattern of Matthew's Jesus, especially his notion of general reciprocity which extended the doors of one's *oikía/oikos* (house) to the *oikouménē* (world).

That Matthew's notion of justice reflected a certain kind of reciprocity becomes clearer when we realize that justice, as Barrington Moore has shown, is at the heart of all forms of reciprocity that characterize various social organizations, whether the traditional form of Matthew's day or the command- and market-oriented forms of our times.[63]

One of Matthew's greatest challenges was to reintroduce to his house churches the image of Jesus whose self-definition (11:2-6) and invitation to his disciples were inseparably linked with solidarity with the poor (19:16-26; 25:31-46; 26:6-13). His house churches, the basic unit of the economy, were called to become a light to all the nations (5:15) so that creation might continue according to God's plan of goodness (5:16). If Matthew's *oikía loikos* horizon will be fused with a twentieth-century *oikouménē* horizon, the question asked by the U.S. Catholic bishops applies here:

> We can rightly ask ourselves one single question: How does our economic system affect the lives of people—*all* people? Part of the American dream has been to make this world a better place for people to live in; at this moment of history that dream must include everyone on this globe. Since we profess to be members of a "catholic" or universal church, we all must raise our sights to a concern for the well-being of everyone in the world.[64]

Just as the social institution of kinship based in the *oikía/oikos* demanded concern for the well-being of all its members, so now, the social institution of post-industrial capitalism demands concern for the *oikouménē* and the preservation of ecological balance as well. What is needed is a new kind of household order based in justice that will help our entrance into the third millennium.

In trying to create justice-based public policy alternatives for our society, a new kind of vision faithful to the fundamental householding vision of Matthew is necessary. Where once this vision revolved around the private household, a new kind of household-based ethic for public policy is needed.

One of the first to call for a new kind of public householding approach for ethics and public policy was Daniel Bell.[65] In his modern classic, *The Cultural Contradictions of Capitalism*, Bell noted how economy was traditionally ordered around the domestic household but then came to be dominated by the market. However, since the 1950s, according to Bell, "a third sector, more important than the other two," came to the fore: the "public household."[66] The public household is not just "the government," or a public economic sector joined to the domestic household and market economies. It now involves all people and demands their welfare. It now is "prior to both and directive of each. It is the *polis* writ large."[67]

As yet we do not have a sufficient theoretical basis for a public householding horizon that joins the economic and the political dimensions, or a political philosophy of the public household that provides decision-makers with rules for the normative resolution of conflicting claims and a philosophical justification of the outcome. In an effort to find some common ground for dialogue between economists and moral theologians, it is important to see justice as the virtue around which social scientists and social ethicists might agree in their effort to bring about rightly-ordered relationships and resources in society today.[68] In addition, any ethic of public householding must balance the values of freedom and equality, while ensuring the necessary reordering of society that will incorporate those who are presently marginated.

1. Balancing Freedom and Equality

The ethical framework sculpted by the Canadian and U.S. Catholic bishops in their pastorals on the economy, as well as that found in Protestant documents like those of the United Church of Christ and the Presbyterians, tries to establish a discussion of ethical principles for economics within the wider framework of philosophical ethics. When philosophical ethics considers justice, a tension always develops between an emphasis on freedom, with its individual rights, and equality, which insists on the meeting of needs. Thus the balance between freedom and equality becomes a major focus.

In chapter 4 we saw that status and patriarchy resulted in a lack of freedom and that disparity of resource-sharing reflected inequality. Since our "horizon" of today equates the lack of freedom and inequity with basic injustices, a reinvestigation of Matthew's gospel today should attempt to find a new promotion of *dikaiosýnē* (justice) which insures freedom and equality for as many people as possible. In order to be faithful to the scriptural demand of *dikaiosýnē*, the bishops note, a concerted effort must be made to insure basic economic rights through efforts at realizing equality as much as U.S. society has insured basic civil rights through the promotion of freedom.[69]

a. Pitfalls in the Libertarian Theory of Justice

Without investigating or counting disagreements about specific policy recommendations of the various church documents, it can be stated that those documents' insistence on the need to have justice expressed in economic rights paralleling civil rights has engendered much of the controversy over the Catholic and Protestant documents on the U.S. economy. Advocates of unencumbered, free-market economics (often called "libertarians"),[70] led by academicians, editorial writers, and columnists in *The Wall Street Journal*, have consistently challenged any idea of balancing freedom and equality. In many ways they reject a concept of "public householding," limiting all economic life to Bell's first two sectors: the individual actors ("private households") and the market, with only a limited role for government, such as the securing of armies. They insist that the foundation of "the West" is civic and political rights, not social and economic rights. For such advocates of the "libertarian" approach to justice, "fairness" exists only if liberty is the most important operational political value. Even though there may be inequity in the sharing of resources, they insist—with one of their chief spokespersons, Irving Kristol—that "the social order we call 'capitalism,' constructed on the basis of a market economy, does *not* believe that 'society' ought to prescribe a 'fair' distribution of income."[71] Instead of a coercive redistribution of income to insure "fairness," they advocate "voluntarism," the free decision to reorder one's own rightfully-gained resources toward those in need. Their "norm" of unencumbered "liberty" is continually proffered as the best way to achieve "equality."

While industrial capitalism was once the biggest employer and empowerer of the poor in the history of the world, what happens when, in the name of "freedom"—be it of the market, of "supply-side" economics, or of free-enterprise—the present form of post-industrial capitalism is moving, as we have seen, toward greater inequality?[72] What happens when, on the political level, economic planning (again overly affected by "corpocracy's" influence on tax-law revision) generates greater inequality? What happens when this greater inequity is not balanced by greater voluntary efforts to right wrongs? An examination of the economic restructuring that took place in the first term of Ronald Reagan serves as a case study.

As a reaction to the stress on the public dimension of householding in the 1960s and 1970s, the Reagan Administration was swept into power in 1981 stressing individual freedom, the market, and a government that functions least as best. Three years after the Reagan Administration enacted a revision of the tax laws based on this theory—during the 1984 Republican Convention— the Orange County, California, edition of the *Los Angeles Times*[73] featured an analysis of "The Reagan Record" under the title of "Fairness." The article's statistics covered three areas: 1) reduction in benefits, 2) reduction in taxes, and 3) total income. Those earning less than $10,000 had a 7.5 percent reduction in benefits, while those with incomes of $40,000-$80,000 had a 0.2 percent reduction in benefits. In the area of tax reduction, those in the bottom fifth of U.S. households had a 0.1 percent reduction in taxes while the top fifth had a 5.9 percent reduction. The purpose of the change in the tax law was to give more to those who had ("supply-side") under the assumption that jobs and income would "trickle down" to the least fortunate. But the third area, regarding total after-tax income from 1980–1984, showed that, "as a result of both economic trends and Reagan policies" the bottom fifth had a 7.6 percent reduction while the top fifth had a 8.7 percent increase. Consequently, the assumption that increasing entitlements to the wealthy would "trickle down" to the poor proved spurious.

The response to inequity and poverty by libertarians, supply-siders, and free-market advocates has been twofold. First, the principle of "entitlement" insures that all people have the right to their earnings on the condition that this wealth has not been gained at the expense of others.[74] Second, where there may be social inequity, voluntarism is the best way to right wrongs.

The data above, plus an understanding of the tendency of human selfishness and desire for more, indicate that the libertarian approach not only has failed to bring good news to the poor to the degree they need it—since the 1981 revision of the tax code, the public household has even more of its members outside the system. Another approach is demanded.

b. Pitfalls in the Liberal Theory of Justice

Because a libertarian approach has not proved capable of establishing equality and justice, many people have looked to a "liberal" theory of justice. While still insuring individuals' freedom at its core, it recognizes the need for structural processes that will insure equality as well.

Probably the best-known ethicist of the liberal school is John Rawls. Writing in his *A Theory of Justice*, Rawls promotes what he calls the "difference principle." In order to ensure a system in which each person will have an equal right to basic liberties, Rawls advocates the implementation of this principle to compensate in situations where there is inequality of freedoms. The principle ensures that "social and economic inequalities are to be arranged so that they are both: (a) to the greatest benefit of the least advantaged . . ., and (b) attached to offices and positions open to all under conditions of fair equality of opportunity."[75] At times, when Rawls's difference principle is used to critique legislation and policies, such as the 1981 tax code, it finds the law wanting in justice. The aim of giving more to those who had more did not result in giving a greater share to those who had little. According to Rawls:

Assuming the framework of institutions required by equal liberty and fair equality of opportunity, the higher expectations of those better situated are just if and only if they work as part of a scheme which improves the expectations of the least advantaged members of society. The intuitive idea is that the social order is not to establish and secure the more attractive prospects of those better off unless doing so is to the advantage of those less fortunate.[76]

On the basis of the "difference principle," then, policies and practices are unjust if they do not help reorder the system to promote meeting the needs of its most disadvantaged. Consequently, the 1981 legislation would have to be judged unable to reflect a contemporary way of implementing the *dikaiosýnē* of Matthew's Jesus and his economics. Another way of taxation that insured liberty and promoted greater equality would have to be discovered.[77]

While the liberal theory of justice promoted by Rawls offers a greater emphasis on equality than the libertarian position, ultimately it keeps true equality from being effectively realized because it grounds all behavior in the primary value of freedom. As a result it depends too much on the good will of certain individuals to change those procedures and institutions which exist for the benefit of those individuals and which, in the process, leave others hurt.

An important reason for the failure of both the libertarian and liberal theories of justice is that both assume a philosophy of private households which cannot be supported by the economic data; that data demand a philosophy of public householding. A philosophical explanation for their inadequacy to cope with present problems is that their ultimate basis lies in Immanuel Kant's emphasis on the radical independence of each person. To construct a theory on such an atomistic approach denies the fact that individuals are essentially communitarian and, as such, are part of the *oikouménē*.

A system based on people's entitlements rests in freedom; yet the cry for freedom may muffle the cry of the poor. Consequently the claim of entitlement and freedom is ensured at the expense of the claim of equality and the meeting of human needs. The libertarian and liberal theories, with their basic emphasis on freedom, have no way of adjudicating between the conflicting claims. Alasdair MacIntyre insists that

> our pluralistic culture possesses no method of weighing, no rational criterion for deciding between claims based on legitimate entitlement against claims based on need. Thus these two types of claims are indeed . . . incommensurable, and the metaphor of "weighing" moral claims is not just inappropriate but misleading.[78]

As an alternative to the continued dependence on the Kantian ethical model which reinforces individualism, MacIntyre suggests a return to the Aristotelian concept of justice and its stress on communitarianism. MacIntyre's suggestion finds an echo in that of Daniel Bell, who envisions a return to Aristotle's vision of the household. Whether based in Aristotelian notions of justice or householding, we are brought back to the first chapter of this book and its discussion of Aristotle's vision of the house and proper house-ordering as the basis of justice. Here we may find a way to fuse the two horizons.

2. Oikos/Oikía, *Ethics, and Communitarianism*

Aristotle's horizon of house-ordering, as well as Matthew's, was applied to a traditional economy radically different from our post-industrial "corpocracy." However, we have seen that the "ethos" contained in Matthew certainly can be used as a judge of our own realization of justice. In this sense William Johnson Everett has written in the *Journal of Business Ethics*:

> Now it is quite clear that we cannot recover the same pattern of integration as that in ancient Greece or in traditional agrarian culture. However, the concept of *oikos* gives us an orientation toward the process of integration. It symbolizes the human desire to relate these crucial dimensions of existence. *Oikos* is a heuristic concept for analyzing a set of relationships that shapes the way people relate to work, family, and faith. It can be applied to individuals as well as to organizations. It is both psychological and structural.[79]

I have emphasized Matthew's approach to church, economics, and justice (from the assumed primary metaphor of "house") as grounded in the relationality of persons to each other and their resources. In this same communitarian sense, Everett writes: "The concept of the *oikos* directs our attention to an ensemble of relationships rather than to its compartmentalized sectors. It prepares us to reflect on the structural as well as motivational aspects of these relationships. It leads us to talk about how our lives are energized and oriented as well as how they are ordered."[80]

A reflection on the way lives were ordered in the first century reveals a structure sustained by differences of rank between rich and poor. While those differences were not called into question in that system of reciprocity, they were challenged if people were made poor because of exploitation and injustice. Thus, if social arrangements in his society were unjust, insofar as they sustained exploitative marginalization of the poor, Jesus challenged these structures. Since we have seen that our world is "marked by the grave sin of social injustice," an application of the horizon of Matthew's justice for his society must be made to ours.

Any structural (re)ordering that took place within his household had its impact on the wider, political society as a whole. In this sense we must understand Matthew's way of supporting the goals of public householding through a new communitarian ethic of responsibility geared to right order in the *oikouménē* and ecological balance. This is best expressed in the notion of the jubilee, which called for a periodic, structural reordering of society that would bring good news to the poor (11:2–6).

a. Jubilee Ethics and Relative Equality

A responsibility ethic of public householding for disciples returns to the jubilee narrative to determine how best communitarian justice and love might be realized in the church and in the economy. If the jubilee called for a kind of "economic structural reordering," one must ask how its values and principles might be applied to contemporary policy and economic structures to create order within the public household. Since essential elements of the implementation of the jubilee were the freeing of the enslaved and debt forgiveness, we can ask how those values of the *oikía/oikos* can be translated into our *oikouménē* today and how those values will promote ecological order.

In reflecting on the growing disparity among peoples, especially among the races, as well as the increasing inequity in the allocation of resources, what constitutes a proper response by those purporting to be part of the household of Jesus Christ? Although a balance should be maintained among principles of merit, equality of life chances, and the autonomy of the family,[81] one concrete step in the United States would be to affirm a 1987 decision by the Supreme Court which supported a kind of jubilee. To correct discrimination, the Court approved, for a temporary period, the deliberate hiring and promotion of a typically small number of qualified minority members and women along with a larger number of others. When evidence shows that the pattern of discrimination has been broken, employers need no longer use quotas or goals.

Another way to promote a contemporary expression of freeing the slaves to announce a jubilee would be through the support of what Drew Christiansen calls the principle of "relative equality," which he considers central to policy recommendations in Catholic social teaching.

An ideal form of justice ensures the maximum amount of freedom and equality for the highest number of people. But our world and nation are not yet in that ideal position. Thus one must choose that ethical norm which best advances this goal. We have seen that a reordering in society that followed a more libertarian mode—stressing freedom and free access to markets combined with voluntary efforts to share with those disaffected by the process—did not bring the desired result: good news to the poor. An alternative approach can be found in the adoption of the norm of "relative equality." This norm tries to balance freedom in relationships, equality in resource-sharing, and solidarity in community as envisioned in recent Catholic and Protestant social thought. According to Christiansen:

> The basic thrust of the norm is that the distance between any set of groups ought to be curbed so that their ability to act in a fraternal/sororal way toward one another is not subverted. It tries to effect this eradication of differences by enjoining repeated distribution of wealth, income, and resources to make a full human life available to all. This description entails three functions: (1) the (re)distribution of resources on egalitarian

lines, (2) for the realization of full human life by all, (3) in a spirit which reduces differences and increases the life shared in common.[82]

A relative equality approach can be best interpreted from a "least difference principle." That principle ensures that "any allocation which decreases the absolute difference between the greater entitlement and the lesser is more equal."[83] In other words, where freedom keeps the "difference principle" from bringing about better equality, the "least difference principle" finds a way of making sure greater equality takes place.

b. Jubilee Ethics and Debt Forgiveness

In chapter 7 I pointed out that, in Matthew's terminology, "forgive us our debts" (6:12) contains an economic as well as relational notion. Only Matthew has the story of the limitless debt that was forgiven (18:21-35). The advocation of some form of debt forgiveness of present-day Third World debt by contemporary disciples of Jesus is one way the value Matthew promoted might be brought to bear upon our economic relations, especially with developing nations which have become burdened with debt.

In the late 1960s, the Third World debt "game" began. The chief player at that time, according to a December 1985 article in *Fortune,* was Citicorp. It had

> set a goal of increasing earnings 15% every year and saw overseas profits as a golden way to do it. Today, of that $437 billion owed by the 15 countries (which are, of course, only some of the Third World borrowers), commercial banks worldwide hold $275 billion. Of that, U.S. banks hold $94 billion, about 85% of it on the books of the 24 largest banks. The leader, still, is Citicorp, whose Citibank has an estimated $12 billion of the debt.[84]

While the capital loaned will never be repaid (nor would it need to be repaid since it would merely be reloaned to others), the issue at stake is whether the interest will be repaid. When the debt crisis broke in 1982, Third World countries moved into austerity programs designed by the International Monetary Fund and the World Bank (effectively controlled by the fiat of the United States). Soon prices skyrocketed. This brought greater economic deprivation among the poor within those countries even though the slashing of imports and greater amount of exports delivered surpluses which could be used to honor the interest payments to the commercial banks and international lending agencies.

However, arguing from the "difference principle," the economic structure set in motion failed to enhance the life of the already economically oppressed and marginated peoples of the Third World. This demands a reconsideration of the issue to create new structural changes that will implement debt forgiveness in a way which will not yoke the poor even more. Country-by-country relief should be targeted to countries with growth plans, but whose growth is not at the expense of the least advantaged.

One of the first steps might involve writing off the debt entirely or in large part. This religiously-grounded position might even make good economic sense, in the long run. Alan S. Blinder, economics professor at Princeton University, has concluded, with other economists, that the debts of many less developed countries cannot be serviced, much less repaid, except at unthinkable cost. Blinder argues: "The rich countries may soon have to choose between partial forgiveness and unilateral repudiation. Forgiveness is the better alternative."[85] While he notes that his reasons supporting debt relief have humanitarian, political, and economic foundations, another statement belies the traditional, periodic, religious rationale for the jubilee: "Debt forgiveness should come with proclamations that the circumstances are special and that we do not plan to do it again."[86]

It is debatable whether the jubilee was ever implemented; the leadership group who would call for the jubilee would be the first to be harmed by its norms. This may be the main reason for its non-implementation. However, their possible resistance to implementing the scriptures does not mean that the purposes or legislation geared to structural reordering is wrong or impossible to implement. As Matthew's Jesus said of the difficulties of another economic reordering on behalf of the poor: "With men this is impossible, but with God all things are possible" (19:26).

The recognition of the need to come under the power of the God who makes all things possible brings us to a further consideration of our society as addictive.

RECOVERING FROM SOCIETY'S ADDICTIONS: IMPLICATIONS FOR SPIRITUALITY TODAY

Previous chapters have shown that, despite Jesus' calls for conversion, the social order of his generation and its leaders developed hardness of heart. In his narrative Matthew incorporated those stories about the intransigency of Jesus' social opposition continually to remind his house churches that what happened to Jerusalem and its leaders could easily happen again—whether in the 80s or 90s of his day or in any of the other days "to the close of the age" (28:20).

Today, as in the day of Matthew's Jesus, the heart of the people seems to have grown hard toward conversion, especially the hearts of the prosperous who are called to work to bring good news to the poor in the form of justice. While many people of the middle and upper classes are generous with their time and service on behalf of the poor and others make individual contributions, when it comes to changing the terms of the relationship between the rich and the poor, hardness of heart all too often seems to develop. Few among the prosperous are open to forms of redistribution of power and wealth that will manifest a just social order.

According to Jennifer L. Hochschild, only 27 percent of those in the highest income bracket supported government involvement in reducing income differences between the rich and the poor.[87] Further data indicate that, in the United

States, even though a growing gap exists between the rich and the poor, the richer people are, the more satisfied they are. For instance, in 1986, 68 percent of the whites said they were "satisfied with the way things are going in the U.S. at this time" while 44 percent of the blacks answered affirmatively.[88] The correlation between increase in personal wealth and satisfaction with society was positive. Wealth creates satisfaction. But satisfaction related to wealth can often represent biblical hardness of heart. This hardness of heart can also reflect forms of denial and psychic numbing which indicate addictive patterns of behavior.

1. Society as Culturally Addictive

In the early 1980s, commenting on the challenge of Matthew's Beatitudes to First World Christians, I noted how much of our social attitudes and behavior reflected patterns of what I then called "cultural addiction."[89] At that time I limited myself to consumerism as a contemporary addiction. Since then my analysis has broadened to include forms of classism, technologism, and militarism which reveal the deeply addictive way of thinking and behaving that exists within "developed" nations. The basis of these addictive patterns of behavior and thinking rests in the system of post-industrial capitalism itself with its insatiable need (addiction) for growth. According to Alwyn Jones:

> In such societies, however politically patterned, there is a universal, and virtually unequivocal, acceptance of economic growth and expansion as the prime objective to be pursued. As such economic expansion depends on advances in scientific and technological knowledge the control and manipulation of nature is given full legitimacy. This attitude towards nature is seen as a central feature of the industrial culture as a whole and reflects the dominance of material over other human values. And it is the asymmetry between these value systems which predisposes the industrial culture to violence and instability: in short it gives ideological support to the use of violence in the resolution of problems, whether these be of a political, social or economic nature.[90]

Jones's description of the culture of advanced industrial society points to it as addictive. The addictive society is based on inequality among its members, the obsession with money and what it can buy, and the need to defend and protect that society at any costs. Thus the parallels among inequality, materialism, and militarism.

Anne Wilson Schaef has gone even further by describing society itself as addictive. Building on her experience of working with individuals suffering from addictions, Schaef discovered the same attitudes and behaviors at work in society. Using a holographic model wherein the individual is contained within the whole and the system in the person, she concludes: "The individual reflects the system and the system reflects the individual. They are the same and different simultaneously. We see exactly the same characteristics operating in the system as we see in the individual addict."[91] Thus the title of her book: *When Society Becomes an Addict*.

Harper's editor Lewis H. Lapham calls the addiction of our culture pathological. This pathology is oriented around biblical mammon and is infused with religious overtones: "Unhappily . . . the pathologies of wealth afflict the whole society, inhibiting the conduct of government as well as the expressions of art and literature. The rituals of worship produce formations of character in institutions as well as individuals. . . .It isn't money itself that causes the trouble, but the use of money as votive offering and pagan ornament."[92]

The characteristics of the pathology of addiction Schaef describes point to forces at play in the social patterns of our culture that have been described throughout this book. Her "self-centeredness" recalls de Tocqueville's fears about self-interest. Her "stress" reflects the anxiety of people "given over to" what they will eat, drink, and wear. Biblical anxiety often refers to concerns which arise from the values and standards of the present age.

The chief characteristic of an addictive thinking process and behavior, Schaef notes, is dishonesty or lying.[93] We saw in the previous chapter that the conflict between Jesus and the leaders of his day, according to Matthew, was mirrored in his calling them liars and hypocrites. We also saw that, in Matthew, hypocrisy is a characteristic of injustice. How, we might ask, does "the lie" get institutionalized in the psyche of advanced industrial societies, be it in political, economic, or even religious manifestations? How does that occur in a way which reflects those societies' addictiveness? And how does the lie reinforce injustice?

a. Institutional Reinforcement of the Cultural Addictions

In a feature article, "A Nation of Liars?," *U.S. News & World Report* offered a perspective on this question: "Government officials dissemble. Scientists falsify research. Workers alter career credentials to get jobs. What's going on here? The answer, a growing number of social critics fear, is an alarming decline in basic honesty."[94] In 1987 England was rocked with stories of the Guiness affair, which involved stock manipulation. At the same time, people in the United States learned more about "Irangate" and the revelations that Wall Street traders were disobeying the law. In late 1986 an article in *Fortune* on "The Decline and Fall of Business Ethics" began with the statement: " . . . a profit-at-any price malaise is spreading through investment banking and reaching into other industries as well."[95] A few months later an investigative article in *The Wall Street Journal* revealed that the Vatican Bank, using "shell-company deals," played a central role in the billion-dollar collapse of Banco Ambrosiano.[96] Each one of these instances of greed and power was wrapped in cover-ups, stonewalling, and denials. All of these serve as synonyms for "the lie." Reflecting on the general malaise of society indicated in such behavior, investment banker Felix G. Rohatyn said with alarm:

Greed and corruption are the cancer of a free society. They are a cancer because they erode our value system. They create contempt for many of our institutions as a result of the corrupt actions of individuals. The continuity of institutions is too important to be sacrificed to the unfettered greed of individuals. I have been in business for almost 40 years and I cannot recall a period in which greed and corruption appeared as prevalent as they are today.[97]

Rohatyn's comments reveal a deep character flaw in the social psyche, a further evidence of addictive behavior. Furthermore, his comments about individuals corrupting systems echo the notion of Schaef's hologram of addictions. According to Schaef, individual and social addictions feed on each other. According to Rohatyn, the corruption of the individual supports the corruption of the system. Corruption has become endemic to the system; it is addictive. When such addictive thinking and behaving become dominant, morality is jettisoned. Thus the 1986 Nobel Prize winner in economics, James M. Buchanan, saw the modern North American "excessively self-interested" in a way that erodes the communal basis of morality. As a result, he says, "homo economicus"—the self-seeking economic individual of the textbooks—has assumed the dominant role in the real world, endangering the community.[98]

Matthew portrays Jesus as contrasting two ways of life that revolve around two opposite forces or authorities—God and mammon: "No one can serve two masters; for either he will hate the one and love the other, or he will be devoted to the one and despise the other. You cannot serve God and mammon" (6:24). We have already seen that Matthew's horizon and language refer to what we know today as addiction. In other words, mammon is addictive.

A 1987 *Fortune* magazine cover feature on "The Money Society" spoke clearly about the way money can become an addiction in reaction to insecurity and anxiety. The article declared, using addiction terminology: "Those cashoholics who fail to get their needed infusion of money . . . become agitated, anxious, combative, and depressed, like addicts deprived of their fix."[99] In suggesting a reason for the addictiveness, the author pointed to the *anomía* and breakdown of values in society, including existing family life and religious institutions: "The money society has expanded to fill the vacuum left after the institutions that embodied and nourished those values—community, religion, school, university, and especially family—sagged or collapsed or sometimes even self-destructed."[100]

We saw earlier in this book that "to serve," in Greek, is *douleúein*. *Douleúein* means "to be given over to" something. The Latin word for addiction—*addicere*—means "to give up or over" to something. One can tell to what people are "given over," what they serve (God or mammon), by discovering what preoccupies them. "Where your treasure is, there will your heart be also" (6:21).

In a market economy companies spend millions in "motivational research" to discover what preoccupies people and what affects their preoccupations so that, having *sought* and *found* what these preoccupations may be, advertisers may sell their clients' goods and services in order to alleviate the preoccupations. Marketing experts know that, on a hierarchy of needs, the most basic human need is survival, but that, after survival, the next most basic need affecting preoccupations is security. As a result, Madison Avenue advertisers can manipulate people's security needs such as acceptance, safety, and protection. Increasing budgets at the Pentagon are justified around security—the Pentagon plays upon people's fear of "the Russians" or claims that "national security" is at stake. Deodorants protect; guns ensure safety; cars indicate acceptance. Whether the advertising of Madison Avenue enticing us to more consumerism or the Pentagon's increasing militarism, both evidence elements of an addicted culture, a nation of addicts plagued by fears needing immediate resolution.

b. The Role of Fear and Faith, Insecurity and Trust

Anxiety or fear is the emotional challenge to security. This was known by Matthew's Jesus in the 80s and 90s as well as by today's psychiatrists and psychologists. According to psychologist Michael E. Cavanaugh, fear is the basic emotion.[101] It is the feeling of anxiety caused by the presence or perception of pending danger. While the danger can be physical, the majority of threats to security are psychological. Psychological threats undermine a person's self-concept; fear is the weapon which can cripple any positive self-image. These fears which can undermine an otherwise positive self-image can involve areas of intimacy, rejection, failure, change and/or freedom.[102] Fear, in Greek, is *phóbos*. The link to phobia is clear.

Karen Horney has shown that a fear-ridden (neurotic) personality flows from and reflects specific social structures and cultures. When reading her description of the neurotic cycle stemming from the neurotic's environment, one becomes aware that this is the same milieu that is ripe for what we earlier called propaganda (the manipulation of fears to achieve certain ends):

Anxiety, hostility, reduction of self-respect . . . striving for power . . . reinforcement of hostility and anxiety . . . a tendency to withdraw in the face of competition accompanied by tendencies to self-depreciation . . . failures and disproportion between capabilities and accomplishments . . . reinforcement of feelings of superiority . . . reinforcement of grandiose ideas . . . increase of sensitivity . . . an inclination to withdraw . . . increase of hostility and anxiety.[103]

We have seen that First World people, especially North Americans, live in a culture dominated not by political propaganda but by sociological propaganda. The main instrument used by those (corporate elites) with enough financial resources to "propagandize" the masses is advertising. If advertising can either create fear and anxiety about security or play on already existent insecurities and offer goods and services to alleviate those preoccupying fears, neuroses, and anxieties about insecurity, it is considered successful. Faith in the product to alleviate the fear is essential for cultural consumerism.[104] Similarly, faith in the weapons to control the Soviet Union is essential for an increasing militarization.[105]

Matthew portrays Jesus making the same connection between fear and faith. However the objects are different. For the advertisers faith in the product alleviates fear; for Matthew's Jesus fear is alleviated by a faith-experience of God's reign. Earlier in this book I noted the significance of the chiastic structure of 6:25-34, which dealt with the juxtaposition of anxiety and faith. Realizing that the emotional challenge to security is anxiety or fear, Matthew's Jesus urged the disciples with little faith (6:30) not to be anxious about what they would eat, drink, or wear[106] in the manner of unbelievers, but to seek first the experience of God's reign and *dikaiosýnē*. Then, such things would fall into place: "Therefore do not be anxious about tomorrow, for tomorrow will be anxious for itself. Let the day's own trouble be sufficient for the day" (6:34).

2. Recovering from Our Cultural Addictions One Day at a Time

Just as those addicted to food or drink learn that they will never be totally converted from their addiction and must, therefore, "take one day at a time," so Matthew's Jesus urged the same to his anxious disciples. The God who gives daily bread will meet all basic needs if people are faithful and just (Ps. 37:25).

"One day at a time" is at the core of the "recovery program" for those working to overcome addictions. At its heart, a recovery program is essentially a program for conversion. Anne Schaef writes:

> In order to understand the system in which we live and help move it toward recovery, the time has come to admit, without reservation, that it is an addict and functions on a systemic level the same as any decompensating or deteriorating drunk. We must move beyond our participation in this disease process, beyond our denial, and see the elephant in its context for what it is, an Addictive System.[107]

Schaef, obviously, is relating substance or object addictions (to drink, gambling, or drugs) that function on an individual level to relational and activity addictions (such as consumerism, militarism, and classism in our political economy and sexism and clericalism in our churches) that function on a social level. Society's addictions are both substance-oriented and relational. In applying the wisdom related to the former type of addiction to the latter types we can begin to develop an approach to discipleship in the First World that will create a truly alternative way of life. At the heart of personal and societal recovery from these addictions are essential elements of spirituality:[108] conversion, contemplation, and community. The next paragraphs will investigate the challenge and relevance of each.

a. Conversion
The first step in overcoming addictions is to convert from their control or authority. Conversion is, at its heart, a movement from and a movement to, a movement from one loyalty to another, be it a thing or a person. The advertisers in today's market depend on "conversion" of others to their products. A

classist, consumeristic, militaristic society plays on people's addictions to reinforce the goals of a market economy. A classic case of this is found in the tobacco companies and how they work for "conversion." This process involves seeking, finding, selling, and buying.

The relationship between advertising and the rise of cigarette consumption in the United States has been well-documented.[109] In recent years, however, cigarette consumption peaked and began to decline. As U.S. tobacco companies realized their market was shrinking, they began to *seek* new markets. When they *found* them in the Third World, they used forms of sociological propaganda (newspapers, magazines, radio, television, billboards, free samples, sponsorships) so that people would *sell* either a non-smoking lifestyle or a local brand to *buy* the new brand.[110] Seeking, finding, selling, and buying are the four stages needed for economic conversion in a consumer society.

Matthew's Jesus uses the same terms to describe the process for religious conversion of disciples that advertisers implement in seeking economic conversion of consumers. Seeking, finding, selling, and buying the pearl of great price or the treasure in the field as images of God's reign (13:44–46) are at the heart of the gospel. If one recalls that we can be "given over to" either God or mammon, what are the implications of being converted to God's reign when consumerism reigns over us? Furthermore, what are the implications of making a "preferential option for the poor" when we, as First World peoples, are running after, or manifest, a "preferential option for consumerism"?

Matthew contrasts the paradigm of the rich young man who parallels Matthew's prospering house church with that of Peter (19:16–30). The rich young man and Peter embody two different approaches to the steps of seeking, finding, selling, and buying. We can diagram this contrast as follows:

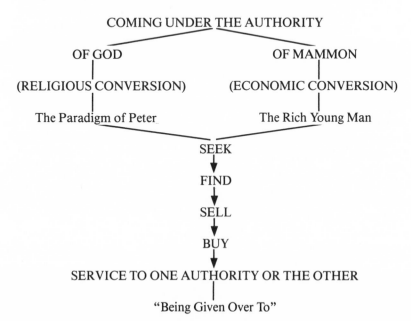

COMING UNDER THE AUTHORITY

OF GOD   OF MAMMON

(RELIGIOUS CONVERSION)   (ECONOMIC CONVERSION)

The Paradigm of Peter   The Rich Young Man

SEEK

FIND

SELL

BUY

SERVICE TO ONE AUTHORITY OR THE OTHER

"Being Given Over To"

Peter "sought" Jesus[111]; so did the rich young man. Both "found" Jesus. Peter was willing to "sell" "all things" (*pánta*)[112]on behalf of the poor (19:21), but when the young man heard that he had to sell what he possessed and give it to the poor he went away sorrowful (19:21-22). There was no "buying" into the reign of God via that discipleship proclaimed by Jesus which demands solidarity with the poor.

Why could Peter enter into a religious conversion and not the rich young man? Somehow the young man's "great possessions" (19:22) had an addictive power over him. Somehow the power of his possessions was more significant than the power of Jesus and his way of discipleship. He was given over to the authority of mammon.

Conversion implies a change of loyalty, a change of gods. It involves "selling" to "buy." One will never "sell" unless what is "bought" is perceived as better. The rich young man did not experience Jesus as better than his possessions. How could it have been different? He would have to come under the influence of a power or force greater than that to which he was "given over." This brings us to the second element in the conversion process: the role of contemplation or religious experience[113] in an addictive society.

b. Contemplation
According to the second step of the various programs to overcome addictions, only the realization and/or experience of a "power greater than that power which has its addictive authority" over someone can free him or her from the addiction. Applying this insight to the addictions reinforcing the industrialized nations, we can say that only a power greater than the market's addictive hold over the First World can enable its conversion to take place. But what power or reality is more real than the materialism surrounding us, continually inviting us to give ourselves over to it? What is more real than a consumeristic approach to life that finds its security in weapons? For the vast majority of people in the First World, the only thing that would be "more real" certainly cannot be anything visible. If visible, material reality and that classism, consumerism, and militarism which are at its heart are so very real to us, then the only possible thing more powerful would have to be something equally or more real, but *non*material or invisible. The only thing nonmaterial that is real must be something spiritual. The only thing spiritual that is real is one's religious experience of a reality or power greater than material reality.

Any psychologist, be it one on Madison Avenue or Matthew himself, will insist that nobody will "sell" anything to "buy" something else unless what is "bought" appears more significant or valuable. If this be the case, the authentic conversion of First World people caught in the addiction of classism, consumerism, and militarism will occur only if those persons experience God's reign as more powerful than the addictive hold of society's consumerism and militarism and ecclesiastical sexism and clericalism.

The first two steps in the twelve-step conversion process show that this beginning of "recovery" occurs in one of two ways.[114] In the first form, one becomes disillusioned with that which addicts by "reaching bottom" or discovering life's unmanageability. This realization makes one open to something else to be given over to. The person stops "running after" the object of the addiction. This enables the person to *seek* another power in life, which, when *found*, provides new meaning for life. The second way involves an actual experience of *finding* a power having more authority than that which currently addicts. The only way to achieve this is through a charismatic or contemplative experience of faith. This demands continually seeking to be touched by God's *exousía* in prayer as well as manifesting that *exousía* by doing God's will through actions that bear fruit in justice.

The experience of faith is the experience of finding God's reign within and around one's self. The contemplative experience of God's reign is the deepest experience of faith any human can have. It is little wonder, then, that, after chiding the disciples on their "little faith" (6:31), Matthew's Jesus challenged the disciples in the house churches to "seek first his kingdom and his *dikaiosýnē*" (6:33).

Everyone has faith in something or someone. One's ultimate faith is in that which constitutes the object of his or her concern. For many this ultimate concern represents an addiction. The experience of that something or someone constitutes a power which can only be altered if one begins to believe in something or someone else. Thus Matthew's Jesus directed the overly-addicted members of his house churches (6:30) to begin to hunger and thirst for God's order in their lives (5:6) and to seek the experience of God's reign and order in their lives (6:32). Then their "little faith" would begin to be deepened. Contemplation begins with seeking the reality of God's reign and God's order in one's life. It is expressed in resting in that reign alone (11:25–30).

c. Community

After "conversion" and "contemplation," the third element in being healed from the addictive authority of First World cultures is to gather regularly with like-minded addicts to create an alternative community for support. In the face of our addictive society with its increasing inequality, consumerism, and militarism, there is a special need for alternative communities or "households" of equality wherein people find their security in the group. In his excellent article on "The Culture of Procurement: Reflections on Addiction and the Dynamics of American Culture," Roland A. Delattre discusses our society's addiction to consumer goods and the armaments we feel are necessary to maintain our security. He concludes:

> I also think it might be a good idea if we, in all seriousness, formed an organization once proposed by Kurt Vonnegut: a new W.P.A., War Preparers Anonymous, modeled after Alcoholics Anonymous and their twelve-step program for recovery. If my analysis of the culture of procurement is correct, such an organization would make an effective contribution towards creating world peace and a sane society.[115]

What Delattre suggests for societal addictions is equally applicable for recovery programs in our churches. Within Matthew's social world the house churches provided an alternative way of life. Today there is an equal need, within the institutional churches of the First World, to create alternative communities, contemporary "house churches," so that like-minded disciples can experience hospitality in places of meaning, mutuality, and empowerment. Some of the deepest forms of religious experience and the most profound alleviation from the suffering caused by various addictions can be found in the regular meeting. Regularly coming together to share in the struggle to be free of addictions, to stop running after society's enticements and clerical power struggles, and to share in a faith-struggle and vision in offering an alternative— that will be at the heart of future discipleship in the First World.

The Compromising of the Church Embedded in Economic Institutions. Earlier, following Malina's notion of kinship, politics, and religion being embedded in the economic institutions of society, I noted how religion, or at least people in their practice of religion, can be compromised by economics. In his "The Socio-Economic Conditioning of the Church," Kuno Füssel has shown that the church's historical nature and involvement in the world are "shaped, limited and oriented in accordance with the particular mode of production that predominates in a specific society."[116] In other words, in post-industrial capitalism, the church's presence in society is highly shaped by the predominant economic attitudes.

Today, one of the biggest obstacles in preaching conversion to the institutions in our political economy is the reality that religious institutions themselves often are part of the problem and/or contradict the message being proclaimed.

It has been argued, with good justification, that Matthew's attribution to Jesus of his diatribe against the scribes and Pharisees in chapter 23 might not only be "biased, unfair and even libelous;"[117] it seems to undermine the command of universal love (19:19; 22:30) and forgiveness of enemies (5:43–48). However, in his masterful study of the composition and structure of Matthew 23, David E. Garland shows that Matthew's interpretation of the material not only was affected by the serious divisions that existed between the synagogues and the house churches and by the events of the Jewish-Roman war, but was also affected in a special way by abuses of power within Matthew's house churches. Garland writes: "Matthew's interest in warning his own church by negative example continually crops up in the text; and he is particularly interested in warning those who have inherited the scribal mantle, the Christian doctors of theology, the teachers and leaders of the 'little ones.' "[118]

Matthew's gospel not only addressed the church of his day but any disciple of Jesus who must accept the challenge of Jesus' teachings "always, to the close of the age" (28:20). Consequently, it can be justifiably stated that Matthew's gospel not only addressed abuses in church authority then, but abuses in authority now as well. Garland makes this connection in the concluding words of his book:

The Christian is to see himself potentially mirrored in the scribe and Pharisee as a type and to recognize that the same judgment which befell the leaders of Israel awaits the unfaithful leaders of Christ's community. In this matter, Matthew would probably wish to say to Christian leaders, who embody everything which is condemned in this chapter all too much and who live out everything which is commended in this chapter all too little, "Do you not see all these things?"[119]

If the church is to be authentic, it must witness to a new kind of contemporary householding of faith that reflects the kind of community Matthew's Jesus envisioned. It must "give light to all in the house," and let its "light so shine before men, that they may see your good works" (5:15–16). In other words, the church must be the first witness of what it proclaims to the world. If it calls for equality at all levels among people in the world, it should proclaim what it preaches by its works. If it calls for justice within economic and political systems, it must witness to justice within its own structures. Thus the 1971 Synod of Bishops states emphatically: "While the Church is bound to give witness to justice, she recognizes that anyone who ventures to speak to people about justice must first be just in their eyes. Hence we must undertake an examination of the modes of acting and of the possessions and life style found within the Church itself."[120]

The reign of God in heaven—where all will be equal and all will share in the fullness of resources—must come on earth. The church must be the first sign of what it preaches. Thus Leonardo Boff concludes: "If conversion does not reach the institution of the church . . . then we cannot speak of Gospel conversion."[121]

Because of the institutional contradictions and the injustice in so many parts of the church, but especially because it too can develop a kind of institutionalized "hardness of heart," there is a need for alternative kinds of communities. These can be found in contemporary house churches and similar gatherings of disciples committed to seeking the reign of God through religious experience and responding to their God by bearing fruit in justice.

Alternative Communities: The Role of Contemporary House Churches. Despite the evident need for contemporary forms of house churches, some people feel they are more suited to a Third World experience. Basic communities by the thousands exist in countries in Latin America and other Third World nations. However, as we have shown, given the addictive nature of our classist, consumeristic, militaristic society (as well as the sexist, racist, and clerical domination of most of the churches), basic household communities are equally necessary in the world of post-industrial capitalism.

Gerhard Lohfink has suggested that the Second Vatican Council's insight in *Lumen Gentium*[122] about the family being the domestic church be expanded to make the Christian family the basis of a new house church.[123] His words are gradually becoming implemented. As of 1982, the house church movement in Britain numbered several hundred churches with over fifty thousand members.[124] Until recently in the United States, "house church" movements have tended to be reactions to negative elements in institutions or have been more therapeutic in nature.[125] However an increasing number of books[126] and even a ten-session program oriented to the creation of house-based churches striving to be converted from society's addictions and to a life formed by Matthew's Beatitudes[127] have become available.

The times now call for a new approach to translating the gospel into our addictive society. The times call for building on the approach of Matthew's gospel as articulated in these pages in order to create continually-converting house churches in solidarity with the poor through justice. Whether based in the house or other kinds of gatherings, and without detailing its dynamics any further, "process over product" should be its aim. In other words it is more important that the group continually comes together (as all co-addicts must do), faithful to the struggle of conscientization, than to expect immediate solutions to infrastructural intransigency or hardness of heart.

A SUMMARY OF THE MAIN THESES OF THIS BOOK

Before making some concluding remarks, it may be good to pause and consider what has been written in this book thus far. As I near my conclusion, I want to highlight the main points which I have developed in the previous pages.[128]

1. Since first-century economics and religion were embedded in the household, an understanding of Matthew, or any gospel, is incomplete if redaction criticism is limited only to the ecclesial dimension. The use of the "primary assumed metaphor" of "house" helps unpack the connections between economics and church.

2. If Matthew's intent was to have his narration about the teaching of Jesus put into practice all days (28:19–20), each age demands an interaction of faith between the horizon of the "then" and the one of "now." This task has not been facilitated by most uses of historical and narrative criticism. An interactive hermeneutic offers an alternative.

3. Since "economics" involves the ordering of scarce resources among competing persons, since "church" involves the gathering of persons with each other with their resources, and since "justice" involves the right-ordering of relationships among persons vis-à-vis each other and their resources, there is an intimate connection among economics, church, and justice.

4. Matthew's theology of discipleship can be understood by examining the image of those faithful elect who are "inside" the house (12:46–50) or who "gather" to be with Jesus, who understand his teachings, and who put them into practice, thus bearing the fruit of justice which is doing the will of the heavenly Father. All this revolves around the notion of the members of the house united with the householder (10:25).

5. While there is an intimate connection between "house" and "church" in Matthew (7:24–27 and 16:17–19; 17:25 and 18:17), not every house is church,

nor is every church a house. Church is also the gathering of at least two or three in the name of Jesus (18:17–20). The authority of binding and loosing rests in both the house-based church (universal and local) and in the gathering of two or three.

6. Just as society was built on the foundation of the *oikía/oikos* for the *pólis* and *basileía*, so Matthew not only sees a connection among the terms (12:25) but makes the house the entrance into the kingdom of heaven. Obedience within the house church is obedience to the heavenly Father.

7. A pivotal passage in Matthew, 12:46–50, depicts the members of the traditional patriarchal family "outside" and the "disciples" inside the house. The transfer of Jesus' presence with those "outside" to those with him takes place in 23:37–24:2 when Jesus says that Jerusalem's house will be abandoned and when he leaves the temple.

8. Matthew's churches were divided along ethnic (Hebrew and Hellenist), geographic (rural and urban), sexual (male and female), and status (power, possessions, and prestige) lines. These divisions were worked out in and between two major kinds of households, the patriarchal model and the collegial/voluntary association model. Matthew's gospel reveals the tensions but offers a vision of a united church (or churches) that is more collegial than patriarchal.

9. The more collegial vision of Matthew for his church is not only reinforced by strong group/low grid dynamics that had leadership but no domination and titles, but also by a unique kind of *haustafel* whose contents were void of traditional patriarchal forms of domestic submission. The first (17:24–18:35) *haustafel* in Matthew is structured on the basis of the traditional *haustafel* that contains a civic component (17:24–27) and domestic component (18:1–35). The second (19:1–20:16) is patterned on the structure of the other major *haustafel* model. Again, however, its content is non-patriarchal. The first part deals with domestic relations (19:1–15), the second with issues related to wealth and acquiring it (19:26–20:16).

10. Given the more urbanized and generally prosperous composition of Matthew's households, Matthew never portrays Jesus or his disciples—in his public life—as unable to have access to resources, i.e., as "poor." Jesus is first presented in a house (2:11) and probably owned a house ([8:14]; 9:1, 10, 28; 13:1, 36; 17:25) in Capernaum (4:13; 8:5; 9:1; 17:24) where he settled (i.e., "made a house"). To prepare for his death a woman with very expensive ointment shared her resource with him in a house; that action had religious and economic implications for evangelical discipleship (26:1–13). Only at his death was he unable to have access to resources. Then "a rich man from Arimathea, named Joseph, who also was a disciple of Jesus" (27:57), shared the resource of his tomb. Given the stratified society of the first century, the issue was not poverty, but justice via the right-ordering of resources.

11. Even though one cannot transpose the gospel of Matthew into the twentieth century, a reader-response interactive hermeneutic finds "justice" or rightly-ordered relationships and resources as an ethical key linking the "then"

and the "now." Justice in church and economics must be seen in the context of Jesus' fulfillment of the Law and the prophets which is the fulfillment of God's will for the whole world. This has spiritual as well as socio-political implications. An ethics of responsibility, modeled on the character of Jesus' response to his "heavenly Father," characterizes Matthean morality.

12. The application of justice to our political economy as well as to the church demands moral policies and practices that will insure the dignity of the human person realized in freedom, the most equitable sharing of resources, and the insurance of solidarity among all respective participants.

13. The service of God and mammon "then" and "now" are the two basic forces around which individuals, groups, institutions, as well as societies will order their lives. Being anxious about and given over (*douleúein*) to what we eat, drink, or wear (6:25–32) is best understood from addiction theory. Recovery or "conversion" is grounded on seeking, finding, selling, and buying, which begin by first seeking God's reign and God's justice (6:33). The spirituality of Matthew's Jesus urges approaching life one day at a time (6:34).

14. Given the need to develop a communitarian ethic of justice and policies implementing justice within post-industrial "corpocracy," the future will be enhanced if, within structures which are constituted of institutions and "isms" and which are reinforced via ideologies ("horizons"), contemporary disciples of Jesus who are awakened (i.e., "understand") create an alternative order. This involves gathering together to become church via communities of conscientization that are in the process of being continually converted from society's addictions and inviting others in society to a similar ongoing conversion. The process to use within these gatherings might reflect the twelve-step recovery program for other addicts.[129]

CONCLUSION

The last judgment scene makes it clear that salvation rests on religion and economy oriented toward the meeting of people's needs. In his first encyclical, *Redemptor Hominis*, Pope John Paul II used the story of the sheep and the goats in Matthew as a moral model for judging human behavior. His interpretation moves the narrative from the past and the level of actions by individuals to present realities and systemic issues of justice. His words also touch upon the addictiveness of First World economic patterns that are extended into the Third World, especially through forms of militarism, creating greater forms of "co-dependency":

> This eschatological scene must always be "applied" to people's history: it must always be made the "measure" for human acts as an essential outline for an examination of conscience by each and every one: "I was hungry and you gave me no food . . . naked and you did not clothe me . . . in prison and you did not visit me" (25:42, 43). These words become charged with even stronger warning when we think that, instead of bread

and cultural aid, the new states and nations awakening to independent life are being offered, sometimes in abundance, modern weapons and means of destruction placed at the service of armed conflicts and wars that are not so much a requirement for defending their just rights and their sovereignty but rather a form of chauvinism, imperialism, and neo-colonialism of one kind or another. We all know well that the areas of misery and hunger on our globe could have been made fertile in a short time, if the gigantic investments for armaments at the service of war and destruction had been changed into investments for food at the service of life.[130]

Pope John Paul II's interpetation of Jesus' words about alleviating hunger and thirst touches upon the addictiveness of economic imperialism and militarism. His interpretation of Jesus' words about meeting the needs of the poor demands working to alleviate unjust exploitation and changing structures that sustain impoverishment. The ethic he outlines stands in sharp contrast to practices in churches in which leaders lord their authority over others (20:25) or in a market economy based on the allocation of scarce resources among individuals competing with each other to have their wants fulfilled. Such a contrast should not be present in the lives of the disciples of Jesus (20:26).

Where Matthew's Jesus demands an economic ethic responding to need, the market-ethic responds to greed or unlimited wants. Given this situation, as the various denominational statements on the economy have made clear, it is essential that new principles guide our production and consumption. While we realize the interdependence of production and consumption, both must be guided by basic priorities which reflect a Matthean ethic. These ethical priorities involve meeting the basic needs of the poor, increasing the active participation in economic life of those presently excluded or vulnerable, and a reordering of the investment of wealth, talent, and human energy to benefit the economically insecure. As the Catholic bishops noted:

> These priorities are not policies. They are norms which should guide the economic choices of all and shape economic institutions. They can help the United States move forward to fulfill the duties of justice and protect economic rights. They were strongly affirmed as implications of Catholic social teaching by Pope John Paul II during his visit to Canada in 1984: "The needs of the poor take priority over the desires of the rich; the rights of workers over the maximization of profits; the preservation of the environment over uncontrolled industrial expansion; production to meet social needs over production for military purposes."[131]

While few would argue with Pope John Paul II's ideal, it is still far from being seriously considered by those who make policy. Thus, the task of the Christian to bring the message of justice into society remains formidable.

Matthew's ethic implies a renewed church and a global economic. With

justice as its goal (5:20, 48), it demands a reordering of familial ties, relationships, and resources (20:29), especially regarding those in need, namely the
poor (19:21). Only those who experience the presence of God's reign within
them (see 28:20) will experience a power (*exousía*) greater than all human
countervailing forces and hear the promise given when the task of this reordering seems unworkable, impractical, inconceivable, unobtainable, or unachiev-
able: "With men this is impossible, but with God all things are possible"
(19:26).

If Jesus was the first to put into practice this "kingdom ethic" of reordering
relationships and resources to meet the needs of the people with justice as the
goal, he did so because of the *exousía* that was part of the "all things" delivered
to him by God (11:27). To the degree he fulfilled his own teaching and ethics, to
the same degree must his disciples.

By baptism, the disciples of all ages are given the same *exousía* Jesus
received. If he could live by his ethic because of that *exousía*, the heart of
everything he taught can and must be observed by his disciples because they
share in that same power. With *exousía* (28:18) all things are possible, even
changing society's economic priorities. If the baptized are to go into the whole
world, and if economic entities collectively are the main social institution in our
world, then the baptized must bring the message of Matthew's gospel about
justice to bear upon the economy—be it domestic or international house-
ordering.

With a growing realization of the basic unity of the world, we are beginning
to return to a realization of the need to see things not just from the perspective
of the *oikía* or the *oikouménē*, but from the viewpoint of the ecological whole.
Just as the world at the time of Matthew's Jesus was seen as a whole with
humans interacting with nature and the divine, so we are beginning to realize
the first part of that horizon—that we are to be one with our world. The justice
demanded of Matthew's households should compel us to work for a new kind
of ecological house-ordering. This ecological perspective will contribute to
what the social philosopher Wendell Berry calls "home economics."[132]

Ecology involves reflection on the world as a cell. Ecology is the study of the
household, or how the household of nature is kept in order.[133] Rooted in the
household, its economic concern addresses the whole of the earth and all
creation—persons and resources in their interrelationships—as a single, unified organism. From a religious perspective ecology is concerned with the
world as the original household created by God. When the relation between
house and ecology is viewed from this perspective, it becomes clear that the
house as an assumed primary metaphor in Matthew's gospel is a microcosm of
the world—Matthew's vision of his justly-ordered house churches is a localized
vision of what the world might become (see 28:16–20). From this perspective
our reflections on house apply to the whole ecological reality, for the root word
of ecology, as ecumenics, is also *oikía/oikos*. Ecology is merely the study of the
world as a basic organism, as a basic global household.

In the Introduction to this book I said that "house" served as an "assumed primary metaphor" in Matthew. Earlier in this book I quoted Leander Keck as saying that the reign of God expressed in right relationships (*dikaiosýnē*) is the "master image" of Matthew's gospel. I also showed connections among reign of God, house, and justice. Thus, any ethic that purports to be Matthean and relevant to religion and economics must include understandings and demands that proceed from Matthew's vision for the "house" in its broadest sense—as a reflection of God's reign of justice. It must be a holistic, ecological ethic. When not only dreams but the scriptures view the house as a symbol of the self (Job 4:19), when the house is the basic social order of society, when the house is the grounding of the *oikoumēnē*, and, finally, when the house is the ecological foundation of the universe itself, then it is clear that the macrocosm is imaged in the microcosm of the house. The house is the image of the unity of the self and the cosmos.

Those who boldly proclaim this ethic need not be afraid when they call for this household reordering, for the words they use will be those of the Spirit (10:20). They can be assured of the abiding promise Jesus gives to those who observe all that he has taught: "lo, I am with you always, to the close of the age" (28:20).

Notes

INTRODUCTION

1. The notion of "horizon" will be discussed later in this Introduction.

2. For a discussion of the use of *oikía/oikos* and related terms see various lexicons, especially Otto Michel's study in Gerhard Kittel and Gerhard Friedrich, eds., *Theological Dictionary of the New Testament*, vol. 5, trans. Geoffrey W. Bromiley (Grand Rapids: Eerdmans, 1981), pp. 119–59. To my knowledge no book in English has yet been oriented to the examination of a gospel or the gospels from the perspective of "house." An excellent book which sets the overall context for house-theology and applies it to a specific scripture is John H. Elliott's *A Home for the Homeless: A Sociological Exegesis of I Peter, Its Situation and Strategy* (Philadelphia: Fortress, 1981). Despite its title, Robert Banks's *Paul's Idea of Community: The Early House Churches in Their Historical Setting* (Grand Rapids: Eerdmans, 1980) stresses community more than household as such. For treatments of house in other languages see the studies by Hans-Josef Klauck, *Hausgemeinde und Hauskirche im frühen Christentum* (Stuttgart: Verlag Katholisches Bibelwerk GMbH, 1981) and "Die Hausgemeinde als Lebensform im Urchristentum," *Münchener Theologische Zeitschrift* 32 (1981), pp. 1–15. For a consideration of the house church as the basic structure of Christianity see Rafael Aguirre, "La casa como estructura base del Cristianismo primitivo: Las iglesias domesticas," *Estudios Eclesiasticos* 59 (1984), pp. 27–51. For bibliography on *haustafeln*, see chapter 2, n. 43.

3. While religion was part of the fabric of first-century life, it is very difficult to define. Today, even from a sociological perspective, definitions of "religion" can be inclusive or exclusive, substantive or functional. Anthropologists also offer different frameworks for their definitions. Building on both sociological and anthropological definitions I see the basic elements of "religion" involving a system of beliefs and practices related to life's ultimate conditions; this system unites people into a single moral community within which a *general order for existence* is offered for dealing with life's ultimate issues.

4. Matthew does not use the word *oikonomía* as such. However he does stress the ordering (*relationships*) taking place among *persons* and *resources* within households. Thus, since economics is the ordering of resources among persons, economics cannot be divorced from Matthew's gospel. It constituted the very social, religious, and economic dynamic of his community. Given the various definitions for "economics," I see its basic elements involving the allocation or *ordering* of limited resources among (competing) persons who have different wants.

5. Contrary to popular usage, the original etymology for management or ordering is not *nomos*, but *némein*, to order. I follow the German practice of using the infinitive

form for verbs rather than the first-person singular. John Reumann has shown quite convincingly that the current practice of finding the root word for house *management* in *nomos* is untenable. Rather *nomos* itself is rooted in *nem*, specifically *nemo* and *nemein*. Thus *nomos* is derived from *nemein*. See John Henry Paul Reumann, *The Use of Oikonomía and Related Terms in Greek Sources to about A.D. 100, as a Background for Patristic Applications*, unpublished dissertation (Philadelphia: University of Pennsylvania, 1957), p. 144; see also H. Kleinknecht, "Nomos," in Kittel, ed., *Theological Dictionary of the New Testament*, vol. 4, trans. Geoffrey W. Bromiley (Grand Rapids: Eerdmans, 1983), p. 1023, n. 1. For a good study on the early meaning of *oikonomía*, see Reumann, " 'Stewards of God'—Pre-Christian Religious Application of *Oikonómos* in Greek," *Journal of Biblical Literature* 77 (1958), pp. 339-49.

6. For further discussion about the house as Mark's locale for Jesus' teaching see Klauck, *Hausgemeinde*, pp. 60-62. For a discussion on Mark's vision of the house as basis of the new family (as well as the context for his teaching) see John R. Donahue, *The Theology and Setting of Discipleship in the Gospel of Mark* (Milwaukee: Marquette University Press, 1983), pp. 37-46, as well as Ernest Moore, " 'Outside' and 'Inside': A Markan Motif," *The Expository Times* 98 (1986), pp. 39-43.

7. John Koenig presents a rough outline for a Lukan house theme in his *New Testament Hospitality: Partnership with Strangers and Promise and Mission* (Philadelphia: Fortress, 1985), pp. 20-51 and 85-123.

8. While it is conceivable that the author of the first gospel may have been a woman, the patriarchal situation of that society tends to preclude this possibility. Thus I refer to Matthew as "he." As will be seen, the word for "Matthew" may indicate any disciple, male or female, who tries to do the heavenly Father's will by putting the teachings of Jesus into practice, thus becoming a member of God's household.

9. The one exception occurs in Luke's Benedictus (Lk. 1:75). Much of the current discussion around justice in Matthew (which will be treated in chapter 7) is well summarized in Benno Przyblyski, *Righteousness in Matthew and His World of Thought* (Cambridge: Cambridge University Press, 1980).

10. Throughout this book I will operate from a concept of justice which defines it as "rightly-ordered relationships of persons with God and of persons with each other vis-à-vis resources." Kleinknecht shows that, in the course of their development, *némein* and *nomos* were often connected and even equated with forms of *díkē* and *díkaion*, the root words for justice (see p. 1023, n. 1).

11. See Kleinknecht, p. 1024. "As the epitome of what is valid in social dealings *nomos* in its unwritten form is first rooted in religion. . . . Even the written law of the *nomos* is still an expression of the will of the deity which holds sway in the city . . . . This rootage in the divine sphere, which always persists, gives to the Gk *nomos* concept its characteristic significance and true strength" (ibid., p. 1025).

12. Michael H. Crosby, *Spirituality of the Beatitudes: Matthew's Challenge to First World Christians* (Maryknoll, N.Y.: Orbis, 1987).

13. Throughout this book, I use the term "prosperity"—rather than "affluence"—to describe the economic situation of a major portion of Matthew's house churches. "Affluence" as such exists only with capitalism, which involves a systematic accumulation of wealth. No such dynamic existed in the precapitalist, slave-based economy of the first century.

14. Anthropologists are divided over the applicability of modern, market-based economic theory to pre-modern, traditional economies. Generally economic anthropologists have followed the "substantive difference" viewpoint which sees traditional

economic activity embedded, rather than separate from, the rest of human activities. There is no formal identification; thus a substantive difference. Consequently modern economic theory cannot be used to understand traditional economies. For an early discussion of this issue—which sees the debate originating in the "oikos theory" of Karl Robertus—see Karl Polanyi, Conrad M. Arensberg, and Harry W. Pearson, *Trade and Markets in the Early Empires: Economies in History and Theory* (Glencoe, Ill.: The Free Press, 1957). For a more thorough discussion on the formal-substantive debate see David Kaplan, "The Formal-Substantive Controversy in Economic Anthropology: Some Reflections on its Wider Implications," *Southwestern Journal of Anthropology* 24 (1968), pp. 228–51.

15. Bruce J. Malina, " 'Religion' in the World of Paul," *Biblical Theology Bulletin* 16 (1986), p. 93.

16. This will be discussed in chapter 2. See also Jack Dean Kingsbury, *Matthew as Story* (Philadelphia: Fortress, 1986), pp. 28,44,123; Elizabeth Struthers Malbon, "Te oikia autou: Mark 2:15 in Context," *New Testament Studies* 31 (1985), pp. 282–92.

17. During the 1970s, this situation began to change. A pioneer in the "sociologizing" of the gospel has been Gerd Theissen. One of his early books in English is *Sociology of Early Palestinian Christianity*, trans. John Bowden (Philadelphia: Fortress, 1977). As will be evident from a quick perusal of this book, I am deeply indebted to the work of more recent biblicists using a social-scientific interpretation of the Bible and its social world, especially John Elliott, Bruce Malina, and Wayne Meeks. Rather than noting their material here, they will be cited throughout the following chapters.

18. Thomas W. Ogletree, *The Use of the Bible in Christian Ethics* (Philadelphia: Fortress, 1983), p. 129.

19. Even if not all members of the house were Christian, there were "internal relations." Indeed it seems that the fact that not all members were Christian contributed to tensions and even persecutions.

20. I am indebted to David Hester and William Herzog for their insights which helped me develop this section. See William R. Herzog II, "Interpretation as Discovery and Creation: Sociological Dimensions of Biblical Hermeneutics," *American Baptist Quarterly* 2 (1983), pp. 105–18.

21. James Barr, *The Semantics of Biblical Language* (Oxford: Oxford University Press, 1961), p. 283. In this reference, Barr considers the relationship between "house" and *hierón,* the word for "temple."

22. Barr, *Biblical Words for Time,* 2nd (rev.) ed. (London: S.C.M. Press, 1969), pp. 11–19.

23. Duncan S. Ferguson, *Biblical Hermeneutics: An Introduction* (Atlanta: John Knox, 1986), p. 4. For other works on hermeneutics see J. Severino Croatto, *Biblical Hermeneutics: Towards a Theory of Reading as the Production of Meaning,* trans. Robert R. Barr (Maryknoll, N.Y.: Orbis, 1987); Anthony C. Thiselton, *The Two Horizons: New Testament Hermeneutics and Philosophical Description* (Grand Rapids: Eerdmans, 1984); Raymond F. Collins, *Introduction to the New Testament* (Garden City, N.Y.: Doubleday Image Books, 1987).

24. Hans-Georg Gadamer, *Truth and Method,* trans. William Glen-Doepel (London: Sheed & Ward, 1975).

25. Ibid., p. 273.

26. Thomas Kuhn was a pioneer in insisting that all scientific method is based in paradigms. His groundbreaking insights were originally contained in *The Structure of Scientific Revolutions* (Chicago: University of Chicago Press, 1962). Since this work,

Kuhn has nuanced his original insights. Despite a debate around his theories—which has taken place in most every scientific field—his insights cannot be discounted. For a critical study of his theories, see Imre Lakatos and A. Musgrave, eds., *Criticism and the Growth of Knowledge* (New York and Cambridge: Cambridge University Press, 1970).

27. Thomas Kuhn defines a paradigm as a "disciplinary matrix" which includes three elements: "symbolic generalizations" which scientists use without questions, such as mathematical formulae; "models" which offer analogies; and "exemplars" or solutions to concrete problems that are accepted as paradigmatic. See his "Second Thoughts on Paradigms," in Frederick Suppe, ed., *The Structure of Scientific Theories* (Urbana, Ill.: University of Illinois Press, 1977), pp. 459–82.

28. For an easy-to-read study of how these elements of criticism are interconnected see John H. Hayes and Carl R. Holladay, *Biblical Exegesis: A Beginner's Handbook* (Atlanta: John Knox Press, 1982).

29. Ibid., p. 26.

30. Seymour Chatman, *Story and Discourse: Narrative Structure in Fiction and Film* (Ithaca, N.Y.: Cornell University Press, 1978).

31. The basic explanation of narrative criticism as applied to Matthew is based on Jack Dean Kingsbury's model in *Matthew as Story* (Philadelphia: Fortress, 1986), pp. 1–38. For another narrative approach to Matthew see Richard A. Edwards, *Matthew's Story of Jesus* (Philadelphia: Fortress, 1985).

32. Ibid., p. 36.

33. See Günther Bornkamm, Gerhard Barth, and Heinz Joachim Held, *Tradition and Interpretation in Matthew*, trans. Percy Scott (Philadelphia: Westminster, 1963), see esp. pp. 110–12.

34. Walter Wink, *The Bible in Human Transformation: Toward a New Paradigm for Biblical Study* (Philadelphia: Fortress, 1980), p. 10.

35. Gadamer, p. 273.

36. Dan O. Via, Jr., *The Ethics of Mark's Gospel—In the Middle of Time* (Philadelphia: Fortress, 1985), p. 14.

37. Wolfgang Iser, *The Act of Reading: A Theory of Aesthetic Response* (Baltimore and London: Johns Hopkins University Press, 1980), pp. 21, 92.

38. For a description of the methodology behind reader-response criticism see Jane P. Tompkins, "An Introduction to Reader-Response Criticism," in her *Reader-Response Criticism: From Formalism to Post-Structuralism* (Baltimore and London: The Johns Hopkins University Press, 1981). This book contains a listing of works in the field.

39. Croatto, p. 50.

40. My approach has been conditioned by the realization of the assets and limitations of my being a white, First World male cleric in the Roman Catholic Church in the last part of the second millennium and the first part of the third. My personal and social location, which is the context for my theologizing, has been described somewhat in my previous writings, especially *Thy Will Be Done* and *Spirituality of the Beatitudes*.

41. Gibson Winter, *Elements for a Social Ethic: Scientific and Ethical Perspectives on Social Process* (New York: Macmillan, 1968), pp. 18–33.

42. Martin Heidegger, *Unterwegs zur Sprache* (Neske: Pfullingen, 1960), p. 267.

43. Winter, *Liberating Creation: Foundations of Religious Social Ethics* (New York: Crossroad, 1981), p. 6.

44. Sallie McFague, *Metaphorical Theology: Models of God in Religious Language* (Philadelphia: Fortress, 1985), p. 40.

45. Elliott, p. 213.

46. Winter, *Liberating Creation*, pp. 6–10.

47. Anders Nygren, "The Role of the Self-Evident in History," *The Journal of Religion* 28 (1948), p. 236. I am indebted to John Reumann for sharing Nygren's ideas with me.

48. Elliott, p. 192.

49. This insight is key to understanding my use of house because there are many times that "entering a house" in Matthew might be simply considered a physical act of motion rather than a relational reality.

50. Wayne A. Meeks, "Understanding Early Christian Ethics," *Journal of Biblical Literature* 105 (1986), p. 4.

51. Karl Polanyi, *The Great Transformation: The Political and Economic Origins of Our Time* (Boston: Beacon, 1957), p. 46.

52. John H. Elliott, "Social-Scientific Criticism of the New Testament: More on Methods and Models," *Semeia* 35 (1986), p. 5.

53. T. F. Carney, *The Shape of the Past: Models and Antiquity* (Lawrence, Kans.: Coronado Press, 1975).

54. Elliott, "Social-Scientific Criticism," pp. 1–26.

55. Carney, pp. 47–281.

56. Carney begins his examination of the cross-cultural model by investigating the spheres of action in ancient bureaucratic politics. Starting with those actions performed by the emperor, he moves next to top bureaucrats, then to middle-level bureaucrats. After this he determines the characteristics of agrarian societies and traditional pre-industrial cities by studying demography; family and socialization processes, culture and social stratification; economics, technology, education, and communications; politics and religion.

57. Carney, p. 83. Carney concludes his section on cross-cultural models with an extended treatment of " 'Economics' in Antiquity" and "The Military and Society in Antiquity."

58. Elliott, "Social-Scientific Criticism," p. 17.

59. In *Liberating Creation* Gibson Winter offers a conceptual framework for an interpretation of Western society by defining its dominant root metaphors and relating these to different orientations in religio-social ethics and theology.

60. Barrington Moore, Jr., *Injustice: The Social Bases of Obedience and Revolt* (White Plains, N.Y.: M. E. Sharpe, 1978), p. 8.

61. Ibid., p. 9.

62. Max L. Stackhouse, "What Then Shall We Do? On Using Scripture in Economic Ethics," *Interpretation* 4 (1987), p. 382.

63. François Houtart, *Religion et modes de production précapitalistes* (Bruxelles: Université de Bruxelles, 1980), pp. 271–72.

64. Stackhouse also sees such a "fusion" of first-century horizons with ours involving justice (p. 394).

65. This conclusion is shared by Stackhouse as well. See pp. 394–97 for his comments on justice as well as those on *oikos* and *pólis*.

66. Chief among these have been T. F. Carney of the University of Windsor and Gareth Morgan at York University. Although Gareth Morgan does not include "house" as a possible metaphor for organization among his others (i.e., organism, brain, political system, culture, psychic prison, flex and transformation), my private conversations with him have supported the notion of house as organization-metaphor. See Gareth Morgan, *Images of Organization* (Los Angeles: Sage, 1986).

67. Various church denominations have prepared material for study groups to reflect on capitalism and the U.S. economy. See especially two study documents: *Christian Faith and Economic Justice* (Atlanta: Presbyterian Church USA, 1984), and *Toward a Just, Caring, and Dynamic Political Economy* (New York: Presbyterian Church USA, 1985). A well-argued position, including notions of household, can be found in the study of the United Church of Christ. See Audrey Chapman Smock, ed., *Christian Faith and Economic Life: A Study Paper Contributing to a Pronouncement for the Seventeenth General Synod of the United Church of Christ* (New York: United Church Board for World Ministries, 1987).

68. National Conference of Catholic Bishops, *Economic Justice for All: Catholic Social Teaching and the U.S. Economy*, no. 4, in *Origins* 16 (1987), p. 410. While our vision of economic life should be shaped by the Bible, this does not mean that Christians have a right to impose their vision on the economic system. When the scriptures were written the economy was house-based; thus the Bible could define how a local economy (house-order) should take place. However, today there is an international economic system with many actors and not all these share the Christian faith. Yet, because North America and Western Europe contain democracies, citizens have the right to bring their concerns to the public forum. This is not imposition of values, but open dialogue. Thus Christians should both model a biblically-based economic and work democratically to bring this vision to society's structures, despite the radical differences between first- and twentieth-century economics.

69. Gareth Morgan's metaphors describe organizations in a way that is geared to their transformation. Since "house" was the basic organization of the first century, this metaphor cannot be limited to that time but must be "imaginized" into our religious, economic, social, and cultural life today (pp. 321-44).

70. Kingsbury, p. 136.

71. Herzog, pp. 114-15.

CHAPTER 1

1. "Periclean Athens had already discovered the paradox that the polis, which gave to the Western world the ideal of direct democracy, could be transformed into an instrument of imperial ambition" (Wayne A. Meeks, *The First Urban Christians: The Social World of the Apostle Paul* [New Haven and London: Yale University Press, 1983], p. 11).

2. While Rome's economy was "quite primitive," it was not "primitive" in the strict sense used by economic anthropologists. According to Marshall Sahlins, "primitive" refers "to cultures lacking a political state, and it applies only insofar as economy and social relations have not been modified by the historic penetration of states" (Marshall D. Sahlins, "On the Sociology of Primitive Exchange," in Michael Banton, *The Relevance of Models for Social Anthropology* [London: Tavistock Publications, 1963], p. 141). Since the first century witnessed "romanization" under Augustus which paralleled the "hellenization" of Alexander, it is not accurate to describe the traditional economy of the first century as "primitive." Furthermore, since economic anthropology deals with primitive economics, all findings of economic anthropology applied to first-century economics in Syria-Palestine must be seriously examined. For some other works treating the anthropological dimension of economics in primitive economies see Melville J. Herskovits, *Economic Anthropology: The Economic Life of Primitive Peoples* (New York: W. W. Norton, 1952); Sahlins, *Tribesmen*, Foundations of Modern

Anthropology Series (Englewood Cliffs, N.J.: Prentice-Hall, 1968); James C. Scott, *The Moral Economy of the Peasant: Rebellion and Subsistence in Southeast Asia* (New Haven and London: Yale University Press, 1977).

3. This section on the economy of ancient Rome does not intend to be exhaustive. Among the many works consulted for this period, some stand out for their excellence. See Michael Avi-Yonah, *The Holy Land: From the Persian to the Arab Conquest (536 B.C. to A.D. 640): A Historical Geography* (Grand Rapids: Baker Book House, 1966); T. F. Carney, *The Shape of the Past: Models and Antiquity* (Lawrence, Kans.: Coronado, 1975); Richard Duncan-Jones, *The Economy of the Roman Empire: Quantitative Studies*, 2nd ed. (Cambridge: Cambridge University Press, 1982); M. I. Finley, *The Ancient Economy*, 2nd ed. (Berkeley and Los Angeles: University of California Press, 1985); Peter Garnsey, Keith Hopkins, and C. R. Whittaker, *Trade in the Ancient Economy* (Berkeley and Los Angeles: University of California Press, 1983); Kevin Greene, *The Archeology of the Roman Economy* (London: B. T. Batsford, 1986); Fritz M. Heichelheim, *An Ancient Economic History*, vol. 3, trans. Joyce Stevens (Leyden: A. W. Sijthoff, 1970), as well as his "Roman Syria" in Tenney Frank, ed., *An Economic Survey of Ancient Rome*, vol. 4 (Baltimore: The Johns Hopkins Press, 1938) and vol. 6 (Paterson: Pageant Books, 1959); François Houtart, *Religion et modes de production précapitalistes* (Bruxelles: Université de Bruxelles, 1980); E. K. Hunt, *Property and Prophets: The Evolution of Economic Institutions and Ideologies*, 2nd ed. (New York: Harper & Row, 1975); Manning Nash, *Primitive and Peasant Economic Systems* (Scranton, Penn.: Chandler, 1966); Karl Polanyi, Conrad M. Arensberg, and Harry W. Pearson, *Trade and Market in the Early Empires: Economies in History and Theory* (Glencoe, Ill.: The Free Press, 1957); M. Rostovtzeff, *The Social and Economic History of the Roman Empire*, vol. 1, 2nd ed. (Oxford: Clarendon, 1957).

4. For an excellent study on the connection between agriculture and urbanization see Max Weber, *The Agrarian Sociology of Ancient Civilizations*, trans. R. I. Frank (Atlantic Highlands, N.J.: Humanities Press, 1976).

5. For a discussion on the role of business in the first century see Finley, pp. 123–49. For a summary of the debate generated by his theories see H. W. Pleket, "Urban Elites and Business in the Greek Part of the Roman Empire," in Garnsey, et. al., pp. 131–44.

6. Heichelheim, *An Ancient Economic History*, p. 249.

7. Greene, p. 15.

8. Douglas C. North, *Structure and Change in Economic History* (New York and London: W. W. Norton, 1981), pp. 109ff.

9. Heichelheim, "Roman Syria," in Frank, vol. 4, p. 158.

10. The denarius was standardized during this era under Augustus and his successor Tiberius. See Heichelheim, *An Ancient Economic History*, pp.213ff.

11. Keith Hopkins, "Introduction," in Garnsey, pp. xv-xxi. Hopkins represents more recent findings about first-century economics than are found in Carney, who posited low agricultural output (p. 101), little technological development (pp. 106–7), and relatively stable city-size (p. 102). See Carney.

12. Mircea Eliade, *The Myth of the Eternal Return, or Cosmos and History,* trans. Willard R. Trask (Princeton, N.J.: Princeton University Press, 1974), pp. 76–77. See also G. van der Leeuw, *Religion in Essence and Manifestation,* vol. 2, trans. J. E. Turner (Gloucester, Mass.: Peter Smith, 1967), pp. 396–402. For the Egyptian notion of the house of God, esp. in Philo, see Elliott, p. 173.

13. Karl Polanyi, *The Great Transformation: The Political and Economic Origins of Our Time* (Boston: Beacon, 1957), pp. 47ff. T. F. Carney sees four types of exchange

systems: reciprocity, redistribution, the market, and mobilization exchange. However, because the latter two were quite minuscule and Carney does not include householding as the basic unit of exchange, Polanyi's approach seems more apropos to my discussion. See Carney, pp. 140–42.

14. Reciprocity and redistribution will be discussed more in subsequent chapters. The fact that the state was the redistribution instrument in first-century Rome is further evidence that Rome cannot be equated with a primitive economy, in which a chief is the instrument of redistribution. "Chiefly redistribution is a centralized, formal organization of kinship-rank reciprocities, an extensive social integration of the dues and obligations of leadership" (Sahlins, "On the Sociology of Primitive Exchange," p. 163).

15. Polanyi, p. 53.

16. For a description of the movement from household to lineage to village to subtribe to tribe see Sahlins, *Tribesmen*, pp. 14–20.

17. Robert David Sack, *Human Territoriality: Its Theory and History* (Cambridge: Cambridge University Press, 1986), pp. 61–62.

18. Weber, pp. 336ff.

19. See Avi-Yonah, p. 112.

20. Meeks, p. 14.

21. It is not clear if *oikos* or *domus* was used to refer to the housing of the lower classes. In his research into second-century Ostia, James E. Packer has concluded that less than 10% of the population lived in private mansions (*domi*) and multi-storied apartment houses (*insulae*); about 20% lived on the streets; and the rest (about 70%) lived in the one- or two-room apartments (James E. Packer, *The Insulae of Imperial Ostia: Memoirs of the American Academy of Rome*, vol. 31 [1971], pp. 70–71).

22. Ramsey MacMullen, *Roman Social Relations* (New Haven and London: Yale University Press, 1974), p. 63.

23. For a description of these forms of redistribution see Finley, pp. 89–94.

24. For a discussion on the role of the state in Rome's grain trade, see Lionel Casson, *Ancient Trade and Society* (Detroit: Wayne State, 1984), pp. 96–116.

25. Houtart, p. 223.

26. Casson, p. 108.

27. For an extended study of the contractual system Rome employed, using the *publicani*, see E. Badian, *Publicans and Sinners: Private Enterprise in the Service of the Roman Republic* (Ithaca, N.Y.: Cornell University Press).

28. M. I. Finley argues that neither Greek nor Latin has a word to express the commonest modern sense of "family" (p. 18). The Matthean use implies a servant who gives the household (i.e., the members of the family) "their food at the proper time" (Francisco Zorell, *Lexicon Graecum Novi Testamenti* [Paris: P. Lethielleux, 1931], p. 30). For an investigation of family relationships see Raphael Patai, *Sex and Family in the Bible and the Middle East* (Garden City, N.Y.: Doubleday, 1959). For contemporary anthropological distinctions between household and family see Donald R. Bender, "A Refinement of the Concept of Household," *American Anthropologist* 69 (1967), pp. 493–504.

29. The connection between *kýrios* and *paterfamilias*—as regards household authority in reference to Jesus and the church—will be examined in the next two chapters.

30. Meeks, p. 30.

31. Polanyi, p. 19.

32. David Herlihy, *Medieval Households* (London: Harvard University Press, 1985), pp. 8–9.

33. Sometimes even the voluntary associations put themselves under the patronage of the rich and powerful or used their households for various purposes, including worship.

34. Carney, p. 90.

35. Xenophon, *Oeconomicus* VI,4, trans. Carnes Lord, in Leo Strauss, *Xenophon's Socratic Discourse: An Interpretation of the Oeconomicus* (Ithaca and London: Cornell University Press, 1970), p. 26. For Strauss's elaboration on this identification of household and possessions see pp. 92–99.

36. Xenophon, V,1,4–19, pp. 22–25.

37. Michel Foucault, *The Use of Pleasure*, vol. 2 of *The History of Sexuality*, trans. Robert Hurley (New York: Vintage, 1985), pp. 158–59.

38. Aristotle, *Politics* I,13, in Richard McKeon, ed., *The Basic Works of Aristotle* (New York: Random House, 1941), p. 1143. *Haustafeln* will be discussed in greater detail in chapter 2.

39. Ibid., I,3, p. 1130. See I,12, p. 1143. For a fuller discussion of philosophical discussions concerning the constitution and management of households, including *haustafeln,* see David L. Balch, *Let Wives Be Submissive: The Domestic Code in I Peter* (Chico, Calif.: Scholars Press, 1981), pp. 21–62. The relationship of *haustafeln* to Matthew will be discussed in chapter 4.

40. Aristotle, *Nichomachean Ethics* V,1–11, in McKeon, pp. 1002–22.

41. Balch, p. 76.

42. Abraham J. Malherbe, *Social Aspects of Early Christianity*, 3rd ed. (Philadelphia: Fortress, 1983), p. 68.

43. Sahlins, pp. 10–11.

44. E. A. Judge, *The Social Pattern of Christian Groups in the First Century* (London: The Tyndale Press, 1960), p. 40.

45. R. E. Witt, "Isis-Hellas," *Cambridge Philological Society Proceedings* 12 (Cambridge: The Philological Society, 1966), p. 62.

46. Speaking of the *collegia*, John Elliott has noted: "In spite of the fact that the voluntary character of these associations was 'one of the critical steps toward breaking the original family domination of Greek society,' and despite the further fact of their suspected potential threat to Roman order and control of the imperial household, there is evidence that they too embraced the self-designation *oikos*" (John H. Elliott, *A Home for the Homeless: A Sociological Exegesis of I Peter: Its Situation and Strategy* [Philadelphia: Fortress, 1981], p. 180, quoting E. A. Judge, p. 40).

47. Balch gives evidence of this on pages 70–71.

48. Meeks, p. 78.

49. John E. Stambaugh and David L. Balch, *The New Testament in Its Social Environment* (Philadelphia: Westminster, 1986), p. 125.

50. Ibid., p. 126.

51. These various elements connected with the house (persons, relationships, and resources) will be used throughout the rest of the book.

52. *Oikeiotēs* meant relationships, especially people living together as husband and wife. It also involved intimacy, friendship, kin, and relationships in general. The basis for *oikos/oikía* referring to such relationships is grounded in this meaning of family, kin, and community. Confer Henry George Liddell and Robert Scott, *A Greek-English Lexicon* (Oxford: Clarendon Press, 1961), p. 1202.

53. Liddell and Scott, p. 1203. I will use "resources" to mean those economic forces of production, circulation, and consumption of goods and services traditionally identi-

fied with land, labor, and capital. A biblical word for "resources" is "possessions." Possessions themselves, which were inherited, were called *oikía* at various times. Confer "You devour widows' houses [*oikías*]" (23:14). This text, which equates inherited possessions with "house," is not found in all Matthean manuscripts. See Mark 12:40 and Lk. 20:47.

54. Notions of rank, status, and class will be discussed at greater length later in this chapter.

55. Probably no one has written as extensively on the kinship and political dimensions of the economy in New Testament times as Bruce J. Malina. Among other works noted throughout this book see his "Wealth and Poverty in the New Testament and Its World," *Interpretation* 41 (1987), pp. 354–67.

56. Bruce Malina, " 'Religion' in the World of Paul," *Biblical Theology Bulletin* 16 (1986), p. 95.

57. Tacitus, "The Annals," 14:44, in Moses Hadas, ed., *Complete Works of Tacitus*, trans. Alfred John Church and William Jackson Broadribb (New York: The Modern Library, 1942), p. 344.

58. See my Introduction, notes 2, 6, and 7, for background on some of the sources.

59. Floyd V. Filson, "The Significance of the Early House Churches," *Journal of Biblical Literature* 58 (1939), p. 112.

60. Hans-Josef Klauck, "Die Hausgemeinde als Lebensform im Urchristentum," *Münchener Theologische Zeitschrift* 32 (1981), p. 2.

61. Elliott, p. 188.

62. G. D. Kilpatrick argues about Mark—the foundation for Matthew—against interchanging *oikía* and *oikos* ("Jesus, His Family and His Disciples," *Journal for the Study of the New Testament* 15 [1982], p. 3). In Matthew *oikos* refers (but not exclusively) to the sphere of relations with cult: house of God (12:4; 21:13; 23:38), the house of Israel (10:6; 15:24), or the house of the demons (12:44). However, *oikos* is also used in Matthew to speak of peoples' place of residence (9:6). Thus, in Matthew, the terms are not essentially distinguishable. Confer Walter Bauer, *A Greek-English Lexicon of the New Testament and Other Christian Literature*, trans. William F. Arndt and F. Wilbur Gingrich, 2nd ed. (Chicago: University of Chicago Press, 1979), pp. 556–61; and Otto Michel, in Gerhard Kittel and Gerhard Friedrich, eds., *Theological Dictionary of the New Testament*, vol. 5, trans. Geoffrey W. Bromiley (Grand Rapids: Eerdmans, 1981), pp. 119–59. Any difference between *oikos* and *oikía* should be established by actual use, not supposed etymological or lexigraphical distinctions.

63. These statements about the various functions of the house build on Elliott, p. 222.

64. Elliott, p. 172. Matthew does not use these words; thus they will not be elaborated here, as Elliott does referring to First Peter.

65. Bauer, p. 240.

66. K. L. Schmidt, "*Ekklēsía,*" in Gerhard Kittel, ed., *Theological Dictionary of the New Testament*, vol. 3, trans. Geoffrey W. Bromiley (Grand Rapids: Eerdmans, 1982), pp. 513–16.

67. Robert Banks, *Paul's Idea of Community: The Early House Churches in Their Historical Setting* (Grand Rapids: Eerdmans, 1980), p. 35.

68. Meeks, pp. 75–84.

69. The third stage, according to Walter Lowrie, came at the end of the first century and extended well into the third century, with private homes given over completely to ecclesial functions. The fourth stage arose before the middle of the third century and

found the building of larger edifices, especially in larger cities, for specific church functions (*Art in the Early Church*, rev. ed. [New York: Pantheon, 1947], pp. 91f).

70. Elliott, p. 223.

71. *Kalein* or "call" is the root word for *ekklēsía*. See Schmidt, pp. 487–91.

72. "In discussing house church we are dealing fundamentally with developments in the setting for Christian assembly. By 'setting' we mean both the manner and place of assembly" (Lloyd Michael White, *Domus Ecclesiae—Domus Dei: Adaptation and Development in the Setting for Early Christian Assembly*, Ph.D. dissertation, 1982 [New Haven, Conn.: Yale University, 1983], p. 5). White considers the "manner" of assembly related to the internal organization and constitution of the house church. Chronologically this represents the earlier period of the first century. The "place" of assembly is considered by White as involving art, architecture, liturgy, and worship. Chronologically it deals with a later period, the Constantinian era. White's dissertation is one of the most thorough explanations of the transition from house church to basilica available.

73. A synagogue was the building in which the congregation (*qahal/ekklēsía*) met. Ten men, not necessarily ten householders, constituted the congregation. It was generally constituted as a voluntary association of equals.

74. This theory has been debated with no resolution of the issue, which often centers around the need for freedom in baptism.

75. Elisabeth Schüssler-Fiorenza, *In Memory of Her: A Feminist Theological Reconstruction of Christian Origins* (New York: Crossroad, 1983), p. 175. See also Meeks, pp. 77–79.

76. Filson, pp. 105–6.

77. Georg Heinrici, "Die Christengemeinden Korinths und die religöisen Genossenschaften der Griechen," *Zeitschrift für wissenschaftliche Theologie* XIX (1876), pp. 465–526; "Zur Geschichte der Anfänge paulinischer Gemeinden," *Zeitschrift für wissenschaftliche Theologie* XX (1877), pp. 89–130; "Zum genossenschaftlichen Charakter der paulinischen Christengemeinden," *Theologische Studien und Kritiken*, LIV (1881), pp. 505–24.

78. These were subsequently published in book form: Edwin Hatch, *The Organization of the Early Christian Church* (London: Longmans Green, 1918).

79. David C. Verner, *The Household of God: The Social World of the Pastoral Epistles*, SBL Dissertation Series 71 (Chico, Calif.: Scholars Press, 1983), p. 64.

80. Floyd V. Filson, *A New Testament History: The Story of the Emerging Church* (Philadelphia: Westminster, 1964), p. 177.

81. For various positions on the Matthean setting and date, sources and structure, use of the Old Testament and attitude toward the Law, christology and ecclesiology, see Donald Senior, *What Are They Saying about Matthew?* (New York/Ramsey: Paulist, 1983).

82. Jack Dean Kingsbury, *Matthew as Story* (Philadelphia: Fortress, 1986), p. 121.

83. John P. Meier, "The Antiochene Church of the Second Generation (A.D. 70–100—Matthew)," in Raymond E. Brown and John P. Meier, *Antioch and Rome: New Testament Cradles of Catholic Christianity* (New York: Paulist, 1983), pp. 12f. One can get the impression that Meier is reluctant to speak of "churches" at Antioch. "The church at Antioch" seems to be favored. However, as will be shown, due to the large numbers of converts alone, there had to be more than one "church." There were many churches (18:17) but one church (16:18).

84. Heichelheim, p. 224.

85. M. P. Charlesworth, *Trade-Routes and Commerce of the Roman Empire*, 2nd. rev. ed. (Chicago: Ares Publishers, 1926), p. 44.

86. Heichelheim, p. 225. Heichelheim notes that costly spices, purple dye, artistic wares, and textiles from Syria were the delight of the upper classes.

87. Heichelheim, "Roman Syria," in Frank, vol. 5 (Paterson: Pageant Books, 1959), p. 123.

88. Rostovtzeff, p. 139.

89. Avi-Yonah, p. 112.

90. Since the first Christians tended to live in the Jewish community, details can be ferreted from studies on Jewish life at that time. See Carl Hermann Kraeling, "The Jewish Community at Antioch," *Journal of Biblical Literature* 51 (1932), pp. 130–60. This article was reprinted in New Haven: Antioch Index Publications, 1932. For detailed studies of the archeology of Antioch, see Richard C. Haines, *Excavations in the Plain of Antioch II: The Structural Remains of the Later Phases* (Chicago: University of Chicago Press, 1971). The research of the Oriental Institute does not deal with Antioch but the area around it. Janine Balty, ed., *Apamée de Syrie Bilan des recherches archéologiques 1965–1968*, vol. 6 (Bruxelles: Centre Belge de Recherches Archéologiques à Apamée de Syria, 1969). Janine et Jean Ch. Balty, eds., *Apamée de Syrie Bilan des recherches archéologiques 1965–1968*, vol. 7 (Bruxelles: Centre Belge de Recherches Archéologiques à Apamée de Syria, 1972). G. W. Elderkiln, ed., *Antioch-on-the Orontes I. The Excavations of 1932* (Princeton: Princeton University Press, 1934). Richard Stillwell, *Antioch-on-the Orontes II. The Excavations of 1933–1936* (Princeton: Princeton University Press, 1938). The French and Princeton works are key archeological studies. However, they concentrate on Daphne, an outlying area, rather than old Antioch's center. Glanville Downey, "Personifications of Abstract Ideas in the Antioch Mosaics," *Transactions and Proceedings of the American Philological Association* LXIX (1938), pp. 349–63. G. M. Harper, "Village Administration in the Roman Province of Syria," *Yale Classical Studies* 1 (1928), pp. 105ff. George Haddad, *Aspects of Social Life in Antioch in the Hellenistic Period* (Chicago: University of Chicago Microfilm, 1949).

91. For a discussion of the archeological findings related to Mediterranean house churches, see Lloyd Michael White, stressing Dura-Europos. For Corinth see the section on "Archeology" in Jerome Murphy-O'Connor, O.P., *St. Paul's Corinth: Texts and Archeology*, Good News Studies, vol. 6 (Wilmington: Michael Glazier, 1983), pp. 153–72. Gustaf Dalman, "Das Haus," *Arbeit und Sitte in Palästina*, vol. 7 (Hildesheim: Georg Olms Verlagsbuchhandlung, 1964), pp. 1–246. P. S. P. Handcock, M.A., *The Archeology of the Holy Land* (London: T. Fisher Unwin, 1916), pp. 6–141.

92. Heichelheim, vol. 4, p. 163.

93. For recent studies on the houses at Dura-Europos see White, Susan B. Matheson, *Dura-Europos: The Ancient City and the Yale Collection* (Detroit: Wayne State University Press, 1982); Graydon F. Snyder, *Ante Pacem: Archaelogical Evidence of Church Life before Constantine* (Macon, Georgia: Mercier Press, 1986), pp. 67–70.

94. Luke Timothy Jones, "The Gospel of Matthew," in *The Writings of the New Testament: An Interpretation* (Philadelphia: Fortress, 1986), p. 177.

95. Mt. 9:6,7; 10:6; 11:8; 12:4; 15:24; 21:13(2x); 23:38.

96. Mt. 2:11; 5:15; 7:24,25,26,27; 8:6,14; 9:10,23,28; 10:12,13,14; 12:25,29(2x),44; 13:1,36,57; 17:25; 19:29; [23:14]; 24:17,43; 26:6. 23:14 is questioned as to its authenticity. It is not in all versions.

97. *Oikía* = 2:11; 5:15; 7:27; 8:6; 9:28; 10:14; 13:1,36; 17:25. *Oikos* = 10:6; 11:8;

15:24. Only Matthew uses *oikiakós* for "household" (10:25,26). While Mark and Luke use *oikodespótēs*, "head of household," Matthew uses the Q source once (24:43) and has six unique usages for the word.

98. John P. Meier, *The Vision of Matthew: Christology, Church and Morality in the First Gospel* (New York: Paulist, 1979), pp. 53–54.

99. Gerd Theissen sees the Jesus movement divided into two groups among the disciples: the wandering charismatics and those who were settled in households. He sees the upper tier of the community as the itinerant charismatics who showed their full commitment to Jesus by homelessness (8:20) and renunciation of possessions (6:25–32; 19:21). See Gerhard Theissen, *Sociology of Early Palestinian Christianity*, trans. John Bowden (Philadelphia: Fortress, 1978), esp. pp. 22–30.

100. Robert H. Smith, "A Response to Donald Hagner's 'The Sitz im Leben of the Gospel of Matthew,' " unpublished paper given at the Society of Biblical Literature, November 1985.

101. Avi-Yonah, pp. 110–11.

102. Building on the Greeks, "Rome added the one element lacking in the picture— the establishment of the *pax romana*. The result was a rapid expansion of the cultivated area onto the steppe. The 'sown' now gained on the 'desert.' Political stability also made possible the extension of the profitable caravan trade across the desert" (Michael Avi-Yonah, "II: From the Time of Alexander the Great to the End of the Roman Period [332 B.C.–324 A.D.]," in Aharon Kempinski and Michael Avi-Yonah, *Syria-Palestine II: From the Bronze Age to the End of the Classical World [2200 B.C.–324 A.D.]* [Geneva: Nagel, 1979], p. 129).

103. For an excellent reference on urbanization at this time, see Carl H. Kraeling and Robert M. Adams, eds., *City Invincible: A Symposium on Urbanization and Cultural Development in the Ancient Near East* (Chicago: University of Chicago Press, 1960).

104. Douglas Edward Oakman, *Jesus and the Economic Questions of His Day*, Studies in the Bible and Early Christianity, vol. 8 (Lewiston, N.Y.: Edwin Mellon Press, 1986). This book contains a wealth of information, including an excellent bibliography of the socio-economic situation of the first century. For more background on the socio-political situation at this time see the discussion on the sub-apostolic period (67–100 CE), especially the Flavian period (from Vespasian [69–79] and his sons Titus [70–81] to Domitian [81–96], whose last name was Flavius), in Bo Reicke, *The New Testament Era: The World of the Bible from 500 B.C. to A.D. 100*, trans. David E. Green (Philadelphia: Fortress, 1968), pp. 253–317.

105. Robert H. Smith, "Were the Early Christians Middle-Class? A Sociological Analysis of the New Testament," *Currents in Theology and Mission* 7 (1980), p. 266.

106. Jack Dean Kingsbury, *Matthew as Story*, pp. 125–26. See also his *Matthew* (Philadelphia: Fortress, 1977), pp. 97–98, and his "The Verb *Akolouthein* (to Follow) as an Index of Matthew's View of His Community," *Journal of Biblical Literature* 97 (1978), pp. 67–68.

107. Samuel Dickey, "Some Economic and Social Conditions of Asia Minor Affecting the Expansion of Christianity," in Shirley Jackson Case, ed., *Studies in Early Christianity* (New York & London: Century, 1928), p. 405.

108. See Rodney Stark, "The Class Basis of Early Christianity: Inferences from a Sociological Model," *Sociological Analysis* 47 (1986), pp. 216–25.

109. Meeks, p. 73.

110. David L. Mealand, *Poverty and Expectation in the Gospels* (London: SPCK, 1980), p. 16.

111. W. D. Davis, *The Setting of the Sermon on the Mount* (Cambridge: Cambridge University Press, 1964), p. 213.

112. Bruce J. Malina, *The New Testament World: Insights from Cultural Anthropology* (Atlanta: John Knox, 1981), pp. 71–90.

113. Malina, "Interpreting the Bible with Anthropology: The Case of the Poor and the Rich," *Literary Journal of Religion and Culture* 21 (1986), p. 155. More recently Malina has expanded on this notion in his discussion of three cultural norms pertaining to wealth and poverty: 1) all goods are limited; 2) no one goes without necessities; and 3) the wealthy are inherently evil. See his "Wealth and Poverty in the New Testament and Its World," pp. 361–65.

114. Among a larger group see Benjamin Bacon, *Studies in Matthew* (London: Constable, 1930); O. Lamar Cope, *Matthew: A Scribe Trained for the Kingdom of Heaven* (Washington, D. C.: The Catholic Biblical Association of America, 1976); M. Goulder, *Midrash and Lection in Matthew* (London: SPCK, 1974); Douglas R. A. Hare, *The Theme of Jewish Persecution of Christians in the Gospel according to St. Matthew* (Cambridge: Cambridge University Press, 1967); R. Hummel, *Die Auseinandersetzung zwischen Kirche und Judentum im Matthäusevangelium* (München: Kaiser Verlag, 1963); Kingsbury, *Matthew as Story* (Philadelphia: Fortress, 1986); Krister Stendahl, *The School of St. Matthew and Its Use of the Old Testament* (Philadelphia: Fortress, 1968).

115. One of the first to advocate Matthew as a gentile was K. Clark, "The Gentile Bias of Matthew," *Journal of Biblical Literature* 66 (1947), pp. 165–72. Another early proponent of this position was Paul Nepper-Christensen, *Das Matthäusevangelium: Ein juden-christliches Evangelium* (Aarhus: Universitetsforlaget, 1958). A strong argument has been made more recently by G. Strecker, *Der Weg der Gerechtigkeit*, 3rd. ed (Göttingen: Vandenhoeck & Ruprecht, 1971).

116. John P. Meier notes Matthew's link of the "leaven" of the Pharisees and Sadducees (16:5–12) and the entrance into Jerusalem where the disciples—to fulfill Isaiah 62:11 and Zechariah 9:9—are told to find a donkey and a colt (21:2), to bring *them*, to have Jesus sit on *it* (21:7). See his *The Vision of Matthew*, pp. 19–22.

117. In general Greek and Hellenistic usage, some specific houses were "treasure houses." Confer Michel, p. 119.

118. Robert H. Gundry, *Matthew: A Commentary on His Literary and Theological Art* (Grand Rapids: Eerdmans, 1982), p. 281. There is a typo in Gundry's text: 2,4 should be 24. Verse 27 is 13:27.

119. For Matthean adaptations of Mark's notation about the disciples' lack of understanding see 13:13 on Mk. 4:12; 14:31 on Mk. 6:52; 16:9 on Mk. 8:17; 16:12 on Mk. 8:21; 17:9 on Mk. 9:10; 17: 23 on Mk. 9:32.

120. This will be discussed in chapter 3.

121. John P. Meier, *Matthew* (Wilmington: Michael Glazier, Inc., 1980), p. 154.

122. The notion of "bearing fruit" will be discussed at various places in the following chapters. See Gerhard Barth, "Matthew's Understanding of the Law," in Günther Bornkamm, Gerhard Barth, and Heinz Joachim Held, *Tradition and Interpretation in Matthew*, trans. Perry Scott (Philadelphia: Westminster, 1963), p. 110.

123. Just as "the beloved disciple" in John's gospel may be a rhetorical device referring to the reader, so "Matthew" may refer to anyone who puts into practice all that is taught in the first gospel, thus fulfilling God's will. By that praxis she or he becomes a disciple (12:49–50).

124. Terry Eagleton, *Literary Theory: An Introduction* (Minneapolis: University of Minnesota, 1983), pp. 205–6.

125. Since St. Augustine it was thought that the chronology of the gospels followed the ordering Matthew, Mark, Luke, and John. That theory was discounted by the "two source" theory (Mark and "Q"), which I follow and articulate below. However that theory also has received criticism, much of it discounted. The first came from Abbot Butler who promoted Mark's dependence on a Greek version of Matthew (Basil C. Butler, *The Originality of St. Matthew: A Critique of the Two-Document Hypothesis* [Cambridge: Cambridge University Press, 1951]). Later W. F. Albright and C. S. Mann suggested that all three Synoptic gospels were written independently but relied on a common Aramaic or Hebrew gospel (W. F. Albright and C. S. Mann, *Matthew*, Anchor Bible, 26 [Garden City, N.Y.: Doubleday, 1971]). Michael Goulder agreed that Matthew depended on Mark, but not on "Q," and "that Luke knew Matthew, and that Q is therefore no longer a valid hypothesis" ("On Putting Q to the Test," *New Testament Studies* 24 [1978], p. 234). C. M. Tuckette showed the fragility of Goulder's points in "On the Relationship between Matthew and Luke," *New Testament Studies* 30 (1984), pp. 130–42. William Farmer posited that Matthew wrote first, Luke expanded on Matthew, and Mark used both (William F. Farmer, *The Synoptic Problem: A Critical Analysis* [Dillsboro: Western North Carolina Press, 1976]). Since that time, other source-theories are variants on the above themes.

126. Matthew's use of *oikía* from Mark includes 8:14; 9:10,23; 12:25,29(2x); 13:57; 19:29; (23:14); 24:17; 26:6. 26:18 does not use the Markan word but the possessive form meaning "house." He shares *oikía* with Mark but not Luke in 12:29(2x) and 13:57. His Markan sources for *oikos* are 9:6,7; 12:4; and 21:13(2x).

127. Matthew shared with Luke *oikía* in 7:24,25,26; 10:12,13; 12:44; and 24:43.

128. Another series of passages about resources and sharing of resources that may have been from Q and that is found in Luke but not in Matthew is Lk. 3:10–14; 6:24–26,34–35; 12:13–21.

129. Anthony J. Blasi, "Role Structures in the Hellenistic Church," *Sociological Analysis* 47 (1986), p. 230.

130. For a good summary of the theological significance of the formula citations see Brevard Childs, *The New Testament as Canon: An Introduction* (Philadelphia: Fortress Press, 1985), pp. 70–71.

131. Traditionally two factions have been seen in the Matthean community. Passages in the first gospel reflect the stresses in these house congregations. However, John P. Meier divides these two factions into other factions and points to places in the first gospel where the stresses of all these various factions can be found. See John P. Meier, "The Antiochene Church," in Raymond E. Brown and John P. Meier, *Antioch and Rome*, pp. 53–57.

132. In a ranked, peasant society there was no "middle class" as such. We are using the term "prosperous" in a figurative sense to indicate some degree of disposable wealth.

133. Wayne A. Meeks, *The Moral World of the First Christians* (Philadelphia: Fortress, 1986), p. 137.

CHAPTER 2

1. Sherman Johnson, "Matthew," *The Interpreter's Bible*, vol. 7 (New York/Nashville: Abingdon-Cokesbury, 1976), p. 232.

2. K. L. Schmidt, "*Ekklēsía*" under "*Kaleo*," in Gerhard Kittel, ed. *Theological Dictionary of the New Testament*, vol. 3, trans. Geoffrey W. Bromiley (Grand Rapids: Eerdmans, 1965), pp. 501–36.

3. In the Sermon on the Mount alone his version of the Lord's Prayer links the hallowing of God's name, the coming of God's reign, and the doing of God's will on earth as in heaven (6:9–10); justice involves almsgiving, prayer, and fasting (6:1–18); he links asking/receiving, seeking/finding, knocking/opening (7:7–8); the Sermon on the Mount concludes with a triad about the narrow and wide gates, the good and bad fruit, and the houses built on rock and sand (7:13–27).

4. For further discussion on the blessing/authority-naming-commissioning triad in Matthew see M. Jack Suggs, *Wisdom, Christology, and Law in Matthew's Gospel* (Cambridge: Harvard University Press, 1979), esp. pp. 120ff. See also Michael H. Crosby, *Spirituality of the Beatitudes: Matthew's Challenge to First World Christians* (Maryknoll, N.Y.: Orbis, 1987), pp. 214–17.

5. It does not suit my purposes here to enter into the debate about either the role of Peter in Matthew's gospel or the applicability of this passage as justification for the Petrine office. Without doubt, Matthew has inflated Peter's role from his sources. Besides retaining the Markan texts of Peter as the one first called (4:18) and who confesses Jesus (16:16), Matthew added Peter's walking on the water (14:28–31), the triad (16:17–18), the temple-tax story (17:24–27), and the request about forgiveness (18:21–22). Despite these positive references, Matthew notes the negative stories as well (16:22–23; 26:33–35,69–75). For a summary of the Petrine debate see Donald Senior, "Peter: Representative Disciple or Symbol of Leadership?," *What Are They Saying about Matthew?* (New York/Ramsey: Paulist, 1983), pp. 73–76.

Two schools dominate regarding Peter's function in the church. One sees him as a representative figure with the same functions given him given to the other disciples as well (binding and loosing [16:19 and 18:18], being called blessed [16:17 and 13:16–17], and confessing Jesus as "Son of God" [16:16 and 14:33]). The main spokesperson for this referent position is Jack Dean Kingsbury ("The Figure of Peter in Matthew's Gospel as a Theological Problem," *Journal of Biblical Literature* 98 [1979], pp. 67–83). The other position has been articulated by Raymond Brown in "The Meaning of Modern New Testament Studies for an Ecumenical Understanding of Peter and a Theology of the Papacy," in *Biblical Reflections on Crises Facing the Church* (New York: Paulist, 1975), pp. 63–83; and *The Churches the Apostles Left Behind* (New York: Paulist, 1984), p. 135. Brown accepts Kingsbury's representative role for Peter but shows that Peter is treated singularly in various places (16:17 and 17:24–27) and that his role cannot be isolated from some connection to the post-resurrection church.

6. John P. Meier, *Matthew* (Wilmington: Michael Glazier, 1980), pp. 181–82.

7. "In the LXX we find the expression *oikodomein tina*, which is important for the NT. 'To plant' and 'to build' are here related concepts (opp. 'to root up,' 'to tear down,' 'to destroy'). God can build, plant, set up or convert Israel, and in judgment He can also overthrow and destroy His work. The image of building is also common in later Judaism, perhaps because it is suggested by the idea of the 'house of Israel.' In the Rabb. God is the builder of the world, cf. also Hb. 3:4: *ho de panta kataskeuasas theos*. There is a good par. to Mt. 7:24–27 in Ab. R. Nat., 24: Elisha b. Abuja (c. 120) said: 'A man who has many good works and has learned much of the Torah, with whom is he to be compared? With a man who below (i.e., the foundation) builds with stones and then with (unfired, only dried in the sun) bricks; even though many waters come and stay at their sides, they will not pry them (the solid stones) from their place. But a man who has no good works and learns the Torah, with whom shall he be compared? With a man who first builds with bricks and then with stones; even though only few waters come, they will at once overthrow them.' The parable demands that one should build in such a way

that the building itself will stand in time of disaster; thus regard must be had to a good relation between good works and study. In a fig. sense 'builders of the Torah' is an honorary title for the scribes, and 'builders' can also be used as a description for students." Otto Michel, *"Oikos,"* in Gerhard Kittel and Gerhard Friedrich, eds., *Theological Dictionary of the New Testament,* vol. 5, trans. Geoffrey W. Bromiley (Grand Rapids: Eerdmans, 1981), p. 137.

8. Most scholars have now rejected the thesis promoted by Reinhart Hummel that, at the time of Matthew's gospel, his audience was not yet separated from the synagogue (*Die Auseinandersetzung zwischen Kirche und Judentum im Mattäusevangelium* [München: Kaiser Verlag, 1963]).

9. See Douglas R. A. Hare, *The Theme of Jewish Persecution of Christians in the Gospel according to Matthew* (Cambridge: Cambridge University Press,1967).

10. Ibid., p. 104.

11. In various places in the New Testament, Jesus is the rock on which the church is built. "For they drank from the supernatural Rock [*pétra*] which followed them, and the Rock [*pétra*] was Christ" (1 Cor. 10:4). Paul told the Ephesians that they were "the household of God [*oikeioi tou Theou*], built [*epoikodomēthéntes*] upon the foundation of the apostles and prophets, Christ Jesus himself being the chief cornerstone [*akrogōniaíou*], in whom the whole structure [*oikodomē*] is joined together and grows into a holy temple [*naon*] in the Lord" (Eph. 2:19–21). First Peter declares about Jesus: "The very stone which the builders [*oikodomountes*] rejected has become the head of the corner," and it calls him "a stone that will make men stumble, a rock [*pétra*] that will make men fall" (1 Pet. 2:7–8). Paul brings these passages from Isaiah together in Romans 9:33 as well. For a discussion on the implications of the meaning of "rock," especially in and about Peter, see John H. Elliott, *The Elect and the Holy: An Exegetical Examination of 1 Peter 2:4–10 and the Phrase* Basileion Hierateuma, Novum Testamentum Supplements, vol. 12 (Leiden: E. J. Brill, 1966). Elliott pays special attention in pages 148–66 to the connection between *oikos pneumatikós* and *basileía*.

12. Augustine Stock, "Is Matthew's Presentation of Peter Ironic?," *Biblical Theology Bulletin* 17 (1987), p. 67.

13. Edward Schillebeeckx, "Problemen rond 'Petrus de Steenrots' (Mt 16,16–20)," in J. van de Ven, ed., *Toekomst voor de Kerk? Studies voor Frans Jaarsma* (Kampen: J. J. Kok, 1985), p. 98, quoted in Stock, p. 67.

14. In his discussion of Peter as referent for all the disciples, Kingsbury fails to comment on this significant passage. Thus he does a disservice to his otherwise important comments.

15. Joachim Jeremias, *"Kleis,"* in Kittel, vol. 3, pp. 744–46,750–51.

16. It would seem that the granting of power to administrate the house reflects a hierarchical and patriarchal form of church organization in Matthew. To this degree it would contradict our previous stress on the Matthean church as a household reflecting the wider society's voluntary associations and more collegial communities. However, the power to bind and loose given in 16:19 will be shared with the local church as well in 18:18. Thus 16:19 must be seen as an example of "normative dissonance" in the early Christian community and should be balanced with stresses on the body of the church having the authority to arbitrate (18:15–18). It would be more correct to conclude that Matthew's community contained both patriarchal and collegial forms of households. For more on normative inconsistency in the gospels, see Bruce J. Malina, "Normative Dissonance and Christian Origins," *Semeia* 35 (1986), pp. 35ff.

17. See John Reumann, "The 'Righteousness of God' and the 'Economy of God':

Two Great Doctrinal Themes Historically Compared," *Aksum-Thyateira: A Festscrift for Archbishop Methodios of Thyateira and Great Britain* (Athens, 1985), p. 618.

18. These notions will be expanded in the last chapter.

19. Hans Windisch, "Die Sprüche vom Eingehen in das Reich Gottes," *Zeitschrift für die Neutestamentlilche Wissenschaft* 27 (1928), pp. 177–86.

20. G. R. Beasley-Murray, *Jesus and the Kingdom of God* (Grand Rapids: Eerdmans; and Exeter: Paternoster, 1986), pp. 184–85. I am indebted to Beasley-Murray for the lead to Windisch.

21. For an interpretation of this narrative as reflecting division in the Matthean community see William P. Thompson, *Matthew's Advice to A Divided Community* (Rome: Biblical Institute Press, 1970).

22. While the traditional way of viewing the structure of Matthew's gospel is somewhat as I propose, there are many exceptions. These might be called the "five book" hypothesis, the "geographical plan," the "three (or four) phases of Jesus' life," and the "literary-critical structure." Benjamin Bacon is an example of one who employed the "five book" hypothesis. Wolfgang Trilling proposed the "geographical plan" of four parts: prehistory of the Messiah (1–2), Galilean activity (3–18), Judean activity (19–25), and the condemnation, death, and resurrection (26–28) (*The Gospel according to St. Matthew*, trans. Kevin Smyth [New York: Herder and Herder, 1969]). The "three phases of Jesus' life" was originally presented by Edgar Krentz, "The Extent of Matthew's Prologue: Toward the Structure of the First Gospel," *Journal of Biblical Literature* 83 (1964), pp. 409–14. A contemporary proponent is Jack Dean Kingsbury, *Matthew: Structure, Christology, Kingdom* (Philadelphia: Fortress, 1975), pp. 1–25. Kingsbury sees the Matthean phrase "from that time" (4:17 and 16:21) as breaking the gospel into three parts. However, 4:17 is echoed in 4:23–25; 9:35; and 11:1, while 16:21 has parallels in 17:22–23; 20:17–19; and 26:2. Wilhelm Wilers sees four phases ordered around Christ's work: the beginning (1:1–4:22), the foundation (4:23–11:24), the operation (11:25–21:46), and the goal (22:1–28:20) ("Die Komposition des Matthaus Evangeliums," *New Testament Studies* 31 [1985], pp. 24–38, esp. pp. 37–38). The "literary-critical structure" was proffered by X. Leon-Dufour ("Les Evangiles Synoptiques," in Augustin George and Pierre Grelot, eds., *Introduction à la Bible, Nouveau Testament*, vol. 2 (Paris: Desclee, 1976), pp. 83ff. This has a "Prologue" (1–2), "The Jewish People Refuse to Believe in Jesus" (3–13), and "Passion and Glory" (14–28). Variations on the chiastic structure can be found in Peter Ellis, *Matthew: His Mind and His Message* (Collegeville: The Liturgical Press, 1974), and Howard Clark Kee, "The Gospel According to Matthew," *Interpreter's One Volume Commentary* (Nashville: Abingdon, 1971), p. 6.

23. Benjamin Bacon, *Studies in Matthew* (London: Constable, 1930).

24. For background on the meaning and significance of "chiasmus," see Nils Wilhelm Lund, *Chiasmus in the New Testament: A Study in Formgeschichte* (Chapel Hill: University of North Carolina Press, 1942).

25. Jack Dean Kingsbury, *The Parables of Jesus in Matthew 13* (Richmond: John Knox, 1971).

26. The conflict between Jesus and the leaders (12:22–32) will be discussed in the next chapter.

27. Jack Dean Kingsbury, *Matthew as Story* (Philadelphia: Fortress, 1986), p. 106.

28. Matthew uses the word for "to gather" (*synágein*) far more than Mark or Luke. Contrasting Jesus with the leaders, he regularly has them gather together in a formal or political assembly (2:4; 22:34,41; 26:3,57; 27:17,27,62; 28:12). They usually "gather" in

order to "scatter" the drawing power of Jesus. In 23:37 and 24:31, the *epi-* form is added.

29. Meier, p. 140. Meier notes that his comments are by "inference from silence," since Matthew never notes specifically that the "brothers" of Jesus (1:25; 13:55) did not believe in him.

30. Much present debate around the notion of discipleship, especially its applicability to women, revolves around the use of the appellation "disciple" for women. Matthew makes it clear that "being discipled" (13:52; 27:57; 28:19) involves more than a word; it reflects a way of understanding and putting into practice the heavenly Father's will.

31. Unlike the pattern in Mark and Luke, Matthew uses references to God as "heavenly Father" or my/your "Father in heaven": 5:16,45,48; 6:1–18,26,32; 7:11,21; 10:32–33; 11:25–27; 12:50; 15:13; 16:17; 18:10,14, 19,35; 23:9; 25:34–35.

32. Matthew's treatment of justice will be discussed further in the sixth and seventh chapters.

33. This section will be expanded upon in the next chapter.

34. Some exegetes see this passage as central to Matthew's ecclesiology. See Daniel J. Harrington, *God's People in Christ: New Testament Perspectives on the Church and Judaism*, Overtures to Biblical Theology (Philadelphia: Fortress, 1980), pp. 89–100; Rudolf Schnackenburg, *The Church in the New Testament*, trans. W. J. O'Hara (Freiburg: Herder; and London: Burns & Oates, 1965), p. 76.

35. It will be seen that Jesus teaches more than the disciples in Matthew (see 5:1–2,28–29); here he explains to those gathered around him—beyond the house. However, it will be shown that discipleship is not centered around hearing (as in Mark) but understanding and putting those words into practice.

36. For an excellent treatment of the differences between Mark's notion and Matthew's meaning of understanding as core to Matthean discipleship see Gerhard Barth, "Matthew's Understanding of the Law," in Günther Bornkamm, Gerhard Barth, and Heinz Joachim Held, *Tradition and Interpretation in Matthew,* trans. Percy Scott (Philadelphia: Westminster, 1963), pp. 105–12.

37. In his section on "The Apologetic Function of Household Codes," David Balch has connected Matthew with elements in 1 Peter 2:11–12,15 that have to do with the persecution of pagans who glorified God because of the Christians' good example: "Several commentators understand that pagans watched the Christians' good deeds over a period of time, reflected on them, and converted. An important parallel is Matt 5:16" (David L. Balch, *Let Wives Be Submissive: The Domestic Code in I Peter* [Chico, Calif.: Scholars Press, 1981], p. 87).

38. This theme is found in other household codes, especially 1 Pet. 2:12 and Eph. 6:8.

39. Kenneth W. Dupar, *A Study in New Testament Haustafeln* (Edinburgh: New College Library, 1971), pp. 261–62.

40. Hans-Josef Klauck, *Hausgemeinde und Hauskirche im frühen Christentum* (Stuttgart: Verlag Katholische Bibelwerk GMbH, 1981), p. 60.

41. The concept of house-light is found also in the *haustafel* in I Peter 2:4–10, especially 2:4,9, and 10.

42. This notion is also part of the *haustafel* in 1 Peter 2:11ff.

43. Several current books on *haustafeln* deserve special mention. Balch, with an extended bibliography; James E. Crouch, *The Origin and Intention of the Colossian Haustafel* (Göttingen: Vandenhoeck & Ruprecht, 1972); Dupar; John H. Elliott, *A Home for the Homeless: A Sociological Exegesis of I Peter: Its Situation and Strategy* (Philadelphia: Fortress, 1981); Dieter Lührmann, "Wo man nicht mehr Sklave oder

Freier ist: überlegnungen zur Struktur frühchristlicher Gemeinden," in Helmut Krämer, ed., *Wort und Diest Jahrbuch der Kirchlichen Hochschule*, Bethel/New Folge 13 (Bethel bei Bielefeld: Verlogshandlung der Anstal & Bethel, 1975), pp. 71–83, and "Neutestamentliche Haustafeln und antike ökonomie," *New Testament Studies* 27 (1980), pp. 83–97; David C. Verner, *The Household of God: The Social World of the Pastoral Epistles* (Chico, Calif.: The Scholars Press, 1981). Unfortunately Dupar's work, written as a dissertation in Scotland, is not available in North America. Consequently his excellent insights have not been critiqued.

44. Alfred Seeberg, *Der Kastechismus der Urchristenheit* (Leipzig: A. Deichert, 1903), pp. 37–39; *Das Evangelium Christ* (Leipzig: A. Deichert, 1903), pp. 125–27; *Die beiden Wege und das Aposteldekret* (Leipzig: A. Deichert, 1906).

45. The passages usually identified as *haustafeln* are Col. 3:18–4:1; Eph. 5:21–6:9; 1 Tim. 2:8–15; 5:1–2; 6:1–2; Tit. 2:1–10; 3:1; 1 Pet. 2:11–3:12.

46. Martin Dibelius, *An die Kolosser, Epheser, und Philemon* (Tübingen: Mohr, 1913), and *Geschichte der urchristlichen Literatur*, vol. 2 (Berlin und Leipzig: Walter de Gruyter, 1926).

47. Karl Weidinger, *Die Haustafeln: Ein Stück urchristlicher Paranäse* (Leipzig: J. C. Hinrichs'sche Buchhandlung, 1928), pp. 40–50.

48. Ernst Lohmeyer, *Die Briefe an die Kolosser und an Philemon* (Göttingen: Vandenhoeck & Ruprecht, 1961).

49. Karl Heinrich Rengstorf, *Mann und Frau im Urchristentum*, Arbeitsgemeinschaft für Forschung des Landes Nordrhein-Westfalen, Abhandlungen Geisteswissenschaften, vol. 12 (Cologne: Westdeutscher, 1954).

50. David Schroeder, *Die Haustafeln des neuen Testaments (ihre Herkunft und theologischer Sinn)* (Hamburg: Mikrokopie, 1959).

51. Elliott, *Home*, p. 208.

52. Dupar, p. 94.

53. Ibid., p. 103.

54. Crouch has proposed that the purpose of the Colossian *haustafel* was to combat "the excesses created by an overemphasis on the equality created by the Spirit" (p. 141; see pp. 120–45).

55. Dupar, p. 279.

56. I find it difficult to agree with George Soares-Prabhu, who argues that 10:6 and 15:24 were not actual sayings of Jesus—who was "unprejudiced"—but rather reflect the biases of the "prejudiced church." In his life Jesus did not see his mission outside the Jewish circles he frequented; his goal was to fulfill, within these circles, the Law and the prophets. These separatist tendencies of Jesus were balanced by the final redactor who found all ethnocentrism subsumed into the mission to the whole world (28:16–20) (George Soares-Prabhu, "The Unprejudiced Jesus and the Prejudiced Church," *The Way* 27 [1987], pp. 4–14).

57. Meier, pp. 106–7.

58. Schuyler Brown, "The Matthean Community and the Gentile Mission,"*Novum Testamentum* 22 (1980), p. 220.

59. The passage in the parallel narrative which preceded this section, about the Son of man having nowhere to rest his head (8:20), must be interpreted in light of the missionary journey and the household economic in chapter 10. Nowhere in Jesus' public life is he or his disciples without resources (i.e., "poor") in Matthew's gospel. On the contrary, the house is to serve as the context for sharing resources, be they the good news or bed and board.

60. A. E. Harvey, " 'The Workman Is Worthy of His Hire': Fortunes of a Proverb in the Early Church," *Novum Testamentum* 24 (1982), p. 218.

61. Klauck, p. 57.

62. Wolfgang Trilling, *The Gospel According to Matthew,* vol. 1 (London: Burns and Oates, 1969), p. 187.

63. E. C. B. Maclaurin, "Beelzeboul," *Novum Testamentum* 20 (1978), p. 157.

64. Sverre Aalen, *Matteus Evangeliet* (Oslo: Universitets Forlaget, 1971), p. 159.

65. The connection between entering the house and entering the reign of God will be further treated in chapter 9.

66. 10:14,40[4x],41[4x]; 11:14; 18:5[2x].

67. Elisabeth Schüssler Fiorenza, *Bread Not Stone* (Boston: Beacon, 1984), p. 91.

68. More on this will be found in the fourth chapter.

69. See George M. Soares-Prabhu, *The Formula Quotations in the Infancy Narrative of Matthew* (Rome: Biblical Institute, 1976), p. 32.

70. Robert H. Gundry, *Matthew: A Commentary on His Literary and Theological Art* (Grand Rapids: Eerdmans, 1982), p. 281.

71. Most exegetes begin the fourth discourse with 18:1. Thompson bases his study of the main body of the fourth discourse on 17:22–18:35. The parallel Markan body is 9:33–48. Mt. 17:24–27 is unique to the first gospel. Within this text is the passage about Jesus going into the house. Since Mark begins (9:33) his pericope with Jesus going into the house and since, in Mark, the passage is significant as the center of Jesus' teaching, it appears more consistent to begin the fourth discourse with the pericope that contains the same concept (17:24–27). The discourse should end as the others end, with the passage about Jesus finishing the discourse (19:1).

72. Another kind of *haustafel* can be found immediately following this one, in 19:3–20:16. In fact, together, they might be considered a unit.

73. 1 Peter 2:13–17 begins with the general admonition and then moves to the civic duty. In 1 Timothy 2:1–4 the civic duty precedes the more specific domestic components. In Titus 3:1, the civic duty follows the domestic admonitions. Romans 13:1–7 has civic duties divorced from domestic duties. It is difficult to determine which approach was closer to the tradition (see Dupar, pp. 27–37).

74. For further discussion about the identification of "sons with members of the household," see Simon Legasse, "Jesus et l'impôt du Temple (Matthieu 17, 24–27)," *Science et Esprit* 24 (1972), p. 369–70, and J. Duncan M. Derret, "Peter's Penny: Fresh Light on Matthew xvii 24–7," *Novum Testamentum* 6 (1963), p. 8.

75. Philip Carrington, *The Primitive Christian Catechism* (Cambridge: The University Press, 1940), pp. 50–51.

76. Because the dynamics involved in bringing peace into the divided house churches will be discussed in the sixth chapter with the beatitude on peacemaking, I will not elaborate the stages here.

77. Floyd V. Filson, "The Significance of the Early House Churches,"*Journal of Biblical Literature* 58 (1939), p. 110.

78. Meier, p. 274.

79. Sebastian Bartina, S.I., "Casa o caserio? Los magos en Belén (Mt 2,11; 10,12–14)," *Estudios Bíblicos* 25 (1966), pp. 355–57.

80. J. Lambrecht, "The Parousia Discourse: Composition and Content in Mt., XXIV–XXV," in M. Didier, ed., *L'Evangile selon Matthieu: Redaction et theologie* (Gembloux: J. Duculot, 1972), p. 314.

81. Fred W. Burnett, *The Testament of Jesus-Sophia: A Redaction-Critical Study of*

the Eschatological Discourse in Matthew (Washington, D.C.: University Press of America, 1979), p. 122. See also his "Prolegomenon to Reading Matthew's Eschatological Discourse: Redundancy and the Education of the Reader in Matthew," *Semeia* 35 (1986), pp. 98–100.

82. Hare, pp. 148–49.

83. Confer Robert M. Grant, *Augustus to Constantine* (New York: Harper & Row, 1970), p. 55. Grant notes that many images and interests of early Christianity were politically motivated. See also John H. Elliott, *Home*, pp. 188–89.

84. Much ink has been spilled on questions regarding the "just" and the "least," with people like Barth insisting that the "least" referred to the Christians themselves (pp. 121–25). While this will be discussed at the end of the ninth chapter, it is important here, for our purposes, that the heavenly Father's love for the *mikroi* be recalled (18:10,14). For a discussion on *mikros*, see Otto Michel, "*Mikros*," in Kittel, vol. 4, pp. 648–59. My opinion is that the "least" is a term referring to rank and that the "just" must be seen in the context of Matthew's entire stress on *díkaios* and *dikaiosýnē*.

CHAPTER 3

1. Barrington Moore, Jr., *Injustice: The Social Bases of Obedience and Revolt* (White Plains, N.Y.: M. E. Sharpe, 1978), p. 9.

2. Ibid., p. 14.

3. For Weber power is derived from established authority that allocates the right to command and the duty to obey. Power means the possibility of imposing one's will upon the behavior of other persons. There are three bases of legitimate authority: the *rational* or legally grounded; the *traditional*, based on established belief in the sanctity of immemorial traditions and their legitimation; and the *charismatic*, whose "recognition on the part of those subject to authority . . . is decisive for the validity of charisma." See Max Weber, *Theory of Social and Economic Organization*, trans. A. R. Henderson and Talcott Parsons (New York: Macmillan, 1947).

4. Aristotle, *Politics*, III, 6, 1278, in Richard McKeon, ed., *The Basic Works of Aristotle* (New York: Random House, 1941), pp. 1184–85.

5. Ibid., I, 2, 1253, pp. 1130–31.

6. David L. Balch, *Let Wives Be Submissive: The Domestic Code in I Peter* (Chico, Calif.: Scholars Press, 1981), p. 34.

7. Aristotle, *Nicomachean Ethics* V, 6, 1134, in McKeon, pp. 1013–14.

8. Moore, p. 18.

9. Max Weber, *Economy and Society: An Outline of Interpretive Sociology*, vol. 1, ed. by Guenther Roth and Claus Wittich, trans. Ephraim Fischoff, et al. (Berkeley, Calif.: University of California Press, 1978), pp. 358–59.

10. "Something of this political power game can be seen during the trial of Jesus" (Derek Tidball, *The Social Context of the New Testament: A Sociological Analysis* [Grand Rapids: Zondervan, 1984], p. 48).

11. For background on their roles see appropriate entries in theological dictionaries. For a summary of the relationship of the leaders and other Jews to Rome see Richard J. Cassidy, *Jesus, Politics, and Society: A Study of Luke's Gospel* (Maryknoll, N.Y.: Orbis, 1983), pp. 114–27.

12. Jacob Neusner, *Judaism in the Beginning of Christianity* (Philadelphia: Fortress, 1984), pp. 45–61. Also S. Safrai, "Home and Family," in S. Safrai and M. Stern, eds. *The Jewish People in the First Century*, 2 (Philadelphia: Fortress, 1976), p. 795.

13. David M. Bossman, "Authority and Tradition in First Century Judaism and Christianity," *Biblical Theology Bulletin* 17 (1987), p. 5.

14. Various authors make strong links between the infancy and passion narratives in Matthew. Most are geared around the image of Joseph and Jesus called *díkaios*, or innocent, in situations of injustice. The opening chapter in Meier's *Matthew* (Wilmington: Michael Glazer, 1980) is entitled "The Prologue Mt 1-2: The Infancy Anticipates The Passion." Unfortunately, Meier does not develop the connection as it deserves. See Meier, pp. 1–17. Originally I had a chapter making these links. Due to the length of this book, it has been excised.

15. Ibid., p. 19.

16. "The element of conflict is central to the plot of Matthew. As the royal Son of God in whom God's end-time Rule is a present, albeit hidden, reality, Jesus is the supreme agent of God who 'thinks the things of God' (3:17; 12:28; 16:23). The conflicts in which he becomes embroiled are with Satan (4:1–11), demons (12:28), the forces of nature and of illness (cf. 4:23–24; 8:9; 11:5; 12:9–14,15,22; 14:14,15–21,22–33; 15:21–28,29–31,32–38; 17:14–21; 19:2; 20:29–34; 21:14–16,18–22), civil authorities (such as Herod and Pilate [cf. 2a; 27; also 14:1–12]), gentiles (including Roman soldiers [cf. 8:28–34; 27:27–31,32–37]), and Israel (cf. 11:16–19,20–24,25; 13:10–13), above all its leaders." Jack Dean Kingsbury, *Matthew as Story* (Philadelphia: Fortress Press, 1986), p. 3.

17. Kingsbury notes that while "the Matthean picture of these several groups does not always square with what is known of them historically, the rhetorical effect of the way they are presented is to make of them a monolithic front opposed to Jesus" (ibid., p. 17).

18. For more background on the nature of Jesus as a charismatic figure, see Martin Hengel, *The Charismatic Leader and His Followers*, trans. James Greig (New York: Crossroad, 1981).

19. Kingsbury, p. 85. It will be important to realize, as we will discuss later, that the leaders of Jesus' day were found also in Matthew's house churches.

20. The separation of the ass and the colt indicates, for John Meier, Matthew's gentleness rather than his Jewishness. Matthew adapted Mark 11:1–10 to include the formula quotation (21:5) from Isaiah 62:11 and Zechariah 9:9, and he also emphasized the quotation's literal fulfillment (21:2,7) regarding Jesus' use of the animal(s). That Matthew misread the text and has two animals (an ass and a colt) that Jesus "mounts" rather than one supposes a non-Jewish origin for Matthew. (John Meier, *The Vision of Matthew: Christ, Church and Morality in the First Gospel* [New York: Paulist, 1979], pp. 21–22).

21. Michael H. Crosby, *Spirituality of the Beatitudes: Matthew's Challenge to First World Christians* (Maryknoll, N.Y.: Orbis, 1984), p. 4.

22. W. D. Davies, *The Setting of the Sermon on the Mount* (Cambridge: University Press, 1964), p. 20.

23. Douglas Meeks, "God as Economist and the Problem of Property," *Occasional Papers*, no. 21 (Collegeville: Institute for Ecumenical and Cultural Research, n.d.), p. 3.

24. Audrey Chapman Smock, *Christian Faith and Economic Life, A Study Paper Contributing to a Pronouncement for the Seventeenth General Synod of the United Church of Christ*, nos. 28–29 (New York: United Church of Christ, 1986), p. 5.

25. Walter Brueggemann, "The Kerygma of the Priestly Writers," *Zeitschrift für die Alttestamentliche Wissenschaft* 84 (1972), p. 410.

26. The first "modern" writers on economics all perceived its evolution in light of the land. Confer Adam Smith, *An Inquiry into the Nature and Causes of the Wealth of*

Nations (New York: The Modern Library, 1965). David Ricardo's whole system revolved around land rents. "The produce of the earth . . . is divided among three classes of the community; namely, the proprietor of the land, the owner of the stock or capital necessary for its cultivation, and the laborers by whose industry it is cultivated. But in different stages of society, the proportion of the whole produce of the earth which will be allotted to each of these classes, under the names of rent, profit and wages, will be essentially different: depending mainly on the actual fertility of the soil, on the accumulation of capital and population, and on the skill, ingenuity, and instruments employed in agriculture. . . . [Without] the true doctrine of rent . . . it is impossible to understand the effect of the progress of wealth on profits and wages, or to trace satisfactorily the influence of taxation on different classes of the community" (David Ricardo, *On the Principles of Political Economy and Taxation*, ed. Piero Saffra with the collaboration of M. H. Dobb, *The Works and Correspondence of David Ricardo*, vol. 1 [Cambridge: Cambridge University Press, 1982], p. 5).

27. Walter Brueggemann, *Genesis* (Atlanta: John Knox, 1982), pp. 244–45. The correct image of Jacob's ladder as uniting heaven and earth by collapsing the heavenly "I am" to the earthly "with you" undermines any attempt to describe Jacob's ladder as a hierarchical notion. The image is one of identification, not patriarchal separation.

28. For a thorough study of genealogy at this time see Robert R. Wilson, *Genealogy and History in the Biblical World*, Near Eastern Researches (New Haven and London: Yale University Press, 1977).

29. Robert H. Smith, "Were the Early Christians Middle-Class? A Sociological Analysis of the New Testament," *Currents in Theology and Mission* 7 (1980), p. 266.

30. Raymond E. Brown, *The Birth of the Messiah* (Garden City: Doubleday Image Books, 1979), p. 143. On pp. 71–73 Brown summarizes the three main positions most interpretations offer regarding the addition of the women in an otherwise male genealogy.

31. Janice Capel Anderson, "Matthew: Gender and Reading," *Semeia* 28 (1983), p. 10. Despite this nod to a more inclusive viewpoint in Matthew, Anderson makes a strong case that, overall, Matthew wrote his gospel "from an androcentric perspective" (p. 7). I will argue, especially in chapter 4, that, while Matthew definitely reflects patriarchal assumptions, his presentation also reflects a definite breakthrough suggesting the ideal of a collegial household.

32. While Matthew's pneumatology is not as developed as Luke's, an examination of various passages referring to the Spirit reveals that Matthew saw the Spirit involved in bringing about a new order through Christ and the community.

33. Eduard Schweizer, *The Good News According to Matthew*, trans. David E. Green (Atlanta: John Knox, 1977), p. 30.

34. For more on this concept see J. A. Ziesler, "Matthew and the Presence of Jesus," *Epworth Review* 11 (1984), p. 58.

35. Eugene LaVerdiere, "God Is with Us," *Emmanuel* 93 (1987), p. 60.

36. Rafael Aguirre, "El Reino de Dios y la muerte de Jesús en el evangelio de Mateo," *Estudios Eclesiasticos* 54 (1979), p. 369.

37. W. F. Albright and C. S. Mann, *Matthew* (Garden City, N.Y.: Doubleday, 1981), pp. 350–51.

38. Hubert Frankemölle, *Jahwebund und Kirche Christi: Studien zur Form- und Traditionsgeschichte des Evangeliums nach Matthäus* (Münster: Verlag Aschendorff, 1974).

39. Kingsbury, p. 105.

40. Eugene LaVerdiere, "The Holy Spirit in Matthew's Gospel," *Emmanuel* 93 (1987), p. 277.

41. Günther Bornkamm, "End-Expectation and Church in Matthew," in Günther Bornkamm, Gerhard Barth, and Heinz Joachim Held, *Tradition and Interpretation in Matthew*, trans. Perry Scott (Philadelphia: Westminster, 1963), p. 38.

42. Joseph A. Fitzmyer, "The Dead Sea Scrolls and the Bible: After Forty Years," *America* 157 (1987), p. 303.

43. Bornkamm, p. 41.

44. 12:27–32 is a key reason why I believe the link between the Spirit and *exousía* in Matthew's gospel can be made stronger. Perhaps because Luke's pneumatology is more fully articulated and developed, Matthew's use of the term has not been given enough credit.

45. Donald Senior, "The Gospel of Matthew and the Ministry of Social Justice," *Spirituality Today* 31 (1979), p. 17.

46. The notion of *exousía* or total power and authority as it applied to the earthly Jesus represents an editorial element in Mark. Only after Easter were the disciples able to begin to understand what brought Jesus' *exousía* into being.

47. "Their," "they," and "them" often refers to people perceived as outsiders. Anthony J. Blasi has shown effectively that the terms are used in opposition to those who are members of the house churches. See his "Role Structures in the Early Hellenistic Church," *Sociological Analysis* 47 (1986), pp. 226–48.

48. James M. Reese, "How Matthew Portrays the Communication of Christ's Authority," *Biblical Theology Bulletin* 7 (1977), pp. 140–41. See also Thomas F. McKenna, "Matthew on Church Authority: Guidelines toward a Healthy Image," *The Bible Today* 17 (1979), pp. 2035–41.

49. Bossman, p. 7.

50. Edward P. Blair, *Jesus in the Gospel of Matthew* (New York: Abingdon), p. 14.

51. Fred Burnett, *The Testament of Jesus-Sophia: A Redaction-Critical Study of the Eschatological Discourse in Matthew* (Washington, D.C.: University Press of America, 1979), p. 385.

52. For a fuller treatment of these themes of authority and their connection to the metaphor of "house," see Letty M. Russell, *Household of Freedom: Authority in Feminist Theology* (Philadelphia: Westminster, 1987), pp. 22–25.

53. Max Weber, *Economy and Society: An Outline of Interpretive Sociology*, vol. 2, ed. Guenther Roth and Claus Wittich, trans. Ephraim Fischoff, et al. (Berkeley, Calif.: University of California Press, 1978), pp. 111–58.

54. Wayne A. Meeks, *The Moral World of the First Christians* (Philadelphia: Westminster Press, 1986), p. 137.

55. Bruce J. Malina, "Jesus as Charismatic Leader," *Biblical Theology Bulletin* 14 (1984), pp. 55–62.

56. Max Weber, *The Sociology of Religion*, trans. Ephraim Fischoff (Boston: Beacon, 1963), p. 47.

57. It is interesting to note that the sociological notion of *anomie* has definite connections in Matthew to charismatic activity and *anomía*. Of all the gospel writers, only Matthew uses the word *anomía* (7:23; 13:41; 23:38; and 24:12) and, except possibly for 13:41, it is noted in relationship with true and false prophets.

58. Weber, *Sociology*, p. 60. It would be wrong to see a person like Jesus as

"charismatic" only in the sense Weber uses the term. He can be viewed as such by social anthropology as well. Sahlins's interpretation of the "chief" of a tribe who becomes so because of his generosity is a parallel: "The process of gathering a personal following and that of ascent to the summits of renown is marked by calculated generosity—if not true compassion. Generalized reciprocity is more or less enlisted as a starting mechanism" (Marshall D. Sahlins, "On the Sociology of Primitive Exchange," in Michael Banton, ed., *The Relevance of Models for Social Anthropology* [London: Tavistock, 1963], pp. 162–63).

59. Bossman, p. 7.

60. Leland J. White, "Grid and Group in Matthew's Community: The Righteousness/Honor Code in the Sermon on the Mount," *Semeia* 35 (1986), p. 75. White bases his work on the anthropological studies of Mary Douglas.

61. Max Weber, *The Theory of Social and Economic Organization*, trans. A. M. Henderson and Talcott Parsons (Glencoe, Ill.: The Free Press, 1947), p. 369.

62. Ibid. A recent study detailing how this evolution took place from gospel communities of equality to patriarchal and hierarchical forms is Edward Schillebeeckx, *The Church with a Human Face: A New and Expanded Theology of Ministry*, trans. John Bowden (New York: Crossroad, 1985), pp. 48–73.

63. Hengel, pp. 34–35. For a theological reflection on this sociological dynamic, especially showing how the more egalitarian house churches became hierarchialized and institutionalized, see Edward Schillebeeckx, *Church*, esp. pp. 42–74.

64. David Garland, *The Intention of Matthew 23* (Leiden: Brill, 1979).

65. Ibid., p. 61.

CHAPTER 4

1. Barrington Moore, Jr., *Injustice: The Social Bases of Obedience and Revolt* (White Plains, N.Y.: M. E. Sharpe, Inc., 1978), p. 32.

2. Bruce J. Malina, *The New Testament World: Insights from Cultural Anthropology* (Atlanta: John Knox, 1981), pp. 99–100.

3. Derek Tidball, *The Social Context of the New Testament: A Sociological Analysis* (Grand Rapids: Zondervan, 1984), p. 79. See also John H. Elliott, *A Home for the Homeless: A Sociological Exegesis of I Peter: Its Situation and Strategy* (Philadelphia: Fortress, 1981), pp. 175–80.

4. See chapter 1, p. 47 for definitions.

5. Joachim Jeremias, *Jerusalem in the Time of Jesus: An Investigation into Economic and Social Conditions during the New Testament Period*, trans. F. M. and C. F. Care (Philadelphia: Fortress, 1969), pp. 271f.

6. There is little agreement among historians and sociologists about the definition, much less the constitution, of these groups. M. I. Finley distinguishes among order or estate, class, and status (*The Ancient Economy*, 2nd ed. [Berkeley and Los Angeles: University of California Press, 1973], pp. 45ff). I have taken the categories from Finley, Malina, and Houtart and collapsed them into the model contained here.

7. Richard J. Cassidy, "Five Jewish Groups," in *Jesus, Politics, and Society: A Study of Luke's Gospel* (Maryknoll, N.Y.: Orbis, 1983), pp. 114–21.

8. François Houtart, *Religion et Modes de Production Precapitalistes* (Bruxelles: Editions de l'Université de Bruxelles, 1980), p. 225.

9. The various rankings, based on power and wealth, were further complicated in households with ethnic differences based on Hellenist and Hebrew backgrounds. For a

discussion on the various kinds of churches in the first century, see Raymond E. Brown, "Introduction," in Raymond E. Brown and John P. Meier, *Antioch and Rome* (New York: Paulist, 1983), pp. 2–8.

10. Malina, p. 75.

11. Lester C. Thurow, *The Zero-Sum Society* (New York: Penguin Books, 1981). Thurow's book purportedly is about economics; however it deals with much of what concerns us in this chapter, namely, the political control of an economy via status. Thurow believes we are already or fast becoming a "zero-sum society." Suppose A and B represent different groups in a population. Since the available resources are limited, they can be represented by a zero, "0." Thus A + B = 0. Because limited resources do not change very much, to improve the condition of A (i.e., to add 1 to A, A + 1), an economic loss must be imposed on B (B-1). Diagrammatically this is shown as (A + 1) + (B - 1) = 0. Thus a "zero-sum." George Foster has shown that peasants saw all "good things" in "finite and limited quantity, but in addition there is no way directly within peasant power to increase the available quantities" (George Foster, "Peasant Society and the Image of the Limited Good," *American Anthropologist* 67 [1965], p. 296).

12. Malina, pp. 75–76.

13. More specifically, culture can be defined as an integrated system of beliefs, values, and traditions which influence the relationships of people and resource-allocation within institutions which express those beliefs, values, and traditions; thus, culture binds society together to give it a sense of identity, meaning, cohesion, security, and continuity. For a discussion of the relationship between culture and ethics, see M. Daniel Carrol R., "The Relevance of Cultural Conditioning for Social Ethics," *Journal of the Evangelical Theological Society* 29 (1986), pp. 308–15.

14. For a discussion on the role of mystification in primitive economies, see James C. Scott, *The Moral Economy of the Peasant: Rebellion and Subsistence in Southeast Asia* (New Haven and London: Yale University Press, 1977), pp. 227–28.

15. Malina, p. 80.

16. Scott, p. 3.

17. Ibid., p. 167.

18. Malina, p. 80.

19. Marshall D. Sahlins, "On the Sociology of Primitive Exchange," in Michael Banton, ed., *The Relevance of Models for Social Anthropology* (London: Tavistock, 1963), pp. 145–49; and Sahlins, *Tribesmen* (Englewood Cliffs, N.J.: Prentice-Hall, 1968), pp. 82–83. See also Elman Service, *The Hunters* (Englewood Cliffs, N.J.: Prentice-Hall, 1966). For an application of the notion of reciprocity to the times of Jesus in the New Testament see Douglas E. Oakman, *Jesus and the Economic Questions of His Day*, Studies in the Bible and Early Christianity, vol. 8 (Lewiston, N.Y.: The Edwin Mellon Press, 1986).

20. For further discussion on the kinds of reciprocity see T. F. Carney, *The Shape of the Past: Models and Antiquity* (Lawrence, Kans.: Coronado Press, 1975), pp. 166ff.

21. Sahlins, "Primitive Exchange," pp. 147–48.

22. Stephen Charles Mott, "The Use of the Bible in Social Ethics II; The Use of the New Testament: Part 1," *Transformation* 1 (1984), p. 25.

23. Confer Edwin A. Judge, *The Social Pattern of Christian Groups in the First Century* (London: Tyndale, 1960), pp. 40–48; Abraham J. Malherbe, *Social Aspects of Early Christianity* (Baton Rouge and London: Louisiana State University Press, 1977), pp. 87–91; Wayne Meeks, *The First Urban Christians: The Social World of the Apostle Paul* (New Haven and London: Yale University Press, 1983), pp. 77–80.

24. Rodney Stark, "The Class Basis of Early Christianity: Inferences from a Sociological Model," *Sociological Analysis* 47 (1986), pp. 216-25.

25. John H. Elliott, "Social-Scientific Criticism of the New Testament: More on Methods and Models," *Semeia* 35 (1986), p. 23.

26. Elisabeth Schüssler Fiorenza, *In Memory of Her: A Feminist Theological Reconstruction of Christian Origins* (New York: Crossroad, 1983), p. 183.

27. Schüssler Fiorenza, *Bread Not Stone* (Boston: Beacon, 1984), p. 80.

28. Ibid., p. 87.

29. Edward Schillebeeckx, *The Church with a Human Face: A New and Expanded Theology of Ministry*, trans. John Bowden (New York: Crossroad, 1985), p. 47. While "free" does not mean "equal," the alternative to the patriarchal form of household indicates the natural ordering would revolve around a voluntary association. While many, if not most, of the voluntary associations had patrons, not all did. Some were able to operate in the form of what we call "cooperatives" today.

30. Meeks, p. 79. In a similar vein, Rafael Aguirre has written: "In the house church people of many diverse situations and social strata participated. It appears that they developed a model which did not normally take place in Graeco-Roman religious settings. They intended to live the Christian spirit in the interior of these communities by promoting a new model of human relations and a very unique kind of fraternity among the members. This interclass movement created something authentically new. It could be historically innovative due to genuine faith." Rafael Aguirre, "La casa como estructura del Christianismo primitivo: Las iglesias domesticas," *Estudios Eclesiasticos* 59 (1984), p. 44.

31. John E. Stambaugh and David L. Balch, *The New Testament in Its Social Environment* (Philadelphia: Westminster, 1986), p. 125.

32. The normal alternative to a patriarchal type of house would be the voluntary association. In the 1930s Filson noted one determinant related to social status: "It is apparent that homes large enough to house a considerable number of Christians in one assembly must have been owned by persons of some means. They need not have been rich. They may have been traders or even workers. But they certainly were not of the dispossessed proletariat. They were established and successful" (Floyd V. Filson, "The Significance of the Early House Church," *Journal of Biblical Literature* 58 [1939], p. 111).

33. See the previous chapter's discussion on *exousía* and the equal sharing of authority and its ramifications for the house churches.

34. Letty M. Russell, *Household of Freedom: Authority in Feminist Theology* (Philadelphia: Westminster, 1987), p. 24.

35. See the passages on "*Patēr*" in Gerhard Kittel and Gerhard Friedrich, *Theological Dictionary of the New Testament*, vol. 5, trans. Geoffrey W. Bromiley (Grand Rapids: Eerdmans, 1981), pp. 945-1014.

36. Such an approach would not eliminate patriarchy but exacerbate it. See Phyllis Trible's critique (in *Theology Today* 37 [1980], pp. 116-19) of Robert Hamerton-Kelly, *God the Father: Theology and Patriarchy in the Teaching of Jesus*, Overtures to Biblical Theology (Philadelphia: Fortress, 1979). The fact that Israel called God "Father" was not so much a reflection of its support of a divine patriarchy as much as it was an effort to overcome idolatry which was geared to female and male gods. The fact that God was "Father" did not exclude "Mother," even though the term is never directly used of God.

37. Joachim Jeremias, "Abba," in *Abba*, Studien zur neutestamentlichen Theologie

und Zeitgeschicte (Göttingen: Vandenhoeck und Ruprecht, 1966), p. 162. For discussion on God and (non)patriarchal notions see Elizabeth A. Johnson, "The Incomprehensibility of God and the Image of God Male and Female," *Theological Studies* 45 (1984), pp. 441–65; Rosemary Ruether, *Sexism and God Talk: Toward a Feminist Theology* (Boston: Beacon, 1983); Gail Ramshaw Schmidt, "De Divinis Nominibus: The Gender of God," *Worship* 56 (1982), pp. 117–31. In interpreting first-century terminology, it is important to preserve a reader-reaction methodology which unites two horizons.

38. Sandra M. Schneiders, *Women and the Word*, 1986 Madeleva Lecture in Spirituality (New York/Mahwah: Paulist, 1986), p. 15.

39. Matthew adapted Q to refer to God as Father. See 5:45 = Lk. 6:35; 6:26 = Lk. 12:24; 7:21 = Lk. 6:46; 10:20 = Lk. 12:12; 10:29 = Lk. 12:6; 10:32 = Lk. 12:8; 18:4 = Lk. 15:7. Since there is probability that Luke reflects the earlier version, Matthew's addition further indicates the word's significance in his theologizing. However, the fact that Matthew makes much use of Isaiah should make its feminine references to God support a more inclusive vision. For a treatment of female imagery for God in Isaiah see Mayer I. Gruber, "The Motherhood of God in Second Isaiah," *Revue Biblique* 90 (1983), pp. 351–59; John J. Schmitt, "The Motherhood of God and Zion as Mother," *Revue Biblique* 92 (1985), pp. 557–69.

40. Gerhard Lohfink, *Jesus and Community*, trans. John P. Galvin (Philadelphia: Fortress; and New York/Ramsey: Paulist, 1984), p. 45.

41. Rosemary Ruether, *New Woman-New Earth: Sexist Ideologies and Human Liberation* (New York: Seabury Press, 1975), p. 66.

42. Lohfink, p. 108.

43. Hans Freiherr von Soden, "*Adelphós*," in Gerhard Kittel and Gerhard Friedrich, eds., *Theological Dictionary of the New Testament*, vol. 1, trans. Geoffrey W. Bromiley (Grand Rapids: Eerdmans, 1964), pp. 144–46; W. Gunther, "*Bruder (adelphós)*," *Theologisches Handwörterbuch zum Alten Testament* 1 (1972), pp. 146–49.

44. The "least" in a patriarchal system implies those who are ranked higher. Thus it would seem Matthew's Jesus supports hierarchy and, thus, patriarchy. However, if all are to become like little children, or the "least," there is no rank left (18:1–6).

45. Edgar Krentz, "The Egalitarian Church of Matthew," *Currents in Theology and Mission* 4 (1977), p. 337.

46. Some exegetes consider Mk. 10:2–31, which is the heart of the Matthean redaction, to be a *haustafel* (Jerome Kodell [noting Eduard Schweizer], "Luke and the Children: The Beginning and End of the Great Interpolation [Luke 9:46–56; 18:19–23]," *Catholic Biblical Quarterly* 49 [1987], pp. 416, 424). I was unable to find the *haustafel* reference in Schweizer. Allen Verhey, *The Great Reversal: Ethics and the New Testament* (Grand Rapids: Eerdmans, 1984), p. 80.

47. These antitheses statements will be further discussed in chapter 7.

48. Bruce J. Malina, *Christian Origins and Cultural Anthropology: Practical Models for Biblical Interpretation* (Atlanta: John Knox, 1986).

49. Mary T. Douglas, *Natural Symbols: Explorations in Cosmology* (New York: Vintage Books, 1973); *Cultural Bias*, Occasional Paper No. 35 of the Royal Anthropological Institute of Great Britain and Ireland (London: Royal Anthropological Institute, 1978); and, with Aaron Wildavsky, *Risk and Culture* (Berkeley/Los Angeles: University of California Press, 1982).

50. Malina, *Christian Origins*, p. 203.

51. Ibid., pp. 14–15.

52. Leland J. White, "Grid and Group in Matthew's Community: The Righteousness/Honor Code in the Sermon on the Mount," *Semeia* 35 (1986), p. 75.

53. Houtart, pp. 252–53.

54. For further elaboration on many of the texts discussed in this section see Schüssler Fiorenza, *In Memory of Her*, pp. 145–51.

55. These terms are explained in the Introduction.

56. Janice Capel Anderson, "Matthew: Gender and Reading," *Semeia* 28 (1983), p. 7. Anderson includes an appendix with Matthean verses concerning women characters, women in Jesus' teaching, female images, and women in direct narratorial comments.

57. Carolyn Osiek, *What Are They Saying about the Social Setting of the New Testament?* (New York/Ramsey: Paulist, 1984), pp. 81–83.

58. Ibid., p. 81. Balch seems to be moving away from an exclusively patriarchal interpretation of Peter. See his "Early Christian Criticism of Patriarchal Authority: I Peter 2:11–3:12," *Union Seminary Quarterly Review* 39 (1984), pp. 161–73.

59. Gerd Theissen, *The Social Setting of Pauline Christianity: Essays on Corinth*, trans. John Schültz (Philadelphia: Fortress, 1982), p. 109. See pp. 11, 37, 118, 138–39, 164.

60. "If democratic equality between husband and wife as it existed in Egypt were allowed to influence Roman households, the government would degenerate into a democracy; and the Romans believed this changed form of government would be morally worse that the aristocracy or monarchy which had brought them to power. The Egyptian Cleopatra's goddess, Isis, who 'gave women the same power as men,' was perceived as a threat to continued Roman rule" (David L. Balch, "Early Christian Criticism," pp. 162–63).

61. This Markan inclusion must be interpreted in the fullest meaning of equality, as recent scripture studies have revealed about the meaning of Gen. 1:26–28. See John W. Miller, "Depatriarchalizing God in Biblical Interpretation: A Critique," *Catholic Biblical Quarterly* 48 (1986), pp. 609–16.

62. Mark S. Smith, "God Male and Female in the Old Testament: Yahweh and His 'Asherarh,' " *Theological Studies* 48 (1987), p. 339.

63. For an elaboration on the levirate see David R. Mace, *Hebrew Marriage: A Sociological Study* (New York: Philosophical Library, 1953), pp. 107–15; Raphael Patai, *Sex and Family in the Bible and the Middle East* (Garden City, N.Y.: Doubleday, 1959), pp. 92f.

64. See 5:46; 6:1; 8:20; 9:6; 12:11; 13:12,44,46; 14:4,17; 15:34; 16:8; 18:25; 19:16,21,22; 21:38; 22:24,25; 15:25,28,29.

65. Marla J. Selvidge, "Violence, Woman, and the Future of the Matthean Community: A Redactional Critical Essay," *Union Seminary Quarterly Review* 39 (1984), p. 219.

66. David C. Vernor, *The Household of God: The Social World of the Pastoral Epistles* (Chico, Calif.: Scholars Press, 1983), pp. 44–45.

67. John P. Meier, *Matthew* (Wilmington: Michael Glazier, 1980), pp. 215–16.

68. Phillip Sigal, *The Halakah of Jesus of Nazareth according to the Gospel of Matthew* (Lanham/New York/London: University Press of America, 1986), p. 116.

69. Schüssler Fiorenza, p. 257; see p. 336, n. 24.

70. Ibid., p. 320.

71. Balch, "Early Christian Criticism," p. 170.

72. Anderson, pp. 16–17.

73. Ibid., p. 16.

74. See my discussion of the sense and structure of Matthew's gospel in chapter 2.

75. Susan Niditch, "The Wrong Woman Righted," *Harvard Theological Review* 72 (1979), pp. 147–48.

76. Jane Schaberg, *The Illegitimacy of Jesus: A Feminist Theological Interpretation of the Infancy Narratives* (San Francisco: Harper & Row, 1987), p. 34.

77. Robert H. Gundry, *Matthew: A Commentary on His Literary and Theological Art* (Grand Rapids: Eerdmans, 1982), p. 295. Gundry notes that the family model is based on that of the Holy Family in chapters 1–2 because the connection is made there between *anēr* (1:16,19) of Joseph, *gunē* (1:20,24) of Mary, and *pais* (2:16; see 12:18) of Jesus.

78. Scott places the notion of "enough" at the heart of the subsistence ethic, which he places "at the center of the analysis of peasant politics" (p. 3).

79. Moore, p. 37.

80. George M. Soares-Prabhu, *The Formula Quotations in the Infancy Narrative of Matthew* (Rome: Biblical Institute Press, 1976), p. 32.

81. This activity reflects a form of economic conversion that is grounded and expressed in religious conversion. It will be discussed in greater length in chapter 8.

82. Despite the title of her book, *In Memory of Her*, Elisabeth Schüssler Fiorenza pays scant attention to this important passage, referring to its account in the four gospels only on pages 128–29 and 330–31.

83. Michael H. Crosby, *Spirituality of the Beatitudes: Matthew's Challenge to First World Christians* (Maryknoll, N.Y.: Orbis, 1984), pp. 55–56.

84. Terming this section a kind of *haustafel* is reinforced if the broader meaning of *haustafeln* is used (as discussed in chapter 2) and if it is remembered that the section immediately before this, 17:24–19:2, is entirely devoted to a *haustafel* of civic submission and reconciliation in a divided household. See chapter 6, below, on peacemaking. As noted earlier, the two sections (17:24–19:1-2 and 19:3–20:16) might be considered one extended *haustafel*.

85. Kodell, pp. 416, 424, and Verhey, p. 80.

86. David L. Balch, *"Let Wives Be Submissive. . ." The Origin, Form and Apologetic Function of the Household Duty Code (Haustafel) in I Peter* (Ann Arbor: University Microfilms International, 1976), pp. 49ff. and his summaries on pp. 70ff. and 112; Verhey, p. 84.

87. In Mark 10:10 this discussion takes place in the house, but Matthew has deleted this phrase. This could be for the sake of consistency, since the dialogue began in Mark 10:1.

88. This phrase has been one of the most debated in all of Matthew. A further discussion does not serve our purposes. For a good summary of the debate see Joseph A. Fitzmyer, "The Matthean Divorce Texts and Some New Palestinian Evidence," *Theological Studies* 37 (1976), pp. 197–226; and John R. Donahue, "Divorce: New Testament Perspectives," *The Month* 14 (1981), pp. 113–20.

89. Sigal, p. 94.

90. David Bakan, "Paternity in the Judeo-Christian Tradition," in Allan W. Eister, ed., *Changing Perspectives in the Scientific Study of Religion* (New York: John Wiley & Son, 1974), p. 214.

91. Either all were to become like children or children were to be considered the greatest. These reversals of Jesus indicate his opposition "to the low estimation of

children common among His people . . .(Mt. 18:2ff,10; 19:13-15; 21:15f" (Albrecht Oepke, *"Pais,"* in Kittel and Friedrich, vol. 5, p. 649).

92. When people approach Jesus in Matthew and call him "Teacher," it invariably is a sign of insincerity. Those with faith never call Jesus "Teacher." They usually call him *"Kýrios,"* which means "Lord," or *Paterfamilias,* or "Head of the Household."

93. Otto Michel, *"Oikía/oikos,"* in Kittel and Friedrich, eds., *Theological Dictionary of the New Testament,* vol. 5, trans. Geoffrey W. Bromiley (Grand Rapids: Eerdmans, 1981), p. 131. This sentence (23:14) is not in all texts; thus in this book I often bracket it to indicate its debated source.

94. Friedrich Büchsel, *"Paliggenesía,"* in Kittel, vol. 1, p. 686.

95. Fred W. Burnett, *"Paliggenesía* in Matt. 19:28: A Window on the Matthean Community?,"* Journal for the Study of the New Testament* 17 (1983), pp. 64, 65.

96. John P. Meier sees Matthew as "remodeling" salvation history in his presentation of Jesus. See his *The Vision of Matthew: Christ, Church and Morality in the First Gospel* (New York: Paulist, 1979), pp. 26-39.

97. John G. Gager, *Kingdom and Community: The Social World of Early Christianity* (Englewood Cliffs, N.J.: Prentice-Hall, 1975), p. 11.

98. Mt. 10:25(2x); 13:27,52; 20:1,11; 21:33; 24:43. Luke uses it four times while Mark uses it but once.

99. Bernhard Lang, "The Social Organization of Peasant Poverty in Biblical Israel," *Journal for the Study of the Old Testament* 24 (1982), p.50.

100. Douglas Oakman sees Jesus as a "broker" between patrons and clients (pp. 194-98).

101. Ibid., p. 209.

102. I will show in the chapter on the Sermon on the Mount that 5:20 and 5:48 represent the beginning and end of the antitheses statements which articulate other requirements for the "new world."

103. Robert L. Heilbroner, *The Making of Economic Society* (Englewood Cliffs, N.J.: Prentice-Hall, 1962), p. 27.

104. Mott, p. 24.

105. I personally find some problems with Mott's thesis, as well as with Malina's. I believe there is an intimate connection between status and class. At the time of the gospel, which came first is difficult to say. Both were intertwined and to argue that poverty had nothing to do with economics but only politics and culture is to do a disservice not only to the tradition but to the fact that both status and class were inseparable at that time. The fact is that Jesus undermined the patriarchal status forms by preaching a new brotherhood and sisterhood of voluntary relationships in the household under God the Father. He also was identified with the oppressed and marginated and poor because he stood in their midst and resourced their needs for bread and healing.

CHAPTER 5

1. James C. Scott, *The Moral Economy of the Peasant: Rebellion and Subsistence in Southeast Asia* (New Haven and London: Yale University Press, 1977).

2. Wayne A. Meeks, *The Moral World of the First Christians* (Philadelphia: Westminster, 1986).

3. Raymond E. Brown, *The Churches the Apostles Left Behind* (New York: Paulist, 1984), p. 125.

4. This is the thesis of John P. Meier's book *The Vision of Matthew: Christ, Church, and Morality in the First Gospel* (New York: Paulist, 1979).

5. Wayne A. Meeks, "Understanding Early Christian Ethics," *Journal of Biblical Ethics* 105 (1986), pp. 3–11.

6. Ibid., p. 5.

7. Ibid., p. 4.

8. Ibid., p. 7.

9. As an effective way of proceeding to describe the ethos and ethics in the emergent Christian movement Meeks comments: "we have learned from several recent studies that there is much to be learned about the early Christian ethos from an exploration of the moral world of the Greco-Roman household," p. 10. He suggests Abraham J. Malherbe, *Social Aspects of Early Christianity*, 3rd. ed. (Philadelphia: Fortress, 1983), chap. 3, and further literature cited on his pp. 121–22.

10. My "examination" has not attempted to duplicate the much broader and exhaustive studies of the environment of the first century. I have drawn on the materials presented by others, especially in the first chapter where I described the social setting of the gospel and in the third and fourth chapters where I discussed the social environment regarding status, subsistence and reciprocity, and the notion of justice. In this sense, I have merely built my argument upon the shoulders (i.e., conclusions) of others.

11. See James M. Gustafson, "Introduction," in H. Richard Niebuhr, *The Responsible Self: An Essay in Christian Moral Philosophy* (San Francisco: Harper & Row, 1978), p. 13.

12. L. E. Keck, "On the Ethos of Early Christians," *Journal of the American Academy of Religion* 42 (1974), p. 440.

13. Keck, "Ethics in the Gospel according to Matthew," *The Illif Review* 41 (1984), p. 39.

14. Ibid., p. 41.

15. The second discourse of Matthew contains significant portions from Mark.

16. Keck, "Ethics," pp. 39–40.

17. Archibald Macbride Hunter, "The Paraenetic Tradition," *Paul and His Predecessors*, 2nd ed. (London: SCM Press, 1961), pp. 52–57.

18. Jack Dean Kingsbury, "The Figure of Jesus in Matthew's Story: A Literary-Critical Probe," *Journal for the Study of the New Testament* 21 (1984), p. 5. See also Kingsbury's *Matthew as Story* (Philadelphia: Fortress, 1986).

19. Keck, "Ethics," p. 45.

20. For more on the wandering charismatics and their influence on the "Jesus movement" see Gerd Theissen, *The Sociology of Early Palestinian Christianity*, trans. John Bowden (Philadelphia: Fortress, 1978); Sean Freyne, *The World of the New Testament* (Wilmington: Michael Glazier, 1980).

21. Bruce J. Malina, "Wealth and Poverty in the New Testament and Its World," *Interpretation* 41 (1987), pp. 362–66.

22. Walter Brueggemann, *The Land* (Philadelphia: Fortress, 1977), p. 29.

23. Ibid.

24. Ibid., p. 3.

25. W. D. Davies, *The Gospel and the Land: Early Christianity and Jewish Territorial Doctrine* (Berkeley: University of California Press, 1974), p. 5.

26. Donald L. Gelpi, *The Divine Mother: A Trinitarian Theology of the Holy Spirit* (Lanham, Md., New York, London: University Press of America, 1984), p. 186.

27. Gelpi, unpublished notes on the divine breath (Berkeley: Graduate Theological Union, 1985), pp. 62–63.

28. Albert Schweitzer, *The Quest for the Historical Jesus: A Critical Study of Its Progress from Reimarus to Wrede,* 3rd ed. (London: Adam & Charles Black, 1956; German original, 1906).

29. Apocalyptic refers to manifestations of cosmic upheaval which reveal the approach of the end times.

30. Eschatology refers to matters having to do with the end times.

31. John R. Donahue, "The 'Parable' of the Sheep and the Goats: A Challenge to Christian Ethics," *Theological Studies* 47 (1986), p. 24.

32. Adela Collins, *The Apocalypse* (Wilmington: Michael Glazier, 1979), p. x.

33. Keck, "Ethics," p. 48.

34. H. Richard Niebuhr has offered one of the best summarizations of the two positions in his *The Responsible Self: An Essay in Christian Moral Philosophy*, pp. 47–68. In applying ethical models to the New Testament other ethicists have developed variations on this model. Gustafson sees Jesus Christ as the Lord who is creator and redeemer, sanctifier, justifier, pattern, and teacher (James M. Gustafson, *Christ and the Moral Life* [Chicago and London: University of Chicago Press, 1968]); Bill Spohn has discovered "six typical ways that Christian theologians are employing Scripture in ethics": as command of God, moral reminder, call to liberation, response to revelation, call to discipleship, and as basis for responding love (William C. Spohn, *What Are They Saying about Scripture and Ethics?* [New York/Ramsey: Paulist, 1984], p. 1).

35. Niebuhr, pp. 60–61.

36. Donald Senior, "Matthew 18:21–35," *Interpretation* 41 (1987), p. 407. According to Allen Verhey, Matthew's ethic is not calculating works-righteousness; but "a response to Jesus' announcement of the kingdom and his summons to a surpassing" justice (Allen Verhey, *The Great Reversal: Ethics and the New Testament* [Grand Rapids: Eerdmans, 1984], p. 92).

37. Stanley Hauerwas, *The Peaceable Kingdom: A Primer in Christian Ethics* (Notre Dame, Ind.: University of Notre Dame Press, 1983), p. 99.

38. Ibid., p. 100. I agree with Hauerwas's conclusions, not his premises.

39. Second Vatican Council, *Dogmatic Constitution on the Church*, no. 11, in Walter M. Abbott, ed., *The Documents of Vatican II* (New York: Guild Press, 1966), p. 29.

40. Max Stackhouse, "What Then Shall We Do? On Using Scripture in Economic Ethics," *Interpretation* 4 (1987), pp. 390–91.

41. Keck, "Ethos," p. 450.

42. Stackhouse, p. 391.

43. Morris A. Inch, "Matthew and the House-Churches," *Evangelical Quarterly* 43 (1971), p. 202.

44. Stackhouse, p. 394.

45. 11:22 = Lk. 10:14; 12:41,42 = Lk. 11:32,31; 23:23 = Lk. 11:42.

46. John R. Donahue, "Biblical Perspectives on Justice," in John C. Haughey, *The Faith that Does Justice* (New York: Paulist, 1977), p. 69. Bruce J. Malina notes that justice ("righteousness") in the first century meant proper interpersonal relationships with all those in one's society, between God and humans, and among humans (Bruce J. Malina, *The New Testament World: Insights from Cultural Anthropology* [Atlanta: John Knox Press, 1981], p. 144).

47. Hans-Hartmut Schroeder, "'Oikos y justicia en los Evangelios Sinópticos," *Revista Bíblica* 41 (1979), p. 25.

CHAPTER 6

1. In secular writings, like Aristotle's, practical wisdom was the quality needed to manage households and to achieve the common good (Aristotle, *Nichomachean Ethics* VI, 5, in Richard McKeon, ed., *The Basic Works of Aristotle* [New York: Random House, 1941], p. 1027).

2. John F. A. Sawyer, "The Ruined House in Ecclesiastes 12: A Reconstruction of the Original Parable," *Journal of Biblical Literature* 94 (1975), p. 520.

3. For a discussion on the chiastic structure of this section see Thomas P. McCreesh, "Wisdom as Wife: Proverbs 31:10–31," in *Revue Biblique* 92 (1985), pp. 35–46.

4. Robert Gordis, *Poets, Prophets, and Sages: Essays in Biblical Interpretation* (Bloomington: Indiana University Press, 1971), p. 162.

5. Aristotle also makes the connection between wisdom and justice. See Aristotle, *Nichomachean Ethics* VI, 12, pp. 1033–35.

6. Krister Stendahl, *The School of St. Matthew and Its Use of the Old Testament* (Uppsala: Allmquist & Wiksells, 1954), p. 30.

7. Surprisingly, Stendahl makes very little reference to wisdom connections in Matthew. Possibly this can be explained by the fact that he limits himself to a consideration of Matthew's direct use of Old Testament passages. However, he does not make connections to wisdom images from Second Isaiah (see pp. 140–42).

8. Walter Brueggemann, *In Man We Trust* (Atlanta: John Knox Press, 1972), p. 120.

9. M. Jack Suggs, *Wisdom, Christology and Law in Matthew's Gospel* (Cambridge: Harvard University Press, 1970), pp. 70–71.

10. Confer Thomas Hoyt, Jr., "The Poor/Rich Theme in the Beatitudes," *The Journal of Religious Thought* 37 (1980), pp. 31–41; John P. Meier, *Matthew* (Wilmington: Michael Glazier, 1980), p. 39.

11. Raymond E. Brown, "The Beatitudes according to Luke," *New Testament Essays* (Garden City: Doubleday Image Books in 1965), p. 336.

12. Donald Senior, *Invitation to Matthew* (Garden City: Doubleday Image Books, 1977), p. 61.

13. For a more extended treatment and application of the Beatitudes to contemporary life see my *Spirituality of the Beatitudes: Matthew's Challenge to First World Christians* (Maryknoll, N.Y.: Orbis, 1986).

14. Dom Jacques Dupont, *Les Béatitudes: Le problème littéraire—Lex deux versions du Sermon sur la montagne et des Béatitudes* (Bruges: Abbaye de Saint-André, 1958), p. 204.

15. Hoyt, p. 39, quoting W. D. Davies, *The Setting of the Sermon on the Mount* (Cambridge: University Press, 1964), p. 213, and Joachim Jeremias, *New Testament Theology* (New York: Charles Scribner's Sons, 1971), p. 113.

16. Many scholars see a connection between this beatitude and the third (or second): "Blessed are the meek" (5:5). For a summary of this discussion see G. R. Beasley-Murray, *Jesus and the Kingdom of God* (Grand Rapids: Eerdmans; and Exeter: Paternoster Press, 1986), p. 158.

17. Eduard Schweizer, "*Pneuma*," pp. 401–4, and Ernst Bammel, "*Ptōchós*," pp. 902–5 in Gerhard Kittel and Gerhard Friedrich, eds., *Theological Dictionary of the New Testament*, vol. 6 (Grand Rapids: Eerdmans, 1982). While this interpretation reflects a "traditional" approach, it must be seen in the entire context of what I have said thus far about Matthew. See Albert Gelin, *The Poor of Yahweh* (Collegeville: The Liturgical Press, 1964), pp. 107–8.

18. Simon Legasse, "Les pauvres en Esprit et les 'Volontaires' de Qumran," *New Testament Studies* 13 (1962), pp. 336–45.

19. Eduard Schweizer, *The Good News according to Matthew*, trans. David E. Green (Atlanta: John Knox, 1977), p. 88.

20. Bruce J. Malina, *Christian Origins and Cultural Anthropology: Practical Models for Biblical Interpretation* (Atlanta: John Knox, 1986), p. 203.

21. J. C. Fenton, *The Gospel of St. Matthew*, Pelican Gospel Commentaries (Baltimore: Penguin, 1963), pp. 119–21.

22. To shepherd meant to have authority over the flock. Here two metaphors are used of Jesus (shepherd and Lord) in relation to those who are evangelized (sheep and harvest). In Aramaic the phrase *rab hesada* means the person having the authority for hiring and dismissing harvest workers (W. F. Albright and C. S. Mann, *Matthew* [Garden City, Doubleday, 1981], p. 114).

23. Hermann Sasse, "*Ge*," in Gerhard Kittel, ed., *Theological Dictionary of the New Testament*, vol. 1, trans. Geoffrey W. Bromiley (Grand Rapids: Eerdmans, 1981), pp. 677–81.

24. Ibid., p. 679.

25. Walter Brueggemann, "The Earth Is the Lord's: A Theology of Earth and Land," *Sojourners* 15 (1986), p. 28.

26. Walter Wink, "Unmasking the Powers: A Biblical View of Roman and American Economics," *Sojourners* 7 (1978), p. 44.

27. Brueggemann, "Earth," pp. 29–30.

28. Walter Brueggemann, *The Land* (Philadelphia: Fortress, 1982), p. 174.

29. H. Hauck and S. Schulz, "*Praüs*," in Kittel and Friedrich, vol. 6, pp. 645–51.

30. Walter Bauer, *A Greek-English Lexicon of the New Testament and Other Early Christian Literature*, 4th, rev. ed., trans. William F. Arndt and F. Wilbur Gingrich (Chicago: The University of Chicago Press; and Cambridge: The University Press, 1952), p. 705.

31. Rodney Stark has shown that the time between the death/resurrection event and the writing of the gospels was one of transition from sect to cult. One of the tendencies of a cult is to reflect the social mores of the surrounding environment or culture (Rodney Stark, "The Class Basis of Early Christianity: Differences from a Sociological Model," *Sociological Analysis* 47 (1986), pp. 216–25.

32. Bruce J. Malina, "Wealth and Poverty in the New Testament and Its World," *Interpretation* 41 (1987), pp. 362–364.

33. Jean Paul Audet, *La Didachè: Instructions des Apôtres* (Paris: Gabalda, 1958), pp. 187–219, esp. the conclusion on p. 219.

34. See Beasley-Murray, p. 158.

35. Malina, "Wealth and Poverty," p. 365.

36. Denis Goulet, *The Cruel Choice* (New York: Atheneum, 1973), pp. 123–52.

37. For the division of the Matthean beatitudes into two groups of four see Meier, p. 39.

38. C. H. Dodd, *The Bible and the Greeks* (London: Hodder & Stoughton, 1935), p. 56. Another word meaning justice or "right" was *mishpat*. Mishpat stressed especially the doing of good deeds. The two words often were used together as in "But let justice [*mishpat*] roll down like waters, and righteousness [*sedakah*] like an overflowing stream" (Amos 5:24). For a fuller treatment of the relationship between justice and mercy see Benno Przyblyski, *Righteousness in Matthew and His World of Thought* (Cambridge: Cambridge University Press, 1980), pp. 99–101.

39. Schweizer, *The Good News*, p. 92.

40. Marcus J. Borg, *Conflict, Holiness & Politics in the Teachings of Jesus*, Studies in the Bible and Early Christianity, vol. 5 (New York and Toronto: The Edwin Mellen Press, 1984).

41. José Miranda, *Marx and the Bible: A Critique of the Philosophy of Oppression*, trans. John Eagleson (Maryknoll, N.Y.: Orbis, 1979), p. 45. In my opinion Miranda offers one of the clearest notions of justice as it would be contained in the Law and the prophets, untainted by Reformation disputes.

42. Marshall Sahlins, "On the Sociology of Primitive Exchange," in Michael Banton, ed., *The Relevance of Models for Social Anthropology* (London: Tavistock, 1963), p. 151.

43. Joseph A. Grassi, " 'I Was Hungry and You Gave Me to Eat' (Matt. 25:35ff): The Divine Identification Ethic in Matthew," *Biblical Theology Bulletin* 11 (1981), p. 84. Also see his " 'You Yourselves Give Them to Eat': An Easily Forgotten Command of Jesus," *The Bible Today* 16 (1978), pp. 1704–9.

44. Jerome Murphy-O'Connor, *St. Paul's Corinth: Texts and Archeology* (Wilmington: Michael Glazier, 1983), p. 153.

45. The original Greek does not contain a word for "house" here. The phrase used is *pros se* from *para soi*. This is like the French *chez toi*, "at your house." The accusative is used, perhaps with the idea of going to the house. See Max Zerwick and Mary Grosvenor, *Grammatical Analysis of the Greek New Testament*, vol. 1 (Rome: Biblical Institute Press, 1974), p. 86. The fact that Matthew did not incorporate the Markan use of "house" at this point, far from denigrating the notion in Matthew, lends support to the thesis that house is a "primary assumed metaphor" in the first gospel. Matthew just assumed the house-context. All major translations of this text include "house."

46. Otto Bauernfeind, *"Haplous,"* in Kittel, vol. 1, p. 386. H. J. Cadbury discusses its meaning as "generous" in "The Single Eye," *Harvard Theological Review* 47 (1954), pp. 68–74.

47. Günther Harder, *"Ponerós,"* in Kittel and Friedrich, vol. 6, pp. 552–55. Notions of the "evil eye" fit here.

48. For an expansion on ideas contained in this section see Michael L. Barre, "Blessed Are the Pure of Heart: Levels of Meaning in the Sixth Beatitude," *The Bible Today* 22 (1984), pp. 236–42.

49. One may even see the relationship between coveting a woman and coveting possessions, since, at that time, divorce and remarriage took place, for some, to obtain a woman's possessions. This could be a reason why Matthew kept the Markan version on adultery (Mk. 10:2–12; Mt. 19:3–12) close to the section about the rich young man and his possessions (Mk. 10:17–31; Mt. 19:16–30).

50. Schweizer, *The Good News*, p. 94.

51. Floyd V. Filson, "The Significance of the Early House Churches," *Journal of Biblical Literature* 58 (1939), p. 110.

52. William P. Thompson, *Matthew's Advice to A Divided Community* (Rome: Biblical Institute Press, 1970).

53. Abraham J. Malherbe, *Social Aspects of Early Christianity*, 3rd ed. (Philadelphia: Fortress, 1983), p. 97, n. 14. I have noted some of the reasons for this in my discussion of Mt. 24.

54. Crosby, pp. 192–98.

55. Leland J. White, "Grid and Group in Matthew's Community: The Righteous-

ness/Honor Code in the Sermon on the Mount," *Semeia* 35 (1986), pp. 75-76.

56. See Douglas R. A. Hare, *The Theme of Jewish Persecution of Christians in the Gospel according to St. Matthew* (Cambridge: University Press, 1967), pp. 19-61.

57. Ibid., pp. 130-40.

58. Meier, p. 42.

59. Audrey Chapman Smock, ed., *Christian Faith and Economic Life, A Study Paper Contributing to a Pronouncement for the Seventeenth General Synod of the United Church of Christ*, no. 47 (New York: United Church of Christ, 1987), p. 7.

CHAPTER 7

1. For background on Matthew's Sermon on the Mount see W. D. Davies, *The Setting of the Sermon on the Mount* (Cambridge: Cambridge University Press, 1966); as well as the entire April 1987 issue of *Interpretation* 41; and Hans Dieter Betz, *Essays on the Sermon on the Mount* (Philadelphia: Fortress, 1985).

2. Audrey Chapman Smock, ed., *Christian Faith and Economic Life, A Study Paper Contributing to a Pronouncement for the Seventeenth General Synod of the United Church of Christ*, no. 29 (New York: United Church of Christ, 1987), p. 5.

3. Otto Michel, *"Hē oikouménē,"* in Gerhard Kittel and Gerhard Friedrich, eds., *Theological Dictionary of the New Testament*, vol. 5, trans. Geoffrey W. Bromiley (Grand Rapids: Eerdmans, 1981), p. 157.

4. The same image is found further in the priestly genealogy in Genesis when Adam is noted as fathering a son "in his own likeness, after his image" (Gen. 5:1). This does not refer to physical likeness as much as to relationship and function.

5. Douglas Meeks, *God as Economist and the Problem of Property*, Occasional Papers, no. 21 (Collegeville: Institute for Ecumenical and Cultural Research, 1984), p. 4. For a fuller treatment of Meeks's ideas on this topic, and others' response to it, see his unpublished paper, with responses, for the American Academy of Religion, *"Oikos* and the Correlation of God and Economics," November 1985.

6. Originally *dikē* had one connotation dealing with judgment or penalty; the other personified justice as a goddess (Walter Bauer, *A Greek-English Lexicon of the New Testament and Other Early Christian Literature*, trans. William F. Arndt and F. Wilbur Gingrich [Chicago: University of Chicago Press; and Cambridge: University Press, 1952], p. 197).

7. Hugh Lloyd-Jones, *The Justice of Zeus* (Berkeley, Los Angeles, London: University of California Press, 1971), p. 161.

8. "It seems that a common perception in the ancient Mediterranean relative to rich and poor was that 'Every rich man is either unjust or the heir of an unjust person.' For this reason, it is not adequate to say that the biblical texts witness to a pervasive concern with the dangers of wealth as such. Rather, there is a pervasive conviction of the wickedness of the wealthy." Bruce J. Malina, "Interpreting the Bible with Anthropology: The Case of the Poor and the Rich," *Literary Journal of Religion and Culture* 21 (1986), p. 155.

9. Jubilee and its implications for discipleship will be discussed further in this chapter, in the section on prayer.

10. Robert Gnuse, "Jubilee Legislation in Leviticus: Israel's Vision of Social Reform," *Biblical Theology Bulletin* 15 (1985), p. 43. Gnuse presents a fine interpretation of the theory and possible practice of the jubilee. However, in explaining why the jubilee

may never have been called, he fails to offer one of the most compelling arguments. It would have to be called by the leaders, who would tend to be the very ones whose interests would be threatened if such legislation was implemented because they were the first to benefit from any injustice in the economic arrangements. Thus to promote justice via the jubilee would be to undermine their own economic basis.

11. Walter Brueggemann, "The Earth Is the Lord's," *Sojourners* 15 (1986), p. 29.

12. A rationale had to be proffered which justified the accumulation of land/ property/wealth in the form of hoards and interest-bearing loans. John Locke did this a few centuries ago. Walter Brueggemann shows its implications for a developed nation like the U.S.: "If *erets* is translated only as 'earth,' we are left with a romantic view of the Bible that does not grapple with social reality. This, I suspect, is what has happened in much of the church in the United States" (p. 30).

13. Classical economic theory has held, since the time of Locke and Adam Smith, that governments arise due to conflicts over property rights. It has been debated whether Locke had any direct influence on the theories of the framers of the early U.S. documents. See Gary Wills, *Inventing America: Jefferson's Declaration of Independence* (Garden City: Doubleday & Company, 1978), especially pp. 169ff. This concept about conflicts arising out of differing perceptions related to property is reflected in the theories in the Federalist Papers that gave rise to the United States of America's Bill of Rights and Constitution. Adam Smith wrote in 1776, "Wherever there is great property, there is great inequality. For one very rich man, there must be at least five hundred poor, and the affluence of the few supposes the indigence of the many. The affluence of the rich excites the indignation of the poor, who are often both driven by want, and prompted by envy, to invade his possessions. It is only under the shelter of the civil magistrate that the owner of the valuable property, which is acquired by the labour of many years, or perhaps of many successive generations, can sleep a single night in security. He is at all times surrounded by unknown enemies, whom, though, he never provoked, he can never appease, and from whose injustice he can be protected only by the powerful arm of the civil magistrate continually held up to chastise it. The acquisition of valuable and extensive property, therefore, necessarily requires the establishment of civil government." Adam Smith, *An Inquiry into the Nature and Causes of the Wealth of Nations* (New York: The Modern Library, 1965), p. 670.

14. From the perspective of a sociologist, this process seems characteristic of all religious movements. What begins as an egalitarian effort gradually is taken over by the *shamans* or priests and becomes patriarchal and clerical.

15. James M. Kennedy, "The Social Background of Early Israel's Rejection of Cultic Images: A Proposal," *Biblical Theology Bulletin* 17 (1987), p. 138. For other reflections on the effort of the original tribal groups to overcome patriarchal gods see David Bakan, *And They Took Themselves Wives: The Emergence of Patriarchy in Western Civilization* (San Francisco: Harper & Row, 1979).

16. Norman K. Gottwald, *The Tribes of Yahweh: A Sociology of the Religion of Liberated Israel: 1250–1050 B.C.E.* (Maryknoll, N.Y.: Orbis, 1981), pp. 330–31. Gottwald's thesis has engendered much debate. Whether all the details are supportable is not our interest here. What is important for our purposes is that the house-base for Israel be established.

17. Ibid., p. 328.

18. This excludes the deutero-canonical books. Daniel I. Block, "Israel's House:

Reflections on the Use of *byt ysr'l* in the Old Testament in the Light of Its Ancient Near East Environment," *The Journal of the Evangelical Theological Society* 28 (1985), p. 260.

19. Some see an etymological connection between "house" and "covenant" in the Hebrew words used for these terms. "Covenant" is *berith*; "house" is *bayith*.

20. Smock, no. 32, p. 5.

21. Meeks, p. 3.

22. Donald E. Gowan, "Wealth and Poverty in the Old Testament: The Case of the Widow, the Orphan, and the Sojourner," *Interpretation* 41 (1987), p. 353.

23. John Reumann, *"Righteousness" in the New Testament: "Justification" in the United States Lutheran-Roman Catholic Dialogue* (Philadelphia: Fortress; and New York: Paulist, 1982), p. 134.

24. Leland J. White, "Grid and Group in Matthew's Community: The Righteousness/Honor Code in the Sermon on the Mount," *Semeia* 35 (1986), p. 63.

25. Malina, *New Testament World: Insights from Cultural Anthropology* (Atlanta: John Knox, 1981), pp. 25–50.

26. Ibid., p. 39.

27. White, p. 63.

28. Among the many articles and books discussing the theories, see Reumann, pp. 22–26, 124–35. For details of the debate, see Benno Przyblyski, *Righteousness in Matthew and His World of Thought* (Cambridge: Cambridge University Press, 1980). Przyblyski opts for a unified connection among the seven uses of *dikaiosýnē*. While supporting these findings, I also see significance in the integration provided in José Miranda (*Marx and the Bible: A Critique of the Philosophy of Oppression*, trans. John Eagleson [Maryknoll, N.Y.: Orbis, 1979]).

29. See my earlier discussion of 3:15 and 21:32 in chapter 2.

30. While Matthew's concept of justice is integrated, it seems that 5:6 and 6:33 refer to an inner orientation toward God—"to know God" as in Jer. 22:16—while 3:15, 5:10, 5:20, 6:1, and 21:32 lay a greater stress on the actual observable deeds of people—"to do justice." In many ways a parallel might be made between 5:6 and 6:33 and the first and greatest commandment; the second commandment can be seen as related to 3:15, 5:10, 5:20, 6:1, and 21:32. You can't have one without the other. On these the whole Law and the prophets rest (22:37–40). For the twofold division of Matthew see Jack Dean Kingsbury, *Matthew*, 2nd rev. ed., Proclamation Commentaries (Philadelphia: Fortress, 1986), p. 90.

31. Jack Dean Kingsbury suggests another schema around *dikaiosýnē*, which he calls righteousness. Unfortunately, besides distinguishing between the "greater righteousness" toward "the Neighbor" (5:17–45) and that "in Other Areas of Life" (6:19–7:12) he not only forgets the key verses of 5:46–48 but makes a determination that is spurious. Is not the neighbor at the heart of "other areas of life"? See his "The Place, Structure, and Meaning of the Sermon on the Mount," *Interpretation* 41 (1987), p. 136. The chiastic structure suggested by Daniel Patte seems too forced and intricate for Matthew (*The Gospel according to Matthew: A Structural Commentary on Matthew's Faith* [Philadelphia: Fortress, 1987], p. 65).

32. Meeks, p. 3.

33. It is significant that Matthew stresses Jesus' *fulfillment* of the Law and the prophets by the special nuance of prophecy (11:13). Of the sixteen times Matthew uses the verb "to fulfill" (*plērousthai*), three-fourths (twelve [1:22; 2:15,17,23; 4:14; 8:17; 12:17; 13:35; 21:4; 26:54,56; 27:9]) introduce Old Testament formula quotations that

discuss Jesus' prophetic fulfillment of the scriptures. The compound verb *anaplérous-thai*, which also means "to fulfill," is used in 13:14.

34. John P. Meier, *Matthew* (Wilmington: Michael Glazier, Inc., 1980), p. 48.

35. Pinchas Lapide, *The Sermon on the Mount: Utopia or Program for Action?*, trans. Arlene Swidler (Maryknoll, N.Y.: Orbis, 1986), pp. 44–45.

36. John H. Elliott, "Law and Eschatology: The Antitheses of the 'Sermon on the Mount'," *Lutheran World* 15 (1968), p. 21.

37. Verses 5:24–26 are shared with Luke 12:57–59.

38. See Richard A. Horsley, "Ethics and Exegesis: 'Love Your Enemies' and the Doctrine of Non-Violence," *Journal of the American Academy of Religion* 54 (1986), pp. 3–31.

39. Also see the discussion in chapter 5 on the temptations of Jesus and the call to trust in God manifested in household sharing.

40. John P. Meier, *The Vision of Matthew: Christ, Church and Morality in the First Gospel* (New York: Paulist, 1979), p. 54.

41. Horsley, pp. 22, 23. Horsley argues that the last two antithesis statements, "understood as pertaining to (complex) social-economic relations (and not to non-violent behavior), could be applied to the use of economic resources for the benefit of the needy and oppressed" (p. 27).

42. Ralph K. White has shown that when people are enemies, they justify retaliation, violence, and even war by a "moral self-image" in which God supports the retaliatory behavior (*Nobody Wanted War: Misperceptions in Vietnam and Other Wars* [Garden City, N.Y.: Doubleday Anchor Books, 1970]).

43. Douglas Edward Oakman, *Jesus and the Economic Questions of His Day*, Studies in the Bible and Early Christianity, 8 (Lewiston, N.Y.: Edwin Mellen, 1986), pp. 215–16.

44. Kenneth W. Dupar, *A Study in New Testament* Haustafeln (Edinburgh: New College Library, 1971), pp. 280–81.

45. See Pheme Perkins, *Love Commands in the New Testament* (New York: Paulist, 1982), p. 40.

46. Leopold Sabourin, "Why Is God Called 'Perfect' in Mt 5:48?," *Biblische Zeitschrift* 24 (1980), pp. 267–68.

47. The Christian community was to manifest its almsgiving to those in need following the manner described 1900 years later by the Second Vatican Council: "The right to have a share of earthly goods sufficient for oneself and one's family belongs to everyone. The Fathers and Doctors of the Church held this view, teaching that men are obliged to come to the relief of the poor, and to do so not merely out of their superfluous goods. If a person is in extreme necessity, he has the right to take from the riches of others what he himself needs. . . . According to their ability, let all individuals and governments undertake a genuine sharing of their goods" (*Pastoral Constitution on the Church in the Modern World*, no. 69, in Walter M. Abbott, *The Documents of Vatican II* [New York: Guild Press, 1966], pp. 278–79).

48. For further treatment of the subversive nature of the Lord's Prayer see my *Thy Will Be Done: Praying the Our Father as a Subversive Activity* (Maryknoll, N.Y.: Orbis, 1977).

49. Joachim Jeremias, *The Prayers of Jesus*, trans. John Reumann (London: SCM Press, 1967), p. 99.

50. R. ten Kate, "Geef ons heden ons 'dagelijks' brood," *Nederlands Theologisch Tijdschrift* 32 (1978), pp. 125–39.

51. For an expansion on the implications of indebtedness at this time see Oakman, pp. 72-77.

52. Eugene LaVerdiere, *When We Pray . . . Meditations on the Lord's Prayer* (Notre Dame: Ave Maria, 1983), p. 132.

53. While Matthew does not have an explicit correlation between Jesus and the jubilee, the underlying image of structurally reordering the economic order, or house, is clear, as I have tried to show throughout this book. To this degree his is very much—at least conceptually—a jubilee-based economic. For a further treatment of the connection between Jesus and the biblical jubilee, see Sharon Ringe, *Jesus, Liberation, and the Biblical Jubilee: Images for Ethics and Christology*, Overtures to Biblical Theology (Philadelphia: Fortress, 1985).

54. John Howard Yoder, *The Politics of Jesus* (Grand Rapids: W. B. Eerdmans, 1972), p. 66.

55. See Ringe; Paul Hollenbach, "Liberating Jesus for Social Involvement," *Biblical Theology Bulletin* 15 (1986), pp. 151-57.

56. Hollenbach, p. 153.

57. Sean Freyne, *Galilee from Alexander the Great to Hadrian: 323 B.C.E. to 135 C.E.: A Study of Second Temple Judaism* (Wilmington: Michael Glazier; and Notre Dame: Notre Dame University Press, 1980), pp. 127, 156-70.

58. LaVerdiere, p. 132.

59. Bruce Malina, *Christian Origins and Cultural Anthropology: Practical Models for Biblical Interpretation* (Atlanta: John Knox, 1986), p. 203.

60. Friedrich Hauck, *"Mamōnas,"* in Gerhard Kittel, *Theological Dictionary of the New Testament*, vol. 4, trans. Geoffrey Bromiley (Grand Rapids: Eerdmans, 1983), pp. 288-90.

61. Bauer, *"Kardía,"* pp. 404-5; Friedrich Baumgärtel, *"Kardía,"* in Gerhard Kittel, *Theological Dictionary of the New Testament*, vol. 3, trans. Geoffry Bromiley (Grand Rapids: Eerdmans, 1982), pp. 605-7.

62. Ivor W. J. Oakley, " 'Hypocrisy' in Matthew," *Irish Biblical Studies* 7 (1985), p. 118.

63. Pierre Bonnard, *L'Evangile selon saint Mathieu* (Neuchatel: Edition Delachaux & Niestle, 1970), p. 399.

64. J. Duncan M. Derrett, "The Merits of the Narrow Gate," *Journal for the Study of the New Testament* 15 (1982), p. 25.

65. 3:8,10; 7:16-19; see 12:33; 13:8,26; 21:19,34,41,43.

CHAPTER 8

1. Matthew's approach to conversion is grounded in the Old Testament. For a study of Old Testament understandings of conversion see William L. Holladay, *The Root Sûbh in the Old Testament—with Particular Reference to Its Usages in Covenantal Contexts* (Leiden: E. J. Brill, 1958). See also Michael H. Crosby, "The Biblical Vision of Conversion," in Francis A. Eigo, ed., *The Human Experience of Conversion: Persons and Structures in Transformation* (Villanova, Pa.: Villanova University, 1987), pp. 31-74.

2. 27:3 features both the literal and relational forms of conversion in speaking of Judas. He returned (*apéstrepse*) repenting (*metamelētheis*). *Katastréphein* = Jesus overturned the tables (21:12); *diastréphein* = a "perverted" generation (17:17); *apostréphein* = do not refuse the borrower (5:42) and return the sword to its sheath (26:52);

epistréphein = the motion of returning to origin (10:13 [peace]; 12:44 and 24:18 [to house]) and a covenantal sense: "and turn for me to heal them" (13:15).

3. Different ways of transliterating the Hebrew word for conversion exist. I have chosen *shûb*. Crosby, p. 35.

4. The example of the second son at first refusing his father, but later feeling sorry (21:29) and going into the vineyard, is a parable about Israel's lack of conversion (21:32) and must be treated in a covenantal sense.

5. This statement does not include the use of the word where it simply refers to a motion (5:39,42; 7:6; 9:22; 10:13; 12:44; 16:23; 21:12; 24:18; 26:52) or gesture (5:42).

6. Leland J. White, "Grid and Group in Matthew's Community: The Righteousness/Honor Code in the Sermon on the Mount," *Semeia* 37 (1986), p. 71.

7. Jacob Neusner, *From Politics to Piety: The Emergence of Pharisaic Judaism* (Englewood Cliffs: Prentice-Hall, 1973), p. 80.

8. Norman Perrin, *Rediscovering the Teaching of Jesus* (San Francisco: Harper & Row, 1976), p. 107.

9. Given the political control of Israel by Rome, the Pharisees had developed a conception of an inner kingdom of God, within the hearts of those whose lives revolved around the Torah. This kingdom had to be expressed in the justice or righteousness (*dikaiosýnē*) of Israel. For them individual and corporate conversion toward observance of the Law would again return God's rule in oppressed Israel in a way that would unseat foreign rule. The Pharisaic notion of conversion was internal. Jesus, while having a concept of God's rule that paralleled this dimension of the Pharisees, called for a conversion based on a higher *dikaiosýnē* (5:20) that did not exclude those outside the social order.

10. Marcus J. Borg, *Conflict, Holiness & Politics in the Teachings of Jesus* (New York and Toronto: Edwin Mellen, 1984), p. 62.

11. Letty M. Russell, *Household of Freedom: Authority in Feminist Theology* (Philadelphia: Westminster, 1987), p. 63.

12. Gerd Theissen, *Sociology of Early Palestinian Christianity*, trans. John Bowden (Philadelphia: Fortress, 1978), pp. 3–4.

13. John T. Pawlikowski, "On Renewing the Revolution of the Pharisees," *Cross Currents* 30 (1970), p. 425.

14. Sverre Aalen, " 'Reign' and 'House' in the Kingdom of God in the Gospels," *New Testament Studies* 8 (1961–1962), esp. pp. 228–32. This connection will be discussed more fully in the next chapter.

15. Dom Marc-François Lacan, "Conversion and Kingdom in the Synoptic Gospels," in Walter E. Conn, ed., *Conversion: Perspectives on Personal and Social Transformation* (New York: Alba House, 1978), p. 109.

16. Dominic Crossan stresses finding (advent), selling (reversal), and buying (action) as paradigmatic elements in the parables. See his *In Parables: The Challenge of the Historical Jesus* (New York: Harper and Row, 1973), p. 34.

17. This should not be construed to mean that the poor are again victimized by God or others. As was discussed in regard to the woman washing Jesus' feet, the reality of poverty is the invitation to discipleship and fidelity.

18. "Possessions" in Matthew involved both status and material goods. In a ranked society that was not based on accumulation, a young man could become rich only by inheritance. Since rich and poor were part of the social structure, a conversion of that structure would be demanded only if riches were acquired at the expense of the poor. Jesus' approach was to reorder his existing social order, and this makes one wonder if

the riches of the young man may not also have been the fruit of exploitation.

19. This will be the foundation for what we later call contemplation.

20. Unlike Matthew who kept the Markan expression, Luke adapts Mark to say the disciples "left everything" (Lk. 5:11). Luke also adapted Mark to demand that the "ruler" (Lk. 18:18) "sell all" that he had (Lk. 18:22). The handling of Mark in Matthew and Luke reflects their approach to conversion as colored by the different communities which they addressed.

21. Rudolf Bultmann, "*Merimnáō, promerimnáǭ mérimna, amérimnos,*" in Gerhard Kittel, ed., *Theological Dictionary of the Bible*, vol. 4, trans. Geoffrey W. Bromiley (Grand Rapids: Wm. B. Eerdmans, 1983), pp. 592–93.

22. I use the word "addiction" as well as addiction theory in analyzing the implications of mammon in our lives not only because the text lends itself to this, but because addiction theory is an analysis of the pressures that impinge on the human condition. If tested sociological and anthropological theories can help students of scripture understand human interaction, so can addiction theory. Finally, it is generally known that the founders of Alcoholics Anonymous found the basis for their theory in Matthew, especially the Sermon on the Mount, this passage in particular.

23. 6:22 contains Matthean images for what we today call contemplation. Thus the need for contemplation to deal with the addictive power of material things.

24. Peter Davids, "The Poor Man's Gospel," *Themelios* 1 (1975–1976), p. 38.

25. This structure is presented in Hans Schieber, "Konzentrik im Matthäusschluss: ein Form- und Gattungskritischer Versuch zu Mt 28, 16–20," *Kairos: Zeitschrift für Religionswissenschaft und Theologie* 19 (1977), pp. 286–307.

26. For a popular book on the link between economic anxiety and faith, see Larry L. Rasmussen, *Economic Anxiety & Christian Faith* (Minneapolis: Augsburg, 1981).

27. The whole narrative (11:2–12:50) might be considered for commentary here. However, since many of the elements in chapter 12 have been discussed elsewhere, a general outline suffices here. Chapter 12 begins with reflections on the Sabbath rest that still continues the creative work of reordering relationships and resources on behalf of those in need (12:1–14); it continues with the justice of Jesus (12:16–21); the conflict between the two households (12:22–38); and the evil generation that will not convert (12:38–45). It concludes with new reordered household relationships based on submission to God's will rather than blood ties (12:46–50).

28. Mt. 11:2–6 is grounded in Is. 61:1–2. This oracle evidences jubilee imagery. Sharon H. Ringe has investigated the imagery in Isaiah in her *Jesus, Liberation and the Biblical Jubilee: Images for Ethics and Christology* (Philadelphia: Fortress Press, 1985), pp. 29–32. She goes on to connect the Isaiah oracle to this passage of Matthew and indicates overtones of jubilee. See pages 45–54.

29. For a discussion on how 11:2–6 reflects Matthew's entire hermeneutic for his house churches see my *Spirituality of the Beatitudes: Matthew's Challenge for First World Christians* (Maryknoll, N.Y.: Orbis, 1987), pp. 16–18.

30. Jan Lambrecht, " 'Are You the One Who Is to Come, or Shall We Look for Another': The Gospel Message of Jesus Today," *Louvain Studies* 9 (1980), p. 126.

31. Matthew does not use the word *érga* for "deeds" in 11:19c. However, from the following sentence: "Then he began to upbraid the cities where most of his mighty *dynámeis* had been done" (11:20), the equation is clear. Suggs shows that the two phrases, "the deeds of the Christ" and the "deeds of wisdom," frame the entire section 11:2–19. Thus when Matthew speaks of Jesus' deeds he speaks of wisdom's deeds (M.

Jack Suggs, *Wisdom, Christology, and Law in Matthew's Gospel* [Cambridge: Harvard University Press, 1970], p. 37).

32. Eduard Schweizer, *The Good News according to Matthew*, trans. David E. Green (Atlanta: John Knox, 1977), pp. 264–65.

33. For instance, Philo wrote: "a house is a city compressed into small dimensions, and household management (*oikonomía*) may be called a kind of state management (*politeía*), just as a city too is a great house (*oikos megas*)." See Philo Judaens, "On Joseph," VIII, 38, in F. H. Colson, *Philo*, vol. VI (Cambridge: Harvard University Press, 1959), pp. 160 (Greek) and 161 (English). Philo was supposed to have spent a year at Antioch.

34. Matthew merely took the material from Q, repeating the tradition.

35. Fred W. Burnett, *The Testament of Jesus-Sophia: A Redaction-Critical Study of the Eschatological Discourse in Matthew* (Washington, D.C.: University Press of America, 1979), pp. 377–78.

36. Ibid., p. 379.

37. For a fine exegesis of chapter 12, highlighting the Isaian passage used in reference to Jesus as son and servant, see O. Lamar Cope, *Matthew: A Scribe Trained for the Kingdom of Heaven* (Washington, D.C.: The Catholic Biblical Association of America, 1976), pp. 322–52.

38. Paul Hollenbach, "Liberating Jesus for Social Involvement," *Biblical Theology Bulletin* 15 (1985), p. 155.

39. J. Lambrecht, "The Parousia Discourse: Composition and Content in Mt. XXIV-XXV," in M. Didier, ed., *L'Evangile selon Mattieu: Rédaction et théolgie* (Gembloux: J. Duculot, 1972), p. 314. See also Burnett, p. 122; Burnett, "Prolegomenon to Reading Matthew's Eschatological Discourse: Redundancy and the Education of the Reader in Matthew," *Semeia* 37 (1986), pp. 98–100; and Douglas R. A. Hare, *The Theme of Jewish Persecution of Christians in the Gospel According to St. Matthew* (Cambridge: Cambridge University Press, 1967), pp. 148–49.

CHAPTER 9

1. In reference to Matthew, "the very fact that the expressions are interchangeable both in the MSS and in the Synoptic parallels forces us to the conclusion that they are used *promiscue* and have exactly the same meaning. It is open to dispute whether Jesus used the one or the other in the original Aramaic" (Karl Ludwig Schmidt, "*Basileía*," in Gerhard Kittel, ed., *Theological Dictionary of the New Testament*, vol. 1, trans. Geoffrey W. Bromiley [Grand Rapids: Eerdmans, 1981], p. 592). For further discussions of the issue, see Barclay M. Newman, Jr., "Translating 'The Kingdom of God' and 'The Kingdom of Heaven' in the New Testament," *Practical Papers for the Bible Translator* 25 (1974), pp. 401–4; Michael Goulder, *Midrash and Lection in Matthew* (London: S.P.C.K., 1974), see esp. p. 63. I prefer "reign" where I can possibly use it since it means the same thing as "kingdom" and is also more inclusionary. Alexander Sand, *Reich Gottes und Eheverzicht im Evangelium nach Matthäus*, Stuttgarter Bibel-studien 109 (Stuttgart: Verlag Katholilsches Bibelwerk GmbH, 1983).

2. Jack Dean Kingsbury, *Matthew* (Philadelphia: Fortress Press, 1978), p. 58. See also his *Matthew: Structure, Christology, Kingdom* (Philadelphia: Fortress Press, 1975), p. 128.

3. John H. Elliott, "Law and Eschatology: The Antitheses of the 'Sermon on the Mount,' " *Lutheran World* 15 (1968), p. 23.

4. 1:19; 5:45; 9:13; 10:41; 13:17,43,49; 20:4; 23:28,29,35(2x); 25:37,46; 27:4,19,24.

5. Mark = 2x, Luke = 11x, and John = 3x. Statistics are from Dr. Alfred Schmoller, *Handkonkordanz zum griechischen Neuen Testament* (Stuttgart: Privilegierte Württembergische Bibelanstalt, 1949), pp. 123-24. I have used this source for much of my statistical data throughout the book.

6. John Dominic Crossan, *The Dark Interval: Towards a Theology of Story* (Niles, Ill.: Argus, 1975), p. 55.

7. Ibid., p. 167.

8. Douglas E. Oakman, *Jesus and the Economic Questions of His Day*, Studies in the Bible and Early Christianity, 8 (Lewiston, N.Y.: Edwin Mellen, 1986), p. 128.

9. Leander E. Keck, "Ethics in the Gospel according to Matthew," *The Illif Review* 41 (1984), p. 47.

10. Ibid., p. 48. Keck's statement about Matthew's ethics being teleological does not contradict our conclusion about it being a character-based discipleship ethics, for the goal of God's perfection is that which ultimately is the norm for all virtue. In fact I noted that Matthew contains elements of the three main approaches to ethics: teleological, deontological, and character/responsibility.

11. Jack T. Sanders, *Ethics in the New Testament: Change and Development* (Philadelphia: Fortress, 1975), p. 75.

12. According to the sociologist Emile Durkheim religion performs five basic functions in society: 1) it legitimizes social norms of its surrounding culture; 2) it provides a sense of shared experience and solidarity for its adherents; 3) it helps people adjust to crises and difficulties in life's breaking points; 4) it offers worship to insure bonds of solidarity among people in a society; and 5) it offers support in times of rapid social change, disorganization, and systems' breakdown. See *The Elementary Forms of the Religious Life*, trans. Joseph Ward Swain (New York: The Free Press, 1915 [1969]).

13. For more on the social dimension see my "The Biblical Vision of Conversion," in Francis A. Eigo, ed., *The Human Experience of Conversion: Persons and Structures in Transformation* (Villanova, Pa.: Villanova University, 1987), pp. 31-46.

14. Stephen Charles Mott, "The Use of the Bible in Social Ethics II: The Use of the New Testament: Part II: Objections to the Enterprise," *Transformation* 1 (1984), p. 20.

15. Stanley Hauerwas, *The Peaceable Kingdom: A Primer in Christian Ethics* (Notre Dame: University of Notre Dame Press, 1983), p. 100.

16. Charles L. Kammer III, *The Kingdom Revisited: An Essay on Christian Social Ethics* (Washington, D.C.: University Press of America, 1981), p. 124.

17. Max Zerwick and Mary Grosvenor, *A Grammatical Analysis of the Greek New Testament*, vol. 1 (Rome: Biblical Institute Press, 1974), p. 9.

18. G. Todd Wilson, "Conditions for Entering the Kingdom according to St. Matthew," *Perspectives in Religious Studies* 5 (1978), p. 42. For a further discussion on this, consult chapter 2.

19. The only other direct objects used are spatial concepts such as "gate" (7:13[2x]), the temple (21:12), and Noah's ark (24:38).

20. Heinz Eduard Todt, *The Son of Man in the Synoptic Tradition*, trans. D. M. Barton (London: SCM Press, 1963), p. 79.

21. Sverre Aalen, " 'Reign' and 'House' in the Kingdom of God in the Gospels," *New Testament Studies* 8 (1961-1962), p. 228.

22. Ibid., pp. 228-29. Aalen links reign with house (*basileía* = *oikos/oikía*) in his commentary on 12:25ff. He also finds parallels in 11:12. He concludes, "The kingdom is the place where salvation is received. It is the state of salvation and deliverance. This place is the house of God" (p. 232).

23. Ibid., p. 223.

24. For a treatment of this spiritual interpretation of *oikonomía* see John Reumann, "*Oikonomía* = 'Covenant'; Terms for *Heilsgeschichte* in Early Christian Thought," *Novum Testamentum* 3 (1959), pp. 282–92.

25. John Koenig, *New Testament Hospitality: Partnership with Strangers as Promise and Mission* (Philadelphia: Fortress, 1985), pp. 43–44.

26. John P. Meier, *Matthew* (Wilmington: Michael Glazier, 1980), p. 243.

27. Wilson, p. 48.

28. Much of the background on this pericope can be found in Neil J. McEleney, "Mt 17:24–27: Who Paid the Temple Tax? A Lesson in Avoidance of Scandal," *Catholic Biblical Quarterly* 38 (1976), pp. 179–82.

29. Richard J. Cassidy, "Matthew 17:24–27: A Word on Civil Taxes," *Catholic Biblical Quarterly* 41 (1979), pp. 571–80.

30. Paul de Surgy, "Rendez a Cesar ce qui est a Cesar, et a Dieu ce qui est a Dieu: Mt 22,15–21," *Assemblées du Seigneur* 60 (1975), pp. 21–24.

31. A. J. Mattil, Jr., "Matthew 25:31–46 Relocated," *Restoration Quarterly* 17 (1974), p. 114.

32. David R. Catchpole, "The Poor on Earth and the Son of Man in Heaven. A Re-Appraisal of Matthew XXV. 31–46," *Bulletin of the John Rylands University Library of Manchester* 61 (1979), p. 389. Catchpole adds: "When the poor and needy as such are seen at the heart of the discourse, and when the form of the material is taken into account, it becomes clear that the listeners are not being invited to identify themselves with the sufferers (as was normal in such apocalyptic contexts) against whom is ranged just one oppressing group, but rather to check whether they should be identified with one or the other of two groups who have in different ways responded to the suffering of others. In other words, the discourse voices demand rather than consolation, just as Jesus had done in the background of Mark ix. 37a,41. Moreover, in both cases the essential demand is defined as *diakonia*. In both cases service shows itself as *dechesthai* and the satisfying of physical needs. In both cases such service is performed for all in need without restriction. In both cases eschatological blessing is promised to the person who takes the role of the servant. In both cases this is affirmed by the speaker with all the authority inherent in *Amen*. And in both cases a similarly expressed declaration affirms the equivalence of the needy and the speaker."

33. Allen Verhey, *The Great Reversal: Ethics and the New Testament* (Grand Rapids: Wm. B. Eerdmans, 1984), p. 90.

34. Ibid., p. 91.

CHAPTER 10

1. Bruce J. Malina, *Christian Origins and Cultural Anthropology: Practical Models for Biblical Interpretation* (Atlanta: John Knox, 1986), pp. 68–111; "Interpreting the Bible with Anthropology: The Case of the Poor and the Rich," *Literary Journal of Religion and Culture* 21 (1986), pp. 148–59; "Wealth and Poverty in the New Testament," *Interpretation* 41 (1987), pp. 354–67.

2. Malina, "Wealth and Poverty," p. 358.

3. Barrington Moore, Jr., *Injustice: The Social Bases of Obedience and Revolt* (White Plains, N.Y.: M. E. Sharpe, 1978).

4. Moore sees the division of labor in society determined by positions of power, or status. See pp. 32–34.

5. Malina, *Christian Origins*, p. 77.

6. Peter Berger, "The Concept of Economic Culture," unpublished paper (Boston: Boston University, Institute for the Study of Economic Culture, 1986), p. 2.

7. National Conference of Catholic Bishops, *Economic Justice for All: Catholic Social Teaching and the U.S. Economy*, no. 37, in *Origins* 16 (1986), p. 416.

8. Ibid., no. 61, p. 419.

9. Synod of Bishops, "Justice in the World," III, no. 29, November 30, 1971, in Joseph Gremillion, ed., *The Gospel of Peace and Justice: Catholic Social Teaching since Pope John* (Maryknoll, N.Y.: Orbis, 1976), p. 519.

10. Charles E. Lindblom, *Politics and Markets: The World's Political Economic System* (New York: Basic Books, 1977), p. 18.

11. Ibid., p. 13.

12. Jacques Ellul, *Propaganda: The Formation of Men's Attitudes*, trans. Konrad Kellen and Jean Lerner (New York: Random House Vintage Books, 1973), p. 61.

13. Ibid., p. 64.

14. Michael Schudson, *Advertising, the Uneasy Persuasion: Its Dubious Impact on American Society* (New York: Basic Books, 1984), pp. 147–77. Schudson's work is a model in balance between those who insist advertising initiates consumer trends (creates needs) and those arguing that it merely reinforces them (responds to needs).

15. Alexis de Tocqueville, *Democracy in America*, trans. George Lawrence, ed. J. P. Mayer (Garden City, N.Y.: Doubleday, 1975), p. 690.

16. Ibid., p. 691.

17. The latent despotic tendency of large bureaucracies has been recently analyzed and critiqued by Alasdair MacIntyre, *After Virtue: A Study in Moral Theory* (Notre Dame: University of Notre Dame Press, 1981), p. 33.

18. Lindblom, p. 356.

19. A major way U.S. corporations and other large institutions try to impact the political processes has been through Political Action Committees (PACs). In 1986 PACs contributed $130 million to congressional candidates. For the same elections, the 10 largest defense contractors (e.g., Boeing, General Electric, General Dynamics, General Motors) contributed almost $3 million to key members of Congress dealing with military matters (Philip J. Simon, *Top Guns: A Common Cause Guide to Defense Contractor Lobbying* [Washington, D.C.: Common Cause, 1987], p. 9).

20. For instance, as an indication of largeness and the ability of larger corporations to have access to the consumer in ways not available to smaller businesses, ad expenditures should be examined. In 1986 the top 100 advertisers spent $27,170,000,000.00 for ads in newspapers, magazines, network cable, spot tv, network tv, spot radio, network radio, and outdoor advertising. Procter & Gamble, the largest advertiser in 1986, spent $1,435,000,000.00 on these various forms of advertising (*Advertising Age*, September 24, 1987). Executives of corporations can control the mass media even to the determination of the way news itself is presented over television. See John Weisman, "Network News Today: Which Counts More—Journalism or Profits?," *TV Guide*, October 26, 1985, pp. 7–13.

21. Warren T. Brookes, "The Economy: U.S. Economy Not Ready to Lay Down and Play Dead," *San Francisco Chronicle*, December 9, 1985. A Dun & Bradstreet survey indicated that the nation's smallest firms projected the biggest employment increases for 1986: those with less than 20 workers projected a 7.4 percent increase and those with 20 to 99 expected a 6.9 percent increase. Companies employing 25,000 or more workers projected increases of 0.6 percent ("U.S. Firms to Create 3 Million Jobs,"

San Francisco Chronicle, March 3, 1986). Businesses with fewer than 100 employees account for more than 90 percent of all corporations in the United States. Small businesses, especially in the technology-based (computer programming, communications, chemicals, engineering, plastics, biogenetics) and service sectors, generated 3 million new jobs between 1982 and 1983. The "Fortune 500" actually lost 310,000 jobs during the same period.

22. This influence can be exercised politically through lobbying, Political Action Committees, and campaign contributions directly to candidates. Its exercise through the media, especially television, is especially prevalent.

23. Synod of Bishops, no. 50, p. 523.

24. Robert N. Bellah, Richard Madsen, William M. Sullivan, Ann Swidler, Steven M. Tipton, *Habits of the Heart: Individualism and Commitment in American Life* (Berkeley: University of California Press, 1985), p. 143.

25. Bellah, p. 250.

26. De Tocqueville, p. 544.

27. Ibid., pp. 545–46.

28. Few, if any, reliable statistics show a positive *causal* connection between the degree of advertising and consumption patterns. This fact is continually raised by advertisers and corporations regarding such products as tobacco and infant formula promoted in the Third World. However, while there may be no demonstrable causal connections, *direct* relationships can be charted.

29. Ellul, p. 251.

30. Ann Douglas, *The Feminization of American Culture* (New York: Alfred A. Knopf, 1977), p. 80. Schudson discusses possible connections between advertising and religion in several places, again with excellent balance. For a more recent approach linking "civil religion" and the dollar, see Lewis H. Lapham, *Money and Class in America* (New York: Weidenfeld and Nicholson, 1987).

31. Ellul, p. 251.

32. "Institutions That Influence American Life," *U.S. News and World Report*, May 20, 1985. Unfortunately in 1985 the magazine discontinued this survey, which was always included in its annual issue on "Who Runs America."

33. The production-consumption dynamic has been described clearly by Amitai W. Etzioni of Columbia University, who noted that the "central project of U.S. society" seems to be the production of resources during working hours and the destruction of them in leisure time. With a veiled reference to the addictive nature of this process, he wonders if it is sillier to think that 6 percent of the world's people can indefinitely go on consuming a third of its energy and other resources than it is to think that millions upon millions of Americans will find ways to jump off the accelerating production-consumption treadmill. See his comments in James P. Gannon, "Getting off the Treadmill," *The Wall Street Journal*, April 12, 1974.

34. Given my definition of culture, we can easily see why such can be applied to our large corporations. This has ethical implications. C. West Churchman has written: "Large social systems seem to take on a character of their own. Since character is closely tied into morality, the conclusion is that large social systems develop an ethics that is independent of the wishes and morality of the individual" (*Challenge to Reason* [New York: McGraw-Hill, 1968], p. 206). For an application of this theory to individual corporations, see Terrence E. Deal and Allan A. Kennedy, *Corporate Cultures: The Rites and Rituals of Corporate Life* (Reading, Mass.: Addison-Wesley, 1982).

35. See Lindblom, p. 356, for a summary. Increasingly there is resistance to

businesspeople being the only "elites." A new class of bureaucrats is rising, with implications for ethics. See Barbara Hargrove, *The Emerging New Class: Implications for Church and Society* (New York: The Pilgrim Press, 1986). There also is increasing pressure from these bureaucrats on the management of corporations. See "The Battle for Corporate Control," *Business Week*, May 18, 1987, pp. 102-9. Peter Davis has given a fascinating description of the new "domestic elites" in his description of the "big-time player" who keeps one foot in Washington and one in New York by riding the Eastern Shuttle (who must have counterparts riding the Concorde!): ". . . they know their purpose as well as their direction. They are not the chosen but the choosing people. These Shuttlers and their fixed goals are reminders that American businessmen, perhaps alone among us, know what they want. Their bottom line is the bottom line. Lincoln told us labor was prior to capital, but we do not believe him. Capital and profits are still sacramental to us. Isn't the lesson of these catnapping Shuttlers, for whom ambition has been elevated to theology, that the ignored history of America is a business history?" (*Eastern Review* [August, 1985], p. 66).

36. "The Reindustrialization of America," *Business Week*, June 30, 1980, p. 78. According to Chicago-based economist David Hale, "the huge concentration of people going into things like finance will make us a society that is good at administering wealth, rather than creating it" (in Alan Murray, "U.S. Economic Role May Face Long Decline," *The Wall Street Journal*, August 17, 1987).

37. Richard G. Darman, quoted in "Treasury Official Assails 'Inefficient' Big Business," *The New York Times*, November 8, 1986.

38. Darman, "In Search of Pioneer Spirit," Executive Style Viewpoint, *The Wall Street Journal*, March 20, 1987.

39. According to T. F. Russell, chairman of Federal-Mogul Corporation, most of the money spent (i.e., over half a trillion dollars between 1980 and 1985) in buying up corporations by other corporations has "added nothing to the economy, and may have diverted investments from areas that needed beefing up" (T. F. Russell, quoted in John Perham, "What CEOs Think of Takeovers," *Dun's Business Month*, November 1983, p. 82). While corporations in this process were small, the large scale mergers by Fortune 1000 companies actually drained the economy of workers.

40. Howard Wachtel, *The Money Mandarins: The Making of a Supranational Economic Order* (New York: Pantheon Books, 1986), p. 163. See Peter F. Drucker, "The Transnational Economy," *The Wall Street Journal*, August 25, 1987.

41. Wachtel, pp. 196–97. Wachtel's words reinforce the thesis of Robert Bellah regarding the consequences de Tocqueville warned of as regards exaggerated individualism. The prospect that this will change in the future is undermined by the data of UCLA's Higher Education Research Institute showing that 70 percent of 1986 first-year college students consider making money their primary goal in contrast to altruistic and social concerns. See Elizabeth Greene, "Shifts in Students' Attitudes Seen Threat to Liberal Arts," *The Chronicle of Higher Education*, November 5, 1986, pp. 32–35. These data were reinforced by the Carnegie Foundation for the Advancement of Teaching, which showed that only 28 percent of the parents and 27 percent of their high school children considered college as a place to become a more thoughtful citizen. See Ernest L. Boyer, *College: The Undergraduate Experience in America* (San Francisco: Harper & Row, 1986). Similar statistics were revealed in 1987.

42. Peter F. Drucker, "The Rise and Fall of the Blue-Collar Worker," *The Wall Street Journal*, April 22, 1987.

43. Rick Wartzman, "Nature or Nurture? Study Blames Ethical Lapses on Corporate Goals," *The Wall Street Journal*, October 9, 1987.

44. Marilyn Cash Matthews, in Wartzman.

45. Canadian Bishops Commission, "Alternatives to Present Economic Structures," in *Origins* 27 (1983), p. 524.

46. Catholic Bishops, no. 170, p. 429.

47. In 1985 the top fifth of U.S. households received 42.3 percent of all after-tax family income while the poorest fifth received only 4.6 percent, the lowest level the Census Bureau has recorded. The gains of the rich came at the expense of the poor and middle fifth or middle class. The middle fifth received 17.9 percent of the national income in 1980 but 17.3 percent in 1985. The next-to-the-bottom fifth received 11.0 percent, down from 11.6 percent in 1980. For background on the Census Bureau statistics see "Release," Center on Budget and Policy Priorities, Washington, D.C., July 13, 1987; A. Kent MacDougall, "Rich-Poor Gap in U.S. Widens During Decade," *Los Angeles Times*, October 25, 1984, p. 28. A columnist in *Business Week* noted that "in 1968 the poorest one-fifth of families with children had 7.4% of the total family income. By 1983 this had dropped to just 4.8%, an incredible loss of more than one-third of their share. During the same period, the richest fifth increased its share to 38.1% from 33.8%. See Robert Kuttner, "A Shrinking Middle Class Is a Call for Action," *Business Week*, September 16, 1985, p. 16.

48. Church of England, *Not Just for the Poor: Christian Perspectives on the Welfare State*, no. 7.55 (London: Church House Publishing, 1986), p. 135.

49. Hodding Carter III, "A Have and Have-Not America," *The Wall Street Journal*, July 24, 1986.

50. Victor F. Zonana, "Is the U.S. Middle Class Shrinking Alarmingly? Economists Are Split," *The Wall Street Journal*, June 20, 1984; Fabian Linden, "Myth of the Disappearing Middle Class," *The Wall Street Journal*, January 23, 1984; and Robert Z. Lawrence, in "The Myth of the Vanishing Middle Class," *Business Week*, July 9, 1984, p. 83.

51. See Kuttner; see also R. C. Longworth, "Our Endangered Middle Class," *Chicago Tribune*, March 3, 1984; "The Middle Class Isn't What It Used to Be," *Business Week*, November 17, 1986, p. 26; Tom Stieghorst, "U.S.'s Bulging Middle Narrows," *Miami News/Sun-Sentinel*, January 18, 1987.

52. Katherine L. Bradbury, "The Shrinking Middle Class," *New England Economic Review*, Sept.-Oct., 1986, p. 45.

53. Lester C. Thurow, "It's Not Just Demographics: The Disappearance of the Middle Class," *New York Times*, February 5, 1984.

54. Jim Fain, in "Who Would Want to Join Rotary?," *San Francisco Chronicle*, May 11, 1987.

55. Claudia H. Deutsch, "The Ax Falls on Equal Opportunity," *The New York Times*, January 4, 1987.

56. Carolyn Hymowitz and Timothy D. Shellhardt, "The Glass Ceiling: A Special Report on the Corporate Woman," *The Wall Street Journal*, March 24, 1986.

57. Audrey Chapman Smock, ed., *Christian Faith and Economic Life: A Study Paper Contributing to a Pronouncement for the Seventeenth General Synod of the United Church of Christ*, 167 (New York: United Church Board for World Ministries, 1987), p. 25.

58. "Third World Income Just Can't Catch Up," *Business Week*, May 18, 1987. The ramifications of increasing global economic inequity were outlined in Pope John Paul's encyclical *Sollicitudo Rei Socialis,* issued February 19, 1988.

59. "Protestant Lead Over, Study Says," *Milwaukee Journal*, October 19, 1975.

60. The NORC figures have been adapted from those of 1975 to reflect the median

household income in the United States as of 1986. The denominational order does not seem to have changed appreciably. See Andrew M. Greeley, "The Economic and Educational Context," *American Catholics Since the Council: An Unauthorized Report* (Chicago: Thomas More, 1985), pp. 26-48.

61. National Conference of Catholic Bishops, *Pastoral Letter on Catholic Social Teaching and the U.S. Economy*, First Draft, no. 63, in *Origins* 14 (1984), p. 348.

62. "The Casino Society," *Business Week*, September 16, 1987. Despite warnings from analysts and journals like *Business Week*, the addictive need for more money grew over the next years. The Dow Jones industrial average, which stood at about 1300 when this article was written, hit a record of 2722 on August 25, 1987. When the October 1987 crash took place, *Business Week* recalled the article on "The Casino Society" and, continuing to use concepts related to addiction theory, asked "Must the Panic Get Worse to Spark Reform?," *Business Week*, November 9, 1987.

63. "The rhetorical and ideological use of the conception of reciprocity testifies to its widespread appeal, to its possible role as the fundamental idea behind popular conceptions of justice and injustice, fairness and unfairness" (Moore, pp. 508-9).

64. Catholic Bishops, *Economic Justice for All*, no. 363, p. 447.

65. Daniel Bell, "The Public Household," *The Public Interest* 37 (1874), pp. 29-68. Bell later expanded his ideas in the last chapter of his *The Cultural Contradictions of Capitalism* (New York: Basic Books, 1978). I am indebted to Larry L. Rasmussen of Union Theological Seminary for reminding me of this connection.

66. Bell, *Cultural Contradictions*, p. 220. Bell uses "public household" to emphasize sociological connotations of family problems and common living in contrast to more neutral terms like "public finance" or "public sector": "The public household, as expressed in the government budget, is the management of state revenues and expenditures. More broadly, it is the agency for the satisfaction of public needs and public wants, as against private wants. It is the arena for the register of political forces in the society" (p. 221).

67. Ibid., p. 252.

68. A common language of justice represents many of the values in which the principles of social scientists and ethicists are grounded. Alvin Pitcher and Gibson Winter have noted that, while religious social ethics is concerned with the possibilities and claims of justice in social and political life, this concern is also present, at least implicitly, in many policy studies by social scientists ("Perspectives in Religious Social Ethics," *Journal of Religious Ethics* 5 [1977], p. 71).

69. Catholic Bishops, nos. 295-325, pp. 441-43. The United Church of Christ Working Document proposes an "Economic Bill of Rights" for adoption as an amendment to the United States Constitution (Smock, *Christian Faith*, no. 205, p. 31).

70. A good summary of the "libertarian" conception of justice promoted by people like F. A. Hayek, Milton Friedman, and Robert Nozick is found in James P. Sterba's *Justice: Alternative Political Perspectives* (Belmont, Calif.: Wadsworth, 1980), pp. 125-71.

71. Irving Kristol, "What Is 'Social Justice'?", *The Wall Street Journal*, August 12, 1975.

72. Besides the discussion earlier, see Thomas Byrne Edsall, *The New Politics of Inequality* (New York/London: Norton, 1984). Edsall's thesis is that in "the United States in recent years there has been a significant erosion of the power of those on the bottom half of the economic spectrum, an erosion of the power not only of the poor but of those in the working and middle classes. At the same time there has been a sharp

increase in the power of the economic elites, of those who fall in the top 15 percent of the income distribution" (p. 15).

73. "The Republican National Convention," *The Los Angeles Times*, August 22, 1984.

74. For the rationale on "entitlement theory" see Robert Nozick, *Anarchy, State, and Utopia* (New York: Basic Books, 1974), pp. 149–82.

75. John Rawls, *A Theory of Justice* (Cambridge: Harvard University Press, 1971), p. 302.

76. Ibid., p. 75.

77. Another approach could be based on a utilitarian philosophy. However, while many practices in the First World reflect a utilitarian approach, its philosophical assumptions are untenable to those stressing the dignity of each human person who never can be compromised for the good of the whole. Consequently, I am not considering utilitariansim as a philosophical approach to justice. Even though it may represent the core of an individualistic approach to life, it has not garnered much support from social philosophers, due to its apparent problems around individuals' freedom. Rawls's effort, in great part, is an effort to challenge utilitarianism.

78. MacIntryre, p. 229. Michael J. Sandel makes a similar argument in his *Liberalism and the Limits of Justice* (Cambridge: Cambridge University Press, 1982). For a summary of his position, see pp. 175–83.

79. William Johnson Everett, "OIKOS: Convergence in Business Ethics," *Journal of Business Ethics* 5 (1986), p. 319.

80. Ibid., p. 320.

81. A good study discussing the interrelationship of these three principles grounding affirmative action can be found in James S. Fishkin, *Justice, Equal Opportunity and the Family* (New Haven and London: Yale University Press, 1983).

82. Drew Christiansen, "On Relative Equality: Catholic Egalitarianism after Vatican II," *Theological Studies* 45 (1984), p. 666.

83. Ibid, p. 667.

84. Carol J. Loomis, "Why Baker's Debt Plan Won't Work," *Fortune* 112 (1985), p. 98.

85. Alan S. Blinder, "It's Time for Rich Nations to Forgive Needy Debtors," *Business Week,* October 13, 1986, p. 27.

86. Ibid.

87. Jennifer L. Hochschild, *What's Fair: American Beliefs about Distributive Justice* (Cambridge and London: Harvard University Press, 1981), p. 18.

88. George Gallup, Jr., "Life Is Wonderful, Americans Report," *Los Angeles Times,* April 10, 1986.

89. Michael H. Crosby, *Spirituality of the Beatitudes: Matthew's Challenge to First World Christians* (Maryknoll, N.Y.: Orbis, 1981), pp. 66–73.

90. Alwyn Jones, "The Violence of Materialism in Advanced Industrial Society: An Eco-Sociological Approach," *The Sociological Review* 35 (1987), p. 19.

91. Anne Wilson Schaef, *When Society Becomes an Addict* (San Francisco: Harper & Row, 1987), p. 95.

92. See Lapham.

93. Schaef, pp. 50–59.

94. "A Nation of Liars?," *U. S. News and World Report*, February 23, 1987, p. 54.

95. Myron Magnet, "The Decline and Fall of Business Ethics," *Fortune*, December 8, 1986, p. 65.

96. Laura Colby, "Vatican Bank Played a Central Role in Fall of Banco Ambrosiano," *The Wall Street Journal*, March 27, 1987.

97. Felix G. Rohatyn, Speech to the Urban League, December 2, 1986, in *The Wall Street Journal*, December 5, 1986.

98. James M. Buchanan, quoted in Leonard Silk, "To Correct Moral Erosion," *The New York Times*, October 24, 1986.

99. Myron Magnet, "The Money Society," *Fortune*, July 6, 1987, p. 31.

100. Ibid. H. J. Clinebell points to addictions as being surrogates for authentic religion: "It is the central thesis of this discussion that one of the significant factors in the etiology of alcoholism is an attempt to satisfy religious needs by non-religious means" ("Philosophical-Religious Factors in the Etiology and Treatment of Alcoholism," *Quarterly Journal of Studies on Alcohol*, 24 [1963], p. 476). For an excellent treatment of the religious dimensions of addiction see Vincent J. Giannetti's article in the special issue on "Spiritual Formation and Problems of Addiction," in *Studies in Formative Spirituality* 8 (1987), pp. 187–98.

101. Michael E. Cavanaugh, *Make Your Tomorrow Better: A Psychological Guide for Singles, Parents and the Entire Family* (New York: Paulist Press, 1980), p. 66.

102. Ibid., pp. 71–81.

103. Karen Horney, *The Neurotic Personality of Our Time* (New York: W. W. Norton, 1937), quoted in Ellul, p. 168.

104. For a well-balanced description of the role of advertising in the promotion of cultural consumerism and its relation to faith, see Schudson. See also Erik Barnouw, *The Sponsor: Notes on a Modern Potentate* (Oxford: Oxford University Press, 1979).

105. In 1986 Ann Markusen noted that "manufacturing employment has begun to fall in absolute terms, and nonmilitary manufacturing in particular has suffered severe losses. For the last several years, every manufacturing category has experienced a trade deficit—with the notable exception of military goods, whose net exports tripled between 1980 and 1984" ("The Militarized Economy," *World Policy Journal* 3 [1986], p. 495).

106. Eating, drinking, and the wearing of clothes all can be objects of addictions. Note the parallels to themes related to these objects in today's advertising.

107. Schaef, p. 95.

108. An entire issue (vol. 8, May 1987) of *Studies in Formative Spirituality* was devoted to "Spiritual Formation and Problems of Addiction."

109. Schudson, pp. 178–208; Peter Taylor, *The Smoke Ring: Tobacco, Money & Multinational Politics*, rev. ed. (New York and Scarborough, Ont.: New American Library, 1985).

110. I have outlined how the Midwest Province of the Capuchin Franciscans tried to bring "gospel values" to bear upon the marketing practices of the two largest U.S.-based supranational tobacco companies. See my "U. S. Exports: Lifestyle Deathstyle: Selling Cigarettes in the Third World," *Christianity & Crisis*, May 30, 1983, pp. 212–15.

111. As noted earlier, I am aware that Jesus initiated all calls to discipleship. However, from the relational element of discipleship, there was a mutual *seeking*.

112. Following John Kenneth Galbraith's description of wealth as power, possessions, and prestige, it is clear from the phrase immediately following Peter's statement that he did not give up the desire for power and prestige: "What then shall we have?" (19:27). Matthean conversion demands a reorientation of life at all levels. See Galbraith, *The Affluent Society* (Boston: Houghton-Mifflin, 1958), p. 88.

113. This religious experience involves a transcendent experience which brings one under a power greater than one's own or greater than that which previously controlled. This experience can be mystical, contemplative, or charismatic.

114. For an elaboration of how the twelve steps might be used to confront society's addictive power, see my *Spirituality*, pp. 66–73.

115. Roland A. Delattre, "The Culture of Procurement: Reflections on Addiction and the Dynamics of American Culture," *Soundings* 70 (1987), p. 142. Delattre declares: "The culture of consumption is so powerful that it has invaded every region of our experience. The family, once a unit of production, has become primarily a unit of consumption. We practice the politics of consumption, entering political life less as citizens than as consumers" (p. 134).

116. Kuno Füssel, "The Socio-Economic Conditioning of the Church," in Virgil Elizondo and Norbert Greinacher, eds., *Tensions between the Churches of the First World and the Third World* (New York: The Seabury Press Concilium Series, 1981), p. 11.

117. Bernard J. Bamberger, *Proselytism in the Talmudic Period* (Cincinnati: Hebrew Union College Press, 1939), p. 272.

118. David Garland, *The Intention of Matthew 23* (Leiden: Brill, 1979), p. 214.

119. Ibid., p. 215.

120. Synod of Bishops, no. 40, p. 522.

121. Leonardo Boff, *Church, Charism and Power: Liberation Theology and the Institutional Church*, trans. John W. Diercksmeier (New York: Crossroad, 1985), pp. 55–56.

122. Second Vatican Council, *Dogmatic Constitution on the Church*, no. 11, in Walter M. Abbott, ed., *The Documents of Vatican II* (New York: The Guild Press, 1966), p. 29.

123. Gerhard Lohfink, "Die Seite der Herausgeber," *Theologische Quartalschrift* 163 (1983), pp. 227–29.

124. Joyce V. Thurman, *New Wineskins: A Study of the House Church Movement* (Frankfurt am Main und Bern: Verlag Peter Lang, 1982), p. 8. Thurman's analysis tends to be historical. For a more practical approach used in areas of Great Britain see David C. Orr, *The House Church*, An Iona Community Pamphlet (Glasgow: Iona Community Publishing Department), and Michael Skinner, *House Groups* (London, Fakenham, and Reading: Epworth Press & SPCK, 1969). None of these works reflects the norms stressing justice which have been articulated in this book.

125. Philip and Phoebe Anderson, *The House Church* (Nashville and New York: Abingdon Press, 1975).

126. See especially Bernard J. Lee and Michael A. Cowan, *Dangerous Memories: House Churches and Our American Society* (Kansas City, Mo.: Sheed & Ward, 1986), and Thomas Maney, *Basic Communities: A Practical Guide for Renewing Neighborhood Churches* (Minneapolis: Winston Press, 1984). Maney and a team offer extended parish renewals based on the house church concept. For information write Parish Neighborhood Renewal Ministry, 1950 25th Street, Hibbing, MN 55746.

127. This program includes the social analysis based on addiction theory and theological reflection geared to the creation of alternative base communities for First World environments. It is based on my book and a ten-part video series on the "Spirituality of the Beatitudes." For information on the program, write Beatitudes Program, 1001 East Keefe, Milwaukee, WI 53212, (414) 964-9697.

128. Hopefully the reader will think that others are main points as well or that my notations need further discussion. This should help in the dialogue which I hope will accompany this book.

129. Crosby, *Spirituality,* pp. 66–73.

130. Pope John Paul II, *Redemptor Hominis*, no. 16.9, in Michael Walsh and Brian Davies, eds., *Proclaiming Justice & Peace: Documents from John XXIII–John Paul II* (Mystic, Conn.: Twenty-Third Publications, 1984), pp. 257–58. Another contemporary application of the last judgment scene can be found in Smock, nos. 298–303, p. 45. See also James Gaffney, "Our Bishops and Our Economy," *America* 156 (1987), p. 46.

131. Catholic Bishops, *Economic Justice*, no. 94, quoting Pope John Paul II's address on "Christian Unity in a Secular Age," Toronto, September 14, 1984, in *Origins* 16 (1986), p. 422.

132. Wendell Berry, *Home Economics* (San Francisco: North Point Press, 1987).

133. The word "ecology" is derived from *okologie*, a word coined by the German zoologist Ernst Haeckel to mean "the relationship of the animal to its organic as well as its inorganic environment." The origin of the word is grounded in *oikía/oikos*. Given the connection to the household, ecology is an extension of economics to the whole world of nature and life itself.

Appendix

The first list does not include references to God as "Father" or other religious concepts related to God or Jesus, such as "Son of Man." Neither does it include references to Jesus as Kýrios or Lord, even when the term might refer to Jesus as paterfamilias or "head of the household." It is interesting to note that, in Matthew, only believers called Jesus Kýrios while non-believers or the insincere used other titles, such as "Teacher."

In the lists an asterisk (*) indicates that more than one Greek word is used for the word in English. The English word I have chosen is my translation from the Greek. It may or may not be the same as the English in the Revised Standard Version, which I have used to translate the biblical texts used in this study.

KINDS OF *PERSONS* IN MATTHEW'S GOSPEL WHO WOULD BE CONNECTED TO A HOUSE

Alien (25:35,38,43,44), those who are anxious (6:25,27,28,31,34; 10:19), babes (11:25; 21:16), banker (25:27), someone betrothed (1:18), boy (2:16; 17:18; 21:15), bride (10:36), bridegroom (9:15 [3x]; 22:10; 25:1,5,6,10), brother (1:2,11; 4:18; 5:22,23,24,47; 7:3,4,5; 19:2,21 [2x]; 12:47,48,49,50; 14:3; 17:1; 18:15,21,35; 19:29; 20:24; 22:24; 23:8; 25:40; 28:10), brothers of Jesus (12:46; 13:55), builders (*oikodomountes* [21:42]), those burdened (11:28), carpenter (13:55), celibates (19:12), child/ren (2:8,9,11,13,14,16,18,19,21; 3:9; 7:11; 8:6,8,13; 9:2; 19:21 [2x]; 11:16,19; 12:18; 14:2,21; 15:26,31; 17:18; 18:25; 19:13,14,29; 21:15,28 [2x]; 22:24; 23:37; 27:25),* daughter (9:18,22; 10:35,37; 14:6; 15:22,28; 21:15), debtor (6:12; 18:24; 23:16,18), disciples (passim), those eating (14:21; 15:38; 24:38), enemy (5:44 [2x]; 10:36; 13:28), evil ones (13:19,38,49; 16:4; 18:32; 20:15; 22:10; 25:26), faithful ones (24:45; 25:21 [2x],23 [2x]), family (*oiketía* [24:45]), father, exclusive of God (2:22; 3:9; 4:21,22; 8:21; 10:21,35,37; 15:4 [2x],5 [2x]; 19:5,19,29; 23:9,30,32), female (19:4), the first (19:30; 20:8,16,27; 21:8,31,36), firstborn (1:25), fisherman (4:18,19), friend (11:16; 20:13; 22:12; 26:50), generation (11:16; 12:39,41,42,45; 16:4; 17:17; 23:36,51; 24:34), girl (9:24,25; 14:11), great ones (5:19,35; 11:11; 12:6; 18:1,2,4; 20:25,26; 23:11), head of a household/ paterfamilias (*oikodespótēs* [10:25; 13:27,52; 20:1,11; 21:33; 24:43]), heir (21:38), humble ones (11:29; 18:4; 23:12 [2x]), those hungering (4:2; 5:6; 12:1,3; 21:18; 25:35,37,42,44), husband (1:16,19), the innocent (27:4,24), those joined together (19:5), the just (1:19; 5:45; 9:13; 10:41 [3x]; 13:17,43,49; 20:4,7; 23:28,29,35 [2x]; 25:37,46; 17:19,24), the last (19:30 [2x]; 20:8,12,14,16), leader (15:14; 23:8,19 [2x],23,24),* the least (2:6; 5:19; 25:40,45), the one at the left (20:21,23; 25:33,41), those of little faith (6:30; 8:26; 14:31; 16:8; 17:20), little ones (10:42; 11:11; 18:6,10,14), lord/ *paterfamilias* (passim), maid (26:69), male (19:4), man (passim), manager (20:8), master (passim), the meek (5:5; 11:29; 21:5), members of household (*oikiakós* [10:25,36]), moneychangers (21:12), mother (1:18; 2:11,13,14,20,21; 10:35,37; 12:46,47,48,49,50; 13:55; 14:8; 15:4 [2x],5,6; 19:5,12,19,29; 20:20; 27:56), mother-in-law (8:14; 10:35), someone naked (25:36,38,43,44), neighbor (5:43; 19:19; 23:39), one who is over others (25:36,38,43,44), an opponent (5:25,18:15-17), parents (10:21), peacemakers (5:6), poor ones (5:3; 11:5; 19:21; 26:9,11), prostitutes (21:31,32), those reclining at table (8:11; 14:19; 15:35; 22:10,11), rich ones (19:23,24; 27:57), the one at the right (20:21,23; 22:44; 25:33,34; 26:64), ruler (9:18,23; 20:25), seller (25:9), servant/slave (8:6,8,13; 12:18; 14:2; 20:26; 22:13; 23:11; 24:45),* shepherd (9:36; 25:32; 26:31), sick ones (9:12; 25:36,39,44,45),* sinners (9:10,13; 11:19; 26:45), sister (13:56; 19:29), slave (8:9; 10:24,25; 13:27,28; 18:23,26,27,28,31,32; 20:27; 21:34,35,36; 22:3,4,6,8,10; 24:24,46,48,50; 25:14,19,21,23,26,30; 26:51), son (1:1 [2x],20,21; 2:16; 5:9; 7:9; 8:12; 9:15; 10:35,37; 12:27; 13:38 [2x],55; 17:15,25,26; 20:20,21; 21:37 [2x],38; 22:2,45; 23:15; 23:25,31; 26:37; 27:56), sower (13:18), stranger (17:25,26; 27:7), suckling babes (21:16; 24:19), tax collector (5:46; 9:10,11; 10:3; 11:19; 18:17; 21:31,32), teacher (8:19; 9:11; 10:24,25; 12:38; 17:24; 19:16; 22:16,24,26; 23:8; 26:18), tenant farmers (21:33,34,38,40,41), thief (6:19,20; 21:13; 24:43; 26:55; 27:38,44),* those thirsting (5:6; 25:35,42,44), trader (13:45), unemployed (20:3,6 [2x]), unjust ones (5:45; 20:13), virgin (1:23; 25:1), woman/wife/daughter-in-law (1:20; 5:28,31,32; 9:20; 10:35; 11:11; 13:33; 14:3,21; 15:22,28,38; 18:25; 19:3,5,8,9,10; 22:24,25,27,28; 26:7; 27:19,55; 28:5), workers (9:37,38; 10:10; 20:1,2,8).

KINDS OF *RESOURCES* IN MATTHEW'S GOSPEL WHICH WOULD BE CONNECTED TO A HOUSE

Abundance (12:34), accounts (18:23; 25:19), alabaster (26:7), altar (5:23,24; 23:18,19,20,35), ass (21:2,5,7), *assárion* (10:29), provision bag (10:10), barn (3:12; 6:26; 13:30), basket (14:20; 15:37; 16:9,10),* belt (3:4; 10:9), boat (4:21,22; 8:23,24; 9:1; 13:2; 14:13,22,24,29,32,33; 15:39), bread (4:3,4; 6:11; 7:9; 12:4; 14:17,19; 15:2,26,33,34,36; 16:5,7,8,9,10,11,12; 26:26), bridechamber (9:15; 22:10), building (*oikodomē* [24:1]), burden (11:30; 20:12; 23:4),* bushel (5:15), something clean (23:26; 27:59), cloak (27:28,31), clothing (3:4 [2x],6:25,28; 7:15; 21:11,12; 27:35; 28:3),* cock (26:34,74,75), coin (22:19), colt (21:2), copper (10:9), cot (9:2,6), couch (23:6), crumbs (15:27), cummin (23:23), cup (10:42; 20:22; 23:25,26; 26:27,39), custom (17:25), darnel (13:25,26,27,29,30,36,38,40), debt (6:12; 18:32), *dēnárion* (18:28; 20: 2,9,10,13; 22:19), *didrachma* (17:24,25), dill (23:23), dish (23:25,26; 26:23),* dog (7:6; 15:26,27),* door (6:6; 24:33; 25:10; 27:60), enough (25:9), everything (11:27; 13:47; 15:17; 19:27; 22:4; 23:3), fatted calf (22:4), field (6:28, 30; 13:24,27,31,36,44; 19:29; 22:5; 24:18,40; 27:7,8,10), fig (7:16), fig tree (21:19,20,21; 24:32), fire (3:10; 7:19; 13:40; 17:15), fish (7:10; 12:40; 14:17,19; 15:34,36; 17:27) fishhook (17:27), fragments of food (14:20; 15:37); frankincense (1:12), fringe (9:20; 14:36; 23:5), fruit (3:10; 7:17[2x],18 [2x],19,20; 12:33 [3x]; 13:8,26; 21:19,34 [2x],41), garment (3:4; 5:40; 6:25,28; 7:15; 9:16,20; 11:8; 14:36; 17:2; 21:7,8; 22:11,12; 23:5; 24:18; 26:65; 27:31,35 [2x]; 28:3),* gifts (2:11; 5:23,24 [2x]; 7:11; 23:19,20 [2x]), goats (25:32,33), gold (2:11; 10:9; 23:16,17), harvest (9:30 [2x],37,38 [2x],13:39), hedge (21:33), housetop/roof (8:8; 10:27; 24:17),* inheritance (21:38),* interest (25:27), keys (16:19), *kodrántēs* (5:26), lamp (5:15; 6:22; 25:1,2,4,7,8),* lampstand (5:15), land/property (5:5,13; 9:6; 10:29,34; 25:18,25), latrine (15:17), leaven (13:33 [2x]; 16:6,11,12), light (5:14,16), market (11:16; 20:3; 23:7), meal (22:4; 23:6),* millstone (18:6; 24:41), mint (23:23), more (5:20; 6:25; 11:20; 12:41,42; 20:10), mustard seed (13:31; 17:20) myrrh (2:11), net (4:18,20; 13:47),* nothing (21:19), oil (25:3,4,18), ointment (26:7,9,12); oven (6:30), oxen (22:4), pearl (7:6; 13:45,46), pigs (7:6; 8:30,31,32), plants (13:32), possessions (19:21,22; 24:47; 25:14),* something precious (13:46; 26:7), ransom (20:28), reward (5:12,46; 6:1,2; 10:41,42), room (6:6; 24:26), salt (5:13 [2x]), sandals (3:11; 10:10), seat (21:12; 23:2), seed (13:24,27,32,37,38; 22:24,25), sheep (7:15; 9:36; 10:6,16; 12:11,12; 15:24; 18:12; 25:32,33; 26:31), silver (10:9; 25:18; 26:15,27; 27:2; 28:12), staff (10:10), *statēr* (17:27), stone (3:9; 4:3,6; 7:9; 21:42,44; 24:2; 27:60,66; 28:2), table (15:27; 21:12), talents (18:24; 25:15-28), tax (17:25; 22:17), tents (17:4), things/material (6:33; 24:17), tower (21:33), treasures/possessions (2:11; 6:19 [2x],20 [2x]; 12:35 [2x]; 13:44,52; 19:21), tribute/tax (17:25; 22:17,19), tunic (5:40; 10:10), vessel (13:48; 25:4), vineyard (20:1,2,4,7,8; 21:28,33,39,40,41), wage (20:8), waste (7:13; 26:8), water (10:42; 27:24),* wealth (6:24), wheat (3:12; 13:25,29,30), winepress (21:33), work (11:2,19; 16:27; 23:3),* words referring to "hers," "his," "mine," "theirs," as possessive of resources (passim).

KINDS OF DYNAMICS AND ACTIVITIES IN MATTHEW'S GOSPEL WHICH WOULD IMPLY *RELATIONSHIPS* WITHIN A HOUSEHOLD

To abound (5:20; 13:12; 14:20; 15:37; 25:29), adultery (5:27,28 [2x],32 [2x]; 12:39; 15:19; 16:4; 19:9 [2x],18),* to agree (18:19; 20:2,13), to be anxious (6:25,27,28,31,34; 10:19), to have authority (7:29; 8:9; 9:6,8; 10:1; 21:23 [2x],24,27; 28:18), to beget (1:1-18), to bestow (3:9), to betray (26:23,24,25,48), to be betrothed (1:18), to bind (16:19 [2x]; 18:18 [2x]), to bless (14:19; 21:9; 23:39; 25:34; 26:26), to share in a blessing (5:3-11; 11:6; 13:16; 16:17; 24:46), to borrow (5:42), to break bread (14:19; 15:36; 26:26), to break-in (6:19; 24:43), to build (*oikodomein* [7:24,26; 16:18; 21:33,42; 23:29,48; 26:61; 27:40]), to bury (8:21,22; 14:12), to buy (13:44,46; 14:15; 21:12; 25:9,10; 27:7), to clean (23:26; 27:59), to clothe (6:29,30; 11:8; 25:36,38,43),* to control (20:25), to correct (18:15), to be covetous (23:25), to be in debt/owe (18:28,30; 23:16,18), to devour (13:4; 23:14), to dig (21:33; 25:18), divorce (19:7), to dominate (20:25), to dress (6:25; 22:11 [2x]; 27:31), to drink (6:25; 9:11; 11:18,19; 20:22,23; 24:38,49; 25:35,42,44; 26:27,29,42; 27:34 [2x]),* to dwell/inhabit (*katoikein* [2:23; 4:13; 12:45; 23:21]), to eat (6:25,31; 11:18,19; 12:4 [2x]; 14:16,20; 15:2,20,27,32,36; 24:49; 25:35,42,44; 26:10,17,26),* to enter (2:11; 5:20; 7:13,21; 8:5; 9:23,28; 10:12; 12:4; 13:36; 15:11; 18:3,8,9; 19:17,23,24; 21:10,12; 22:12; 23:13 [2x]; 25:10,21,23),* to think or do evil (5:11,29; 7:17,18; 9:4; 15:19), to exchange (16:26), to fast (4:2; 6:16,17,18; 9:14,15; 15:32; 17:21), to feed (25:35,37,42), to forgive (6:12,14; 9:2,5,6; 12:31,32; 18:21,27,32,35), fornication (5:32; 15:19; 19:19), to bear fruit (3:8; 7:16), to gain (25:17,20,22), to gather (6:26; 25:24,26), to give (4:9; 5:42; 7:6,7,11; 10:8,19; 13:11,12; 19:11,21; 20:4,14,23,28; 26:15; 28:18), good works (3:10; 5:16; 7:17 [2x],18 [2x],19; 12:33 [2x],34,35 [2x]; 13:8,23,24,27,37,38,45,48; 19:16 [2x],17 [2x]; 20:15; 22:10; 25:21,23; 26:10),* to greet (5:47; 10:12; 23:7), to grind (24:41), to hire (20:7), to honor (15:4,5,8; 19:19), to inherit (5:5; 19:29; 25:34), to invite (22:3,4,8,9), justice (3:15; 5:6,10,20; 6:1,33; 21:32), to knock (7:7,8), to labor (6:28; 11:28), to lead (15:14), to leave (2:6; 4:13; 9:32; 10:11; 12:44; 13:1; 16:4; 19:5; 21:17),* to leaven (13:33), to loose (16:29 [2x]; 18:18 [2x]), to love (5:43,44,46; 6:24; 19:19; 22:37,39), love (24:12), to marry (5:32; 19:9 [2x],10; 22:25,30 [2x]; 24:38), acts related to mercy (5:7 [2x]; 6:2,3,4; 9:13,27; 12:7; 18:33 [2x]; 20:30,31; 23:23), to minister (25:44), nonresistance (5:38-42; 12:18-21), to obey/hear (7:24,26; 10:14,27; 11:5,15; 13:13,16,17,19,22,23; 15:10; 17:5; 18:15), to open (7:7,8; 25:11), to be over others (25:21,23), to pay (5:26; 16:27; 17:24; 18:25,26,28,29,30,34; 20:8; 21:41; 27:58),* to give peace (10:12,13,34), to persecute (5:10,11,12,44; 10:23; 23:34), persecution (13:21), to plant (21:33), to plunder (12:29), to possess/have (5:23; 8:20; 13:12,44,46; 14:17; 18:12,25; 19:21,22; 21:38),* to pray (5:44; 6:5,6,7,9; 14:23; 19:13; 24:20; 26:36,39,41,42), prayer (6:5; 21:13,22; 23:14), to price (27:9 [2x]), to put on (6:24), to reap (6:26; 25:24,26), to receive pay (17:25; 20:7,9; 25:18,20,22), to receive something (19:29; 21:22; 25:22,27),* to recline at a meal (9:10 [2x],14:9), to be reconciled (5:24; 18:5-7), to remain (10:11; 11:23; 15:32; 26:38), to rent (21:33), to repay (18:25,27,29 [2x],30,34), to rest (11:28,29; 12:43; 26:45), to reward (16:27), to be satisfied (5:6; 14:20; 15:33,37), scandal (13:41; 16:23; 18:7), to scandalize (5:29,30; 11:6; 13:21,57; 15:12; 17:27; 18:6,8,9; 24:10; 26:31,33), to scatter (25:24,26), to sell (10:29; 8:15; 20:28 [2x]; 25:44),* service (24:45), to shelter (25:35), to shepherd (2:6), to sin (18:15; 27:4), sin (1:21; 3:6; 6:14,15 [2x]), to sing a hymn (26:30), to sit (5:1; 13:41; 19:28; 20:21,23; 23:2; 25:31; 26:36), to sleep (9:24; 13:25; 25:5), to sow (6:26; 13:4,19 [2x],20,22,23,24,25,27,31,37,39; 25:24,26), to spin (6:28), to steal (6:19,20; 19:18; 27:64; 28:13), to submit (5:38-42; 12:18-21), to sue (5:40), to give thanks (15:36; 26:27), theft/robbery (15:19; 23:25),* to tithe (23:23), trading (22:5), to turn away (5:42; 26:52), to visit (25:36,44), to welcome/receive (10:14,40 [4x],41 [4x],42, [2x]; 11:14; 18:15 [2x]; 25:35,38,43),* to work (7:23; 21:28; 25:16; 26:10), to worship/bend the knee/bow (2:2,8,11; 4:9,10; 8:2; 9:18; 14:33; 15:25; 18:26; 20:20; 28:9,17).*

Scripture Index

NEW TESTAMENT

General Index

Aalen, Sverre, 67, 221-23
Acts, 47, 101
Addiction, 3, 18, 207-9, 264, 312*n,* 317*n,*
    320*n,* 322*n*; community and, 259-62; con-
    templation and, 258-59; conversion and,
    256-58; cultural, 252-62; recovering from,
    251-62; society as, 252-56
Adultery, 113, 120
Advertising, 233-34, 255-57, 316*n,* 317*n*
Affluence, 4, 40, 239, 270, 270*n,* 307. *See also*
    Prosperity; Wealth
Agriculture, 21-2, 174, 238, 273, 275
Aguirre, Rafael, 89, 296*n*
Alienation, 71, 72, 242
Almsgiving, 187
Anderson, Janice Capel, 87, 112, 114
Androcentrism, 87, 111-12, 292
Anger, 183
Anomía, 192, 254, 293*n*
Anthropology, 173-74
Antioch, 36, 37
Antithesis statements, 183-86, 199
Anxiety, 207-9, 255-56, 264
Apocalyptic, 122, 139, 302
Archeology, 37-38, 280
Aristotle, 28-29, 76-77, 120, 247-48, 303*n*
Associations, in patriarchal system, 29-31
Augustus, Roman Emperor, 21-22
Authority, 14-15, 17, 18, 47-48, 57, 71-72, 126,
    133, 230, 257, 265, 290*n*; charismatic, 95-
    98; conflicts of, 79-80, 90-93; democracy
    and, 233-34; first-century Jewish religious,
    78-79; house-based, historical setting for,
    76-78; Matthean basis of, 80-89; nature of,
    76-80; post-industrial capitalism, nature
    of, 232-37; religion and, 234-37
Avi-Yonah, Michael, 39, 40
Bacon, Benjamin, 54-55
Bakan, David, 120
Balch, David L., 29, 30, 112, 114
Banco Ambrosiano, 253
Banks, 34
Baptism, 96, 106
Barr, James, 5
Basileía, 24-26, 29, 52, 100, 106, 109, 112, 116,
    175, 190, 217, 263
Bauer, Walter, 159

Bearing fruit, 57-58, 61, 114-15, 141, 145-46,
    184, 194, 262; conversion and, 197; in jus-
    tice, 204
Beasley-Murray, G. R., 53
Beelzebul controversy, 66-67, 91-93
Bell, Daniel, 244, 245, 247
Bellah, Robert, 234, 235, 318*n*
Berger, Peter, 230
Berry, Wendell, 266
Blacks, resource allocation disparities and, 240
Blair, Edward, 95
Blasi, Anthony J., 47
Blinder, Alan S., 251
Block, Daniel I., 176
Boff, Leonardo, 261
Bonnard, Pierre, 193
Borg, Marcus, 163, 199
Bornkamm, Günther, 91-92
Bossman, David, 79, 95, 96
Bourgeoisie, 101
Brown, Raymond E., 37, 86, 127, 152
Brown, Schuyler, 64
Brueggemann, Walter, 84-85, 134, 135, 149-50,
    158-59, 173-74, 307*n*
Buchanan, James M., 254
Bureaucracy, 14, 27, 318*n*
Burnett, Fred W., 74, 95, 213-14
Business, 21, 148, 237, 275, 316-17. *See also*
    Capitalism, 316-17*n*
Business Week (magazine), 237, 241, 243
Buying, 204-5, 257-58
Capitalism, 2, 15, 174, 179, 270*n*. *See also*
    Business; Post-industrial capitalism
Care, 190-91
Carney, T. F., 13
Carrington, Philip, 71
Carter, Hodding, III, 240
Cassidy, Richard J., 226
Catchpole, David R., 227, 315*n*
Catholic Bishops, 231, 234, 239, 242, 243, 261,
    265
Cavanaugh, Michael E., 255
Celibacy, 120
Character/responsibility ethic, 140-42
Charisma, 95-98, 281*n,* 290*n,* 293-94*n*
Charity, 187
Chrēmata, 28